# TACITUS

RONALD MARTIN

# TACITUS

*Auguror . . . historias tuas*
*immortales futuras*
I prophesy that your
histories will be immortal

<small>PLINY</small> Ep. 7.33

B.T. Batsford Ltd   London

Typeset by Photobooks (Bristol) Ltd
and printed in Great Britain by
Billing & Sons Ltd, Worcester
for the Publishers
B.T. Batsford Ltd
4 Fitzhardinge Street
London W1H 0AH

ISBN 0 7134 2723 X

VXORI
MARITVS

# NOTE ON JACKET ILLUSTRATION

The photograph shows part of the eleventh-century Beneventan manuscript (Laurentianus 68, 2—'the second Medicean'), containing Tacitus, *Annals* 15.44 (*mariti erant . . . plebi uel circulo*). The passage refers to the Great Fire of Rome (*incendiu(m)*, line 3) during the reign of Nero (line 4, text and margin), and is the earliest non-Christian account of the origin of the Christians and of the execution of their founder (*Christus*, first word in line 7) in the reign of Tiberius (*Tiberio imperitante*) by the procurator, Pontius Pilate (*p(er) p(ro)curatore(m) pontiu(m) pilatu(m)*). Tacitus goes on to explain that, because it was popularly believed that the fire of Rome had been started on Nero's orders, Nero caused the Christians to be put forward as scapegoats, and executed as a public spectacle by crucifixion or being torn to pieces by wild dogs or by being set alight as human torches.

*Transcription of first eight lines; expanded abbreviations are italicised*

mariti erant; sed n*on* ope humana n*on* largitio-
nib*us* principis aut d*eum* placam*en*tis decedebat
infamia qu*in* iussu*m* incendiu*m* crederet*ur*; ergo
abolendo rumori nero subdidit reos & qu*a*esitissi-
mis poenis affecit quos p*er* flagitia inuisos uul-
gus christianos appellabat. auctor nominis ei*us*
christus tiberio imperitante p*er* p*ro*curatore*m* pon-
tiu*m* pilatu*m* supplicio affectus erat

# CONTENTS

|  | Note on jacket illustration | 6 |
|  | Preface | 9 |
| I | The Tradition | 13 |
| II | Tacitus and the Contemporary Scene | 26 |
| III | The Lesser Works | 39 |
| IV | The *Histories* | 67 |
| V | The *Annals* · Tiberius | 104 |
| VI | The *Annals* · Claudius | 144 |
| VII | The *Annals* · Nero | 162 |
| VIII | The Sources · *Histories* | 189 |
| IX | The Sources · *Annals* | 199 |
| X | Style | 214 |
| XI | Postscript | 236 |
|  | References and Notes | 244 |
|  | Bibliography | 269 |
|  | General index | 279 |
|  | Index of passages translated or discussed | 286 |

# PREFACE

When the *Agricola* was published in AD 98, Tacitus was over forty; in the previous year he had held the consulship, and he had already established himself as one of Rome's leading orators. His writings bear the stamp of a man experienced in politics and public life, and in all of them, except the *Germania*, the same question, spoken or unspoken, is posed: what is to be the public behaviour of a Roman under what is nominally a republic, but in fact an autocracy? The search for an answer to that question was to take him back to the origins of the principate under Augustus. In common with other Romans he tended to judge politics in moral terms and, like them, he is free with expressions of praise and (more often) blame for those who figure in his pages. But in seeking the causes of the present in the past he showed a historical sense rare among his countrymen. In one respect he is unique among Roman historians. His sense of historical perspective enabled him to grasp the antinomies of the age in which he lived; liberty with its tendency to licence had to be balanced against order that tended to regimentation. In his public life Tacitus loyally served the imperial régime, but as a writer he asserted his freedom to criticise despotism in a *princeps* and subservience in his subjects.

His five extant works were written over a period of about twenty years, and it is to be expected that in the course of time some changes in style should occur. But much of what has been demonstrated consists of minor lexical details, and the more noticeable differences are due to other factors. Thus the neo-Ciceronian style of the *Dialogus* is due, not (as used to be thought) to the fact that it is the product of Tacitus' youth (which it is not), but to the accepted convention that this is the appropriate style for a literary dialogue. In the case of the *Histories* and *Annals*, though they belong to the same genre, their different characters reflect differences in the subject matter of the surviving parts as much as a progressive move by Tacitus towards the sparer style of the *Annals*. So the first three books of the *Histories* consist mainly of

9

swift, unbroken narrative, much of it military, whereas the *Annals* depend much more on the interweaving of domestic and foreign affairs.

But such differences between one work and another are of small importance compared with the persistence throughout Tacitus' writings of a certain sort of political judgment based on a moral concept of how the public man in Roman life ought to behave. This ideal, overwhelmingly aristocratic in its formulation, is epitomised by the word *uirtus*, the idea of 'doing the state some service' both in peace and war. It is Tacitus' realisation of the gulf that exists between that ideal and men's practice that gives to his work such a general air of pessimism, and it is his attempt to explain the reasons for the gap between a man's public *persona* and his inner self that leads to what is most profound in his writing, the probing analysis of the political relationship between *princeps* and senators.

Tacitus is, by common consent, the greatest of Roman historians, and I shall have achieved my aim if what I have written helps those who read him, in English or in Latin, to understand why this is so. It will be an added bonus if a few readers are encouraged to look at some of him in Latin: no one who succeeds in reading even a little of Tacitus in the original is likely to feel that the effort has been wasted. I know of no English translation that, for any sustained length of time, conveys the flavour of his Latinity. For this reason I have tried in the chapter on style to keep in mind the needs of the Latin-less reader, and to give him some insight into what makes Tacitus' style original and memorable. But there is more to him than an original style. His language is peculiarly adapted to the expression of his thought, which is both subtle and complex, with its intermeshing of objective and subjective, and its frequent displacement of emphasis from the statement of action to the suggestion of motive or the reaction of interested parties. Only by understanding the nature of Tacitus' linguistic virtuosity can one understand what purpose he seeks to achieve by it.

It is necessary also to be aware of the tradition within which he wrote, and what he imported into that tradition. The aim of Greco-Roman historiography was not simply to record what actually happened, *was eigentlich geschah*, but to write with distinction. For Tacitus, however, fine writing was not enough; it had to serve his interpretation of historical events. That interpretation was conveyed in an imaginative reconstruction of the past, whose character may, in modern terms, more fairly be described as impressionistic than pragmatic or scientific. Material is selected, arranged and emphasised for effect, but the unity of the whole is sustained by a style that combines brilliance and tonal subtlety. However, it should not be assumed that, because the finished product is a work of art, it is not based on a solid foundation of fact. The nature of Tacitus' sources and the way he has used them are vexed problems of modern scholarship. Some have maintained that Tacitus has done little more than transmute by stylistic alchemy a pre-existing literary source, others that he has investigated and weighed all available evidence with the scrupulousness of a modern historian. Neither extreme is inherently very plausible, nor is it certain that the answer is identical for the *Histories* (as far as they survive) and the *Annals*. The problems receive separate consideration below (Chapters 8 and 9), but a solution falling midway between those two extremes is implicit in all that follows.

Since much of Tacitus' originality consists of putting new wines into old bottles, an introductory chapter briefly surveys the Roman tradition of historical writing. To that tradition, with its right to speak freely and fearlessly, Tacitus proudly claims allegiance. But since he lives in an age whose literature and politics reflect a society in which the effective supremacy of the *princeps* is accepted, Tacitus must also be seen within the context of his own times (Chapter 2). Each of his five works (*Agricola, Germania, Dialogus, Histories, Annals*) is then considered in chronological order (Chapters 3–7). There follow chapters on his sources (Chapters 8 and 9) and style (Chapter 10). A brief postscript describes the thread (or, rather, threads) by which his text has been transmitted to modern times, and gives some indication of the changing fortunes and influence that his writings have enjoyed from the Renaissance to the present.

There remains the pleasant duty of recording my gratitude to three friends and colleagues: to Harold Mattingly, Professor of Ancient History in my own University, for his careful reading and helpful comments on the first two chapters, to Kenneth Wellesley, Reader in Humanity in the University of Edinburgh, and to Frank Goodyear, Hildred Carlile Professor of Latin at Bedford College in the University of London. Both of them have commented extensively on all but the initial chapters, and—as befits friends of long standing—have done so uninhibitedly. Professor Goodyear has put me still further in his debt

11

by comments on many sections that I have submitted to him in revised drafts. What I have written has been greatly improved by their criticisms: the imperfections that remain must be laid firmly at my door.

# I

# THE TRADITION

There are several fields in the ancient world in which the Roman achievement is unchallenged: government, law, military organization, structural architecture above all. In other spheres the Romans readily acknowledged an inferiority, and although there is an element of disingenuousness in this modesty, it is true that in the fine arts they were neither originators nor capable of surpassing the best that others, especially the Greeks, had produced. The dependence on Greek models is particularly conspicuous in literature, where, according to Quintilian (writing just before AD 100), satire alone could be claimed by the Romans as their own. The case of drama illustrates the general truth. Although many types of dramatic entertainment existed in the Italian peninsula from an early date, including one, the Atellan farce, which seems to have been a precursor of the *commedia dell'arte*, it was not until the second half of the third century BC that formal tragedy and comedy were established in Rome; and when they did come, they were direct adaptations of Greek plays.

The same is true of historical writing: only about 200 BC did the Romans begin to write history as a distinct literary genre. When they did so, they turned, as in drama, to Greek models, and, significantly, the first native Roman history[1] was written in Greek,[2] not Latin. Only fragments remain of Fabius Pictor's history, and the same is true of the works of all Roman historians until the second half of the first century BC. But from these fragments and the circumstances in which they were written much can be learned that is to remain valid for the main stream of Roman historiography until the time of Tacitus and beyond. For in literature, as in political and social organization, the Romans were fundamentally conservative; an appeal to tradition (*mos maiorum*, lit. 'the practice, custom of one's ancestors') was assured of a ready response.

The Roman tradition of historical writing, then, evolved gradually, adding to native Roman elements, mostly non-literary, an awareness of structure and style derived from the Greeks, but tenaciously preserving as much as it could from what had gone before, adapting it, where necessary, to the changed circumstances.

Before the Greek sense of structure and style began to be applied to Roman historical writing, the native Roman element already provided a firm warp on which the fabric could be constructed. Among the native strands, a number call for special mention because of their importance and persistence. From an early date the chief priest, the *pontifex maximus*, inscribed on a wooden tablet a list of public events. Though Servius (on *Aen.* 1.373) may ascribe to these *tabulae pontificum* more than they actually contained, it is reasonably certain that, in one form or another, there were available for consultation lists giving 'the names of consuls and other magistrates . . . and memorable events that had occurred at home and abroad, on land and sea, day by day'.[3] The detail contained in these lists is likely to have been meagre and the style jejune; the brief political, religious and military details that frequently occur in Roman historians at the end of a year's narrative may reasonably be thought to reproduce something of their nature.

Though the essence of the *tabulae pontificum* was their factual credibility, their function was, in the broadest sense, political. More overtly political in its purpose were the aristocratic funeral oration (cf. OCD *laudatio funebris*) and a good deal of deliberative and forensic oratory. Though Cicero might make superior remarks about the inadequacy of their style, their purpose was to persuade; to do so they must have made use of emotive language. Language as the servant of political ends was to continue as a powerful current in Roman historiography, for even if history came to be regarded as a literary genre, most of its practitioners were, or had been, active politicians, and for some history was to be used quite explicitly in furtherance of their political views and aims. Added to this strongly political bias in the Roman outlook was a basic tendency to judge political action in moral categories. This not only means seeing the aim of writing history as moral improvement (that can be paralleled from Greek historians, though the attitude is more all-pervasive among the Romans), but affects judgment of motive and (thus) interpretation of events.

In the weft that the Greek influence contributed a number of strands can be discerned. They belong primarily to the sphere of literary technique, and derive from Hellenistic historians of the late fourth century and after.[4] The first strand, that of rhetorical history, comes from the 'orator' Isocrates[5] through Timaeus to Rome, where its imprint is most clearly visible in Cicero's statement that history is a task that above all others calls for rhetorical treatment (*historia. . . opus unum oratorium maxime: De legibus* 1.5. See further p. 19, below). The second strand is that of dramatic history, whose aim was to select and organize material in such a way that it would produce the emotions of pity and horror. It refrains from discussing causes and effects, since objective comment would spoil the dramatic illusion. In Greek it is particularly associated with the names of Duris and Phylarchus.

At times, if the subject matter were itself tragic, rhetorical and dramatic tendencies might coincide, nor is it wise in general to draw too sharp distinctions between the two, though Polybius, who is the source of most of our knowledge of the two foregoing types of history, does make such a distinction. Polybius himself is a representative of a third type of historical writing, which he calls *pragmatikē historia*—not 'pragmatic' history so much as 'serious' history. His work emphasised political and military history, aiming not at literary or dramatic effect, but designed to be of use to those engaged in political life. For the Romans Polybius' importance is manifold; the idea of history as concerned with, and as an aid to, politics was congenial to the senatorial ethos, while as a primary source for Livy's account of Greek affairs from Book XXI and as contributor to the political thought of Cicero's *De re publica* his influence is immense and palpable.

Roman history comes into its own with the figure of M. Porcius Cato ('Cato the Censor', born 234, died 149; cf. OCD Cato (1)). In history, as in politics, Cato is a giant, and a giant about whom we are exceptionally well informed.[6] His background is important. A country-man from Tusculum (15 miles SE of Rome) he served as a military tribune in the later stages of the Second Punic War, and began a political career as quaestor in Sicily in 204. After serving as praetor in Sardinia in 198 he reached the consulship in 195, and became censor in 184 at the age of fifty; he was to continue as an active figure in politics for another thirty-five years. Although a 'new man' in Roman politics[7] he was a staunch upholder of traditional morality, and strongly opposed what he believed to be the subversive effect of the philhel-lenism of aristocrats such as Scipio Africanus—in public he concealed his own not inconsiderable knowledge of Greek culture. The attitude of being *plus royaliste que le roi* in the sphere of morality becomes almost a stereotype with politicians of non-Roman origins.

His surviving *De agri cultura*, the earliest extant work in Latin prose, is an important social and economic document, showing the

15

completely unsentimental approach of a successful farmer determined to secure a good return on his capital. A considerable orator (fragments of over eighty speeches survive) and inveterate litigant, the writer of a (lost) encyclopaedia for his son, Cato is the first Latin historian of whom sufficient remains to enable us to make reasonably sure judgments on the work as a whole. Its title, *Origines*, recalls the foundation histories of the Greeks, and the first three of its seven books are truly *origines* (I Rome; II and III other Italian cities). But Book IV takes Roman history as far as the battle of Cannae in 216, and since the fifth book comes down at least to 167, the last two books must have been on a larger scale than the preceding ones; not for nothing did Livy describe Cato as not given to self-disparagement (Livy 34.15.9 *haud sane detrectator laudum suarum*), for while in the military narrative of the earlier books Cato had deliberately excluded the names of generals, he included a number of his own speeches in the later books.

Three features of Cato's *Origines* are of particular relevance to Tacitus. First, his assertion at the outset of the work that men must be accountable as much for what they did in their leisure as in their public life indicates that he believed that for a senator the writing of history was 'a continuation of politics by other means'. Secondly, the disdain he expressed (frag. 77) for the jejuneness of what was recorded on the *tabulae pontificum* shows a consciousness that history called for a more organized structure and a more elevated style. Lastly, Cato's advocacy of an austere morality and his outspoken hostility to extravagance affords a theme congenial to Tacitus, even though Tacitus is aware that increased prosperity must necessarily bring some relaxation in standards.[8]

The example set by Cato was followed in many respects by L. Calpurnius Piso Frugi. Consul in 133 and censor in 120, he had already made his mark in politics when, as tribune in 149, he carried the law that established a permanent court for the trial of provincial governors for extortion. His history, like Cato's, covered from the origins of Rome to his own day, and even more than Cato he emphasised the moral element, contrasting contemporary vice with earlier virtue.[9] The idea of a progressive moral deterioration is a commonplace of Greek and Roman thought, but by seeking to identify a specific cause and a specific date for its inception Piso adapts the idea in a way that was to have a decisive influence on Roman historiography. Fragment 34 states that it was the conquest of Asia Minor by Cn. Manlius Vulso in 187 BC that saw the introduction of luxury into Rome (cf. Livy 39.6.7), while fragment 38 gives 154 as the date when morality (*pudicitia*) was undermined. But though Piso shares with Cato his strong advocacy of moral rectitude, he diverges from him by calling his work *annales*, thus acknowledging his indebtedness to the annalistic tradition of the *tabulae pontificum*;[10] his style, in keeping with that tradition, is described by Cicero (*Brutus* 106) as 'thin'.

The publication by the *pontifex maximus*, P. Mucius Scaevola, some time after 130 BC, of the *annales maximi* in eighty books gave a new direction to Roman historiography. Now that a firm annalistic framework was readily available outside the senatorial class, senators turned away from writing annalistic history, and non-senators, for the first time, come into the reckoning. It is at this time that political autobiography begins to be practised by leading senators, such as M. Aemilius Scaurus (consul 115) and P. Rutilius Rufus (consul 105).[11] In spite of Tacitus' claim at *Agricola* 1.3 that such autobiographies were common during the period of the Republic, this is a new development that shows a decline from earlier Roman *modestia* and self-effacement.

Among non-senators one of the first to make a name as a historian was L. Coelius Antipater (OCD Coelius (1)), the teacher of Cicero's oratorical model, L. Licinius Crassus. Antipater marks a new stage in Roman historiography. His originality is visible in at least three aspects—his work is a monograph (on the Second Punic War), not an extended history; he deliberately set out to be an *exornator* ('embellisher') rather than a mere *narrator*; and he is the first Roman historian to include wholly invented speeches. His invention is not restricted to speeches, for he introduces dreams and storms at sea to heighten his narrative. Though Cicero laughs at the faults of his style, such as affected rhythms and excessive hyperbaton, he wins Cicero's acclaim as being the first Roman historian who even begins to approach Cicero's own ideal, essentially the Isocratean ideal.

Although Coelius blazed a new trail for Roman historiography, and one that was eventually to exert a decisive influence on it, the way he had shown was not immediately followed by others. Sempronius Asellio, who had served as a military tribune at Numantia, wrote a history of his own times, at least as far as 91 BC, on the model of Polybius' 'pragmatic' history. The lack of style, which Cicero criticises in him, may have been a factor in helping to consign him to almost total oblivion. Yet, though his history seems to have remained virtually unread (Aulus Gellius, 200 years later, is the first person to quote him), the concept he had of history's function is an important one. He distinguishes between *annales*, which simply state what happened in each year, and a higher type of writing that sought to explain cause and motive. The former type of writing is 'to tell tales to children, not to write history'. Only by the latter type of writing can the historian achieve what, according to Asellio, is its true purpose, to make the reader more ready to serve and defend his country; that is a note that will recur in many subsequent historians.[12]

The half century that lay between the tribunate of Tiberius Gracchus and the dictatorship of Sulla (133 to 81) was one in which intense political rivalry escalated from acrimony to bloodshed and civil war. Though the next thirty years—until the outbreak of civil war between Pompey and Julius Caesar—saw little abatement in factional politics, there was (apart from the Catilinarian Conspiracy) a tacit agreement to pursue political power within the traditional structure of government.[13] During this period historians continue to divide, broadly speaking, into two categories, writers with first-hand experience of politics and those for whom history was primarily a literary pursuit. The former category is represented by two writers of opposing political views. C. Licinius Macer reached the praetorship by 68 but, being convicted of extortion, committed suicide in 66. In politics he was an anti-Sullan *popularis* upholding the sovereignty of the people,[14] and in writing of the history of Rome from its foundation he interpreted the Struggle of the Orders in the light of contemporary struggles between *populus* and self-seeking nobles. An older contemporary, L. Cornelius Sisenna, who was praetor in 78, defended Verres in 70, and was legate to Pompey in 67, concentrated on contemporary history, especially the Social War and the Sullan Civil War, and earned Sallust's rebuke for his partisanship for Sulla (*Jug.* 95.2).

By contrast Q. Claudius Quadrigarius, also writing in the post-Sullan period, had first-hand knowledge of neither politics nor warfare. His history in at least twenty-three books covered the period from the sack of Rome by the Gauls (traditionally 390) to his own day. It provided neither political enlightenment nor moral improvement, but had as its primary purpose the entertainment of the reader. In furtherance of this aim letters, speeches and decrees seem to have been freely invented by him and, like his contemporary, Valerius Antias (see below), he had a penchant for exaggerating the number of enemy slain. His style showed that admixture of archaic and poetic vocabulary, accidence and syntax that by now had become a feature of

Roman historical writing. Because of this he attracted the attention of that lover of all things archaic, Aulus Gellius, who provides a number of lengthy fragments, some of which admit of a direct comparison with Livy, who drew heavily on him.[15]

Valerius Antias so 'fully observed the Isocratean canons of (in fact) plausibly detailed mendacity' (Badian, op. cit. 21) that his gross exaggeration of numbers earned the rebuke even of Livy's easy-going credulousness. Elaboration and invention were extensively employed to win and hold the reader's attention. Whether or not he marks 'the nadir of historiography' (Badian), he represents conspicuously one direction in which Greco-Roman historical writing might go, when divorced from an understanding of the workings of politics. Parodying Plato's remark about the need for philosopher-kings (*Republic* 5.473) Polybius had written 'History will never be written properly until either men of action undertake to write it . . . or historians become convinced that practical experience is of the first importance for historical composition' (12.28.3–5). By that criterion Valerius Antias stands condemned. The fact that Livy, in spite of his reproaches, uses him extensively—his most enduring monument is in the pages of Livy[16]—tells us a good deal about Livy.

By now all the main strands that contribute to Roman historiography had been developed, but as yet no Roman historian had succeeded in combining them in a work that could challenge the best work of the Greeks. That deficiency is a subject to which Cicero gives much attention during the period of leisure forced upon him by the triumvirs after his return from exile in 57 BC. For Cicero the way in which that Roman shortcoming might be remedied was clear. It could be taken for granted that the historian must tell the truth and the whole truth, without favour or malice, but the crucial quality that he is looking for—and which no Roman historian had so far produced—was rhetorical embellishment. That aim, stated most clearly in the *De oratore*, published in 55 (see especially 2.52–54 and 62), proclaims in Latin the Isocratean ideal of historical writing (see p. 15 above). It is a view to be epitomised by Cicero a few years later in the aphorism, already quoted, that 'history is a task that above all calls for the orator's skill'.

In spite of his lip-service to the need for the historian to tell the truth, a much-quoted letter, written the year before the *De oratore*, shows that Cicero regarded rhetorical embellishment as an important weapon of tendentious political interpretation. He writes to his friend, Lucius

Lucceius, asking him to write a historical monograph on Cicero himself from the beginning of the Catilinarian conspiracy (crushed by Cicero during his consulship in 63) to Cicero's return from exile in 57. The theme had dramatic possibilities, and Cicero begs Lucceius— even though it would involve him in ignoring the 'laws of history'—to be generous to him, even beyond the strict limits of truth (*plusculum etiam quam concedet ueritas*; *Ad fam.* 5.12.3). The dangers inherent in such a manner of writing history need no underlining.

Lucceius never wrote the monograph that Cicero had asked of him, and a generation was to pass before Livy realised the style that Cicero had envisaged for a historian. Before then a younger contemporary of Cicero had achieved signal success by writing history in a manner that is the complete antithesis of Cicero's ideal.[17] It is on him, more than on any other writer, that Tacitus models his historical style. C. Sallustius Crispus (Sallust), after a chequered political career, during which he was expelled from the senate and escaped conviction for extortion as governor of Africa only through the intervention of Caesar, abandoned politics for writing after (or shortly before) the death of Caesar. In the prologues, which are as conspicuous a feature of his works as they are of Tacitus', he draws a close analogy between the making of history and the writing of it, even claiming in the later work, the *Bellum Iugurthinum*, that in view of the political circumstances then obtaining (about 40 BC) the product of his leisure was more beneficial to the state than the political activity of others.

From the outset Sallust decided to write history 'selectively' (*carptim*), and, as a result, his first two works are monographs.[18] Details are accordingly selected and arranged in such a way as to emphasise themes and lessons of Sallust's own choosing. In his *Catilinarian Conspiracy*[19] Sallust has chosen his subject because it is 'particularly memorable through the unprecedented nature of the crime and the danger it brought', and its main emphasis is on the moral crisis of the Republic.[20] Since, however, for the Romans morals and politics are inseparable, Sallust judges moral standards by the touchstone of *uirtus*, more nearly 'excellence as displayed in public life' than our 'moral virtue'.[21] For the writing of his *Jugurthine War* Sallust gives two reasons: it was a great and bloody war, with fluctuating fortune; and it was the first occasion on which the arrogant behaviour of the aristocrats (*nobiles*) was challenged. Dramatic and political motives thus combine, and this conjunction will be seen to be a prominent feature of Tacitus' writing, as is the emphasis on the concept of *uirtus*.

But one conspicuous feature of Sallust's writings, his popularist sympathies, plays no part in Tacitus. By Tacitus' day popularist politics no longer existed.

However, Tacitus' main indebtedness to Sallust is in style. The jibe that Sallust plagiarised the works of the Elder Cato for unusual words is a distortion of the fact that Sallust sought to add dignity and elevation to his style by a liberal recourse to the vocabulary of earlier writers. But more important than archaising vocabulary (which is indeed a significant feature of much of Roman historiography) is the fact that Sallust looks to Cato in Latin and Thucydides in Greek for certain qualities of mind; from Thucydides a stark recognition of the contrast between political profession and reality, from Cato—a *nouus homo* like himself—a political stance that questioned the aristocrats' judgment of their own worth. Along with this questioning spirit went a rejection of the bland, measured phrases that betokened comfortable acceptance of the political *status quo*. The deliberate disruption of syntactical balance[22] means that Sallust's style is the complete antithesis of the Ciceronian. So, when Quintilian, to whom the name of Cicero was synonymous with that of eloquence, is recommending models for the would-be orator, he warns his reader against imitating Sallust. But though Sallust is an unsuitable model for the orator, he is, in Quintilian's judgment, Rome's outstanding historian. Quintilian notes two qualities in particular, brevity (*breuitas*) and speed—of the latter quality he admiringly says *illa inmortalis Sallusti uelocitas* (10.1.102). Syntax and sentence structure are the external features that contribute to those qualities—omission of verb forms, use of historic infinitives and historic present tenses are among the means—but, in the last resort, speed and brevity are more the product of a certain mental attitude. Sallust is particularly effective in two spheres, in rapid narrative (where speed is combined with colour and drama) and in descriptions of character (primarily of human beings, but also of places). In this latter sphere Sallust's gift for pithy expression, often accompanied by antithesis, finds particular play.[23] But sometimes, especially in the extended reflections on politics and society, the pithiness of the individual phrase is diluted by a tendency to repetitiveness.[24]

There is one other conspicuous feature of Sallust's style in which, though his penchant for antithesis and aphorism is manifest, there is displayed an expansiveness that is more in keeping with the tradition of rhetorical historiography than with the brevity and speed of his narrative style. That is the use of the long invented speech. Such speeches, which occur in all his works,[25] far exceed in length (some of them are well over a hundred lines) anything that Tacitus permits himself, and they inevitably contain some rhetorical padding. But a number of them[26] have a clear political import, mostly with a strong popularist bias. So Marius places merit above birth and privilege; *ex uirtute nobilitas coepit* ('nobility starts from merit'; *Jug.* 85.17).

The Sallustian style, though it fits within the Roman historical tradition, is a new creation. For a time 'chopped off sentences, words ending unexpectedly, and an obscure brevity were all the rage' (Seneca, *Epist.* 114. 17). But within a generation fashions had changed, and at last there appears a work that matched up to the Ciceronian ideal. The 142 books of Livy's history *Ab urbe condita* ('From the Founding of the City') would occupy something like nine thousand pages of a modern book. The magnitude of the task would have precluded the possibility of close investigation of sources, even had that been the custom in antiquity. Moreover Livy, alone of the major Roman historians, had no experience of political life. Neither profundity nor acute political analysis are to be expected of him. Nevertheless he has considerable merits. Each new historian, he tells us (*Preface* 2), hopes either to establish the facts with greater certainty or to surpass his predecessors by the excellence of his style (*arte scribendi*). Though he does not make the claim, it is on the second score that Livy merits the reader's attention. His style is not quite so uniform as Quintilian's 'milky richness' (*lactea ubertas*) might suggest, but by his ability to sustain an equable flow in his narrative style, coupled with a purely classical vocabulary, he achieves, more fully than any other Roman historian, Cicero's ideal of a *genus orationis fusum atque tractum* ('copious and flowing'; *De oratore* 2.64).

Livy's style, itself a striking example of the Augustan Age's striving for perfection of form, is well suited to its subject matter, which also reflects the spirit of the Age. The *Pax Augusta*, after a generation of civil wars, offered the Roman world hope of peace and prosperity, built upon the traditional virtues. A line of Ennius, *moribus antiquis res stat Romana uirisque* ('It is through her ancient ways and men that the Roman state stands firm'), might stand as the text on which Livy wrote his history;[27] 'ways', 'men', 'discipline' all figure in a key sentence in the *Preface* (para. 9), and the following sentence states what, in Livy's view, should be the historian's aim: it is to provide examples of good and bad behaviour for his readers to follow. The full extent of Livy's contribution to Tacitus has not yet fully been investigated, but it seems that Livian echoes may be commoner in the *Histories* than in the *Annals*. Certainly it is in conspicuous moments of valour or shame (*uirtus* and *pudor*) that Tacitus has recourse to Livian analogues (see the Dillius Vocula episode, pp. 97–8).[28]

Though Livy is in many respects a typical representative of the Augustan Age, he may in other ways be regarded as the last of the Republican historians.[29] After Livy no one could write history without the realisation that power ultimately lay in the hands of a single person. Of all those who wrote Roman history during the hundred years between Livy and Tacitus only the most meagre fragments survive.[30] Names can be given, and something said about the men or their writings, enough perhaps to throw some doubt on Tacitus' assertion (*Ann.* 1.1.2) that (himself, of course, excepted) the works of historians of the Principate from Tiberius to Nero were all vitiated by flattery of an emperor during his lifetime and hatred after his death.

Cremutius Cordus, a victim of Sejanus in AD 25, was outspokenly republican in his sentiments (See *Ann.* 4.34 and p. 137, below), the consular Servilius Nonianus (d. AD 59) receives a warm obituary tribute from Tacitus (*Ann.* 14.19),[31] while the Epicurean Aufidius Bassus' history was so well known that the Elder Pliny could designate his own history simply as *a fine Aufidi Bassi* ('From the point where Aufidius Bassus stopped').[32]

What influence any of the above historians may have exercised on Tacitus defies rational speculation. With three writers of the next generation (or generations), though their historical work too is lost, we come to historians on whom Tacitus certainly drew in some measure (See cc. VIII and IX). Of the three only Cluvius Rufus was a senator (consul probably during the reign of Gaius). A letter of Pliny (9.19), in which Cluvius apologises to Verginius Rufus for his outspokenness, may give an exaggerated idea of his candour; he found himself able to serve in turn Nero, Galba, Otho and Vitellius. It is possible (but not certain) that he included an element of spicy gossip in his history.[33] Pliny the Elder, who had a notable equestrian career and died in the eruption of Vesuvius in AD 79, was clearly an important source for Tacitus for German affairs and for at least some of the domestic events of Nero's reign, but it is unlikely that he could have contributed much to the senatorial sections of Tacitus' work. The third writer, Fabius Rusticus, may have been of a younger generation than Cluvius and Pliny,[34] but though Tacitus speaks highly of him in the *Agricola* ('most

23

eloquent of recent writers'; 10.3), there is no evidence that he had a senatorial career, and Tacitus seems to regard his evidence as suspect because of his allegiance to Seneca (see *Ann.* 13.20.2; 14.2.2; 15.61.3).

Tradition endures. As it was for politics, religion, and institutions, so was it for Roman historiography. Tacitus wrote with full consciousness of that tradition. But in doing so it is to the historians of the Republic that he looks: for those who wrote of imperial times during the first century AD he has only contempt—their work is vitiated by flattery or hatred. Yet Republican historiography was not without its contradictions. Above all there was a dichotomy between those who wrote, without political understanding, to entertain rather than to instruct, and those whose motives for writing were, explicitly or implicitly, political.

Tacitus clearly stands with those who believe that history has a political purpose. In an important excursus in the *Annals* (4.32-33), while regretting that the imperial historian has no glorious military victories to record, and at home only an unbroken tale of political persecution and treachery to tell, he asserts that his history will be of use, since 'few are able to distinguish in advance what is honourable from what is base, and what is useful from what is harmful, whereas the majority are instructed by what happens to others' (4.33.2). And at the beginning of the *Histories* (1.4.1) he emphasises that his aim is to reveal to the reader 'not only the course of events and their outcome (for these are generally a matter of chance), but also their underlying causes' (see p. 69). He thus places himself firmly in the tradition of serious ('pragmatic') historical writing that was exemplified by Sempronius Asellio (see p. 17-8).

But, unlike Asellio, he also regards history as a literary genre. Rhetorical technique is most apparent in the invented speeches, which (in common with many Greek and Roman historians) he inserted in his works, but it is also obvious in the colourful language of much of his descriptive narrative, and in the telling comment—often made in the form of an epigram—which he himself appends to men's actions or motives. But whereas many writers, like the non-senatorial Coelius Antipater (see p. 17), regarded rhetoric and colourful language merely as means to entertain the reader, Tacitus mostly[35] uses them to drive home his interpretation of events or persons. In this way he seeks to resolve the dichotomy between 'pragmatic' and literary history.

It is to the elder Cato (see p. 15f.) and Sallust (see p. 20f.) among earlier historians that Tacitus' debt is the greatest. Like Cato he was neither aristocrat nor Roman born, and like Cato he advocated an austere code of public morals and conduct, which the scions of the old aristocracy seemed in many cases to have abandoned. But it is on Sallust, not on Cato, that Tacitus draws both for the basic elements of his style and for the dominating importance he assigns to the concept of *uirtus* as both the spring and the touchstone of political action by the senatorial class.

But since Tacitus is living under, and writing of, the Principate, he interprets *uirtus* in a different way from Sallust. During the Republic the values attached to the concept were principally determined by two factors, factional rivalry within the senatorial class, and the social and political superiority that the senate as a class enjoyed over all other classes. These factors continued to operate to some degree under the Empire, but they did so beneath the inescapable supremacy of the *princeps*, which decisively circumscribed the manner and sphere in which a senator could now hope to display his *uirtus*. Consequently there runs through all Tacitus' historical writings (the *Agricola* included) a continuous thread: how was a senator to 'do the state some service' without either sycophancy or offence to the princeps?

The publicly proclaimed fiction that the emperor was only *primus inter pares* ('first among equals') was a fertile source of friction and misunderstanding. It is perhaps in his handling of this material that Tacitus is both most traditional and most original. He is traditional because he writes of senatorial politics as one who was himself a successful senator and politician. But he also shows an awareness of the disparity between the republican concept of a senatorial career, limited only by competition with one's peers, and the senator's actual position in an era in which his freedom was restricted by the autocracy of the emperor. That awareness generates in his writing a nervous tension that is unique among Roman historians. Though he might claim to be free from factional politics in the old sense, his assertion (*Ann.* 1.1.3) that he will write *sine ira et studio* ('without anger or partisanship') scarcely applies to his treatment of the relationship between *princeps* and senate. On that issue he writes with understanding, but also with passion. In so doing he remains true to the tradition of senatorial historians of the Republic.

# III

# TACITUS AND THE CONTEMPORARY SCENE

Neither date nor place of Tacitus' birth are known; there is uncertainty even about his *praenomen*, Gaius or Publius.[1] From the dates at which he held various magistracies it can be inferred with reasonable accuracy that he was born in AD 56 or 57, a date that fits with his description of himself as *iuuenis admodum* ('just a young man'; *Dial.*1.2) at the time of the dramatic date of the *Dialogus*, namely AD 75. An extensive literature has developed on the place or region of his birth, Gallia Narbonensis (Provence) and Transpadane Italy being the most likely candidates.[2] A letter of Pliny, which is important in another context, makes it probable that the question 'Are you an Italian or a provincial?' (9.23.2) applies equally to Pliny, born in Comum (Como in north Italy), and Tacitus. The Elder Pliny knew a Cornelius Tacitus, who as a Roman knight was procurator of Gallia Belgica. It is possible that this person was the father, or an uncle, of our historian; equestrian status in his father would open the way to a young man for a political career at Rome.

It is probable that he came to Rome to complete his education, combining the study of rhetoric with attendance at the courts as a pupil of one of the leading orators of the day. Whether he studied under Quintilian, first holder of the imperial chair of Latin rhetoric, as did his younger contemporary, Pliny, is uncertain. The *Dialogus* makes it clear that he was well acquainted with Quintilian's theories, but was neither convinced by them as an explanation of the contemporary decline in oratory nor as a prescription for its revival on neo-Ciceronian lines.

Law and convention laid down within close limits the ages and stages of political advancement for those who sought a senatorial career. In the first chapter of the *Histories* Tacitus admits that under each of the three Flavian emperors his career moved forward, making considerable advances under Domitian. To Vespasian (d.79) he must have been indebted for the grant of the right to wear the broad purple stripe on his toga that indicated that he intended, and had been given permission, to aim at a senatorial career. Before he was twenty he would serve in one of the minor civilian posts of the vigintivirate, and that would be followed at about the age of twenty by a short period of military service as a military tribune. We learn from the *Agricola* (9.6) that in AD 77[3] he married the daughter of Britain's newly elected governor, Iulius Agricola.

The next, crucial step on the ladder was election to the quaestorship, for it brought with it membership of the senate. It is to this that Tacitus must allude when he states (loc. cit.) that his *dignitas* (roughly 'status') was extended by the emperor Titus. As 25 was the lowest age at which this post was normally held, Tacitus must have held it in 81 or 82.[4] Half of the annually appointed quaestors served abroad under the proconsuls of senatorial provinces, the remainder had duties in Rome. After the quaestorship came either the tribunate of the plebs or an aedileship, a step in the ladder from which sons of patrician senators were excused. The next magistracy, rarely held before the age of 31 or 32, the praetorship, would constitute the highest office to be held by a number of those who had passed through the earlier positions. Here, for the first time, we are on firm ground for Tacitus. In *Annals* 11.11.1, talking of the Secular Games held during the reign of Claudius in AD 47, he mentions that the games were also held in Domitian's reign (in the year 88),[5] and that he himself was particularly involved with them, because he was one of the priestly college of fifteen 'and praetor at the time'. Tacitus thus attained the praetorship in the earliest year that might be expected of him.[6] Membership of the quindecimviral college, on the other hand, was a signal honour. The four major religious colleges[7] totalled about sixty persons in all, and, since membership was for life, only a portion of those who attained the praetorship could expect to achieve the honour. The Younger Pliny, though covetous of the distinction, had to wait till after his consulship before becoming an augur.[8]

After the praetorship the number of available posts contracts, and their nature and prestige begin to be differentiated. A three-year post as *legatus legionis* (legionary legate) was the first goal of the man who sought to advance further.[9] Perhaps half of those who had reached the praetorship might expect, not always immediately after vacating that office, to become legionary legates. From *Agricola* 45.5 we learn that Tacitus and his wife had been absent for a period of four years (*quadriennium*) at the date of Agricola's death in August AD 93. Since few *noui homines* (lit. 'new men'; see p. 15) reached the consulship in this age without previously having held the post of legionary legate,[10] it is natural to assume that Tacitus' absence from Rome immediately after he had been praetor is due to the fact that he was for most of that time a legionary legate; the fourth year of his absence might be accounted for by tenure of the proconsular governorship of a minor province. It should be remembered that the rebellion of the governor of Upper Germany (Antonius Saturninus) at the beginning of AD 89, coupled with heavy military pressure on the Danube, would make Domitian more than usually glad to have reliable legionary legates in post.

Tenure of the post of legionary legate afforded a strong presumption that the holder might at some time reach the consulship, since the practice of appointing suffect consuls had multiplied the number of annual appointments,[11] but the age at which a man could expect to reach the consulship differed. A small class who had shown exceptional ability in the military sphere (not necessarily restricted to fighting a successful war) might quickly be called on to govern as the emperor's legate a non-consular imperial province. Such men could expect a swift elevation to the consulship. A striking example of the type is Tacitus' father-in-law, Agricola. After serving as legionary legate of the Twentieth Legion under Petillius Cerialis in Britain he was appointed as governor of Aquitania with the certainty of a consulship to follow.[12]

But such men were exceptional, and Tacitus was not one of them. He was appointed one of the suffect consuls for the year 97 at the age of 41 or 42. To have reached that goal earlier would have signified something exceptional.[13] What is not certain, but reasonably probable, is that his consulship was decided by Domitian, before his murder in September 96; not for nothing did Tacitus later admit (*Hist.* 1.1.3, referred to above) that his position had been considerably advanced by Domitian.

During the months that he held his suffect consulship Tacitus was called on to deliver the funeral oration at the public funeral of Verginius Rufus, who had entered on his third consulship as *consul ordinarius* for the year with the emperor Nerva. Verginius' hour of greatness had come thirty years earlier, when he had both crushed the Gallic revolt of Iulius Vindex and refused himself to accept the offer of the Principate from the troops of Upper Germany, whose legate he was. His support for Otho after the murder of Galba gained him a second consulship in AD 69, but throughout the whole of the Flavian dynasty (69–96) he was without further employment or honour. His consulship with Nerva in 97 may well have been a deliberate gesture by that emperor to point the contrast with the neglect Verginius had suffered under the preceding dynasty.

Our knowledge of Tacitus' part in Verginius' funeral comes, as does so much else, from Pliny's letters. To Verginius Pliny owed a special debt of *pietas*, for Verginius had been his legal *tutor* after the death of his father. Pliny's description of Tacitus on this occasion as *laudator eloquentissimus* ('a most eloquent panegyrist'; 2.1.6) is a reminder that at this point in his career Tacitus' reputation depends on his public oratory. The next public act of Tacitus of which we have knowledge (Pliny is again our informant; *Ep.* 2.11) is his appearance as joint prosecutor, along with Pliny, of the proconsul of Africa, Marius Priscus, on charges of cruelty and maladministration. The investigation, begun in late 98 or early 99, was not concluded until January 100, when Trajan himself was present. Tacitus' performance on that occasion is described by Pliny (2.11.17): 'Cornelius Tacitus replied most eloquently and with that elevation that is a particular feature of his oratory.'[14] Two years after his consulship it is still for his eloquence that Tacitus is known.

After holding the consulship a man might, or might not, find further public employment; even if he did nothing, his status as an ex-consul (*consularis*) gave him prestige and influence both within the senate and outside. Those who had reached the consulship after governing one of the lesser imperial provinces might generally expect to find further employment in one of the major imperial provinces, from Britain and the two Germanies in the West to Syria in the East. There were also a number of civilian posts in Rome and Italy. There is little likelihood that Tacitus would be appointed to a major military province, and no evidence that he held a further civilian post. An absence from Rome is attested by Pliny 4.13.1, but there is no indication that this was on official business, while a later paragraph in the same letter (4.13.10) indicates that at this time (104 or 105) he still had around him a number of 'pupils', attracted to him by his success at the bar. A later letter, already referred to (p. 26), suggests that as late as 107 or 108 Tacitus' reputation, like Pliny's, depended mainly on oratory.

Nevertheless the scope for grand oratory diminished, as the reign of Trajan progressed. The example of Pliny is again instructive. When he wished in the ninth Book of his Letters (publication date between 106 and 108) to include an account of an important political trial, he had to go back to the trial of Publicius Certus in AD 97. After the prosecution of Marius Priscus it is in civil cases in the centumviral court that Pliny furthers his reputation as a speaker. The same is likely to have been true of Tacitus.

In a letter in Book V (publication date probably 105–6) Pliny talks of the possibility of writing a history of either past or contemporary events. In the upshot he discards the idea; the task is too difficult, and he is too busy revising his speeches for publication (5.8.6 and 12). The letter suggests (though it does not prove) that Pliny had so far heard nothing of Tacitus' intention to write what was to become the *Histories*, covering the period from 69 to 96. But in a letter in the next Book (6.16) Pliny sends Tacitus a detailed account of his uncle's death in the eruption of Vesuvius in August of AD 79 for inclusion in the forthcoming work. In the following Book (7.33) he writes to Tacitus with an account of his own part in the prosecution of Baebius Massa in 93 for extortion as governor of Baetica (southern Spain): 'I prophesy (and my prophecy will surely come true) that your histories will be immortal; and that (I will readily admit) makes me all the more eager to find a place in them' (*auguror nec me fallit augurium, historias tuas immortales futuras; quo magis illis (ingenue fatebor) inseri cupio*). The publication dates of Pliny's sixth and seventh Books of Letters seem to be between 106–7. Since it was Tacitus who had requested information about the Elder Pliny's death, it is reasonable to assume that at this time Tacitus expected shortly to be dealing with events of AD 79. The information about the trial of Baebius Massa was unsolicited, and it cannot be inferred that Pliny knew that by now Tacitus was coming to deal with events of 93. But at least we may take it that by 107 Tacitus was well on with his task of writing the *Histories*.

Two more milestones in Tacitus' career still remained to be reached. A dozen or more years after the consulate governorship of the senatorial province of Asia was open as the culmination of a senatorial career. Election was by lot, but along with the proconsular province of Africa the lot was restricted to the most senior ex-consuls who had not already held the post, and it was possible by one means or another to discourage an unsuitable candidate.[15] An undated inscription names Tacitus as proconsul of Asia; the year must have been 112/13 or 113/14.

No firm date exists for Tacitus' last work, the *Annals*, nor for his death. For the former an important clue is given by a passage at the end of 2.61, where, speaking of Germanicus' visit to Egypt, Tacitus says, 'he reached Elephantine and Syene, once the limits of the Roman empire, which now extends to the "red sea"' (*rubrum mare*). If (as here seems probable)[16] the 'red sea' is the modern Red Sea, this gives a date after 106, when the governor of Syria, Cornelius Palma, formally annexed Arabia Petraea, and before 114, when Trajan's drive towards Mesopotamia began. If, however, the 'red sea' means the Persian Gulf (as, in some contexts, it can), a date between 115–17 is given, since Hadrian, on his accession in 117, made no attempt to hold Trajan's gains in the East. On either interpretation we gain a date only for this passage. Later books of the *Annals* may have been published in Hadrian's reign. But there is no reason to think that Tacitus needed the events of 118 to teach him the lesson of imperial concealment and intrigue.[17] His view of the Roman world from the time of Augustus had been fully formed by what he had seen and experienced during nearly thirty years of the Flavian emperors and the decade that followed the assassination of Domitian in 96.

Two general questions remain to be asked, the first about Tacitus as a politician, the second about him as a writer. The fact that we know as much as we do about Tacitus as a person is due partly to chance, partly to Pliny's cultivated ingenuousness. Even so we cannot easily estimate how successful a politician Tacitus would have seemed to himself or his contemporaries. A modern authority on Pliny[18] describes the careers of both Pliny and Tacitus as 'of moderate distinction'. That is perhaps unfair to both men. Since neither of them had the aptitude nor, seemingly, the inclination for a military career, they must be judged by their attainments in the civilian sphere. A very small number of men, whether by ability, influence or intrigue, achieved a second and, even more rarely, a third consulship.[19] Neither Tacitus nor Pliny were of that number. In the case of Tacitus we have also to remember that we do not know the whole history of his career. The nature of the employment (certainly a public post) that kept him away from Rome for four years from 89–93 is not known, nor can we say for sure whether or not he held any office or post in the fifteen years between his consulship and governorship of Asia. The evidence, such as it is, of Pliny's letters makes it reasonably certain that he was not continuously away from Rome during those years, but that does not mean that he was without employment. Certainly it would be unwise to believe that from an early date in Trajan's reign he withdrew from public life, only to be brought forth at the appropriate time for election to the proconsulate of Asia. Voluntary retirement from public life was not the way of the senatorial class.

If there is anything 'moderate' in the career of Tacitus, it is in the consistency with which he avoided extreme political positions. That is a trait that is conspicuous too in the judgments he applies to those he writes about in the *Annals*.[20] But the same attitude is stated explicitly in his first work: 'Let those who are accustomed to admire what is forbidden realise that . . . devotion to duty and moderation, if accompanied by resoluteness and strength, can attain a height of renown that many have achieved by paths of danger, crowned by an ostentatious death that brings the state no advantage' (*Agr* 42.4; see p. 47).

The history of Tacitus' own times can illustrate the point. Four classes of persons may be considered. First the *uiri militares*, those who had distinguished themselves in the military sphere. A number who had made names for themselves before the accession of Vespasian or during his reign remained inactive during Domitian's reign, only to re-emerge under Nerva or Trajan. Such men included Verginius Rufus, Vestricius Spurinna, and Iulius Frontinus, all of whom reached a third consulship between 97 and 100. Even under Domitian military men might secure advancement, but it was exceptional loyalty that was rewarded. Lappius Maximus, who crushed the revolt of Antonius Saturninus on the Rhine in 89, received from Domitian in 95 the rare distinction of a second consulate. The future emperor Nerva is the only other man to be so honoured in the last ten years of Domitian's reign. Another act of loyalty by a military commander had its reward. The legate of the seventh legion in Spain had marched north against the mutinous Saturninus in 89; Lappius Maximus had made his journey unnecessary. But in 91, still under forty, the legate reached the consulship; he was Ulpius Traianus, the future emperor.

It could perhaps be argued that military men of ability were denied continuing employment under Domitian. Such, Tacitus maintained, was the case with his father-in-law, Agricola, dissuaded (perhaps with veiled threats) from letting his name go forward for the proconsulate of Asia; such too may have been the case with Tettius Iulianus, who had won an important victory for Domitian against the Dacians in 88. But only with the revolt in 89 of Antonius Saturninus, governor of Upper Germany, were the lives of governors in peril, with the deaths of Sallustius Lucullus, possibly Agricola's successor in Britain, and of Vettulenus Civica Cerialis, governor of Asia.

In the civilian sphere three types of prominent men require notice. High prizes were available to those senators who, as friends of the emperor (*amici Caesaris*), were prepared to play on his suspicions and, if needs be, prosecute members of their own order. In the *Dialogus* Aper singles out Eprius Marcellus and Vibius Crispus as shining examples of contemporary eloquence: in reply Maternus asks, 'What is so enviable about their lot? That they fear? Or that they are feared?' Crispus reached a third consulate early in Domitian's reign. Eprius seemed set for no less distinguished a career when, in the year of Vespasian's death (79), he was convicted of conspiracy with Vitellius' former general, Caecina, and committed suicide. Four other names may be mentioned. Valerius Catullus Messalinus is coupled with Fabricius Veiento in a satire of Juvenal (4.113). Messalinus was consul for the second time in 85, Fabricius Veiento had been consul for the third time by 83 and lived on to share the table of the emperor Nerva.[21] Baebius Massa, a notorious *delator* ('informer', more particularly 'an initiator of political prosecutions'), was hoist with his own petard, being condemned in 93 on a charge of maladministration as governor of Hispania Baetica.[22] Aquilius Regulus, who had gained notoriety at the end of Nero's reign, seems to have abandoned criminal prosecution thereafter. But his undoubted success in the centumviral court did not erase his unsavoury reputation. As late as 97 Pliny contemplated prosecuting him, and his personal dislike of the man continued until Regulus' death about 104.

A second class of men comprises those whose opposition to Domitian, particularly in his last years, was fired by a philosophical anti-imperialism, in many cases handed down from the previous generation. In *Agricola* 2 and 45 four victims of the Domitianic terror are mentioned. Arulenus Rusticus had been consul as recently as 92; he had written a biography of Thrasea Paetus victim of Nero in 66. Herennius Senecio had not only written a biography of the elder Helvidius Priscus, executed in Vespasian's reign; he had had the audacity to join with Pliny in prosecuting Baebius Massa. The younger Helvidius Priscus was executed for an alleged libel of Domitian. The brother of Arulenus Rusticus escaped with banishment. Linking all these men is an adherence to Stoic principles. The persistence of that link as part of a family tradition can be traced in the references in Pliny's letters.

For those who accepted the necessity of the principate but sought to sustain the tradition of senatorial independence the question was whether there was a safe way between the extremes of contumacy and grovelling.[23] Such, clearly, was Tacitus' own ideal, and it must be asked how far that ideal could be realised in practice during the reign of Domitian. If we leave on one side those whose career was primarily military,[24] a number of names can be mentioned of those who matched or surpassed the careers of Tacitus and Pliny. In addition to those who held a first or second consulship during Domitian's reign must be considered holders of the consulship in the ten or fifteen years after his death, since such men must in most cases have been progressing through the earlier stages of a political career during Domitian's reign. Though their early careers are rarely as fully documented as that of Pliny, the regularity of the pattern of a normal senatorial career makes it almost certain that they will have held the customary appointments before the consulship.

Two men, whose first consulship fell at the beginning of Vespasian's reign, reached a second consulship in or about 85, and also held the prestigious and powerful post of City Prefect (*praefectus urbi*). Rutilius Gallicus, recipient of a poem of Statius (*Siluae* 1.4), in which he is described as Domitian's right-hand man, was dead by 91 or 92; Aurelius Fulvus, who also became City Prefect, was the paternal grandfather of the later emperor, Antoninus Pius. Domitian's successor, Nerva, also held one consulship early in Vespasian's reign and a second one under Domitian (in 90); his greatest talent, however, was not integrity, but the ability to survive. Other survivors who had held a first consulship under Vespasian had to wait till the reigns of Nerva or Trajan. Such were Arrius Antoninus and Domitius Tullus,[25] the former maternal grandfather of Antoninus Pius and proconsul of Asia, the latter, in addition to his two consulships, a wealthy man and former proconsul of Africa. Iulius Ursus, a man of equestrian family, had held the prefectships of Egypt and the praetorian guard before reaching a first consulship under Domitian (84) and a second under Trajan (98).[26] His adopted son, Iulius Ursus Seruianus, also held a first consulship under Domitian and subsequent ones under Trajan (102) and Hadrian (134).[27] Another man of equestrian descent, Attius Suburanus, was Trajan's first praetorian prefect before holding consulships in 101 and 104.[28] Annius Verus, consul in 97, 121 and 126, and *praefectus urbi*, was also grandfather of Marcus Aurelius. Lastly, mention should be made of Licinius Sura, three times consul (97?, 102, 107) and close adviser of Trajan till his death about 110. For although much of his success was in the military sphere, his forte seems to have been diplomacy, and he may first have caught Domitian's eye for such skills. It is interesting that the two letters addressed to him by Pliny (4.30 and 7.27) are both on natural curiosities (on a siphoning spring; ghosts); as Pliny himself says, these are the sort of things that their leisure gives them time to discuss.

A remarkable feature of the men referred to in the preceding paragraph is how many of them come from Spain or Narbonese Gaul.[29] A network of family ties helped to tighten bonds formed by a shared place of origin and a community of interest, which produced Rome's first Spanish emperor, Trajan. The purpose of the foregoing remarks is not, however, to show the part that good connections and influence could play in politics, but to give some indication of the scope there was for a successful senatorial career during Tacitus' lifetime. At the end of Nero's reign and for the latter half of Domitian's, conspiracy or suspicion of it in the emperor's mind might put the life of any senator at risk, and the execution in the first year of Hadrian's reign of four of the most eminent military consulars was to reaffirm the lesson; but it is clear that even during Domitian's reign political advancement was, with discretion and good fortune, possible for many, as it was for Tacitus and Pliny, while the reign of Trajan saw a period of twenty years when, within an admittedly autocratic framework, it was open to a senator to promote at the same time the well-being of the state and his own self-advancement.

The pages of the *Histories* and *Annals* show that Tacitus recognised the precariousness of a balance between principacy and senatorial freedom, but except on the unlikely theory that most of the *Annals*, including the crucial portrait of Tiberius, was written after the accession of Hadrian, it would be unwise to see in his writings a projection of his disillusionment with Trajan. Whether he was disappointed in his own career is another matter. On the whole he is likely to have been realist enough to understand that further honours, such as a second consulship or the highly prized post of City Prefect, would scarcely come his way. A public career that ended (as it seems to have done) with the proconsulate of Asia cannot be said to have been a failure. But there was another field in which Tacitus could hope to win preeminence—the writing of history. That would allow him both to comment on and interpret the political fabric of Rome's last century and to stake a claim to that undying fame which, for the Roman upper class, stood in place of immortality.

At the beginning of the *Agricola* (2.2-3.2) Tacitus had written of an

35

imposed silence lasting throughout the fifteen years of Domitian's reign. It is clear that he is talking primarily of history and historical biography and of the right of free speech in the senate. The facts bear out his statement. Fabius Rusticus may have lived on into the reign of Trajan, but there is nothing to suggest that his history was published as late as the reign of Domitian; indeed, his description of the shape of Britain, to which Tacitus alludes in *Agr.* 10.3, can scarcely have been written after AD 84, when Agricola's circumnavigation of Britain had established the shape of the island. The history of Vibius Maximus, which may have been published in Domitian's reign, was a rehash of Sallust and Livy; its theme was sufficiently remote in time to be politically safe. Tacitus' point is confirmed by the fate of Arulenus Rusticus and Herennius Senecio, both executed in 93. They had written political biographies of, respectively, Thrasea Paetus (forced to commit suicide in 66) and his son-in-law, the elder Helvidius Priscus (executed in 74).

Outside the political sphere literature flourished, though much of the verse fell short of the first class, e.g. the epics of Valerius Flaccus (the *Argonautica*), Statius (*Thebaid*),[30] and Silius Italicus, whose long poem on the Second Punic War was written, according to Pliny (3.7.5) 'with greater diligence than talent'. Silius is an interesting figure in that, before turning to poetry, he had had a successful political career (consul in 68, proconsul of Asia c. 77). For his epic poem, written over a number of years, immortality is promised in an epigram of Martial, the other major verse writer of this period (see 7.63.1–2, written about 92). Like Silius, Martial lived on, and continued to compose, into the reign of Trajan. If the verse of the period lacked distinction, it was not for shortage of patronage, both imperial and aristocratic. Domitian himself fostered verse competitions as part of the Capitoline games, while in Arruntius Stella and Vitorius Marcellus, both destined to reach the consulship under Trajan, Statius found patrons (the former was also a patron of Martial) who themselves practised the arts they supported.

Though politically orientated prose is missing, for the reasons already mentioned, the reign of Domitian produced two significant prose writers. M. Fabius Quintilianus (Quintilian), like so many of the prominent figures of this period a native of Spain, was the first teacher of Latin rhetoric to receive a stipend from the *princeps*, Vespasian. After twenty years of active teaching he retired about 88 to write the *Institutio Oratoria* ('The Training of an Orator') in twelve books; it seems to have been completed before Domitian's death in 96. Although Quintilian had speculated, in a work now lost, on the reasons for the contemporary decline in oratory, the tone of the *Institutio Oratoria* is generally optimistic; to Quintilian a revival of public oratory on Ciceronian lines seemed a possibility.[31]

The other notable prose writer is the distinguished military man, Sex. Iulius Frontinus, who after a first consulship in 73 or 74 went on to hold the post of governor of Britain immediately before Agricola. Twenty years later (98) he was to be consul for the second time, and in 100 he was *consul ordinarius* with the emperor Trajan himself. During the reign of Domitian he may have served in 83 in the campaign against the Chatti, but seems otherwise to have held no further appointment until he was appointed by Nerva as *curator aquarum* with the task of overseeing Rome's water supply. Of his writings, all of which reflect his professional interests, two survive. Four books on military strategems (*Strategemata*; the authenticity of the fourth book is uncertain) were written during Domitian's reign; the two books on the aqueducts of Rome (*De aquis*), published early in the reign of Trajan, were the direct outcome of his employment as curator of the city's water supply. Though the *De aquis* is post-Domitianic, the *Strategemata* demonstrate that it was possible, even for a military man, to write under Domitian, provided that he kept clear of contentious matters.

After the assassination of Domitian, when first Nerva, then Trajan, combined those polar opposites 'the principate and freedom' (*Agr.* 3.1), it might have been expected that there would be a great literary revival. Such indeed is what Pliny the Younger would have us believe: 'The present year has brought forth a great crop of poets . . . I am delighted that literature is flourishing' (*uigent studia*; 1.13.1 Cf. 1.10.1 on the liberal arts.). Certainly there was much reading of one's own compositions, both prose and verse (cf. A. N. Sherwin-White on Pliny 7.17.2), but Tacitus strikes a more sceptical note (*Agr.* 3.1): 'it is easier to crush talent and literature than to restore it'. The next two decades show that Tacitus' scepticism was well-founded. If 'the mad passion for scribbling' (Juvenal 7.51–2) seized many, it was an age of dilettante versifiers and poetasters, while the *longeurs* of the published version of Pliny's *Panegyricus* give some idea of the prevailing taste in literary prose.

The *Lives* of Suetonius and (in Greek) of Plutarch are an important reflection of the changing taste and values of the period; biography is beginning to be a substitute for history. Along with the carefully composed letters of Pliny they deserve to be ranked as literature, but literature of a minor order. Real distinction is given to the age only by the *Satires* of Juvenal and the writings of Tacitus himself. In view of the mediocrity that now begins to descend on Latin letters their eminence is all the more striking.

Though there is a marked similarity in the pungency with which Juvenal and Tacitus attack their targets in society, their own situations are quite different. For whereas tradition allowed the verse satirist to adopt the *persona* of detached observer and to speak his mind without fear of penalty,[32] Tacitus writes of a political society in which he himself played an active part; he needed no reminding of the dangers that threatened anyone who gave offence to those in high places. The fact that as an historian he dealt with an earlier period of the principate afforded no defence, for he knew that among his readers were those who, 'having similar characters, think that the crimes ascribed to others are aimed at them; while even fame and integrity have their enemies, for they seem to come too close to criticising their opposites' (*Ann.* 4.33.4). That cap might fit both Tacitus' senatorial colleagues and the emperor himself.

We have no direct testimony to show how Tacitus' historical works were received by his contemporaries,[33] but his appointment to the prestigious governorship of Asia in 112 or 113 (see p. 30, above) must indicate that at that time his political career still prospered. By then the *Histories* had been published and (probably) at least the opening books of the *Annals*. The career and writing of Tacitus thus present a paradox, unique in his time, that a man who had advanced without hindrance through all the stages of a senatorial career should write of the political system under which he himself had prospered in a way that starkly underlined how that system tended to bring out the worst in both *princeps* and senate. In the chapters that follow there will often be mention of an element of ambiguity in his attitude to situations and persons. That (it seems to me) is the product of his awareness of the paradox in himself. That awareness, unique among his contemporaries, is perhaps one of the chief reasons why the writings of Tacitus make so immediate an appeal to our own age.

# IIII

# THE LESSER WORKS

## 1 · AGRICOLA

The fifteen years of the reign of Domitian (81–96) had witnessed increasing tension between *princeps* and senate, culminating in a period when political opposition, or even the suspicion of it, could incur the death penalty. Domitian's assassination in the autumn of 96 was greeted with delight by the senate, which forthwith decreed the removal of his name from all inscriptions and the public execration of his memory. The relief felt by the senatorial aristocracy finds expression in Pliny's *Letters* and *Panegyricus*, and is mirrored too in the opening chapters of the *Agricola*, in which Tacitus speaks of the fifteen years of Domitian's reign as a period of enforced silence. Since Tacitus' political career had advanced without interruption during these years, the manner in which he insists on his past silence may seem a little surprising. But clearly the *Agricola* could not have been published in its present form during Domitian's life-time. Indeed, only after the elderly Nerva had made his own position secure by the adoption of Trajan, the military governor of Upper Germany, was publication really safe. From internal references to Nerva and Trajan (3.1; 44.5) it is probable that the *Agricola* was published in 98, in the same year as, but earlier than, the *Germania*.

The title of the work, *de uita Iulii Agricolae* ('about the life of Julius Agricola'), promises the reader of this short work of under a thousand lines a biography of Tacitus' father-in-law, Gnaeus Iulius Agricola. But it is no ordinary biography, for within its brief compass it contains, and integrates in a unique manner, five or six different elements. To each of these is given an appropriate style and tone, most notably a historical tone in the account of Agricola's governorship of Britain, and an oratorical one, expecially in the final chapters, which virtually constitute a *consolatio* on the death of Agricola.

This variety of tone and tempo is already apparent in the first three chapters, which serve as a preface to the whole work. The first chapter, in a style reminiscent of the prefaces of Sallust's monographs, contrasts the attitude of past and present to biographical writing. In former days the motives of those who wrote the lives of great men were not questioned; even the writing of autobiography did not expose an author to an accusation of conceit or arrogance.[1] In the present age Tacitus has to beg indulgence before he can embark on the biography of a dead man: such is the bitter hostility of the times towards merit.

A personal note has crept into this last sentence. This is continued in chapters 2 and 3, where Tacitus movingly describes how the Domitianic reign of terror numbed him and his peers into silence, and how at last, with the encouragement first of Nerva, then of Trajan, spirits are beginning to revive. Consonant with the personal and contemporary theme of this section the language is that of contemporary eloquence, such as is exemplified for us by Pliny's *Panegyricus*; there is in the sentences a sonority and amplitude that verges on the orotund. Then at the very end of the section (3.3) the language, while still personal, becomes simpler and more direct. After a promise to write at some future date a record of past servitude (the reign of Domitian) and present blessings (Nerva and Trajan) the chapter concludes: 'in the meantime this volume, designed to honour my father-in-law Agricola, will win praise, or at least acceptance, through my claim to be fulfilling the demands of filial piety.'

The mention of Agricola by name (the first time he has been named in the work) in the last sentence of the Preface leads easily to the next main section (cc. 4-9), the life and career of Agricola until his governorship of Britain. This in turn is separated from the account of that governorship, which constitutes the central core of the work (cc. 18-38), by sections on the geography and ethnography of Britain (cc. 10-12) and on the Roman advance in Britain before Agricola's governorship (cc. 13-17). Before attention is paid to the main body of the work, the first chapter deserves closer consideration, for it displays some significant features of Tacitus' thought and language, and their interrelationship:

> To record the deeds and characters of distinguished men for posterity (*clarorum uirorum facta moresque posteris tradere*) was a customary practice of bygone days: even in our time, in an age indifferent to its own achievements, the habit has not been abandoned, whenever some great and remarkable talent (*uirtus*) has crushed and overcome that vice, which small and great states alike share, a disregard for what is right, and envy. In former times the

performance of memorable deeds was easy and open to all; similarly men of distinguished talent (*celeberrimus quisque ingenio*) were encouraged to produce a record of eminence (*uirtutis memoriam*), not by a desire to win influence or advancement, but by a sense of duty well done. Indeed many thought that to give an account of their own lives was a proof of integrity rather than a sign of pride. . . . So true is it that merit (*uirtutes*) is highest esteemed in those times when it most readily occurs. But at the present time, when I am about to record the life of a man who is dead, I have had to crave an indulgence that I should not have had to seek, had my purpose been to accuse: so bitterly hostile to excellence (*uirtutibus*) are the times.

In the opening phrase prominence is given both to the writing of biography and to its subject matter. The conjunction of the ideas of *making* history and of *recording* it is a theme that recurs in the Prefaces of both the *Histories* and the *Annals*. That conjunction is made quite explicit here: *celeberrimus quisque ingenio* refers to the writer, *uirtutis memoriam* to his subject matter.

It will be noted that the noun *uirtus* (perhaps best translated by 'merit' or 'excellence') occurs four times in this first paragraph. Though many of the social values that the Republic had cultivated had necessarily been modified or downgraded under the Principate, the idea of public service publicly recognized, which is inherent in the concept of *uirtus*, persisted. The way in which a man's 'deeds and ways' (*facta moresque*) are related to the ideal of *uirtus* is a cardinal element in all Tacitus' writings. The prominence given to it in the first chapter of the *Agricola* is quite deliberate; Tacitus was over forty when he wrote the words, and the main lines of his political thought were already firmly established.

One last point remains to be made about the opening words. The importance that their initial position gives them is emphasised by the fact that they are designed to remind the reader of the opening words of that seminal work of Roman historiography, the *Origines* of the elder Cato (see chapter 1, p. 16).[2] It must be remembered that a Roman author, writing for an educated public that shared a closely knit cultural and literary heritage, could employ reminiscences and resonances of language in the knowledge that many of his readers would be conscious of the emphasis that these overtones were intended to give. If one tries to assess the effect that Tacitus is aiming at by this reminiscence of Cato, one may suspect a double purpose. In style he is acknowledging a direct line of succession from Cato through Sallust, for whom Cato had been an important model; but, more significantly, he indicates an allegiance in thought to Cato, who had sought to champion the view that political advancement should be won by personal merit (i.e. *uirtus*), not by birth and privilege. He thus underlines the main purpose of his biography of his father-in-law: it is to show that Agricola exemplified in his life that ideal of *uirtus* which the first chapter so insistently drives home.

Agricola's claim to be accounted a 'great and famous man' depended primarily on his governorship of Britain over an extended period of seven years (a period of three or four years would be the usual term of office). It is this fact that gives a markedly historical cast to the central core of the work. Yet the treatment accorded to it is far from that of a straightforward historical narrative, and though it provides precious evidence on which we can build a coherent account of the Roman conquest of Britain, there is a conspicuous paucity of geographical detail and historical event. The account Tacitus gives of Agricola's second year in the field illustrates the point well.

> But when summer arrived, assembling his forces, he was present everywhere on the march, praised discipline, chastised stragglers; camp-sites he selected in person, river estuaries and woods he explored in person. He gave the enemy no rest, but with sudden attacks caused devastation. Then when he had spread sufficient terror, he offered the inducements of peace. As a result many communities that had hitherto preserved their independence offered hostages, and laid aside their animosity. They were ringed round with garrisons and forts, with such skill and care that no previous part of Britain came over to us with so little attack (sc. subsequently, from those who still remained outside our control) (20.2–3).

No name of person or place is mentioned, and it is only by inference, supported by archaeology, that we can say that the second year of campaigning brought Agricola to the Tyne-Solway isthmus. Moreover, until the last sentence almost every phrase is a commonplace, stating the sort of thing that was expected of any good Roman general.[3] But we should not be misled into thinking that Tacitus is attributing to his father-in-law only what might apply to any good general. In the first half of the paragraph there is one telling word—'estuaries'— which is especially appropriate to the West coast of England between the Dee and the Solway. The final sentence of the chapter also seems at first sight only to express commendation of any good general: but seen in the context of Agricola's spectacular advance first to the Solway-Tyne isthmus, and then, in the next year, without time for consolidating in his rear, to the Clyde-Forth line, it suitably stresses the effectiveness of his disposition of fortified posts in North England. Thus

Tacitus' seemingly general remark illustrates a specific trait of Agricola's generalship.

The account of Agricola's first six campaigns is often allusive rather than explicit, and the space given to them is in marked contrast to that allocated to the battle of Mons Graupius[4] in his final year in Britain. That Tacitus should give to Agricola's final campaign more space than he gives to the whole of the narrative of the six preceding years is a clear indication that he regards the battle as the climax of Agricola's career, the action that not only set the seal (so Tacitus would have it) on the conquest of Britain, but also established Agricola's right to be regarded as a *magnus uir*. In case there can be any doubt in the reader's mind of the importance that is to be assigned to the battle Tacitus has deliberately separated his account of the final year from that of the previous six years by the insertion of a remarkable, indeed melo-dramatic, episode, the mutiny and subsequent voyage of a German auxiliary cohort recruited from the Usipi (c. 28). Apart from its intrinsic interest this digression has a double purpose. Structurally it affords a break before the narrative of the culminating events of Agricola's governorship is reached, and its content, the tale of how a crew of mutineers circumnavigated the North of Britain without knowing where they were going, makes a clear contrast with the very last episode of Agricola's campaign, the (anti-clockwise) circumnavigation of Britain by the fleet under Agricola's specific instruction.[5]

To a modern reader it is not only the amount of space devoted to the battle of Mons Graupius that surprises, but even more so the manner in which that space is used. Before the battle begins, and occupying about half the space allocated to the year's narrative, Tacitus records the speeches of exhortation to their troops given by the opposing generals, the Caledonian Calgacus and Agricola himself. It is a convention of Greek and Roman historical writing (though not of its biography) to put invented speeches in the mouths of historical personages.[6] By using the convention here Tacitus is asserting for the *Agricola* a claim to be considered as history.[7]

The two speeches are surprising, though in different ways. It is unlikely that Calgacus delivered a formal pre-battle harangue, and, if he did, it was certainly not couched in neat, Tacitean Latin. Yet, though it is derivative in both form and content, it has a real fire and vigour. Not only does it make an impassioned call to liberty, but it contains a savage indictment of Roman imperialism, including the memorable sentence:

Plunder, murder, rapine they euphemistically call 'empire'; and where they produce desolation, they call it peace.

*auferre trucidare rapere falsis nominibus imperium atque ubi solitudinem faciunt pacem appellant* (30 fin.)

Much of what Calgacus says comes straight from the language of Roman declamations.[8] But the speech seems to have a bite that goes beyond the purely conventional, and the belief that Tacitus is not simply making a debating point is strengthened by another passage (21.2), when Tacitus is speaking in his own person:

Gradually they (sc. the Britons) were led astray by the attractions of vice— the colonnade, baths, elegant banqueting. In their ignorance they called it 'culture', when really it was a part of their enslavement (*idque apud imperitos humanitas uocabatur, cum pars seruitutis esset*).

Are we then to assume that Tacitus himself believed what he put into Calgacus' mouth? Would that not be tantamount to suggesting that his dead father-in-law had been the effective instrument of imposing oppression and servitude on an erstwhile free society? It must be recognized that in all Tacitus' writings there seems to be an ambivalence in his judgments. It appears in the *Germania*, in which he shows a sympathetic understanding of a dangerous enemy, it appears in the *Dialogus*, where both Principate and Republic are seen to have their respective merits and defects, and it is shown in the major historical works, where successful characters are shown to have their flaws, and villains and cowards their redeeming features. Calgacus is therefore allowed his jibe at the Romans. Tacitus understands the sentiment, though he does not endorse it. At the same time, by portraying Agricola's enemy as a determined and worthy opponent, he shows Agricola's own *uirtus* to greater effect.

By contrast with Calgacus' speech that of Agricola is shorter and more restrained—the comparative brevity and 'stiff upper lip' suit a Roman as well as a British military man. Even if Agricola did not deliver a formal oration to his assembled troops, he may well have addressed words of encouragement to groups of his men. It is probable that he would have appealed to their loyalty and patriotism, and he may well have pointed out to them that the only alternatives open to him and them were 'death or glory'. Since Tacitus must have heard the details many times from Agricola's own lips, we might have expected the speech to include some individualising touches. Instead Tacitus elevates the speaker's person by according him a formally organized oration, whose style is clearly influenced by Livy and Sallust. That is a technique that he will employ many times in the *Histories* and *Annals*.

To attempt to understand the *Agricola* within the context merely of military success in Britain is not enough. Tacitus clearly had no doubt of the magnitude of what his father-in-law had achieved. In the Preface to his *Histories* (1.2.1), written perhaps some seven or eight years later than the *Agricola*, he speaks of Britain being completely conquered, and then abandoned (*perdomita Britannia et statim missa*). This statement, once regarded as Tacitean exaggeration, is now confirmed, at least as far as the rapid evacuation of Scotland is concerned, by archaeological evidence based on a careful scrutiny of pottery. The statement that Britain was *perdomita* probably came to Tacitus from his father-in-law. Whether Agricola's belief was justified is open to question. It is a remarkable fact that the only case in the whole of the military narrative (cc. 18–38) for which Tacitus quotes the express testimony of his father-in-law is for the assertion, frequently repeated (*saepe ex eo audiui*; 24.3), that Ireland could be conquered and held by a single legion plus auxiliaries.

Considerations of strategy and, even more so, of logistics play a very small part in Roman historical writing. Their omission from a biography should therefore cause no surprise. But it is possible to suggest reasons which may have weighed with the emperor or his advisers in calling a halt to the Roman advance and for recalling Agricola from his command. The last is the easier point to deal with. Agricola's governorship had been extended well beyond the term granted to the notable predecessors whom Vespasian had appointed, when the decision had been taken to pursue a more aggressive policy in Britain. Even if at this moment no decision had been taken to stage a withdrawal from the more northerly parts of the island, it was consolidation, not further conquest, that was called for; that was a task that did not require the further extension of Agricola's command. But on any realistic assessment consolidation would have called for substantial additions to his forces. It may be doubted whether that was something that Domitian would have been prepared to contemplate even in 84, for at that time his German policy was clearly dictated by the urge to establish a frontier that could be more easily defended and would make fewer demands on the available manpower. The wisdom of this policy was to show itself almost at once, when unrest and warfare in Moesia and on the Danube made heavy and continuing demands on the army's resources. By AD 92 at the latest one of Britain's four legions (*Legio II Adiutrix*) had to be withdrawn for service in the East, and then,

45

if not before, it would have been impossible to hold the whole of Britain. Of these considerations we hear no word in the *Agricola*.

From the time that Agricola left Britain until his death nine years later he held no further post in the service of the emperor, and though it is possible that towards the end of his life his health was impaired, it is likely that Domitian's suspicion or personal hostility were factors. If Agricola was a disappointed man—the more so, because he saw his achievements in Britain so quickly sacrificed—his son-in-law was undoubtedly fired by resentment at the treatment his father-in-law had suffered. But if Agricola's claim to fame through the *uirtus* he had shown in Britain was not to run into the sand, the last part of his biography required particularly careful handling. Disparagement of the dead Domitian—a congenial theme to readers of the *Agricola* when it was published in AD 98—was not enough: the studied calm with which Agricola had accepted Domitian's rebuffs might be stigmatised as cowardly passivity.

In the section that takes us up to the time of Agricola's death in 93 (cc. 39–43), it is clear on a first reading how the material is selected and organized to blacken Domitian's character. But within the section there are a number of passages of particular importance, of which three repay attention. In 40.2 Tacitus mentions that Domitian, fearing that Agricola, with an army at his back, might not accept the instruction to give up his governorship of Britain, sent a private messenger to Agricola with the instruction that if Agricola were still in Britain (and thus still in command of an army), the messenger was to offer him the governorship of Syria—as a bribe, it is to be assumed, to persuade him to leave Britain peacefully. In the upshot, Agricola had already left Britain, and it was not necessary to communicate to him the offer of Syria. It is important to note how Tacitus introduces the incident: *credidere plerique*, 'many believed'. We are therefore dealing, not with a fact, but with a malicious rumour. While disclaiming all responsibility for the authenticity of the statement, Tacitus has made sure that it has made its impact on the reader. The manner in which Tacitus employs rumours as a device to direct the reader's attention and influence his judgment will concern us when we consider his major historical writings: here, in his first work, the technique is already fully at work.

The report of Agricola's death is similarly organized. At his death Tacitus says (43.1 fin.): 'no one rejoiced or forgot him straight away. People's compassion was increased by a persistent *rumour* that he had been poisoned. I could not venture to affirm that we have any certain evidence (the Latin is no less contorted than the translation: *nobis nihil comperti adfirmare ausim*). But it *is* true that throughout his illness the emperor took unusual pains to keep himself informed of the invalid's condition.' We learn later (45.5) that Tacitus and his wife (Agricola's daughter) were out of Italy—we may assume that it was on official business—at the time of Agricola's death. Consequently he was not in a position to give an authoritative denial to the rumour of poison. So much we may allow to Tacitus: but there is little doubt that the reader is intended to give full weight to the innuendo.

The two preceding passages are more concerned with blackening Domitian's character than with praising Agricola's; Agricola is portrayed as a tyrant's victim rather than as a hero or an example of *uirtus*. A third passage attempts an answer to the question: in the face of the ruthless and unpredictable tyranny of Domitian as depicted by Tacitus—a portrait that was readily accepted by those members of the upper classes who had lived through Domitian's reign—what was a responsible senator to do? One possible line of conduct was that of vigorous, outspoken opposition to the emperor; a few notable men (often, like Cato the Younger at the end of the Republic, adherents of the Stoic philosophy) practised this opposition till they were silenced by death or exile. After Domitian's assassination this was a course that in safe retrospect found many vocal advocates. Another, less flamboyant course was to discharge conscientiously all duties that were properly and constitutionally imposed on one, and to decline or refuse to become an instrument of the emperor's despotism, while avoiding a direct confrontation with the emperor himself. Tacitus' own political career suggests that this was the course that he himself chose. In a much-quoted passage (42 fin.) he insists, almost with passion, that this is the course that Agricola too had followed:

> Despite Domitian's proclivity to an anger that was the more inexorable as it was more concealed, he was appeased by the restraint (*moderatione*) and wisdom of Agricola, who did not by a defiant and futile parade of liberty court a renown that must result in his death. Let those who like to admire what is forbidden realise that even under bad emperors great men can exist (*posse etiam sub malis principibus magnos uiros esse*); a quiet fulfilment of duty (*obsequium ac modestiam*), if backed by a keen determination, can achieve a renown such as many have attained only by perilous courses that have brought an ostentatious death without any advantage to the state.

The task of biography is preeminently to record for posterity the lives of those who have gained fame (*gloria*) through *uirtus*. Though it is difficult for *uirtus* to be displayed unless political liberty is assured, Agricola had managed, despite the tyranny of Domitian, to exemplify *uirtus* in his life. It is for this reason that, time and again (e.g., c. 20 and in Agricola's speech before the battle of Mons Graupius), Tacitus chooses to portray in Agricola those general qualities that typify the ideal commander rather than record things that are individual and peculiar to Agricola. There is enough personal information in the *Agricola* that would distinguish him from other men, and to this extent the work is a fitting tribute from son-in-law to father-in-law. But the work was designed for a wider audience than Agricola's family and close acquaintances. It is intended to demonstrate to Tacitus' contemporaries, above all those senators who with him had lived through the tyranny of Domitian, that 'even under bad emperors great men could exist'.

The final chapters are devoted to the personal tribute that Tacitus wishes to make to his dead father-in-law. A short account of Agricola's death (with the innuendo already discussed, that the suspicion of poisoning by Domitian's agents could not be conclusively denied) is followed by an epilogue cast in the form of a *consolatio*.[9] Many of the themes and topics that are employed are conventional elements of the genre. But into them Tacitus has infused a personal warmth of feeling. In keeping with the tone of the section the language becomes more elevated and the style, with its repetitions and balanced clauses, more Ciceronian, even to the extent of incorporating reminiscences of Cicero's consolatory remarks on the death of L. Licinius Crassus at the beginning of *De oratore* III. Though Agricola was only a little over fifty when he died, he had lived long enough to win lasting fame. Moreover, his death, just before the final excesses of Domitian's reign, could be judged a blessing; the dead man is apostrophised as 'fortunate even in the timeliness of your death' (*felix. . . etiam opportunitate mortis*).

The upper-class Roman of Tacitus' day had no belief in a personal after-life; sedulous cultivation of dead ancestors along with a keen desire to pass on the family tradition took its place. Tacitus' biography is the best means he has of seeking to perpetuate the memory and example of Agricola's life, and the final chapter underlines this point when it says that Agricola will best be remembered by his family, if they follow his example: that is the truest honour, that the mark of deepest affection. Rather than seeking to perpetuate his memory in the traditional way of the Roman noble[10]—not that Tacitus opposes this way too—they should embrace the form and shape of his mind; that is something that is everlasting, but cannot be expressed in physical form, but only through one's own way of life.

> Whatever we have loved in Agricola, whatever we have admired, remains and will surely remain in the minds of men throughout the everlasting passage of time, through the fame of his achievements; for many men of old will be[11] buried by oblivion, as if they had won neither name nor glory: Agricola, with his story written and recorded for posterity, will survive (46.4).

The closing words, 'Agricola *posteritati* narratus et *traditus* superstes erit', deliberately recall the opening words of the work, 'clarorum uirorum facta moresque *posteris tradere*'. The deeds and character of Agricola entitle him to be considered as one of the *clari uiri*, but that alone does not guarantee the survival of his name; for that a worthy biographer is needed. The diffident tone in which Tacitus had written of his undertaking at the beginning of the work has vanished, and though he does not explicitly refer to himself at the end, there is a confident ring; Agricola *will* survive, but he will do so only because, in his son-in-law, he has found a worthy biographer.

## 2 · GERMANIA

A reference (37.2) to the second consulship of Trajan dates the composition of the *Germania* to the first half of AD 98, but after the death of Nerva at the end of January in that year. It is thus contemporary with the *Agricola* (though the opening chapters of the *Agricola* make it clear that the *Agricola* was the first of the two works to be published), and might be expected to reflect the same attitude towards the present and recent past. At first sight this is far from the case. The *Germania* seems to be (and is) an ethnographical essay, written with a strong emphasis on the similarities and dissimilarities in morals and customs between Germans and Romans. Indeed it has been argued that the aim of the work is to encourage Romans to return to the moral code of their ancestors by contrasting the virtues of the noble savage (or, rather, barbarian) with the decadence of contemporary Rome. But though moral comment and judgment are important elements in the work, they are clearly not its main purpose, for the shortcomings of the Germans are no less emphasised than their virtues, and, as will be seen, the bipartite structure of the whole is such that moral comment plays only a small part in the second half (28–46); and, where it does occur, it no longer involves criticism, explicit or implicit, of the Roman way of life.

Another, though less prominent, strand runs through the *Germania*, that of political comment, and it has been argued by others that Tacitus' main reason for writing the essay was to bring home to his readers the continuing threat to Roman security that the Germans presented. The fact that Trajan was with the Roman armies on the Rhine when Nerva's death was announced and that he made no attempt to come to Rome on hearing the news—he did not arrive there till the following year, and did so (significantly) only after visiting the Danube—might suggest either that the situation was too dangerous to permit him to leave or that he was on the point of launching an aggressive campaign against the Germans. Something will need to be said later about Tacitus' estimate of the current situation in Germany, but the political element in the *Germania* plays only a restricted and intermittent role in the work, and should be regarded as an ingredient, but a minor one, of the whole. There is nothing surprising in the fact that, in writing about a foreign people, a Roman should use those categories of thought and judgment that came naturally to him. Morals and politics were such categories.

Understanding of the *Germania* must begin with the realisation that the ethnographical treatise or essay was a well-defined genre of Greek and Roman writing. It had an accepted structure and style of its own. Under the two general headings of place and people(s) a number of topics were customarily treated: geography, climate, mineral and agricultural resources, physical characteristics of the inhabitants, their origin (indigenous or immigrant), their social organization in both peace and war. The digression on Britain and its inhabitants in the *Agricola* (10–13.1) follows the pattern.[12] This pattern effectively determines the way Tacitus organizes his material in the first half of the *Germania* (to c. 27)[13]: the second half, dealing with individual tribes, has its own arrangement.

The existence of a traditional set of topics appropriate to ethno-graphical description, far from restricting Tacitus' freedom, provided him with a framework within which he could accommodate all he wished to say about the Germans. The initial chapters, which begin with a very generalised description of the geographical location of Germany,[14] next describe the people—they are indigenous and have preserved the purity of their race by rejecting intermarriage—and then pass to a physical description of the land and its products. Mention of its metals leads by an easy transition (6.1) to weapons and armour, which in turn introduce a long section (6-15) on public life and institutions. In this section the theme of war is prominent, and Tacitus pays particular attention to the relationship between the leading nobles (*principes*) and their retinue (*comitatus*). Though that relationship is basically designed for fighting, the moral obligations it imposes are not unlike those between a Roman *patronus* and his *clientes*. The fame of the leader depends on the number and valour of his retinue. In battle neither leader nor retinue can endure to be outdone in valour by the other; for the members of the *comitatus* it is their paramount duty to defend their *princeps*, and any success they have in battle adds only to his glory. But, while expressing his admiration for these qualities in battle, Tacitus also notes that, when they are not fighting, they become indolent and slaves to eating and sleeping.

The next main section (16-27) is devoted to the private life of the Germans, and it is here that the contrast between German and Roman ways is most emphasised. After describing their habitation and dress Tacitus turns to marriage (18.1): 'no aspect of their behaviour (*mores*) deserves higher praise'. Both men and women take one partner for life, and the exchange between them of gifts that will be of service in war cements their union. At this point Tacitus' prose becomes almost lyrical:

> They consider this their closest bond, these their sacred rites, these their marriage gods . . . at the outset of their marriage the bride is reminded that she comes to share her husband's toils and dangers; in peace, in battle she will suffer and dare the same. This is the message of the yoked oxen, of the caparisoned horse, of the gift of arms. So she must live, so she must die.[15] She is receiving gifts to hand on to her children inviolate and fit for her daughters-in-law to receive, to be handed down in turn to her grandchildren.

Consequently they live with their chastity firmly guarded, and adultery is rare. 'For no one there laughs at vices, nor is corruption and being corrupted considered *à la mode*' (19.1; *nemo enim illic uitia ridet, nec corrumpere et corrumpi saeculum uocatur*). It is clear from the warmth of his language[16] how much Tacitus admires this aspect of the German character, while the references to allurements to vice and clandestine correspondence, both unknown to the Germans, allude to the practices of contemporary Roman society. It should be noted too that the concept, which Tacitus praises, of a wife marrying only once

51

corresponds to the older Roman ideal of a woman being *uniuira* (lit. 'a one-man woman'; but the Latin word is solemn, unlike the English phrase).

The reliability of Tacitus' information needs a more general consideration, but it is worth pointing out that here, where his feelings are so clearly engaged, he (or his source) has misunderstood the significance of the exchanged 'gifts'; for what the husband gave was in fact a 'bride-price', which he paid to the woman's parents, while the sword given to the bridegroom was a present from the bride's father or guardian symbolising the transfer to the husband of the power of life and death over the woman.[17]

The praise that Tacitus gives to the German attitude towards marriage is extended to other aspects of family life. There is a brief eulogy of a policy of eugenics (20.2), and a favourable comment on their treatment of old age; the childless are not, as they are at Rome, besieged by legacy-hunters. Their open-handed hospitality is, in itself, an attractive trait, but they are generous to a fault. Their fondness for banqueting is coupled with a socially accepted addiction to heavy drinking, which—since they go armed—leads to brawls, wounding and manslaughter. It is at banquets, too, that they deliberate on all manner of business, ranging from private feuds to decisions on peace or war. But, Tacitus says, having deliberated one day, when they are drunk, they meet the next day to take a decision, when they are sober (22.2-3). This paradox seems to be a feature of ethnographical writing, for Scythians and Persians[18] act similarly. But the use of such a transferred motif, deliberately phrased in similar language, does not prove that the essence of the statement is not true also of the people to whom the motif is transferred.

Mention of banquets leads to other forms of amusement—or rather their one notable form of entertainment, the sword dance. For dicing was practised with deadly seriousness, so much so that as a last resort the thrower was prepared to hazard his freedom. Tacitus then (c. 25) passes to slavery and the German treatment of freedmen. In a clear allusion to the important posts held by freedmen in the emperor's household at Rome Tacitus remarks that among the Germans freedmen carry little authority, except among those peoples that are ruled by kings: elsewhere the inferior status of freedmen is a sure proof of the existence of political liberty. The last item in the section on private life deals with funeral customs; it ends with the statement that 'for women it is honourable to mourn, for men to remember' (27.1).

The avoidance of conspicuous display contrasts forcibly with the pomp of the funeral of a Roman aristocrat, but it should be remembered that at the end of the *Agricola* Tacitus, while not opposing marble and brass memorials, insists on the greater importance of remembering the dead man and seeking to emulate his example. In this respect the German practice coincided with Tacitus' own ideal.

The second half of the *Germania*, dealing with the individual tribes, has a geographical basis, and is itself divided into two. In cc. 28–37 Tacitus begins with the tribes who abut on the Rhine, and then moves eastwards as far as the Elbe and northwards to Jutland. The section ends (c. 37) with a digression on the long and sustained resistance that the Germans have made against the Romans. Then Tacitus passes to the tribes (to whom he gives the general name of Suebi) further east, including those along the Danube, and to the north-east. As he moves further away from the Rhine the information he gives becomes less detailed, and finally he admits that he has reached the realms of the fabulous. At this point Tacitus prudently abandons his task.

In this half of the *Germania*, where over fifty individual tribes are named, two devices are principally employed to prevent the reader's attention from straying. First, along with the geographical progression away from the Rhine there runs another strand of development, that of political organization as a reflection of moral fibre. In the section from c. 28–37 the keyword is *uirtus*, which in the German context approximates in meaning to 'valour'. So the Batavi are 'pre-eminent in valour' (*uirtute praecipui*), the Chatti—who combine skill and intelligence with bravery—'count fortune as doubtful, but valour as sure' (30.2; *uirtus* is applied to them also at 31.1 and 3), while it is said of the Chauci (35.2) that their valour and strength is demonstrated by the fact that they do not need to resort to aggression to assert their superiority. The last tribe to be mentioned in this section are the Cimbri; of them Tacitus does not need to predicate *uirtus*, since it is attested by their former ability to engage the might of Roman armies from 113 BC. The whole section ends with the statement that the Germans (i.e. those so far discussed) are a more dangerous enemy than were the Samnites, Carthaginians, Spaniards and Gauls, more dangerous even than the Parthians. And the reason? The freedom (*libertas*) of the Germans is more vigorous than the despotism of the Arsacids (viz. the kings of Parthia). In Tacitus' mind *libertas*, 'political freedom', is almost a prerequisite for the exercise of *uirtus*.

When Tacitus passes, at c. 38, to the Suebian Germans, *uirtus* is still applied to the most western of the tribes on the northern banks of the Danube (sc. Naristi, Marcomani, Quadi), but he soon comes to tribes who are ruled by kings. Within this class, though, there is a marked gradation. The Gotones (44.1), though strictly ruled, have not utterly forfeited liberty, whereas the Sitones[19] have sunk still lower: they are ruled by a woman!—'so far have they fallen not only from freedom (*libertas*) but even below the state of slavery' (*seruitus*; 45.6).

The other way in which Tacitus holds his reader's attention is by the insertion from time to time of some more graphic feature or incident, which is then treated at some length. So the Chatti not only show in war a discipline such as is normally shown by Romans; their warriors let their hair and beard grow until they have killed an enemy in battle (cc. 30–31). After dealing with the Suiones, in addition to some highly dubious oceanography and astronomy (45.1), Tacitus inserts a digression on amber. A group of tribes worship a Nature goddess under the name of Nerthus, and details of the ritual attached to her cult, including the use of a cult wagon, are given. Among another group of tribes (the Lugii 43.2) the Nahanarvali worship twin gods who can be identified, Tacitus says, with Castor and Pollux, but it is another of the same group, the Harii, who particularly attract his attention. They prefer to fight by night, having previously blacked their weapons and their bodies to create terror among their enemies: 'for in all battles it is the eyes that are first defeated' (43.4). Transitions and contrasts are effectively used, as in cc. 35 and 36 where the powerful, but peace-loving, Chauci are contrasted with the Cherusci, who were equally peace-loving, but lacked the strength to preserve it. And, lastly, the Roman reader is repeatedly reminded of the contact and conflict between the Germans and Rome.

The most notable of these passages (already referred to) is c. 37, which not only dates the publication of the *Germania* to AD 98 and emphasises that the Germans are a more dangerous enemy because of their keenness to maintain their liberty; it also serves to mark a major structural division in the work, the point at which Tacitus turns from considering those tribes, living mainly between the Rhine and the Elbe, whom he considered as 'non-Suebian' to the 'Suebian' tribes, a name he gives virtually to all other German tribes, whether living along the Danube or east of the Elbe.

The manner in which these historical passages are used to emphasise the ethnographical structure of the work, when taken in conjunction with the matter they contain, is the clearest proof that the *Germania* is not a political pamphlet written to advocate a specific course of action to deal with a contemporary situation. Chapter 37 makes the point. It begins with a mention of the Cimbri, who are described as *parua nunc ciuitas* ('now a small people/state'). We are told nothing about them, and they are introduced simply to facilitate what follows, an account of the menace that German tribes have been to Rome in the past. Beginning with a series of disastrous Roman defeats between 113 and 105 BC Tacitus passes, via the Roman victories of Marius against the Cimbri and Teutones (who are nowhere mentioned in the *Germania*), to Julius Caesar, then to Drusus, Tiberius and Drusus' son Germanicus, and finally to the much derided campaign of the emperor Caligula (Gaius). Even though Tacitus' own comment, *tam diu Germania uincitur* ('so long is the conquest of Germany taking'), implies that the conquest is not yet complete, it does not press upon the new emperor, still on the Lower Rhine, a new policy of aggression against the trans-Rhenane Germans. What Tacitus speaks of is past history. The truth is that the centre of gravity had already moved in the direction of the Danube. From the time that Tiberius recalled Germanicus from Germany in AD 16 no Roman emperor seriously thought of pursuing a policy of annexation in Germany.

But the establishment of a *cordon sanitaire* on the eastern bank of the Rhine was another matter, and if this could be combined with a similar occupation of territory to the north of the upper reaches of the Danube, the elimination of the re-entrant angle would mean an immense shortening in the Roman frontier. By the time that the *Germania* was written that shortening of the frontier had in fact been achieved, but it had been so done under the Flavian dynasty, not least by the detested Domitian. Even though the finishing touches were being put to this new defensive line by Trajan at the very time at which the *Germania* was published, Tacitus effectively ignores it. At 29.3 there is a dismissive reference to the *Decumates agri*,[20] which seems to refer to the land on the eastern bank of the Rhine from the Black Forest to the Neckar and (possibly) the Main. The inhabitants of these areas, according to Tacitus, are not even Germans, but displaced and impoverished Celts. They are now (at the time of the publication of the *Germania*) part of the Roman province (sc. of Upper Germany). The southern parts of this territory had been annexed under Vespasian, while the reduction of the Taunus region (to the north-east of Mainz (Moguntiacum)) was the result of Domitian's conflict with the Chatti in 83. According to Tacitus himself (*Agr.* 39.1) and those writers who

followed the tradition hostile to Domitian (*aliter* Frontinus, who may
have taken part in the campaign) Domitian's victory was a sham:
archaeology reveals a solid achievement, even if it cannot prove a
major defeat of the Chatti on the battlefield. In the next chapters of
the *Germania* (30–31) the Chatti are described in some detail, but
though their military organization receives considerable comment, no
attempt is made to indicate how that organization has affected their
relationship with the Romans, and there is certainly no hint that the
Domitianic campaign has put an effective end to their attacks on
Roman territory.

There are other instances where Tacitus' narrative seems to ignore
recent history[21] and it is possible that this betrays the fact that Tacitus
is using as his main source an account that ended some forty or fifty
years before Tacitus published the *Germania*. But even if this is the case,
it does not explain why Tacitus used an out-of-date source or why,
using an out-of-date source, he nevertheless thought it worth while to
publish the monograph. There is no sure answer to these questions, but
the almost total exclusion of recent history must be the result of
deliberate choice on Tacitus' part. Why should this be? One reason,
already mentioned, is that it would have involved him in giving an
account of the frontier policy of the Flavian emperors, especially
Domitian, very different from that which was alluded to in the *Agricola*.
At the same time he would have been on awkward ground, for Trajan
was not only rounding off Flavian policy on the Rhine at the very time
the *Germania* was being published, but he had also been actively
engaged there in support of Domitian during the abortive revolt of the
governor of Upper Germany, Antonius Saturninus in 89. A further
reason has been suggested: the *Germania* is an expanded version of an
excursus he intended to include in the historical work he already had it
in mind to write. But that work, though it turned out to be the *Histories*,
with a starting point of 69, was envisaged (*Agr.* 3.3) at the time the
*Germania* was published as starting only with the reign of Domitian
(81–96). The studious avoidance of a picture contemporaneous with
the Flavian period makes this suggestion improbable; and even if it
were true, the *Germania* as we have it is a work of much greater size than
could have been accommodated within a historial narrative, and it has
a significant structure of its own.

In short, the *Germania* should be judged on its own merit. Any
attempt to explain its genesis must be speculative, but two points may
be made. The presence on the Rhine of the new emperor would give

the work a topical interest. More important is the fact that the province of Germany was clearly of abiding interest to Tacitus himself. If his father was the Roman knight who served as procurator of Gallia Belgica in the fifties, an important link is established; at that time the procurator was responsible for controlling the revenues and civil administration of the area controlled by the armies of the Rhine.[22]

For the Germanist the content of the work elevates it to the status of a precious document, whose every word needs careful examination and weighing; an important German edition, which claims only to supplement other editions, has nearly 600 pages of comment on 700 lines of text.[23] For the reader of Tacitus it is enough to say that where Tacitus makes specific statements they are more often than not borne out by the finds of archaeology. Two statements in c. 5 illustrate the sort of problem that is involved. Tacitus' assertion that the Germans had little regard for Roman silverware is belied by the finds, and must be regarded as an erroneous generalisation about the attitude of primitive peoples to luxury and civilisation. On the other hand the statement that it is only those Germans closest to the Rhine who value gold and silver coinage is verified by archaeology. Though coins have a wide distribution later, the finds of the first century AD are almost exclusively confined to a strip of two hundred kilometres beyond the Rhine and Danube frontiers.

The *Germania*, then, was written because the subject interested Tacitus and was likely to interest his contemporaries at the time of publication. It is basically an ethnographical essay, following the well-established canons of the genre. But in looking at the Germans Tacitus has injected comments that reflect his own interests and perspectives. These are primarily moral and political, and the categories of thought by which he makes his judgments are those which he will apply in his subsequent historical writings. Two values in particular stand out, those of *uirtus* ('valour') and *libertas* ('political freedom'). Circumstances alter the meaning of those two concepts, but they retain a core that is valid, whatever the society the author is talking about. The comparison between the relatively primitive Germans and the perhaps over-civilised Romans throws light from different directions on the two qualities. The comparison is by no means weighted wholly in favour of the primitive. But those elements that were admirable in the German offered a challenge to the Roman. It is a challenge, not to throw away civilisation and the advantages of the *pax Romana*, but to purge Roman society of its dross.

There is a special aptness in the fact that Tacitus makes a comparison with a Germany that had largely ceased to exist by the time he wrote the *Germania*. Tacitus' future vocation was to be a historian, and the more he wrote, the further back in time he found it congenial to go. The writing of the *Germania* enabled him to stand back from the immediate present and to look at the underlying values, both for good and ill, that obtained in two very disparate societies, German and Roman. Having done so, he was better able to focus a more penetrating gaze on the history of Rome under the Principate. In this sense the *Germania*, besides its intrinsic interest as an ethnographial essay—for it is that, not a scientific treatise—is a part of Tacitus' preparation for his new vocation, the writing of history.

## 3 · DIALOGUS

'You often ask me, Fabius Justus, why—in contrast with previous generations, which were illumined with the talent and distinction of so many outstanding orators—our own age, void and bereft of renown for eloquence, scarcely retains even the name of orator.' In well-balanced phrases the opening sentence of the *Dialogus* announces a theme and the genesis of the work. The author responds to a friend's repeated enquiry for an explanation of the contemporary decline in oratory. Tacitus can offer an answer, because it requires no more of him than to put into writing the discussion he had heard as a young man, when the same question was considered by some of Rome's outstanding speakers.

Although all the participants in the dialogue were historical personages,[24] the Roman reader would be aware of the convention that the arguments ascribed to them are the author's own composition. But apart from that well-understood convention there is nothing on a cursory reading that would seem to belie the impression of a relaxed and urbane discussion of a literary topic by men of culture and taste. In fact, the surface blandness of the dialogue conceals a number of problems, the solution of which, to a greater or lesser extent, is important for our understanding of the work's meaning and purpose.

First there is the question of authorship. The manuscript tradition[25] affords a strong presumption that it is the work of Tacitus. The main reason for doubting his authorship[26] is the unlikeness of its style, with its uninhibited use of balanced phrases and figured speech, to that of

Tacitus' other works. The argument is less cogent than may at first appear, since it is now well understood that, like the Greeks, the Romans regarded different styles as appropriate to different literary genres; there is no reason to think that a talented author could not master more than one style—indeed, within the *Agricola* alone Tacitus had already demonstrated his command of at least three separate styles[27]. For a dialogue, and particularly a dialogue on a literary theme, a Ciceronian (or neo-Ciceronian) style was almost obligatory.

Early in the nineteenth century all doubt of Tacitus' authorship seemed to be removed, when Lange pointed out that in a letter to Tacitus (9.10.2) Pliny the Younger makes what seems to be a *verbatim* reference to the *Dialogus*. Pliny writes from his country retreat that he is not at present writing any poetry 'which you think can be most readily done "amid glades and groves"'. In his first speech in the *Dialogus* Aper, disparaging the practice of poetry, says (9.6) that, to achieve anything worthwhile, poets have to leave the business and pleasure of the city and 'retire, as the poets themselves say, "to the glades and groves", that is, into solitude' (*utque ipsi* (sc. *poetae*) *dicunt* in nemora et lucos, *id est in solitudinem, recedendum est*). Maternus' reply to Aper begins (12.1) with the same words, 'glades and groves'; far from being a disadvantage, he says, one of the greatest attractions of composing poetry is that it takes one into the pure air of the country. The phrase 'glades and groves' is, as Aper remarks, a commonplace of poets, but it is not simply the use of the phrase, but the context it occupies in Pliny's letter and Tacitus' *Dialogus* that makes it almost certain that the letter is alluding to the dialogue.

The *Dialogus*, then, can be safely ascribed to Tacitus.[28] The next problem is the date of its composition. Since *Agricola* 3.2 explicitly states that he has published nothing during the reign of Domitian (81-96) and implies that the *Agricola* is the first thing he has published since, the *Dialogus* must be either earlier than 81 or later than 98. Until a generation ago the earlier date was commonly accepted, for two main reasons. The gap of nearly twenty years was thought to allow time for Tacitus' style to move away from its Ciceronian phase. At the same time the intervening years of Domitian's tyranny would account for the change from the cheerfulness and light of the *Dialogus* to the sombre tones of Tacitus' other works.

Neither argument is convincing. Difference of style is related to difference of genre, not time of composition, while the idea that the *Dialogus* is without sombre undertones comes only from a superficial

59

reading. Today scholars agree that the work belongs to Trajan's reign (98–117). Many pointers help to confirm the view. The dramatic date of the dialogue is in the mid-seventies. When Tacitus speaks of recalling what he had heard as a young man (1.2 *iuuenis admodum*), he seems to be speaking of a distant past, perhaps a quarter of a century or more ago, not of a time only four or five years previously. The fact that the dialogue is dedicated to Fabius Justus is virtually conclusive against the earlier date. He was some years junior to Tacitus and could scarcely be the recipient of a work published in 79 or 80, when he would still be in his 'teens. Fabius was *consul suffectus* in 102 and governor of Syria by about 109; some time between these two dates seems the most likely date for the publication of the *Dialogus*. By the time he composed it Tacitus may well already have started work on the *Histories*. That fact should be borne in mind, when one attempts to look below the surface of the *Dialogus*; the whole truth is not necessarily apparent on a superficial reading.

The dramatic date of the dialogue is in the sixth year of Vespasian's reign, that is in 74 or 75.[29] It was about this time (the exact date is not known) that the running battle between Eprius Marcellus and Helvidius Priscus, referred to in 5.7, came to a head with the expulsion and subsequent execution of Priscus,[30] and it is against this unspoken background that the *Dialogus* must be read. Curiatius Maternus, once a notable orator, has turned to the writing of dramatic poetry. At his house in (or near) Rome he is visited by two friends on the day after he had given a reading of his *Cato*, some of whose allusions had given offence to people in high places (2.1). The two friends, Marcus Aper and Iulius Secundus, have both established a reputation in the courts; they are accompanied by Tacitus, who, however, as their junior, takes no part in the discussion. Secundus asks Maternus if he is going to tone down his *Cato* before publication, but receives the reply that, far from doing so, he intends to be even more outspoken in his next play, the outline of which he has already formed in his mind.[31]

The dialogue has a simple framework; there are three pairs of speeches. First Aper and Maternus argue over the respective merits of oratory and poetry; Secundus agrees to act as referee, but neither now nor later makes any contribution to the argument. At the end of the first two speeches they are joined by Vipstanus Messalla, a young senator and the only native Roman among them. In the second pair of speeches Aper and Messalla champion, respectively, the merits of contemporary oratory and the 'ancients' (*antiqui*), by whom Messalla essentially means Cicero and his contemporaries. Finally, when all but Aper agree that there has in fact been a decline in oratory, Messalla and Maternus in turn give their explanation of that decline. To Messalla the reason is simple: it is the result of a decline in the standard of morals and education. Maternus sees the matter differently. For him great oratory is the product of troubled times: under the settled régime of an enlightened *princeps* there is no place for contentious oratory. At the end of Maternus' speech the discussion ends, and in a mood of good humour his guests leave.

Though it is only in the last two speeches that the discussion gets to the theme that was announced in the opening sentence—the reasons for the decline in oratory—it is not difficult to see how the earlier speeches relate to this theme. It is because of oratory's decline that Maternus has transferred his talent and energies to the writing of poetry, and it is because Aper contests Maternus' premise that the second pair of speeches, discussing the relative claims of the moderns and ancients, becomes necessary. And it is only when the superiority of the ancients (and the inferiority of the moderns) has been established to the satisfaction of all but Aper that discussion of the main problem can be begun.

The contribution that Messalla makes to the discussion presents few difficulties. Though the youngest of the speakers, probably in his early thirties, it is he who most uncompromisingly puts forward the conservative view, a not unfitting role for the only aristocrat among the speakers. His view is essentially one that had been advocated a decade before the *Dialogus* was written by the imperial professor of rhetoric, Quintilian.[32] In his *Institutio Oratoria* ('The Training of an Orator') Quintilian had sought to promote a revival of Ciceronian oratory by a return to the broader educational principles that Cicero had advocated in *his* writings on rhetoric. Messalla was convinced, as Quintilian professed to be, that a return to the good old days was feasible, and it is this point of view that Maternus' final speech sets out to demolish as anachronistic and lacking in historical understanding.[33]

Aper's arguments cannot be so easily dismissed, though it is clear that he convinces none of the other participants in the debate; indeed, it has often been argued that he speaks with tongue in cheek, as *advocatus diaboli*.[34] He both represents and defends contemporary eloquence, and though, in keeping with that eloquence, he too readily resorts to exaggeration, he speaks with understanding of the real state of affairs under the principate. Amid the perils of public life there is no more powerful weapon for offence or defence than oratory; it brings fame, wealth, self-satisfaction. Aper cites two names; without advantage of birth or wealth, without even high moral principles (8.3 *neuter moribus egregius*—a surprising remark this from one who is recommending their example) Eprius Marcellus and Vibius Crispus have for years been among the most powerful men in the state and enjoyed the friendship of Vespasian himself.[35] By contrast, Aper argues, the rewards of poetry are small and its fame transitory; and in the case of Maternus poetry has not even enabled him to escape the dangers that attend involvement in politics, since his *Cato* had given offence, presumably by its republican and anti-tyrannical sentiments. The allusions to Maternus' *Cato* and to Eprius Marcellus are there to warn the reader that the *Dialogus* is not simply to be taken at its face value.

In his second speech Aper does not so much defend modern oratory as attack that of the ancients. His underlying argument is based on relativism; Cicero did very well before the untutored public of his own day, but now a more sophisticated approach is called for. His attempts to disparage Cicero are not (and are not perhaps intended to be) very convincing, but his attempt to see the problem in an historical perspective is an important feature of the dialogue. In the final speeches of Messalla and Maternus it is the refusal of the former to see that, because times have changed, the old solutions will not work, and the awareness of the latter that the solution of the problem they are discussing can only be found by considering its social and political context, that give the victory to Maternus.[36]

As one reads the two speeches of Maternus two questions present themselves: are the arguments of the two speeches compatible with each other, and can one, to all intents and purposes, maintain that Maternus' opinions are those of Tacitus himself? Maternus' first speech, in defence of poetry, is comparatively brief. Its main theme is the contrast between the environments in which oratory and poetry are composed and function. In contrast to Aper's rosy-coloured view of the milieu of contemporary eloquence Maternus shows its darker side; it is mercenary and sanguinary. What, he asks, is so enviable about the position of Crispus and Marcellus? To the emperor they seem insufficiently servile, to us insufficiently free. By contrast poetry takes one far from the madding crowd, to a pure and crime-free atmosphere, such as existed in the golden age, when there were bards and poets in abundance, but no law courts and no orators. Innocence is a better shield than eloquence, and Maternus expresses the hope that he will never need to speak in the senate save in defence of another. As for himself, he prays to die, when his time comes, as a man of modest means, so that no one will wish to overturn his will through envy. The quietist ideal was a commonplace of imperial literature, and Maternus is saying nothing original here. But there is an air of unreality about his reference to the rôle of the poet in the golden age, and this unreality is underlined at the end of his speech, where the expression of hope for a peaceful life and death may possibly be intended to remind the reader that Maternus' end was not, in fact, a peaceful one.[37] In any case, whatever Maternus' ultimate fate, though his criticisms of Aper are well founded, his belief in the poet's immunity from danger is unjustified; the fate of Lucan during Nero's reign is sufficient evidence to the contrary.

But it is Maternus' second speech that presents the real difficulty. There is a small problem at the beginning. At the end of c.35 Messalla's speech breaks off in the middle of a sentence. After a gap in the manuscript,[38] when the text resumes, the speaker is clearly Maternus. Consequently the end of Messalla's speech and the beginning of Maternus' is missing. It is, however, unlikely that a substantial part of the argument of either speaker is lost. Maternus' speech demolishes Messalla's contention that a revival of great oratory is possible, if only there were a return to a better morality and a better system of education. On the contrary, Maternus maintains, great oratory needs fuel to feed its flames, and it prospers most in troubled times. So the period of Rome's greatest orators was that of the Republic's death throes. By contrast, in his own day, Maternus concludes, when a dutiful people is ready to obey its ruler, and decisions are taken by one man, in whom all wisdom rests, there is neither need nor occasion for oratorical display.

It is at this point that a number of questions must be faced. Though the attempt to account for the rise and fall of great oratory in political terms is found in other authors than Tacitus,[39] the answer that Maternus gives is unique. But his assertion that 'that great and renowned eloquence of which I speak is the nursling of licence, which fools call freedom, the companion of civil disorders . . . which does not arise in well-organized states' (40.2 *est magna illa et notabilis eloquentia alumna licentiae, quam stulti libertatem uocant, comes seditionum . . . quae in bene constitutis ciuitatibus non oritur*) is phrased in words deliberately chosen to contradict Cicero, who in his *Brutus* (in essence a history of Roman oratory in dialogue form) had said (45): 'Eloquence is the companion of peace, the associate of leisure, and the nursling of a well-organized state' (*pacis est comes otique socia et iam bene constitutae ciuitatis quasi alumna quaedam eloquentia*). Cicero's formula 'the well-organized state produces great eloquence' has been stood on its head to yield the new equation 'state not well-organized: great eloquence (= late Republic) :: state well-organized: no great eloquence (Principate)'.

Maternus' argument is quite unequivocal. The fact that there still remains some call for the advocate's services is only a proof that the organization of the state has not yet reached perfection. When that stage has been reached, orators will be no more necessary than are doctors for a healthy body. Two questions need to be asked here. How valid is Maternus' argument? How does it relate to the political attitude found in Tacitus' other works? On the first question it is necessary to make a political judgment. To me it seems that, while Maternus accurately diagnoses many of the shortcomings of the last years of the Republic, the ideal state that he envisages is both unrealisable and undesirable. The 'well-constituted' states he mentions (40.3) are Sparta, Crete, Macedon and Persia. The first two were quoted by philosophers as examples of states where the rule of law obtained: others might describe them as authoritarian and illiberal. The other two were, frankly, despotisms. In his opening speech Maternus' picture was coloured by the idea of a golden age (*aureum saeculum*, 12.3); in his present speech he seems to favour societies in which law and order may be a euphemism for regimentation. Belief in rule by one man who is also the wisest (*sapientissimus et unus*, 41.4) can easily become a recipe for totalitarianism.

In that case Maternus' views cannot simply be equated with those of Tacitus. For though Tacitus accepted that the interests of peace necessitated the rule of one man (*Hist.* 1.1.1 *omnem potentiam ad unum conferri pacis interfuit*), he also believed that within such a political framework there was both room and need for independence, above all senatorial independence.[40] If Maternus is not simply Tacitus' mouthpiece, an important conclusion follows. In the dialogues of Cicero, though different topics and points of view are contributed by different speakers, there is clearly one major character who represents Cicero's own views (e.g. Crassus in the *De oratore*): among Latin dialogues the *Dialogus* is unique. No single speaker gives its author's view, and no authoritative answer is offered to the question why the standard of eloquence has declined. The reader is left to piece together his own conclusions from the arguments he has heard. In so doing he must not ignore the contribution made by Aper; for though he exaggerates when he claims that contemporary eloquence matches that of the Ciceronian Age, he is right—as against Maternus—when he affirms that there is a place in contemporary society for eloquence to flourish and prosper.

Finally, a word must be said about the relationship of the *Dialogus* to Tacitus' other works. One tempting hypothesis must be rejected. It has been suggested that when Maternus declares his intention to give up oratory and turn to poetry, this can be taken to mean that Tacitus is declaring *his* intention to give up oratory to turn to history.[41] But Tacitus did not turn his back on public life—he was to go out to the prestigious post of governor of Asia c. 112—and it is unlikely that he regarded history as a form of escapist literature.

A fundamental quality of Tacitus' writing is a certain obliqueness of expression; it is never wise to take his statements at their face value too readily. The limpid style of the *Dialogus* is apparently matched by the transparency of the views it enunciates. But the transparency is more apparent than real—for a number of reasons. The author's avoidance of making any one speaker his mouthpiece throws on the reader the onus of forming his own judgment from the conflicting views before him; and account must be taken of the contrast between what the speaker believes his position to be and what it really is—a contrast particularly clear in the case of Maternus. Far from taking him 'away from it all' his poetry has embroiled him, both in the past and the present, in conflict with the authorities and their henchmen, and on his own admission it is likely to continue to do so in the future.

The *Dialogus* is ostensibly a discussion of a literary problem, as the *Agricola* was ostensibly a biography of Tacitus' father-in-law. But in both works a further purpose is served. The *Agricola* is also a political testament in which Tacitus indicates and defends his belief that 'even under bad emperors great men can exist' (42.4 *posse etiam sub malis principibus magnos uiros esse*); intransigent resistance is not the only way. The underlying lesson of the *Dialogus* too is a political one. It is for this reason that Aper and, particularly in his second speech, Maternus argue historically, and it is Messalla's failure to do the same that makes his argument, though firmly based on traditional Roman respect for moral values, an anachronism. Maternus and Aper were agreed that changes in the political and judicial system had affected the nature and quality of oratory, but it is Aper, not Maternus, who has right on his side when he insists that forensic and political oratory still have a necessary part to play. On this point Maternus is doubly wrong; he is wrong in thinking that it was open to a member of the senatorial class to opt out of the demands and dangers of public life,[42] and he is wrong in maintaining that such a withdrawal is made possible by the fact that the state is now ruled by the *sapientissimus et unus* ('the one and wisest').

Paradoxically, if one is to look for Tacitus' own view in Maternus, it is best done by turning the coin over to its reverse side. If Tacitus abandoned forensic oratory to turn to the writing of history, it was not because he thought that oratory no longer had a function to perform under Trajan, but because he believed that his own talent could be more effectively employed in the service of history. For him the writing of history was not a refuge for one who had turned his back on political life, but an attempt to comment on the present through the interpretation of the past. A study of the changed nature and function of oratory could illuminate the changes that had come about in Rome since the last years of the Republic. For this reason the *Dialogus* is not merely a work of literary analysis; it is also an attempt to study and explain the nature of one area of political change.

# IV

## THE *HISTORIES*

In the Preface of the *Agricola* Tacitus had announced his intention of composing 'a record of past slavery and a tribute to present blessings',[1] that is, an account of the tyrannical reign of Domitian followed by the happier days under Nerva and Trajan. Since Trajan had just succeeded Nerva at the time of the publication of the *Agricola*, Tacitus cannot be promising, even for the future, a history of the whole of Trajan's reign. But clearly the intended starting point is the reign of Domitian. When, some seven or eight years later, the promised historical work began to take shape, the plan of the work had altered. The reigns of Nerva and Trajan are now put aside as fitting material for Tacitus' old age, and for the starting point Tacitus chooses to go back to the civil wars that followed the death of Nero and ushered in the Flavian dynasty with Vespasian.

The extension of the project backwards in time is a significant change, with manifest advantages. The historical perspective is widened and allows Tacitus to explore those underlying causes that occasioned the rise and fall of a hereditary dynasty. A second reason arose from compositional considerations. Apart from the highly dramatic possibilities that were offered by the inclusion of a year that saw four emperors on the throne, the work would now begin with the aftermath that followed the violent death of the last of the Julio-Claudians and end with the assassination of the last of the Flavians. It is difficult not to believe that Tacitus felt that some pattern existed in the sequence of events he now chose to relate. In the upshot the accident of transmission has seen to it that we are denied the possibility of reading what Tacitus had to say about events closer to his own time. The whole work was contained in twelve or fourteen books:[2] of these only four and a quarter have survived, and these bring us down only to AD 70. *Habent sua fata libelli.*

Our estimate of the *Histories*, then, has to be based on not much more than a quarter of the whole, covering less than two of the twenty-eight years it originally dealt with. Yet what remains is feast enough. It contains some of the most brilliant descriptive writing of any age or language, and it proclaims Tacitus, notwithstanding the limitations imposed by the conventions and outlook of Greco-Roman historiography, as a historian of the first rank.

First, where to begin? An obvious starting point would be the death of Nero (June 68). Tacitus chose differently—and better. 'My work will begin with the year when Servius Galba was consul for the second time, along with Titus Vinius.' More than one consideration may have weighed with Tacitus in choosing this date (1 January 69). First, by using the annalistic formula of dating by consular year Tacitus asserts a claim to be considered as a continuer of a long line of Republican historians. Next, the words seem to promise an immediate start to the narrative of events, and though that promise is not at once fulfilled, the reader's interest is aroused and held through the introductory chapters, until, with almost the same words ('Such was the state of affairs in the Roman world, when *Servius Galba, consul for the second time, along with Titus Vinius*, began a year that for them was to be their last, and almost saw the end of Rome'; 1.11.3), the narrative finally gets under way. Most important of all, by beginning at 1 January, the dramatic impact of the turbulent events is enhanced. Within the space of fifteen days the reigning emperor, Galba, is murdered, Otho established as his successor at Rome, and Vitellius proclaimed as rival emperor in Germany. Nowhere in the whole of Latin literature does the narrative move with such speed and urgency as it does between cc. 12 and 49 of Book I of the *Histories*.

But before the narrative begins, the opening eleven chapters lay the foundation of the whole work. This introductory section splits into three distinct parts (c. 1; cc. 2-3; cc. 4-11), each longer than the one before it. In the first chapter Tacitus draws a clear distinction between historians of the Republic—they were eloquent and outspoken—and historians of the Empire, whose judgment was impaired by changed political circumstances; excluded from the 'corridors of power', they reacted to the imperial régime with excessive flattery or excessive hostility. Tacitus claims that he is influenced by neither of these motives, for though he had secured political advancement under each of the Flavian emperors (including Domitian), 'partisanship and hatred must be equally eschewed by a writer of integrity' (*sed incorruptam fidem professis neque amore quisquam et sine odio dicendus est*). The mere profession of integrity, it must be said, is no guarantee of its possession. But the claim is a proud one; it is by the standards of Republican historiography that Tacitus asks to be judged. A final, more conventional, sentence alludes to the felicity of the present age, when thought and utterance are both free; to tell of that age will be the task of Tacitus' declining years. Tacitus never fulfilled that promise: advancing years saw in him an increasing interest in a still earlier period, the period in which the rule of one man was established and then perpetuated over a citizen body that was still nominally free.

The second and third chapters announce, in the most general terms, the subject matter of the whole of the *Histories*: it will be a work 'rich in disasters, full of bitter fighting, torn by civil strife, and even in time of peace beset with cruelty' (*opus adgredior opimum casibus, atrox proeliis, discors seditionibus, ipsa etiam pace saeuom*). 'Four emperors perished by the sword'—no names are mentioned, since that would slow the pace—'there were three civil wars, more foreign ones, and often a combination of the two.' After rapid mention of the extremities of the Empire attention is focused on Italy and Rome. A single mention of prosperity in the East, then unmitigated gloom, including natural disasters, crimes, and outrages against the moral order. Chapter 3 begins with some examples of individual heroism and probity, but the mood quickly darkens again; the emphasis is on human suffering, matched by prodigies and thunderbolts that seemed to be a form of divine chastisement, demonstrating, in Tacitus' words, that 'the gods are indifferent to our well-being, but not to our punishment'.

Whereas the first three chapters refer to the *Histories* as a whole, cc. 4–11 refer more specifically to the period of the civil wars from the death of Nero to the final victory of Vespasian at the end of *Histories* III. Before the narrative proper starts Tacitus undertakes to describe the state of the city of Rome, the temper of the armies, and the attitude of the provinces. The purpose of this review is to enable the reader 'to understand not only the course of events and their outcome (for these are generally a matter of chance) but also their underlying causes' (*ut non modo casus euentusque rerum, qui plerumque fortuiti sunt, sed ratio etiam causaeque noscantur*). What Tacitus means by 'underlying causes' is revealed by the chapters that follow; what he gives is primarily an analysis of the significant civilian and military groups within the Roman world, their general mood, and their reaction to Nero's death. In his narrative Tacitus gives a great deal of prominence to individuals: in the present section he concentrates on the underlying social and political structure. Though he viewed with distaste much of what he saw—a spirit of aristocratic aloofness permeates his writings—his analysis is carried out with penetration and skill.

In c. 8 Tacitus begins his review of the provinces. But it is the armies of the provinces (and in some cases their commanders) that interest him; and he is interested in them only so far as they can influence the struggle for power—a power that would ultimately be exercised from Rome. He begins with Spain, since it was there that Galba had been proclaimed governor; thereafter his course follows roughly a clockwise spiral—Gaul, Germany, Britain, Illyricum, Syria, Judaea, Africa, Mauretania, then (once more on the north of the Mediterranean) Raetia, Noricum, Thrace, and lastly Italy. In this survey Tacitus spends longest time in Germany and the East—understandably so, since it is they who, along with Rome will provide the emperors during this turbulent year. Since Tacitus' concern at this point is with groups, it is not surprising that when he deals with the situation among the troops in Rome, he does not even mention Otho. But when he turns to the East, there is a significant change. Here emphasis is given to individual commanders, but it is Mucianus, governor of Syria, not Vespasian, the future emperor, who catches the eye.[3] Indeed Tacitus stresses the fact that Vespasian was prepared to remain loyal to Galba, and entered the lists largely at the instigation of Mucianus. A briefer mention of Vespasian ends with the warning not to believe all those who, after his elevation to the throne, claimed that it had been foretold by prodigies and the like; for the most part belief came only after the event.

The end of c. 11 brings us back to the point at which the opening words of the Book had promised the reader that the narrative would begin, the first day of 69. Until the end of c. 49, when Tacitus pronounces his obituary on Galba, the narrative deals with the struggle between Galba and Otho. But the first words of c. 12 remind us of another dimension to that confrontation. Already on the first of January the legions in Upper Germany had refused to take the oath of allegiance to Galba, though as yet they were prepared to leave it to the senate and people of Rome to choose a successor. News of their disaffection came from the imperial procurator of the adjoining province of Gallia Belgica. Bad news travels fast, but the information can scarcely have reached Rome in less than seven or eight days, and even that would necessitate a daily rate of more than 150 miles. A small but important point of detail is involved. The Lower German army proclaimed Vitellius as emperor on 2 January, and the Upper German legions threw in their lot with them a day later. According to Tacitus, when Galba decided on 10 January to adopt Piso Licinianus as his successor, he knew of the defection of the German legions, but had no definite news of Vitellius. Plutarch has a different version, and asserts that it was news of Vitellius' proclamation that caused Galba to adopt Piso. The time-distance equation makes it likely that Tacitus' version is the correct one. Mention of the German revolt at this point has an important function, whose purpose, though unstated, the reader is meant to realise. To Galba and Otho their struggle seemed to be for the right to rule the Roman world: in fact all that the victor would gain would be the right to confront Vitellius and, in due course, be defeated by him. The news of the defection of the German legions also gives urgency to Galba's thoughts of adopting a successor.

The public proclamation of Piso's adoption[4] meant the end of the hopes that Otho had nursed of becoming Galba's successor—unless he were to achieve that position by force. Otho was a colourful character; extravagant, dissolute, he had a personal charm that could win both affection and loyalty. For some time he had sought to ingratiate himself with members of the imperial bodyguard. Two of its number were approached by one of Otho's freedmen and 'undertook to transfer the empire of the Roman people—and transferred it' (1.25.1). Near the temple of Saturn Otho was greeted as emperor by no more than twenty-three soldiers. Others joined them as they made their way to the praetorian camp. The audacity of the deed brought it success: 'a few dared this dastardly deed, more welcomed it, all accepted it' (1.28 fin.).

The coup made its imprint on the common source which was at the disposal of Tacitus, Plutarch and Suetonius; for here, even more than in what precedes, their accounts show close, and sometimes extended, similarities. The account of Galba's death and its aftermath similarly had its main lines already laid down in the common source. For the moment, however, there is room for Tacitus to develop his own picture of the confusion that reigned among Galba and his supporters, when news of Otho's revolt reached them. As they deliberated whether to remain within the palace or march, with such forces as they had, against Otho, a great crowd collected, clamouring for the execution of Otho and his fellow conspirators. Tacitus, always contemptuous of crowd behaviour, says of them (1.32.1), 'They might have been demanding some show in the circus or theatre; they showed neither judgment nor sincerity, for they were going, on the same day, to

71

demand with equal enthusiasm an exactly opposite course—it was their usual habit to shower flattery on the emperor, whoever he was.' Galba had scarcely taken the decision to pursue the bolder course, when a rumour sprang up that Otho had been killed. Circumstantial embellishments were soon added; eye witnesses came forward, even a soldier brandishing a bloody sword, claiming that it was he who had slain Otho. Galba's stern response to this claim was: 'Who gave you your orders?' (1.35.2). Plutarch too has the riposte, but waters it down by allowing the soldier to answer back.

In the meantime in the camp Otho was surrounded with great enthusiasm, particularly from the ordinary praetorian. In return he reached out his hands to them and threw kisses to the crowd, 'acting the slave to become the master' (*omnia seruiliter pro dominatione*; 1.36.3). Then, when he was assured of their allegiance, he addressed them in a speech (1.37-38.2) that was nicely calculated to play upon both his audience's fears and hopes—'it is clear that we can neither perish nor survive except together'. As he embarks on his peroration, truisms give way to falsehoods: 'the senate and the Roman people are of one mind; they await the display of *your* valour—you from whom honourable counsels derive all their strength, and without whom enterprises, however noble, are of no avail.' Then a concluding exhortation: 'there is no room for delay in an undertaking that can win praise only if it is successful.' With these words Otho orders the armoury to be thrown open. The soldiers seize arms and band together without regard for due form or order, each man his own leader.

At this point (1.40) we return to Galba and the narrative of the common source. 'Galba was driven this way and that by the shifting tides of the crowd (Plutarch has 'his litter was carried hither and thither as though in a billowing tide'), while the basilicas and temples all around were filled with spectators, a mournful sight before them' (Plutarch: 'the multitude rushing to the porticoes and the vantage points of the forum, as though taking seats for a spectacle'). The climax of the drama follows quickly. In the midst of the milling throng Galba's litter was overturned and he himself thrown out. Othonian troops closed in on him. In a moment he was dead, and his head cut off from his body. Tacitus was not one to lose the opportunity of painting a striking scene. But once more the scene is not entirely of his own construction, for Plutarch's version has many close similarities:

When the litter was overturned at the place called *lacus Curtius*, Galba was thrown out; as soldiers rushed up and struck at him in his breastplate, he proferred his neck and said, 'Do your work, if it is better so for the Roman people'. After receiving many wounds on his legs and arms, he was killed, according to the account of most writers, by one Camurius, a soldier of the fifteenth legion. But some say that he was killed by Terentius, others by Lecanius, while others say that the deed was done by Fabius Fabulus, who also cut off his head and carried it wrapped up in his cloak, because its baldness made it hard to grasp. . . . (Plutarch, *Galba* 27.1-2)

According to Tacitus:

Close to the *lacus Curtius* the panic of his bearers caused Galba to be thrown out of the litter on to the ground. His last words were variously reported, according as men were moved by hatred or admiration. Some say that he humbly asked what he had done to deserve this, and begged to be allowed a few days to pay the donative; the more general account is that without more ado he offered his throat to his assassins, bidding them do their job and strike, if that seemed best for their country. His killers were not interested in what he said. There is some disagreement about who struck the blow: some say that it was the veteran Terentius, others that it was Laecanius; the more generally accepted version records that Camurius, a soldier of the fifteenth legion, drove home the sword and gashed his throat. The others in brutal fashion hacked at his legs and arms (for his breast was protected); many wounds were inflicted on his headless body in a spirit of uncontrolled savagery. (Tacitus, *Histories* 1.41.2-3)

The relevant portions of Suetonius' account are:

Some report that at their first onrush he cried out, 'What are you doing, comrades? I am yours, and you are mine', and that he promised a donative. The more general account is that without more ado he offered his throat, and urged them to do their job and strike, since such was their will. . . . He was murdered beside the *lacus Curtius* and left as he was, until an ordinary soldier . . . came and cut off his head; and since he could not grasp it by the hair, he tucked it into his cloak; then he thrust his thumb into the mouth and brought it to Otho. (*Galba* 20)

Three points call for note. The close similarity between the accounts of Tacitus, Plutarch and Suetonius makes it certain that alternative versions of what Galba said before he was killed, and who killed him, already existed in the source used by all three writers. Secondly, Tacitus is alone in trying to explain—he does so by a mordant epigram—why there should be different versions of Galba's last words. Tacitus is alone, too, in suppressing the macabre details of what happened to Galba's head. His practice elsewhere suggests that he judged it beneath the dignity of history to record such sordid details.

Galba's death was quickly succeeded by the deaths of Vinius and Piso. Then, after an obsequious senate had voted Otho tribunician power, the name of Augustus, and all imperial honours, he gave permission for the burial of the dead. A whole chapter (49) is devoted to the obituary of Galba. Many of the elements are found also in Plutarch's last chapter of Galba's life, and some occur too in Suetonius, but the construction of the whole, and the inimitable language is Tacitus' own. Not for the first or the last time in his character sketches there is an unmistakable Sallustian flavour, which at one point becomes palpable.[5]

> Such was the end of Servius Galba, who for seventy three years had lived through the reigns of five emperors with an attendant good fortune that was more marked during the reign of others than in his own. . . . he himself had a modest talent, more without faults than with merits. He was neither indifferent to fame nor ostentatious of it; not covetous of other men's money, thrifty with his own, he was grasping where the public purse was concerned . . . the distinction of his birth and the terror of the times served as a cloak, so that what was actually sloth was called prudence. In the prime of his life he gained military renown in Germany, as proconsul he governed Africa with moderation, and nearer Spain with a similar fairness, being regarded as destined for greater things, as long as he remained a private citizen; in the opinion of all he was fit to be an emperor—until he became one.

The passage ends with a brilliant (and literally untranslatable) epigram: *omnium consensu capax imperii, nisi imperasset* ('in the judgment of everyone capable of being emperor, had he not been emperor').

With his obituary of Galba Tacitus concludes the first major section of *Histories* I. With Galba dead, the way is clear for him to focus his attention on the conflict between Otho and Vitellius. The second half of the Book is divided between the two new protagonists: cc. 51–70 deal with Vitellius and his generals and their advance to, and across, the Alps; cc. 71–90 deal with Otho at Rome, until at the very end of the Book he leaves the capital to march against Vitellius, thus setting the scene for the main action of the first half of Book II.

Chapter 51 begins: 'Now I will expound the origin and causes of the Vitellian rising' (*nunc initia causasque motus Vitelliani expediam*). The words *initia causasque* have a double function. They recall Tacitus' opening promise to explain the underlying causes of events (*ratio causaeque*; 1.4.1), and will themselves be recalled when they are used to introduce the new theme with which Book III opens, the rise of Vespasian to power. But they also allow Tacitus to go back to a point in time earlier than that reached by the narrative in c. 49 (15 January). Once more his account of the circumstances leading to the proclamation of Vitellius has such similarity with Plutarch's account (*Galba* 22) that dependence on a common source is again the only reasonable explanation. Yet even where this is the case, there are differences that reveal Tacitus' superiority. Plutarch, for instance, confuses the distinct rôles of the Upper and Lower German armies on the first and second of January, whereas Tacitus makes it clear that on 1 January the Upper army's insubordination was restricted to overturning Galba's statues, refusing to take the oath of allegiance to him, and instead swearing loyalty to the Senate and Roman People: the thought of proclaiming Vitellius emperor originated with the troops of Lower Germany, that is, from Vitellius' own command.

According to Tacitus it was the arguments of Fabius Valens, legionary commander in Lower Germany, that moved Vitellius' slothful temperament (*segne ingenium*) so that 'he began to desire rather than hope for the throne' (1.52 fin.). The indolence of Vitellius, coupled with his extravagance and debauchery, is to become almost a leitmotiv of his appearances in the *Histories*, and it forms an effective contrast with the energy that Caecina and Valens showed on his behalf. It is on them that attention is focused in cc. 61–70, after Vitellius had given them instructions to advance into Italy with separate armies, Valens taking a route that would lead him through Gaul and the Cottian Alps, entering Italy via the pass of Mont Genèvre: Caecina was to take the more direct route via the Great St Bernard. Vitellius would follow later with what Tacitus rather vaguely calls 'the whole mass of war' (*tota mole belli*; 1.61 fin.).

The departure of Valens from Cologne took place about the middle of January. It is possible to deduce the main stages of his route from Tacitus' narrative, but his interest is not in the geography of the itinerary, but in the behaviour of Valens' forces and the reaction to them of the communities through whose territories they passed. They were received with friendliness in Trier and Metz, but in the latter town a sudden and groundless panic seized the army, and four thousand inhabitants were killed. If any Gauls had previously had any doubts whom to support, these were now resolved: 'they had an equal hatred for Otho and Vitellius, but for Vitellius they had fear as well' (1.64.1).

The core of Caecina's army, drawn from the troops of Upper Germany, was the twenty-first legion from Vindonissa (Windisch, near Lake Constance). Caecina's journey was therefore shorter as well as more direct: it was not less bloody or less expensive for those through whose territory he passed. As he approached the Alps, Caecina learned that an auxiliary cavalry unit stationed on the Po had declared for

Vitellius, under whom it had earlier served in Africa. More important still, it had brought over with it to allegiance to Vitellius a number of towns north of the river. Though the Alps were still in the grip of winter, Caecina led his troops over the Great St Bernard into Italy. The date—Tacitus, as often, does not give it—was some time early in March.

The last twenty chapters of Book I return the reader to Rome, and take up the story from the death of Galba on 15 January. Much of the material of these chapters is also found in Plutarch's life of Otho. Again the similarities between the two accounts must derive from the use of a common source, again the differences in treatment are revealing. Plutarch's account begins with three episodes—the pardoning of Marius Celsus, who had remained loyal to Galba; the enforced suicide of Tigellinus, the detested favourite of Nero; the quelling by Otho of an outbreak of nocturnal violence among the praetorian guard. Of Marius Celsus Plutarch says that the behaviour of both pardoner and pardoned won applause: in Tacitus Otho is said to have had an ulterior motive—'he sought to win a reputation for clemency': the real honour goes to Celsus,[6] who, Tacitus tells us (there is nothing of this in Plutarch), showed to Otho a loyalty as great as he had shown to Galba.

In their accounts of the mutiny of the praetorians and their irruption into the Palace, where Otho was entertaining leading citizens and their wives to a banquet, Tacitus and Plutarch have similarities that at times descend to close verbal resemblances.[7] So Plutarch's

> while he feared for his guests, he was a source of fear to them is paralleled by Tacitus

> Otho, being in fear, was himself feared (*cum timeret Otho, timebatur*).

But Plutarch wrongly thinks that the mutiny started at Ostia. Tacitus (along with Suetonius) has the truth: it began in the praetorian camp just outside Rome, whither the seventeenth cohort had been summoned from Ostia. On the following day, after the distribution of 5,000 sesterces a man had made it safe for him to do so, Otho entered the camp and addressed the guard. The long speech (fifty lines of *oratio recta*) is a masterpiece of eloquence—and insincerity (1.83.2-84). Otho lays great stress on the praetorians' valour (*uirtus*) and their devotion to him (*pietas*), but asks for some moderation in their zeal. Then, warming to his peroration, he draws the contrast between themselves and Vitellius' troops; it is through the bright glory of the senate that their side dazzles the dull meanness of the Vitellian cause. 'Tell me', he ends, 'do you believe that this fair city stands by reason of its fine houses, its buildings, and its piles of masonry? They are dumb and lifeless, they can fall and rise again: but the immortality of our empire, the peace of nations (*aeternitas rerum et pax gentium*), your lives and mine, are based on the continuing safety of the senate. This institution was established after solemn taking of the auspices by the founder and father of our city; it has passed in unbroken and deathless continuity from kings to emperors; thus have we received it from our ancestors, thus let us hand it down to posterity. For as senators come from your ranks, so do emperors come from the ranks of senators.'

The disparity between the grandeur of the language and the meanness of the actual situation is palpable. And it is by design that the next chapter (1.85) describes the sycophantic behaviour of that senate on whose continuing safety was based *aeternitas rerum et pax gentium*. The senate avoided flattery: its insincerity would be too obvious to Otho who, as one of their number, had used it towards Galba. Instead they resorted to abuse of Vitellius, but muted it in case Vitellius should prove to be the victor!

The final chapters of the Book describe the preparations Otho made for the impending war with Vitellius and the mood in the city. A number of portents are recorded, most of them of ill omen. Tacitus shrewdly observes that in earlier days such portents occurred even in times of peace: now they are heard of only when men are afraid. Otho would not listen to those who urged religious objections against his departure; he knew that Caecina and his army were already south of the Alps. On 14 March he handed over the safe keeping of the state to the senate and addressed the people, who greeted him with cries of adulation that were as fulsome as they were false. On the next day he put the city in charge of his brother, Salvius Titianus, and left for the front. Exactly two months had passed since Galba's murder and his own elevation; the day of his departure was the Ides of March.

The end of Book I leaves the reader looking forward to the engagement of the opposing armies of Otho and Vitellius. But it is not with this conflict that Book II opens. As the struggle in Rome between Galba and Otho had been set against the backcloth of the impending threat of Vitellius, so the contest between Otho and Vitellius is preceded by a section in which the ultimate triumph of Vespasian and the Flavian cause is foreshadowed.

In a very different part of the globe fortune was already devising the first steps that would give rise to a new dynasty that proved by turns fortunate or disastrous to the state, and prosperous or fatal to the emperors themselves.

77

The sentence, gaining prominence as the first sentence of a new Book, includes the same phrase, *initia causasque*, that had been used when Tacitus began to explain the underlying reasons for Vitellius' rising (1.51.1). But here, instead of analysis of motives and resources, Tacitus immediately gives an account of the part played at this juncture by Titus, Vespasian's elder son (and later emperor). It is difficult to see how he is to form part of the *initia causasque imperio*. Neither his journey to Rome to pay homage to Galba, interrupted on receipt of the news of Galba's murder, nor his visit to the temple of Venus at Paphos in Cyprus, where he is said to have learned that the omens were favourable to a mighty undertaking, influenced Vespasian and Mucianus. Flavian propaganda was to proclaim that Vespasian took up arms reluctantly, for the good of his country. Tacitus does not controvert that claim explicitly, but his statement that 'they deferred a resort to arms until the time was ripe' (2.7.2) leaves no doubt that Vespasian and Mucianus were already agreed on a concerted bid for supreme power; only the time remained in doubt.

At this point the narrative returns to the point at which it had broken off at the end of Book I. The war had begun well for Otho; the four legions stationed in Dalmatia and Pannonia had already declared for him and were on their way to join him.[8] From Rome itself came a force of considerable numerical strength, but of somewhat motley constitution. These troops were sent on ahead to occupy the banks of the Po, since Otho's first plan—we are told of it now for the first time (2.11.2), only after it had failed—to prevent Caecina from leaving Gaul, was now rendered inoperative by the fact that Caecina had already crossed the Alps. It is clear that control of the central reaches of the Po valley was likely now to be the objective whose attainment would decide the issue; on it hinged Otho's ability to protect Italy from the invader and to keep open the lines of communication with the armies of the East who had been summoned to his aid.

For the next thirty chapters Tacitus concentrates on military narrative, and here, for the first time, it is possible to estimate what justification there is for Mommsen's much quoted aphorism that 'Tacitus is the most unmilitary of authors'. For much of the material we possess a parallel account in Plutarch's *Life of Otho* (clearly drawn from the same source as Tacitus), and important inferences can be drawn from a comparison of the two accounts; but it is also necessary to set Tacitus' account against the best reconstruction we can make of what actually happened.

The initial contacts between units of the opposing sides took place in an area forming a shallow triangle bounded by Ticinum and Cremona (on the north bank of the Po) and Placentia, roughly half way between them on the south bank and guarding the junction of the Aemilian and Postumian ways—the former leading directly into the heart of Italy and to Rome, the latter the route by which support for Otho from the East would come. Two minor successes encouraged the Vitellians to make a brief raid to the south bank of the river near Placentia, and this sortie gave rise to a report that Caecina had arrived with the whole of his army. Though Vestricius Spurinna, whom Otho had sent on ahead to hold the banks of the Po, could not hope to contest the advance of Caecina, his troops, who included three praetorian cohorts, demanded that they be led out against the enemy. Spurinna deemed it prudent to fall in with their demands. At nightfall, when the order to set up camp was given, the unwisdom of their precipitate action began to dawn upon his men, and they allowed themselves to be led back to Placentia in a more sober and disciplined frame of mind; their first task was to strengthen the city's defences.

In his narrative of this episode[9] Tacitus concentrates on those things that he regarded as most important, above all the interrelationship, causal or consequential, of mood and event; facts that we should like to know are often omitted unless they serve that purpose. A cohort of Pannonians was captured near Cremona. We are not told what this cohort was doing in that neighbourhood, nor does Tacitus tell us that Cremona itself passed into Vitellian hands, which it certainly did about this time.

Shortly afterwards the Othonian side had a small, but striking success. Gladiators, who formed part of the Othonian contingent from Rome, made a light raid across the river and inflicted casualties on some Vitellian auxiliaries. Martius Macer, who was in command of the gladiators, aware of the danger if reinforcements came to the assistance of the enemy, ordered his men to withdraw across the river, in spite of his troops' eagerness to continue the action. The incident, which Plutarch does not even mention, was too slight to exert any significant influence on the campaign as a whole. But to it Tacitus appends a paragraph that has important implications for understanding his method of writing history. Macer's order to withdraw aroused the suspicion of his men, for the Othonian troops put the worst possible interpretation on everything their generals did. Annius Gallus, Suetonius Paullinus, and Marius Celsus all came under the lash of their tongue. . . . The men's complaints were conveyed in secret missives to Otho, who, always ready to listen to the lowest elements, sent for his brother, Titianus, and made him commander-in-chief (2.23.4–5, abridged).

Essentially the same method is found in Plutarch (*Otho* 7.23 ff.):

> But most of the soldiers actually accused him of treachery, and sought to incense Otho by their loud protests that victory had been cut short by the cowardice of the generals. Otho did not believe what they said, but did not wish to seem to disbelieve them. So he sent his brother, Titianus, to the army along with Proculus, the Praetorian Prefect, who held effective power, while Titianus was only a figurehead. Those about Celsus and Paullinus, too, enjoyed the empty names of friends and advisers. . . .

The material surely comes to both writers from a common source, but in Plutarch it is attached to a different incident, the failure of Suetonius Paullinus to press home the advantage in a later, much more substantial engagement against the whole of Caecina's army at Castors (it is Tacitus who supplies the name). If, as is probable,[10] it is Plutarch who keeps the position that the paragraph occupied in the common source, why has Tacitus chosen to locate it differently? The likely explanation is simple. The battle at Castors took place on 5 or 6 April. That news could not have reached Otho, marching North through Italy, in time for him to summon Titianus from Rome, and for Titianus to reach Bedriacum, where he was present for the council of war, held not later than 12 April.

Tacitus, then, rejects an impossible chronology, but is unwilling to sacrifice the material he found in the common source that accounted for the appointment of Titianus as commander-in-chief. But because the incident involving Macer and the gladiators could not in itself have provoked the change in command, Tacitus depicts it as the last straw in a series of disagreements between the generals serving Otho and the men under them.

The manner in which Plutarch and Tacitus treat the council of war itself is instructive. In Plutarch Proculus and Titianus urge an immediate engagement, and the arguments for delay, advanced by Paullinus (supported by Marius Celsus and Annius Gallus) were unavailing. According to Tacitus,

> Suetonius Paullinus, thinking it in keeping with his unmatched reputation as a military expert to express an opinion on the overall strategy of the war, declared that haste was to the advantage of the enemy, delay in their own interest (2.32.1).[11]

But rational argument was powerless against the demands of Titianus and Proculus, who further insisted that Otho himself should retire with a powerful bodyguard to the safety of Brixellum, where, we presume, he had his headquarters. Tacitus and Plutarch agree in regarding that decision as disastrous both to Othonian morale and fighting strength.

In his next chapter (*Otho* 9) Plutarch adds further reasons that are alleged to have influenced the opposing sides in the Othonian council of war. There was, he says, some belief that the rival armies had considered calling a truce and either proclaiming one of their own generals as emperor or leaving the choice to the senate. Plutarch seems to accept that such thoughts may have been seriously entertained by the more sensible and experienced soldiers, and he adds that the same source opines that it was for this reason that Celsus[12] and his supporters proposed delay, and, conversely, Otho and *his* supporters were eager to force a battle.

The same material appears in Tacitus, but once again he has placed it differently. After his description of the council of war and Otho's withdrawal to Brixellum he takes the narrative up to the eve of the battle of Bedriacum (cc. 34–36).[13] It is at this point (37.1), introduced by the words 'I find it stated in some authorities' (*inuenio apud quosdam auctores*), that Tacitus inserts the rumour that through dread of war or loathing of both commanders the armies hesitated whether to lay down arms and choose, or leave it to the senate to choose, a new emperor. Tacitus deals with this suggestion in a long digression, in which he shows a sense of historical perspective, that is not significantly impaired by the rhetorical moralising of its penultimate sentence ('It was the same wrath of the gods, the same madness among men, the same motives for crimes that drove them into conflict'). He first gives three personal reasons for disbelieving the rumour; Suetonius would not have believed that, in such a corrupt age, the common herd would lay war aside through love of peace, it was physically impossible for armies of such different origins to reach a consensus for peace, nor (lastly) would officers and generals, themselves so steeped in extravagance and crime, have accepted any but an equally corrupt emperor.

To justify his suppositions Tacitus appeals to a broader historical generalisation, supported by the facts of Roman history. After the Romans had achieved world domination, internal conflict broke out. Fractious tribunes alternated with domineering consuls, the arms of the plebeian Marius and the aristocratic Sulla destroyed constitutional government and political liberty, establishing despotism in its place.

81

Pompey was no better, only less overt. Thereafter the prize was always sole power. Legions of citizens did not lay down their arms at Pharsalia or at Philippi: there was no reason to think that the armies of Otho and Vitellius would voluntarily have abandoned war. What Tacitus says, it must be admitted, is not very original. Many of the details appear in Plutarch (*Otho* 9), and presumably were in the common source, while significant elements of thought and language in c. 38 can be paralleled from Sallust. But what is peculiarly Tacitean is how, after divorcing it from its original context, he uses the material he has borrowed to create a major digression. The theme of that digression, the interrelationship of political power and moral corruption, is a recurrent leitmotiv of Tacitus' thinking.[14]

Though the victory of his armies at the first battle of Bedriacum was to give Vitellius only an uneasy eight months' mastery of the Roman world, the defeat of Otho had immeasurable consequences; for without it Vespasian and the forces of the East might well have continued in the allegiance they had already proclaimed to Otho, and Rome would not have experienced the retrenchment of the early Flavian régime and the absolutist tendencies of its last years. The accounts of the battle given by Plutarch and Tacitus will not satisfy the demands or expectations of the modern reader. Plutarch's account is, as often, simpler, though not necessarily more accurate. Tacitus' account, roughly the same length as Plutarch's, is much more dense and complicated. But in spite of the fact that he omits details that would help to clarify the picture, in order to concentrate on the vivid incident and the critical moments at which moods changed or action was decided, his description of the battle has a more solid basis in time and place, and is both more coherent and more credible.

When news of the defeat of his army reached Otho at Brixellum, he resolved to sacrifice his own life rather than seek to prolong the war. The nobility of his decision would be forfeited if it could be demonstrated that he knew that his generals (including his brother) had already capitulated at Bedriacum. Tacitus clearly intends us to believe that Otho made a free choice. If so, we must assume that news of the capitulation of his generals did not reach Brixellum, twenty miles away, till after daybreak on the following day. That is just possible, especially if we allow some reluctance on the part of the generals to inform their emperor of what they had done without his authority.

Otho's suicide not unnaturally claimed the attention of historians;

even Suetonius, who despatches the whole of Otho's campaign in twenty lines, treats the final episode of his life at some length (9.3-11), drawing heavily, as do Tacitus and Plutarch, on the lost common source. In both Tacitus and Plutarch (c. 15), after those around Otho have urged him to continue the fight, Otho delivers a speech of some twenty lines. Both are highly rhetorical and abound in antitheses, but Tacitus' version is much more compact and compressed in thought, and it is used to convey his own historical judgment on Otho. He does not imply that Otho's final act of heroism outweighed his earlier crimes; but he is equally insistent that a tarnished past is not inconsistent with ability to show nobility, even if it is only briefly and at the end of a man's life. The speech that Tacitus puts in the mouth of Otho (2.47) is truly Roman, in a way that Plutarch and Dio Cassius cannot match. There is in it, too, a note of Stoicism, a note that will recur in the last moments of many of the characters in the pages of the *Annals*.

On the last details of Otho's life there is substantial agreement between Tacitus, Plutarch and Suetonius: a frugal drink of water, the choice of the sharper of two daggers, a night of deep sleep (Tacitus, more guardedly, says only that it was not without sleep), and, at first light, his suicide. As he had requested, his funeral was performed without delay; a number of soldiers slew themselves by his pyre. There remains only the obligatory obituary notice. One item appears alike in Tacitus, Plutarch, Suetonius, and Dio Cassius. Plutarch says:

> When he died, there were no fewer and no less honest men who praised his death than those who blamed his life.

Suetonius has:

> many who had utterly loathed him in his lifetime loudly praised him in death.

Dio Cassius:

> having lived the worst of lives he died the noblest of deaths.

Tacitus follows the same model, showing beyond doubt that all four authors, directly or indirectly, drew on the same common source, a source that had a liking for rhetorical antithesis. But in Tacitus there is an important difference:

> By two deeds, the one most dastardly, the other noble, he earned with posterity as great a share of renown as of obloquy.

Tacitus contrasts Otho's death, not with the rest of his life, as do the other writers,[15] but with one other act in his life, his treachery towards Galba. For the period between these two acts Tacitus' narrative has made his judgment abundantly clear: Otho had neither the power nor strength of character to impose his will on events. But at the end he took one decisive action that spared his country the shedding of much blood. Tacitus is determined that nothing should rob him of the praise which that decision deserved.

With the death of Otho there ends that section of narrative for which Plutarch provides a continuous account drawn substantially from the same source as Tacitus. But it is not only for that reason that Otho's death marks a significant point in Tacitus' narrative. The conflict between Galba and Otho had taken place in Rome, and when Otho moved into north Italy to oppose the armies of Vitellius, he still in some measure carried with him the interests of a Rome-centred power bloc. In the struggle that was to follow his death, even though the issue was finally resolved within the walls of the capital, Rome itself could no longer exert a decisive influence on the result. At this point in time Tacitus had to manipulate a number of diverse strands. The victory had gone to Vitellius, but he himself had not been present at the battle; so it was necessary to trace his movements from the time he left Cologne till his entry into Rome not later than the middle of July. But by then Vespasian had already been proclaimed emperor in Egypt and the near East, and the steps leading up to that proclamation have to be told.

Chapter 74 begins *at Vespasianus . . .*; *at* ('But . . .'), as often, marks a change of place and theme, the second word puts Vespasian in its forefront. Vespasian could reasonably expect the support of his own troops, of Mucianus, governor of Syria, and of the prefect of Egypt, Tiberius Alexander. He could also count on the third legion, which had recently been transferred from Syria to Moesia, and there was a good hope that they would bring the Illyrian legions on to the Flavian side. This would give him the support of fourteen legions (three each in Judaea, Syria, and Moesia; two each in Egypt and Pannonia; one in Dalmatia). But he was not blind to the risks that would attend a bid for power, and it was only after many private conversations that Mucianus ventured to address him openly (2.76-77). There is no reason to think that Tacitus could have had any knowledge of what Mucianus actually said. What we have is, according to the conventions of ancient historiography, a totally Tacitean creation. As if to underline the fact, it begins with a sentence clearly modelled on

Sallust, and ends with an epigram (*qui deliberant, desciuerunt*, 'those who contemplate revolt, have already revolted'), which in turn is borrowed from the source common to Plutarch and Tacitus, but used in that source at the point where Vinius urges Galba to revolt from Nero (Plutarch, *Galba* 4: 'for to consider whether we are to remain loyal to Nero is the act of those who no longer are loyal').

So far there has been singularly little hint of dates. With c. 79 we are at last given something concrete. The first move towards proclaiming Vespasian emperor was taken on 1 July at Alexandria by Tiberius Alexander, and this date was thereafter treated by Vespasian as his *dies imperii*, even though his own Judaean army did not make its proclamation until 3 July. Vespasian's authority was unquestioned throughout the seaboard provinces as far as Asia and Achaea, and inland as far as Pontus and Armenia. A council of war was held at Berytus. The outcome of its deliberations was the raising of levies, the recall of veterans to the colours, the commissioning of armaments, and the minting of gold and silver at Antioch. References to the sinews of war are not frequent in Tacitus, and it is interesting that it is in connection with the Flavian campaign that they should be mentioned. There is mention too of strategy. It was agreed that Vespasian should secure Egypt and its corn supply, while Mucianus was to move against Vitellius with a portion only of their troops. In the event the issue was to be decided, not by Mucianus and Vespasian, but by the daringly rapid advance of a legionary commander in Pannonia, Antonius Primus. Antonius, who, more than any other single man, was to be responsible for the Flavian victory, is introduced by a Sallustian character sketch: a ready speaker and shrewd intriguer, he was without principle in time of peace, but in war he was a man no one could afford to ignore (2.86.1–2).

With c. 87 Tacitus reverts to Vitellius, whose advance towards Rome showed him daily more contemptible and more indolent. The date at which he entered Rome cannot be fixed exactly, but it is likely to have been only a short time before 18 July.[16] Tacitus' narrative therefore demolishes as chronologically impossible the pro-Flavian version of Josephus, which implies that it was Vitellius' entry into Rome and the behaviour of his troops there that provoked Vespasian's proclamation as emperor.

When news came of revolt in the East, Vitellius at first made light of it. Only when it was reported that the vanguard of the Flavian forces, under Antonius Primus, was on the move did Vitellius at last order

Valens and Caecina to take the field. As Valens was ill, Caecina went ahead. Caecina sent an advance cavalry force to occupy Cremona; substantial infantry followed. Caecina himself diverged to Ravenna, where he sought to concert with the admiral of the fleets of Ravenna and Misenum a plan of defection from Vitellius, against whom both had grudges. In a final, important chapter (2.101) Tacitus notes that pro-Flavian writers alleged that the two defectors were motivated by concern for peace and patriotism (*cura pacis* and *amor rei publicae*). Tacitus will have none of this; they were motivated by jealousy and self-interest.

'Histories III has some claim to be considered the best book Tacitus ever wrote.'[17] It has pace, incident, and variety. A decisive night battle, the capture and sack of a famous north Italian city (Cremona), fighting in the streets of Rome, culminating in the burning of the Capitoline temple of Iuppiter Optimus Maximus, the humiliation and brutal murder of the emperor Vitellius—all this offered the sort of challenge that ancient historiography welcomed. Some of the incidents are handled also by Suetonius and Dio: nowhere is Tacitus' superiority in the art of writing more apparent, and a modern account of the events he describes is likely to be little more than a watered-down version of Tacitus' narrative. But the impetus with which the reader is swept along should not blind him to the problems that Tacitus leaves unsolved. Questions of time, distance, and strategy are, as often as not, left unmentioned, and we are forced to make inferences—not always with complete certainty—where a word from Tacitus would have made everything clear. The omissions underline the fact that Tacitus' purpose and interest are different from those of most modern historians.

'Better fortune and fidelity attended the Flavian generals, as they discussed strategy.' The opening words are designed to draw a contrast with the closing sentences of Book II, where the treachery of Caecina and Bassus on the Vitellian side has been related. The Flavian generals who are here referred to are the Pannonian commanders. In a council of war, held at Poetovio, the forcefulness of Antonius Primus persuaded his colleagues to move into northern Italy and seek to resolve the issue of civil war by an immediate confrontation with the forces of Vitellius. Such a plan ran counter to the strategy decided on by the high command at Berytus (2.81.3), according to which Mucianus was to make a swift but not precipitate advance into Italy. The audacity of Antonius is staggering. Though the measures taken to prevent a descent via the Brenner Pass of forces loyal to Vitellius show that Antonius did not cast all care to the winds, his willingness to denude the Danube of its legionary defences against the Dacians indicates either ignorance or culpable disregard of the strategical needs for the empire's defence.

Antonius' arrival in north-east Italy quickly brought the towns from Aquileia to Patavium (Padua) and Ateste over to him, and he had decided to make Verona the centre of his operations, when he learned that he had already exceeded Vespasian's instructions, which were to wait at Aquileia for the arrival of Mucianus. Antonius' disobedience (albeit unwitting) could best be justified by success, so he decided to seek a swift and decisive action against the Vitellian forces at Cremona; if he himself wished to advance further towards Rome, he could not afford to leave a substantial enemy force in north Italy to threaten his lines of communication. Two days' march brought him from Verona to Bedriacum, where he pitched camp. On the following day a small cavalry detachment, sent forward with auxiliaries to gather provisions and to plunder, had the better of a series of attacks and repulses. As evening approached, the enemy withdrew towards Cremona, and Antonius too decided to break off the engagement. At this point the main weight of the Flavian army arrived, and insisted that they should press on to take Cremona. Antonius' attempts to dissuade them had not fully convinced them, when news was brought that the whole of the Vitellian legionary force, six legions in all, was preparing to give battle. At last Antonius' troops were ready to listen to him (3.21.1). All that was left was to draw up the order of battle.

Tacitus on this occasion does not disappoint us. The disposition of the Flavian troops at the outset of the battle is given precisely—with the warning that because of the darkness precision applied only to the location of the eagles and standards; troops were not able in every case to find their own standard, but grouped themselves as best they could. It is possible that the detailed account of the Flavian line of battle derives from Tacitus' friend, Vipstanus Messalla, who took part in the battle, and is mentioned by name in cc. 9, 11, 18, 25 and 28 (for the two latter see p. 189 below). From the topographical hints given by Tacitus it is possible to locate just where astride the Via Postumia the Flavian army took up its position. When Tacitus turns to the Vitellian line of battle, he professes himself unable to give sure information, but reports what 'others have recorded' (*quamquam alii tradiderint*; 3.22.2)—a phrase that probably indicates that Tacitus here departs from his primary source.

The battle began about 8.30 p.m. and continued for almost ten hours. Tacitus' account is graphic and memorable.[18] It concentrates on a number of striking incidents or features—the heroism of two anonymous soldiers who managed to spike the Vitellian 'Big Bertha' (an incident also recorded by Dio Cassius 65.14.2), the way in which the rising moon gave an advantage to the Flavians, who could now see their enemies clearly, whereas the Vitellians were firing into shadows and often falling short. The turning point of the battle occurred when the soldiers of the third legion greeted the rising sun, and since this was a habit of the Syrian legions, there was a general belief that Mucianus and his legions had arrived. As the Vitellians begin to retreat, Tacitus gives another colourful incident, one that epitomises the horror and the inhumanity of civil war: a son kills his father; the son tearfully begs his dying father's forgiveness. Those around notice the incident, and execrate civil war, which produces such enormities. Then, in typically Tacitean fashion, the chapter ends: 'but none the less they kill and despoil kinsmen and brothers; they call it a crime—and do it' (*factum esse scelus loquuntur faciuntque*; 3.25.3.).

Though the Vitellians had been defeated in the field, an immense task still faced the Flavians; unless they were to retire to Bedriacum or set up camp where they were, the Vitellian camp had still to be taken, and that by troops weary with continuous fighting. But the Flavian troops were more ready to endure danger than delay, and an assault was launched. With Roman military skill on both sides, it was beginning to look as if the Flavians would have to admit failure, when their leaders pointed to Cremona, with the implication that it could be looted as the prize of victory. With a new access of energy the Vitellian camp was stormed. The subsequent surrender and sack of Cremona is described with dramatic effectiveness in the next chapters—such subjects (*expugnationes urbium* (*Annals* 4.32.1)) are stock themes for rhetorical embellishment by the historian, and Tacitus rises to the occasion, laying particular emphasis on the element of pathos. The section ends on a more matter-of-fact note; arrangements were made for the dispersal of the defeated legions and for sending news of the Flavian success to the Western provinces (c. 31).

At c. 36 the scene switches to Rome, and reverts in time to events beginning about a month earlier: 'hidden away in the shady retirement of his gardens, like those slothful creatures, who, if you feed them, lie in a sluggish torpor, Vitellius was equally oblivious of past, present, and future.' Any hope that the Vitellian cause would be furthered by resolute action by his general Fabius Valens now proved illusory. Leaving Rome for the front about 25 September, accompanied (according to Tacitus) by a large retinue of concubines and eunuchs, he was moving north at a leisurely pace, when express messengers brought news of the defection of Lucilius Bassus and the Ravenna fleet. Any slim chance he had of influencing events was ended with his departure by sea for the Narbonese and his subsequent capture in the Stoechades (Iles d'Hyères).

'With the capture of Valens all sides rallied to the victorious cause . . .' (44.1). In fact it was the victory at Cremona rather than Valens' capture that gave the initial impulse; Spain, Gaul, Britain all came over to the Flavians—Vespasian, after all, had served with distinction in Britain. Mention of the last province effects a transition, by way of a colourful tale about the headstrong queen of the Brigantes, Cartimandua, to the theme of unrest in the provinces. In Britain trouble arose from Cartimandua's discarded husband, Venutius; in Germany the first hints of Civilis' revolt could be discerned, while in the East the withdrawal of the Moesian legions was seen by the Dacians as an opportunity to invade the province. Having crossed the Danube, they were on the point of attacking the legionary camps, when the good fortune of the Roman People (*Fortuna populi Romani*) brought Mucianus and his troops, en route for Italy, to those parts; the fact that the Flavians had in the meantime won the decisive battle of Cremona made it safe for Mucianus to detach the sixth legion to deal with the Dacian invader (3.46.2–3).

When Vespasian heard in November of the victory of Cremona, he continued on his way to Alexandria, intending to cut off the corn supply from there and Africa for Rome and Italy. The blockade was part of a combined strategy, in which the military penetration of Italy from the north-east was to be carried out by Mucianus, while Vespasian was to occupy the *claustra Aegypti* (2.82.3). That plan had been altered only by the precipitate action—and success—of Antonius: for Vespasian there was nothing to do but press on with his part in the grand strategy. Even if he had wished to change that strategy (and there was no reason why he should), the time-lag in communications would have made it virtually impossible; by about 8 December Antonius was little more than fifty miles from Rome, and although he delayed at Carsulae for about a week to allow the legionary troops to join him, it is unlikely that instructions from either Mucianus or Vespasian could have caused him to hold back his further advance. He had already ignored too many orders; only the capture or capitulation of Rome could justify his insubordination.

With winter now at hand Antonius left the main legionary strength for the time being at Verona; the auxiliary infantry and cavalry with some legionary detachments moved south to Fanum Fortunae, where they halted, undecided what to do in view of the report that the praetorian guard had left Rome, intending, it had to be assumed, to occupy the Apennine approaches.

The narrative now returns to Rome and Vitellius. After his death there was no one to defend his memory, and much of what Tacitus says of him seems only to underline a picture of indolence, indifference and indecision. At first he sought to conceal news of the disaster of Cremona, but was eventually persuaded to send fourteen cohorts of the praetorian guard north to hold the line of the Apennines (3.55). These troops were content to guard the southern foothills of the range, but when news of the revolt of the fleet at Misenum and the seizure of Tarracina led Vitellius to recall half their number, the remaining praetorians at Narnia soon capitulated. At about the same time approaches were made to Vitellius, offering him terms for a cessation of hostilities and his own surrender. Vitellius haggled about the exact terms and did nothing: 'such torpor (Tacitus uses the choice Sallustianism, *torpedo*) had seized his mind that, had not others reminded him of the fact, he would have forgotten that he was emperor' (3.63.2).

The rest of Book III falls into two sections, separated by two chapters (76–7), which tell of the only Vitellian success during this period, the recapture of Tarracina by the emperor's brother. The first section (64–75) is one of high drama—and muddle: the second section (78–86) tells in a vivid and tense narrative of the bitter fighting for Rome, and ends with the death of Vitellius.

Chapters 64–75 focus on the part played by Vespasian's elder brother, Flavius Sabinus, in the momentous events in Rome during the four or five days from 17 December. The events are also narrated by Suetonius (*Vitellius* 15.2 ff.) and Josephus (*BJ* 4.645 ff.).[19] Nowhere perhaps in the whole of the *Histories* is Tacitus' superiority more clearly demonstrated. Suetonius is muddled and inaccurate. Even when allowance has been made for the fact that he is writing a biography, not continuous history, his account has two major flaws. According to him, Vitellius made three attempts to abdicate: Tacitus is quite definite that there was only one attempt, and for that attempt, most unusually, he gives (3.67.2) a precise date, 18 December. The rumour of Vitellius' abdication brought Sabinus into the open, and that in turn led to a skirmish with some Vitellian troops and the flight of Sabinus and his followers to the safety of the Capitol.[20] According to Suetonius the refusal of soldiers and people to accept his abdication gave Vitellius fresh courage; he thereupon 'drove Sabinus and the other Flavians . . . into the Capitol, and, after setting fire to the temple of Jupiter Optimus Maximus, he destroyed them'. All that, according to Suetonius (it is clear), took place on the same day. Not long afterwards (*non multo post*)—this must be on the morning of the 19th—Vitellius summoned an assembly, and once more tried to abdicate;[21] once more the offer was refused, and Vitellius declared that he would keep the dagger.

There is no plausible reason for Vitellius' third attempt to abdicate, but though it is in itself unlikely, it is not inconceivable. But the crucial flaw in Suetonius' account is that the siege and capture of the Capitol take place on the same day. This leaves no time for Sabinus to summon his son and Domitian to join him on the Capitol, and no time to get an urgent message for help to Antonius Primus at Ocriculum, some forty miles from Rome. By late next day (*multo iam noctis*) Antonius had covered over thirty miles with his men to reach *Saxa Rubra*, a few miles north of Rome, and was ready next day (20 December) to launch a three-pronged attack on the city. In short, Tacitus' narrative fits exactly into a framework that allows the interrelationship of time, person and place involving Sabinus, Vitellius and Antonius Primus: Suetonius' version, which places within a single day (the 18th) the siege and capture of the Capitol, does not.

The final chapters of Book III deal with two main topics, the fight for Rome and the death of Vitellius. To many Romans the terrain of many of the famous battles of their history could not have been known in any detail: every one of Tacitus' readers could have followed a detailed description of the fighting through Rome itself. But, with the minimum of topographical information, Tacitus concentrates first on the morale of the opposing sides—the Flavians buoyed by success, the Vitellians fighting desperately, and, as they are pushed back, regrouping time and time again. But what interests Tacitus still more is the reaction of the non-combatants. For the Roman crowds it was a spectacular holiday entertainment; with enthusiasm and impartiality they urged the victors to butcher the vanquished—Tacitus' moral indignation is apparent in every word.

Meantime Vitellius had sought to make a furtive escape. First he had gone to his wife's house on the Aventine, but then returned to the

Palatine, where all was deserted. What follows is graphically told by Tacitus, Suetonius and Cassius Dio. He sought to hide in what Tacitus calls a demeaning bolt-hole (*pudenda latebra*); Suetonius says it was a doorkeeper's room, Dio a kennel. The humiliation of Vitellius' final moments was redeemed only by his last words. Before he fell under a stream of blows, he cried out to his taunting captors, 'Yet I *was* your emperor' (3.85).

The last chapter of the Book (3.86) begins with Vitellius' obituary. The gist of it is that he owed his position to his father's political distinction, not his own merits. But the sting is in its last sentence, which passes judgment, not on Vitellius, but on those who conspired to overthrow him: 'Doubtless it was in the state's interest for Vitellius to be defeated, but no credit could be claimed for their treachery by those who betrayed him to Vespasian, when they had already deserted Galba.' The theme of treachery at the end of Book III thus echoes the end of Book II. There (2.101) Tacitus had contradicted the Flavian version of history, which claimed that the motives for which Caecina and Bassus deserted Vitellius were 'concern for peace and love of their country'.

The very last sentence of the Book states that, when all was quiet, Domitian at last dared to show his face and was greeted as Caesar. Josephus, who gives the Flavian version at its clearest and most tendentious, states that on the next day 'Mucianus entered with his army and restrained the troops of Antonius from further slaughter... and bringing Domitian forward recommended him to the people as their ruler until the arrival of his father'. There are two falsehoods here: first the statement that Mucianus entered the city the day after it had been captured by Antonius—in fact several days intervened, and the likely date is about 25 December. Secondly, Josephus deliberately eliminates any connection between Domitian and Antonius, and ascribes to Mucianus the credit of Domitian's appearance in public. Thus, as Book II ends with explicit denunciation of the Flavian distortion of history, so Book III ends by giving the lie, though only implicitly, to another falsehood of Flavian propaganda.

The first three books of the *Histories* form a compact unit, both structurally and historically. With the death of Vitellius, for the first time since the starting point of the work, an emperor is in undisputed possession of supreme power, without the threat of a pretender, proclaimed or impending. The loss of the whole of the *Histories* after chapter 26 of Book V makes it impossible to make any meaningful comment on the articulation and tone of the rest of the work, but the character and structure of Book IV is palpably different from what has gone before. After two and half chapters, which form a coda to Book III, Book IV reverts to a more traditional approach to the writing of Roman history, with the material divided into separate and continuous sections on affairs at home and abroad (*domi militiaeque*). Domestic matters are principally business in the senate and the senate's relations with the absent emperor and his family and representatives in Rome (chiefly Domitian), while the major preoccupation in foreign affairs is the revolt of Civilis on the Rhine. Book IV also shows the annalistic division of material that is common to Roman historiography; everything up to 4.37 belongs to the year 69, at 4.38 the new year begins with the statement 'Meanwhile Vespasian, consul for the second time, took office along with Titus, both being absent from Rome.'

The senatorial matters contained in cc. 3–10 belong to a period of only a few days between the death of Vitellius and the arrival in Rome of Mucianus (11.1), which must have occurred a few days before the end of the year. At its first meeting after Vitellius' death the senate voted to Vespasian 'all the usual imperial honours' (*cuncta principibus solita*; 4.3.3).[22] A mood of confident joy prevailed, for it seemed that the whole world had now been cleansed of civil war. This optimism was reinforced by the reading of a letter from Vespasian, written after the Flavian victory at Cremona, but before he knew of the death of Vitellius. The diplomatic language used in the letter evoked a corresponding show of deference from the senate, who conferred the consulship on Vespasian and Titus, and the praetorship along with consular *imperium* on Domitian. A letter from Mucianus created a much less favourable impression: why, senators asked each other, had he written, when in a few days he could give his opinion in person in the senate? But openly they showered praise on him, and voted him triumphal *insignia*; and since it was not possible for a triumph to be granted when the defeated were one's own fellow citizens, Mucianus' defence of Moesia against the Sarmatians was adduced as the reason for the award.

Mention of the praetor designate, Helvidius Priscus, who had won the senate's applause by praising the new *princeps* without resort to flattery or insincerity, leads Tacitus into a biographical digression (5.1–6.2). Priscus, son-in-law of Thrasea Paetus, was an outspoken member of that Stoic opposition[23] to the principate that so interested

Tacitus himself, and which figures prominently both in the *Agricola* and the later books of the *Annals*. For the moment Priscus' aim was to exact retribution from those leading figures who in the later years of Nero's reign had prospered by bringing political prosecutions against those whom the *princeps* hated or feared. His immediate target was Eprius Marcellus, who had brought the prosecution that had led to Thrasea's forced suicide. While praising Priscus' unflinching adherence to his principles, Tacitus also remarks that some people regarded him as too keen on renown, 'since even with philosophers the desire for fame is the last to be discarded' (*quando etiam sapientibus cupido gloriae nouissima exuitur*: 'fame . . . that last infirmity of noble mind'; 4.6.1).

A proposal to send envoys to Vespasian was followed by a debate on the manner of choosing the delegates, in the course of which there arose an acrimonious exchange between Priscus and Marcellus. Priscus, speaking first, argued that the envoys should be chosen individually by the magistrates, while Marcellus urged that the traditional procedure of selection by lot should be followed. Priscus' speech needs no comment: but in what Marcellus says there is both a sense of urgency and of relevance to the position of Tacitus and his contemporaries. Marcellus first stressed the need for circumspection in their behaviour at the start of a new reign, and then used the occasion as a peg on which to hang a discussion of how one should behave under the rule of a *princeps*; one should pray for a good emperor, but put up with whatever sort heaven sent (4.8.2). Yet, he warned Priscus, even a good emperor would not tolerate limitless freedom.[24]

Not for the first time a speech in Tacitus faces us with the problem of deciding how far Tacitus' personal view is reflected in it. Tacitus' own career, which had continued to advance even under Domitian, seems to have been an embodiment of Eprius Marcellus' advice. The modern reader may be surprised that this prudent advice comes from the lips of a notorious *delator*, but it is one of the features of Tacitus' writing that the devil is given a fair share of the good tunes. Whatever opinion the senate may have held of Marcellus, the majority voted with him. The moderates wished to preserve the established custom—it would have been surprising if a traditionally conservative body had done otherwise —while the more eminent senators had their own good reasons for favouring the anonymity of the lot. The final vote was thus determined, not by the speeches of Priscus and Marcellus, but by habit and self-interest. The two speeches are revealed for what they were, the continuation of a personal vendetta.

The time seemed ripe for the settling of a number of old scores, but at this moment, about a week before the year's end, Mucianus entered Rome, and immediately assumed control. In everything but name he exercised the authority of the emperor (*uim principis amplecti, nomen remittere*; 4.11.1). There was an immediate demonstration of what that authority could do: a young noble, the son of that Piso who had led an abortive conspiracy against Nero four years earlier, was put to death without trial. By contrast—Tacitus leaves the reader to draw the comparison for himself—the judicial processes by which senators sought to bring to justice those of their number who had acted as Nero's tools seem almost trivial.

The domestic scene at Rome is now left in suspense till Tacitus' account of the new year begins at c. 38. The rest of the narrative of the year 69 is devoted to an account of the first stages of the revolt of Civilis, a Batavian noble. In the extant books of the *Histories* two further sections are devoted to this revolt (4.54–79 and 5.14 ff.) and it will be convenient to consider all three sections together, as forming a continuous narrative. Though his account lacks specific dates, and there are occasions where troop movements have to be inferred, the narrative forms a coherent whole that belies Tacitus' reputation as an inadequate military historian.[25]

The revolt of Civilis falls into three phases. The first lasted until news of the Flavian victory and Vitellius' death reached Germany. During this period Civilis was able to pretend that his attacks on Vitellian troops in Germany were being undertaken in support of the Flavian cause. Once Vitellius' death became known in Gaul and Germany, Civilis could no longer pretend to be acting in support of Vespasian, and he proclaimed open rebellion against Rome. He also now, for the first time, began to receive an active response from Gallic tribes, who had at last become convinced that the power of Rome was on the wane. During the first two phases of his revolt Civilis had to face only those Roman troops, legionary and auxiliary (the latter often of doubtful loyalty), that had not been drawn off to form the effective strength of the Vitellian advance into Italy against Otho. The lines, both military and supply, of those troops that remained along the Rhine were impossibly stretched, and since there was a strong current of suspicion between the mostly pro-Flavian higher ranking officers and the ordinary troops, who steadfastly supported Vitellius, military success during this period mostly favoured the rebels. But they failed to achieve any degree of political cohesion. The Gauls had joined with

Civilis in order to establish an *imperium Galliarum*, but that was an ideal to which Civilis and his Batavians would not take an oath of allegiance.

The last phase of the revolt began when at Rome Mucianus appointed Petilius Cerialis and Annius Gallus, both experienced generals, to command a massive legionary army. The brunt of the fighting fell to Cerialis, whose generalship was by turns resolute and audacious, well-considered and foolhardy. In the upshot the superior discipline of the Romans, perhaps aided by good fortune, began to turn the tide decisively in their favour. Gallic support for the revolt quickly dwindled, and Civilis was forced to withdraw further and further north. At the point where our manuscripts end Civilis had sought a parley with Cerialis. We do not know what happened to Civilis, but a compromise solution seems to have been reached, for the Batavians returned to their allegiance to Rome, but were allowed to retain the privilege of serving under arms rather than pay taxes to the Roman government.

In what way does Tacitus put his own stamp on the narrative? The great amount of detail that his account contains might simply reflect the fact that he is using a particularly good and detailed source for these events.[26] But it is not so much the detail as the organized complexity of his narrative that is its most striking feature. At the beginning of the revolt, though the first overt act of rebellion comes from Brinno, leader of the Canninefates, Tacitus makes it clear that it is preceded by a chain of undercover events originating with the Batavian Civilis. As the revolt proceeds, Tacitus continues to give a rounded picture of the action. There is no attempt to oversimplify by drawing only in black and white. Military success and failure are not ascribed unvaryingly to one side or the other, and within the ranks of the Romans and their enemies full weight is given to the tensions and conflicts that influenced decisions and, through decisions, events.

The manner in which Tacitus organizes a multiplicity of details into a clearly envisaged whole leaves little doubt that the overview he presents is his own. Yet it is not here that the most strikingly Tacitean features are to be found. Apart from the considerable use he makes of the invented speech (discussed below) one element that immediately strikes the eye is the graphic description of pathetic incident. The straits endured by the Roman garrison at Vetera before its final surrender are described as follows:

> The besieged were torn by honour and desperate need between glory and disgrace. As they hesitated, all supplies, both normal and extraordinary,

failed, for they had consumed mules, horses and other animals, which, however abhorrent and repulsive, dire necessity compelled them to use. Finally they tore up shrubs and roots and the grass growing between the stones, and afforded a signal example of privation and endurance, until they tarnished a heroic stand by shamefully sending envoys to Civilis to beg for their lives. (60.1)

Shortly afterwards the sixteenth legion capitulated at Novaesium (Neuss). Its departure is depicted in language deliberately moulded on Livy's description (9.5.11) of another day of Roman ignominy, the passing of the Roman army under the yoke after its humiliating surrender to the Samnites at the Caudine Forks in 321 BC.

In these pathetic scenes a note of moral comment is implicit. Elsewhere moral comment is made directly. When the centurions and soldiers of Dillius Vocula's army agree to take the oath of allegiance to the enemy, sealing their compact by a promise to murder or incarcerate their commanders, Tacitus roundly describes it as 'an unheard-of act of shame'.[27] At an earlier juncture, to cover up their own defeat in a minor skirmish, the troops accused the governor, Hordeonius Flaccus, of treachery and threw him into irons. Only the arrival of Vocula rescued him. But next day the army made no protest when Vocula executed the ring-leaders.

> Such extremes were there in that army of insubordination and obedience. Undoubtedly the ordinary soldier was firm in his loyalty to Vitellius, whereas the highest ranking officers favoured Vespasian; hence crime was followed by punishment, and blind frenzy mixed with willing obedience. In short the men could not be controlled, but could be punished. (27.3)

But there is more to this passage than a moral judgment, terminated by a neat epigram (*ut contineri non possent qui puniri poterant*); it also contains an element of intellectual diagnosis—the cause of it all lay in the differing loyalties of men and high command.

In his account of Civilis' rebellion Tacitus makes considerable use of the invented speech, both by direct quotation (*oratio recta*) and by indirect or reported speech (*oratio obliqua*). The latter type is influenced by the nature of Latin syntax, and although it is less graphic than *oratio recta*, it favours a compact manner of utterance, often giving the impression more of succinct précis than of word-for-word transcription. The manner in which such speeches can be used may be illustrated by the *oratio obliqua* speech of Civilis, in which he whips up enthusiasm among his fellow Batavians for the revolt he is planning (4.14). The speech makes three main points. The first of these (that

97

rebellion is necessary because of the harshness of the Vitellian recruiting officers) reinforces what has already been mentioned in the narrative (14.1f.). The last point (rebellion will not be unwelcome to the Romans) underlines a fact that the official Flavian account preferred to ignore, that Antonius Primus and Hordeonius Flaccus had originally urged Civilis to do all he could to occupy the Vitellian forces on the Rhine. An epigram concludes the speech—if things go wrong, they can put the blame on Vespasian: if they succeed, they need give explanations to nobody (*ambiguam fortunam Vespasiano imputaturos: uictoriae rationem non reddi*; 4.14.4).

Two further speeches by Civilis (4.17 and 32—the latter a short speech in *oratio recta*) make much use of catchwords such as freedom and valour (*libertas* and *uirtus*), and are little more than rhetorical exercises. The same is true of a number of other speeches, including the balancing pair in *oratio recta* in cc. 64 and 65, where the fate of Cologne is debated among the Germans, with the violently anti-Roman legate of the Tencteri urging that the city walls should be dismantled and all Roman citizens within put to death, while the representatives of Cologne argue for a milder, temporising solution.[28]

Two *oratio recta* speeches of particular importance remain to be considered, that of Dillius Vocula in 4.58 (over 40 lines) and that of Petilius Cerialis in 4.73-4 (just over 50 lines). When Vocula discovered that the legionary troops under his command at Novaesium (Neuss) had made a compact to swear allegiance to the *imperium Galliarum* after butchering or imprisoning their officers, he made an earnest appeal to his troops not to commit the ultimate impiety of renouncing their allegiance to their country. His plea carries a note of conviction and is underlined by its strongly Livian language.[29] Shortly afterwards Vocula is murdered and his troops surrender; the pathos of their departure from their camp is suitably described in language which again borrows from Livy's description of the Roman army being sent under the yoke after their surrender at the Caudine Forks. Heroism in adversity is the main feature that Tacitus seeks to bring out by Vocula's speech, but the speech has to be read in the context that Tacitus gives it. Vocula is no idealised hero, and failures in his generalship are more than once noted. The speech that Tacitus puts in his mouth is therefore a tribute to a brave man, no more.

Similarly the imposing speech that Cerialis delivers in defence of Roman imperialism must be seen in its context. His victory at Rigodulum on the Mosel (4.71) marked the turn of the tide for Roman fortunes. That military success now needed to be backed up by winning the hearts of those who had risen against Rome. Addressing the assembled Treveri and Lingones, he poured scorn on the naïve belief that the Germans had the well-being of the Gauls at heart. Mention of 'freedom' and other fine-sounding words was just a pretext: 'never has anyone sought to impose slavery on others without using those same words' (4.73 fin.). An empire, it was true, had to be paid for, but were Roman demands greater than what a Gallic empire would require to defend its frontiers against German or British invaders? He warms to his peroration:

> It is through the good fortune and the discipline of eight hundred years that this fabric of empire has been knitted together; it cannot be torn apart without the destruction of those who tear it apart. But yours is the greatest danger, for it is you who have the gold and wealth that are the principal causes of war. Accordingly you should love and foster peace and that city which victors and vanquished alike have the same right to enjoy. Be warned by the examples of fortune, both good and bad, not to place defiance that will bring destruction above an obedience that ensures your safety. (4.74. 3-4)

Tacitus has given Cerialis a speech such as (allowing for the rhetorical embellishments permitted within the genre) a Roman commander might have made on such an occasion. But does the speech also reflect Tacitus' own most deeply held views on the Roman empire? It is meant as a public oration for a public occasion, designed to give a plausible account of the acceptable face of Roman imperialism. It is unlikely that its oversimplified picture represents all that Tacitus, that master of light and shade, felt; but it is equally unlikely that he would disagree with it as a partial expression of the truth.

The problem of interpretation that faces us over the speech of Cerialis is equally obvious in those sections where Tacitus treats of internal politics. Chapter 38 of Book IV marks the beginning of a new year (AD 70) with a variation of the traditional consular formula: 'In the meantime Vespasian, consul for the second time, entered office with Titus, though absent from Rome.' Real power rested with Mucianus (*uis penes Mucianum erat*; 4.39.2). For the moment, though, the condemnation of Publius Celer seemed to give the signal for a spate of trials of revenge upon those who had undertaken political prosecutions under Nero. The young Vipstanus Messalla (source for at least some of Tacitus' information on Antonius Primus' campaigns in Book III, and a speaker in the *Dialogus*—clearly Tacitus had a soft spot for him) won

great renown by his loyal defence of his step-brother, the notorious
Aquilius Regulus. But Tacitus' tribute to Messalla is merely a way of
leading in to the speech delivered by Regulus' prosecutor, Curtius
Montanus. This is the only speech in the whole of Tacitus that in
oratorical rhythm and vocabulary shows a markedly Ciceronian
tone.[30] Why has Tacitus chosen to emphasise it in this way? As often,
we must look at the speech in its context. It is followed by great
applause from the senate, and Helvidius Priscus, already singled out
for special mention in 4.4 ff, took it as a sign that now was the time for
him to pursue his vendetta against Eprius Marcellus. Heated exchanges followed, the meeting ended with bitterness on both sides. The
next meeting of the senate found Domitian urging senators to let
bygones be bygones. Mucianus was more direct. He defended the rôle
of the prosecutors and criticised those who blew hot and cold in
starting prosecutions and then letting them drop—remarks clearly
aimed at such people as Helvidius Priscus. The moment they were
opposed by Mucianus the senators abandoned their newly redis-
covered freedom of speech (*patres coeptatam libertatem, postquam obuiam
itum, omisere* 4.44.1). This is the context in which Curtius Montanus'
speech is to be seen: a brief interlude of high flown Ciceronian
eloquence on themes that befitted the free Republic of Cicero's day,
but dropped like a hot brick, the moment the reality of power politics
under an emperor (here displayed by his vice-gerent) was asserted.

The second, long section on the Rhine rebellion (already dealt with)
occupies cc. 54-79. In the final chapters of Book IV interest oscillates
between Mucianus and Vespasian. At Rome Mucianus exercised his
authority by ordering the execution of Vitellius' young son. He also
refused to allow Antonius Primus to join Domitian's retinue. As a
result Antonius departed to Vespasian, by whom he was well treated,
but stripped of all power and influence. Vespasian's own authority was
authenticated in the eyes of the citizens of Alexandria by his
performance of miracles; his interest in Serapis leads Tacitus to a
digression on that god. The last two chapters revert to Mucianus and
Domitian. As they reach the Alps en route for Germany, they hear of
Cerialis' success among the Treveri. Domitian is believed to have
sounded Cerialis to see if he would hand over his army to him.
Receiving an evasive answer, he abandoned interest in military and
political matters, and turned his attention to literature.

What remains of Book V consists of two continuous sections dealing
with foreign affairs. The first (cc. 1-13) gives, with a curious mixture of

fact and fantasy, an introduction to what must have been one of the most colourful episodes in AD 70, Titus' siege and capture of Jerusalem. Victory over a stubborn and fanatical enemy was a theme that would appeal alike to the historian and his readers. Chapters 14–26 (already considered) return to the Rhine frontier and give an account of the concluding stages of the revolt of Civilis.

If nothing of Tacitus had survived but those portions of the *Histories* that have come down to us, his name as an historical writer of the first rank would still have been assured. The events of the twelve months from 1 January, which form the subject matter of *Histories* I–III, have a dramatic momentum of their own, and others besides Tacitus were attracted to their narration—Plutarch and Suetonius among his contemporaries, and before them the lost anonymous narrator on whom Plutarch, Suetonius and Tacitus all drew liberally. Comparison with Plutarch and Suetonius shows Tacitus' superiority alike in language, thought, and organization. That superiority is at once apparent in the opening chapters of Book I. Tacitus begins by placing his own position as a writer firmly in its historical perspective; though he writes in imperial times, he does so as the conscious continuator of the republican tradition of historiography. The second and third chapters, composed mostly in terse, staccato phrases, outline the subject matter of the *Histories* and foreshadow its sombre tones. In the fourth chapter Tacitus turns his attention to the underlying causes of events (*ratio causaeque*), which are for the most part, he believes, to be sought in men's moods and motives.

His masterly control of language quickly becomes evident as the account of the year of the four emperors develops. He equals or surpasses Sallust in the speed and brevity of his narrative and in his ability to draw pithy and telling character sketches, while his gift for timely epigram is used to illuminate or to drive home a point. To the invented speeches, which, following tradition, he inserted in his work, he brings all the skill of a practised orator, and he turns the artificiality of the convention to advantage by using the speeches not only to underline the speaker's character, but also to reveal the gulf that lies between men's professions and reality. The same contrast between public *persona* and private thought is reflected in other ways too. Reported speech, often echoing divergent groups of opinion, is used as a means of exploring motive, where the fact is not in dispute, while rumour is similarly employed, where facts are not, or can not, be known.

The interweaving of subjective and objective elements produces a texture that is both subtle and brilliant, while their rapid alternation gives to events an immediacy that engages the reader's attention and interest. Vividness is consciously aimed at by the historian, and as a result he has a tendency (carried to excess by the more rhetorical historians) to focus on moments of high drama or pathos. Such a tendency might lead to emphasising the sensational or the bizarre— faults not always avoided by the Younger Seneca in tragedy, or in declamation by the orators recalled by the Elder Seneca—but Tacitus, for the most part, was careful to choose instances where the dramatic and the significant coincide: the moment when Otho raised the standard of rebellion against Galba, the last hours of Otho before his suicide, the turning point in the second battle of Bedriacum.

Brilliance of style is not necessarily prejudicial to the writing of history, but it needs to be regulated by an understanding of the salient points in a chain of events. The manner in which Tacitus organizes his material is instructive. Since his aim is not simply to give an unvarnished narrative, he selects his material and emphasises or omits, as it suits his purpose. It is irritating not to be given details of time and place that are necessary for the construction of a timetable of events, but where we are able to reconstruct such a timetable, it usually underpins Tacitus' version. Much of the material he uses in the earlier books of *Histories* is drawn from the same source that Plutarch (as far as the death of Otho) and Suetonius used, but on both the larger and the smaller scale Tacitus imposes his own imprint. The introductory overview of cc. 4–11 of Book I is wholly his own, even though much of the material is drawn from the common source. The same is true of the way in which the conflict between Galba and Otho is set against the backcloth of the German armies' proclamation of Vitellius, and it is true of the synchronism of the actions of Flavius Sabinus and Vitellius *within* Rome and the approaching Flavian forces under Antonius *outside* the city. Tacitus' organizational skill is equally apparent in his handling of material within sentence and paragraph. Here too it is instructive to observe how Tacitus deals with material he shares with Plutarch or Suetonius, and though it is his stylistic individuality that first strikes one, on closer inspection this can be seen to be the instrument by which a personal interpretation of events is conveyed.

It is particularly regrettable that nothing of the *Histories* after AD 70 survives, since from about the middle of the decade Tacitus begins to have first-hand knowledge of politics, and his own experience must have been supplemented by conversations with many of the leading notables of the day. But in the two years after the death of Nero arms were the main instrument of politics, and for that period what was required of the historian was, above all, mastery of a complex narrative. That mastery the surviving portions of the *Histories* show in ample measure. To find Tacitus seeking for a deeper understanding of the springs of political action under the principate it is to the *Annals* that we must turn.

# V

## THE *ANNALS* · TIBERIUS

Though the title by which the modern world knows Tacitus' latest work, the *Annals*, has no ancient authority, it is a happy choice in that it reminds the reader that Tacitus, most original of Roman historians, wrote within the traditional framework of year-by-year narrative. But that is only part of the picture, for the annalistic reckoning stands in counterpoint to a new factor that determines the structure of the work as a whole—the reign of the individual emperor. Within the broad framework other considerations also operate: the point at which a book is to begin or end, the division of material within a year into home and foreign affairs. Selection (including the powerful weapon of omission), arrangement, emphasis lie entirely within the historian's choice. The shape that he finally gives to his work is an important instrument of a historian's interpretation of events. Ranke, whose most quoted dictum is that the historian should write history as it really was, also wrote, 'Only through form are they (sc. works of the mind) elevated above the commonplace.' The first insight into the *Annals* is to be gained by seeing how the work is organized.

The *Histories* had begun at the beginning of the year AD 69, six months after Nero's death, and when complete had taken the tale to the death of Domitian in 96. The *Annals*, consisting of sixteen or eighteen books[1] covered the period from the accession of Tiberius in AD 14 to the death of Nero in 68. The reign of Tiberius occupies six books, all of which except much of Book V survives; Gaius and Claudius were dealt with in a further six books, of which only the last book and a half of Claudius' reign (47–54) survives; for Nero's reign three and a half books (XIII-XVI) are extant, taking the narrative from his accession in 54 to a point in the middle of 66.

The six books of Tiberius' reign are clearly divided into two triads. The dichotomy is not merely an artistic convenience, but corresponds (as will be seen) to Tacitus' belief that the reign of Tiberius fell into two distinct halves: the first was, in the main, a time of prosperity for both

104

state and ruling dynasty, the second saw a swift and progressive deterioration. The division, over-simplified and over-theoretical, reflects a concept of character that other ancient writers besides Tacitus shared; according to the stereotype the reign of a tyrant could generally be divided into two such halves. Tacitus is clear that the change for the worse took place at a certain point in time—in the ninth year of Tiberius' reign when C. Asinius and C. Antistius were consuls (that is, AD 23)—and that the responsibility for it lay with the then prefect of the praetorian guard, Lucius Aelius Seianus (Sejanus).

But at the end of Book VI, which is concluded by Tacitus' obituary notice on Tiberius, a different and more detailed subdivision of Tiberius' life is offered:

> His character too passed through different phases: (i) excellent both in achievement and reputation, as long as he was a private citizen or held commands under Augustus; (ii) given to concealment and an artful simulator of virtue (*occultum ac subdolum fingendis uirtutibus*), as long as Germanicus and Drusus survived; (iii) a similar mixture of good and evil during his mother's lifetime; (iv) then a period of loathsome cruelty, but concealed lusts, as long as he had Sejanus to love or fear; (v) then, finally, he threw himself into crimes and vices alike, casting aside all sense of shame and fear, following no inclination but his own. (6.51.3)[2]

According to this passage it is only at the very end that the real Tiberius is revealed, and rather than a single turning point marked by the rise of Sejanus, a number of stages of progressive moral decline and gradual unmasking of the emperor's true character are listed, each of them signalised by the removal of one more person's restraining influence. Whether the two types of explanation are mutually compatible, and whether either of them is true are questions that are best left to the end of the chapter. For the moment it is enough to observe how each explanation affects the structure and interpretation of *Annals* I-VI.

Behind the obituary of Tiberius lies an attitude towards the understanding of human character that differs radically from our own. In general the ancient world regarded character as immutable—the *Characters* of Theophrastus epitomise that view. Consequently, if a person seemed to change his character, it could only be that in the earlier stages of his life his real character was not yet revealed. Where events of the earlier part of Tiberius' reign seemed to conflict with the character that manifested itself at the end, Tacitus[3] concluded that Tiberius earlier sought deliberately to conceal his true character from those about him. The task of the historian, conversely, must be to unmask that hypocrisy. For this reason it was important for Tacitus that the truth about Tiberius should be brought home to the reader at the earliest possible moment. This is one of the purposes that is fulfilled by the opening chapters of Book I, in which Tacitus describes as a sham Tiberius' apparent hesitation to accept from the senate the power which he already exercised in fact.

The final stage in Tiberius' moral degeneration (translated above) is marked by heavily Sallustian language.[4] Tacitus' borrowing is not merely verbal; it implies an important parallelism in thought. Just as in the history of the Roman Republic the removal of the threat of Carthage marked the point at which political corruption and degeneration set in, so with Tiberius the removal of the last external restraint upon his conduct marked the critical point at which the final degeneration and corruption manifested itself.

The Sallustian echo at the end of Book VI is balanced by a two-fold borrowing at the beginning of Book IV. The first of these underlines the fact that AD 23 marked a major turning point in the reign of Tiberius:

> The consulship of Gaius Asinius and Gaius Antistius saw Tiberius in the ninth year of his reign; the state was in good health and the imperial household prosperous, (for he considered Germanicus' death as a piece of good fortune), when suddenly fortune began to run amok, and Tiberius himself to turn to cruelty or lend support to those who practised it *(turbare fortuna coepit, saeuire ipse aut saeuientibus uires praebere)*. The cause and origin lay with Aelius Seianus.. . . (*Ann.* 4.1.1)

In the historical survey in his *Catiline* (10.1) Sallust had written:

> But when the state grew great through toil and justice, and mighty kings had been conquered in war . . . and Carthage, rival of Rome's power, utterly annihilated and every sea and land lay open—then fortune began to turn cruel and throw everything into confusion *(saeuire fortuna ac miscere omnia coepit)*.

For Sallust *fortuna* is something of a *deus ex machina*, and it is she who turns cruel: for Sallust's *saeuire fortuna coepit* Tacitus substitutes *turbare fortuna coepit*, so that the crucial verb *saeuire* ('to be cruel') can be transferred to the following phrase. In Tacitus it is on the human level, not in the realm of *fortuna*, that *saeuitia* ('cruelty') is to be found. Moreover, the *saeuitia* is shared between two persons, the emperor and his new evil genius, Sejanus.

Although some indication has been given earlier of Sejanus' future significance, only now is he given an extended character sketch—a sketch that is directly modelled on Sallust's description of Catiline.

Here the borrowing is more direct and more sustained than anywhere else in Tacitus. Its purpose is plain. The literary dress implies a judgment; something of the *persona* of Catiline—his qualities of daring, physical courage, uncontrolled and unprincipled ambition—is to be applied to Sejanus. But the significant adjective *subdolus* ('full of underhand cunning') and the phrase *cuius rei simulator ac dissimulator* ('able to pretend or dissemble anything he chose') find their direct echo, not in Sejanus, but in Tiberius, who in these respects is Sejanus' superior.[5]

The prominence given to Sejanus at the beginning of Book IV not only marks in the clearest fashion the bipartite division of the six Tiberian books; it also has an important consequence for the structure and content of the preceding Book. Others beside Tacitus had looked for a cardinal turning point in Tiberius' reign, and many had found it in the death of Germanicus in AD 19, since Germanicus was the only member of the imperial family who had the ability, prestige and popularity to supplant the emperor; his death would (it might be argued) have set Tiberius free to follow his own bent. The obituary notice of 6.51 makes it clear that Tacitus regarded Germanicus as only one of several restraining influences on Tiberius, whereas—against these negative restraints—he saw Sejanus as providing a positive incitement to villainy. But Germanicus had an important part to play in the opening Tiberian triad, as Sejanus had in the second. He serves as a foil to the emperor, displaying those amiable qualities that the older man lacked. On his death Tacitus records that there were those who compared him, not to his disadvantage, to Alexander the Great. Tacitus himself does not go so far, and attentive reading reveals some hints of criticism, but in *Annals* I and II he is given, at least in terms of space, a prominence at least as great as that accorded to Tiberius.

But since Germanicus died in 19 and since Tacitus has chosen the year 23 and Sejanus' climb to power as the watershed for his account of Tiberius' reign, there is a period of four years when the theme of 'Germanicus as the foil of Tiberius' can no longer operate. This interval presented Tacitus with problems—and opportunities. The annalistic framework that Tacitus follows imposed certain obligations upon him, but the intervening years could have been despatched quite briefly. Instead Tacitus seems to have welcomed the breathing space that the gap between the themes of Germanicus and Sejanus allowed him. Here, for the only time in the first five books of the *Annals*, Tacitus is free to give extended consideration to the interrelationship of *princeps* and senate. It is in this section that we get the first major digression—on the origin and development of Roman Law—the first obituaries (marking the ends of AD 20, 21 and 22), the first senatorial debate reported *in extenso* (albeit in *oratio obliqua*) on a motion (eventually defeated) that, as in Republican times, provincial governors should not be accompanied abroad by their wives, a speech in *oratio recta* by the estimable Marcus Lepidus—an unsuccessful attempt to secure the mitigation of the death penalty on a Roman knight—and the longest speech (or rather a letter to the senate) in *oratio recta* by Tiberius on the subject of luxury, with Tiberius sensibly declining to take legal action against it. In these chapters full scope is given for the display of what is perhaps Tacitus' greatest talent, his acute observation of the realities of senatorial and imperial politics. The ability to see behind the façade and to crystallise that vision in sinewy, pungent Latin belongs to Tacitus as to no other Roman writer.

At the beginning of Book IV the preceding eight or nine years (the period covered by *Annals* I-III) are described as a time when 'the state was in good shape and the imperial house prospered'. But that is a façade. The same period is described in retrospect[6] as one in which Tiberius showed himself a master at concealment and the artful simulation of virtue. The reader must be alerted from the outset to this truth. The first fifteen chapters of Book I, marked off as a self-contained unit by the opening words of c. 16 ('Such was the state of affairs in Rome, when . . .')[7] are paradeigmatic; besides serving as an introduction to the whole work, they show what Tacitus believes to be the true Tiberius. All Tiberius' subsequent actions are to be measured by the standard of this model.

It has been argued that Tacitus should have started at some point in Augustus' reign, but reasons both historical and dramatic suggested the beginning of Tiberius' reign as the best starting point. It was only at the moment of the transition of power that the dynasty became a reality. Moreover, by plunging *in medias res*—just as he had done in the *Histories* by beginning with January 69 rather than with the death of Nero in the previous June—he was able to give a brief and concentrated retrospect on just those aspects of Augustus' policy that seemed to him relevant for his main theme: 'my plan is to say a few words about Augustus, especially the final details'.

The second chapter consists of two sentences only, the first being of unusual length and complexity. It describes how Augustus gathered sole power into his hands; the complexity of the task is matched by the syntactical complexity of the sentence that describes it.[8] Shrewd calculation and political bribery are prominent among his instruments. The next chapter describes what steps Augustus took to try to secure the succession for one of his family, and how the death of one preferred successor after another finally left him with no choice but his stepson, Tiberius. For the most part the language sounds coolly objective, but there is an unsupported hint that the untimely death of Augustus' grandson Gaius may not have been from natural causes but from the scheming of Livia, who sought the throne for her own son Tiberius.

The theme of Livia's intrigue occurs a number of times during these introductory chapters, and the question arises whether Tacitus is giving us history or invention. Suspicion is increased when Tacitus says that some people suspected that his wife (Livia) had a hand in his death, supporting the suspicion with the statement that a rumour had got about that a reconciliation had been effected between the aged Augustus and his only surviving grandson, Agrippa Postumus—an event which, if it happened, might have jeopardised Tiberius' chances of succeeding Augustus. There is almost certainly no truth in the rumour,[9] and it is important to note that Tacitus clearly designates it as rumour, presumably realising that the innuendo will nevertheless leave its mark.

'Be that as it may'—with this dismissive formula Tacitus returns to statement of fact: Tiberius, who had just reached Illyricum, was urgently recalled to the bedside of the dying Augustus. Then, once again, we are in the realm of speculation: 'It is not certain whether he found Augustus still breathing or dead.' Suetonius (*Augustus* 98.5 and *Tiberius* 21.1) states unequivocally that Augustus was still alive and conscious when Tiberius arrived, and the attendant circumstances that he relates make this seem the more probable version. What then of the circumstantial details that Tacitus adds—that Livia had prevented access to the house and issued reassuring bulletins, until she had taken steps to secure Tiberius' position and could announce simultaneously that Augustus was dead and Tiberius in charge of the state? These details occur in no other writer, but they appear also in Tacitus' account of the death of Claudius and the proclamation of Nero as emperor. Moreover we can point with some probability to the source from which Tacitus drew these details; Livy (1.41) has almost the identical succession of events in his account of how Tanaquil concealed the death of her husband, Tarquinius Priscus, until she had taken steps to secure the throne for Servius Tullius. Tacitus, it seems, is here adding invented detail to lend credibility to an otherwise doubtful version.[10] One can perhaps guess why he preferred this version. It is the version that best fits with Tacitus' interpretation of the other events surrounding Tiberius' accession: a *de facto* usurpation of power precedes the senatorial discussion that was necessary before its *de iure* conferment.

'Le roi est mort: vive le roi!' Effective rule by Tiberius began with the announcement of Augustus' death (1.5.4 fin.). The first deed of the new reign was an act of murder, the killing of the banished Agrippa Postumus, once a possible candidate to succeed Augustus. Tacitus begs leave to doubt Tiberius' assertion that Augustus had left orders for Agrippa's execution: more likely, he says, that it was the joint responsibility of Tiberius and Livia—the former motivated by fear, the latter by a step-motherly hatred of the young man. When Tiberius proposed to have the matter discussed in the senate, he was quickly reminded by a confidential adviser that the books of empire would not balance if they were scrutinised by more than one auditor.

'At Rome (sc. on the news of Augustus' death) there was a rush into slavery by consuls, senators and knights' (7.1). The oath of allegiance to Tiberius was taken by the consuls, and then by the prefects in charge of the praetorian guard and the corn supply. Next the oath was taken by 'the senate *and the army* and the people': The intrusion of 'the army' into the traditional formula, 'senate and the Roman people' (SPQR), is deliberate, and prepares the way for the following paragraphs: Tiberius acted with constitutional propriety and great modesty in all his dealings with the senate, but immediately on Augustus' death he had given orders to the army as their commander-in-chief, as though the principate was already his. For Tiberius' hesitancy in dealing with the senate Tacitus, without equivocation, states three causes: he was apprehensive about the loyalty of Germanicus, who was in charge of the eight legions in Germany; he wished public opinion to believe that he was the state's constitutional choice, not the product of a wife's influence on an aged husband; lastly, as it subsequently emerged, his hesitation was a deliberate pretence, assumed so that he could see what the reaction of individual senators would be.

The three reasons have little or no plausibility, but each of them has its place in Tacitus' scheme of things. The third suggestion is a mere stereotype;[11] it enables Tacitus to emphasise what he regards as crucial in Tiberius' character, the concealment of his true character until the final stage of his life. As Augustus had adopted Tiberius ten years before his death, any allegation that he had crept into power by Livia's scheming seems groundless.[12] The first reason, which Tacitus describes as the principal reason, is not Tacitus' own invention;[13] he chooses to use it at this point in order to alert the reader to Germanicus and his relationship with his uncle and adoptive father, which forms an important *leitmotiv* until the beginning of the Third Book of the *Annals*.

At the first meeting of the senate after Augustus' death (Tacitus gives no date, but it was probably in early September, just over a fortnight later than Augustus' death at Nola on 19 August) business was restricted to the reading of his will and the making of funeral arrangements. The funeral took place perhaps a week later. Tacitus makes no mention of the pageantry of the occasion, but comments ironically on the fact that it was felt necessary to line the streets with soldiers to ensure that the funeral passed off quietly. For the moment the reader's interest is concentrated on Augustus, and the next two chapters (9-10) show Tacitus at his most imaginative. As people reflected on the dead man, what interested most of them were trivialities and idle coincidences; more discerning critics discussed his political career. Some found more to praise, others to blame. Tacitus reports the views of both parties in *oratio obliqua*. The device is transparent; without committing himself to an unequivocal judgment on Augustus, Tacitus is able to convey to the reader a critical assessment of the dead emperor, in which the ostensibly balanced evidence nevertheless comes down clearly on the side of condemnation.

The same phrase begins both sides of the argument: *pietatem erga parentem*, 'filial duty towards his father' (i.e. Augustus' adoptive father, Julius Caesar). *Pietas* is a political catchword of the times. In the *Res Gestae*,[14] Augustus' own account of his achievements, he prides himself that the senate and Roman people, in recognition of his services to the state, had set up in the Curia Iulia a golden shield testifying to his *uirtus, clementia, iustitia* and *pietas* ('valour, clemency, justice, "piety" '). What follows in Tacitus is in essence a commentary, obverse and reverse, on the claims of the *Res Gestae*; indeed, in the arguments on both sides there is allusion to, though never direct quotation of, the *Res Gestae*. But because Tacitus is ostensibly reporting the strongly held views of opposing schools of thought, he is able to use emotive language to represent the heat of the exchanges. As often in such circumstances he draws upon Sallust—particularly to express the contempt which, according to his defenders, Augustus felt for the indolence of Lepidus and the sexual vices of Antony. Some of the details of the 'speech for the

111

defence' occur also in Dio Cassius, who on the whole takes a favourable view of Augustus. It is possible here that Dio is drawing directly on a source used also by Tacitus, who, it should be noted, uses the common material only in c. 9, the *apologia pro vita Augusti*: the adverse comment of the opening paragraphs of c. 10 shows a typically Tacitean movement of thought, and there is no further borrowing from the common source until 10.7 (see next paragraph).

The argument of c. 9 follows the customary line of Augustan apologetics in seeking to distinguish between Octavian the triumvir, reluctantly driven into civil war, and Augustus, beneficent founder of the principate and worldwide peace. The case is put incisively, and an attempt is made to disarm criticism by admitting that even under the *pax Augusta* force was occasionally used in order to secure peace for the rest. Chapter 10 shows the reverse of the coin. The appeal to 'filial duty' and 'state emergency' were nothing but pretexts: the actuality was a lust for autocratic power, achieved by bribery and corruption and the levying of a private army;[15] Sextus Pompey was deceived by the semblance of peace, Lepidus by the guise of friendship, while Antony, enticed by the treaties of Tarentum and Brundisium and marriage to Octavian's sister, paid with his life for that deceitful alliance ('semblance', 'guise', 'enticed', 'deceitful' are all loaded words: *imagine . . . specie . . . inlectum . . . subdolae*). So much for the period of the civil war: after that there *was* peace, but it was stained with blood—disasters in Germany, executions or enforced suicide for alleged conspiracy at Rome. Augustus' private life was attacked too, and a further mention is made of Livia the baleful stepmother. Finally the themes of Augustus and Tiberius enmesh when it is suggested that the choice of Tiberius as successor had been dictated by Augustus' desire to enhance his own posthumous fame by comparison with a successor whose lack of charm and social graces was well known to him. This astounding and improbable allegation (the so-called *comparatio deterrima*), of which Dio also has knowledge, is convincingly refuted by Suetonius (*Tiberius* 21.2-3) in a passage that makes it clear that the calumny does not originate with Tacitus. The surprising thing is not that Tacitus should have utilised the allegation—it is, after all, in *oratio obliqua*, the alleged report of what people thought and said—but that it should form part of the opinion of those whom Tacitus has described (9.3) as *prudentes*, 'discerning'.

But—and here Tacitus returns to the main narrative line— whatever people said about Augustus, his funeral passed off without a hitch and the dead emperor was deified. The stage is now Tiberius' alone. No precedent existed for confirming a successor to a *princeps* and the constitutional position was a delicate one. Tiberius showed great reluctance to accept what was offered to him, urging that the task was too great for any one man other than Augustus. The sentiment was noble but, according to Tacitus, insincere:

> Even in matters which he did not seek to conceal Tiberius' words, whether by nature or through habituation, were always carefully weighed[16] and obscure; on that occasion, when he was striving to keep his thoughts completely concealed, they were still further wrapped in doubt and uncertainty. (11.2)

Here in a single sentence is what Tacitus regards as the clue to the understanding of Tiberius' character. Tacitus does not entertain the possibility that there could be any reason for Tiberius' hesitancy other than hypocrisy. He had acted as emperor from the moment of Augustus' death: *ergo* any hesitation, any show of deference to the senate must be a charade.

In the exchanges that followed in the senate Tacitus singles out for mention a number of individuals who, according to Tacitus, incurred Tiberius' animosity by their attempts to get him to declare his hand. Two names are mentioned directly, two more are brought in by a curious story, in which Augustus is said to have discussed on his death-bed the names of the senators who had the ability or wish to take his place. All of them, Tacitus says, with the exception of Marcus Lepidus,[17] were subsequently destroyed on various charges engineered by Tiberius. Though all were dead before the end of Tiberius' reign, only of Asinius Gallus can it be strictly said that his death was directly attributable to Tiberius. It is difficult not to conclude that mention here of the four names is a literary device to draw the reader's attention to men who will be prominent in later pages.

Because it is typical of Tacitus' approach to the writing of history, it is worth noting how he concentrates on the behaviour of Tiberius and the senators who crossed swords with him. We are not told how the constitutional position was settled; indeed we are not told that Tiberius accepted any proposal, and it is only from an incidental reference that we learn that a formal proposal was put by the consuls. Nor is the ending of the senate's meeting marked in the text, any more than is that of the earlier meeting.

The first thirteen chapters of the *Annals* show Tacitus at his most selective, impressionistic, and neglectful of factual details we should like to know. There is not a single date in the whole of this section. But even if a skeleton timetable is worked out on the basis of internal and external evidence,[18] much remains unexplained. Apart from the omission of much-needed information it is not always clear what happened when, since even what is recorded does not always follow a strictly chronological order. Rather there are a number of aspects that Tacitus pursues, and these are at times treated separately, at times interwoven. Two strands in particular can be observed running through the fabric.

First the themes of Augustus and Tiberius. Until Augustus' death is announced at the end of c. 5, it is he who stands in the foreground, but the figure of Tiberius (with or without his mother, Livia) is given some prominence in the middle of c. 3 and dominates the second half of c. 4. Conversely it is Tiberius who comes to the fore at the beginning of c. 6 (naturally enough, after Augustus' death). But the funeral of Augustus (8.6) leads Tacitus back to Augustus and the long bipartite assessment of him that occupies cc. 9–10. Only after Augustus has been safely buried (*sepultura more perfecta*) and deified (10.8) does Tiberius begin to command our undivided attention.

The second strand comes from the tension between the *de facto* and the *de iure* position of Tiberius during the period between Augustus' death and the meeting of 17 September, at which the senate regularised his position. During the intervening weeks Tiberius still possessed, and could act in virtue of, his tribunician and proconsular powers (*tribunicia potestas* and *imperium proconsulare*), but vis-à-vis the senate his position was unprecedented and ambivalent. Accordingly c. 6 describes Tiberius' *de facto* power in the elimination of Agrippa Postumus and the urgent advice of his close counsellor, Sallustius Crispus, not to refer the matter to the senate: some things should be hidden from the public gaze—palace secrets, the advice of friends, and the activities of the armed forces. Chapter 7 turns to the civil sphere. First the reality: Tacitus describes it as a 'stampede into slavery' (*ruere in seruitium*). But a *modus vivendi* between emperor and senate had to be worked out and clothed in a decent constitutional dress. That was something that must wait till the second meeting of the senate on 17 September; till then an uneasy air surrounded the relationship.

From the interweaving of these two strands comes the initial portrait of Tiberius. Details can be filled in as the narrative of his reign proceeds, but the first broad strokes of the portrait are decisive. Incidents are selected and arranged with the finished picture already in mind. Artistically, at least, the portrait is compelling. But the artistic execution is based on an intellectual analysis that seeks to probe the gap between façade and reality. Augustus had schemed his way to power, and the power he exercised was a despotism (*dominatio*—the word already used in 1.1.1 to describe the despotisms of Cinna and Sulla); all the more was that likely to be true of Tiberius. His behaviour during the first month after Augustus' death seemed to Tacitus to prove it. Convinced of the justness of his interpretation, Tacitus sought to persuade his reader of its validity by applying a whole range of emotive techniques. In so doing he was writing entirely within the tradition of Greco-Roman historiography.

The introductory chapters of *Annals* I form a frontispiece to the reign of Tiberius. In them the total impression is more important than strict chronological sequence. But by the time c. 14 is reached the narrative is firmly fixed in time and place (17 September, AD 14, at Rome in the senate house), and the annalistic framework can now assert itself. Events are divided into yearly blocks, and within each year into events at home (*domi*) and abroad (*foris*). But the annalistic framework is a servant, not a master, and within each Book it is manipulated differently.

Book I covers (effectively) from September 14 to the end of 15. Its introductory and final chapters (1-15; 72-81) are located at Rome; except for three chapters (52-4) placed at the year end—AD 15 begins with consular names (55.1)—everything else belongs to the sphere of *foris*: first (16-30) the mutiny of the Pannonian army and its suppression by Drusus, the emperor's son; then the mutiny of the German legions, its suppression by Germanicus, and his subsequent campaigns against the Germans (31-71, less 52-4).[19] The revolt of major legionary armies, before Tiberius' position as Augustus' successor was assured, was a matter of considerable political importance, but neither the mutinies nor Germanicus' German campaigns justify the amount of space that Tacitus gives them. Part of the reason is his desire to enhance the picture of Germanicus (who is allotted more than twice the space given to Drusus), but partly (and this applies equally to Drusus) it is because of the scope the subject matter allowed for graphic description and pathetic detail.

*Annals* II covers the four years 16-19, with the two middle years occupying only eighteen of its eighty-five chapters. Germanicus continues to claim much of the limelight.[20] After a further campaign in Germany he believed (contrary perhaps to the evidence that Tacitus himself offers) that one further year could bring the war to a final conclusion: Tiberius, veteran of many German campaigns, thought otherwise and recalled Germanicus to a triumph and the prospect of a second consulship. In the next year (17) he was given an extraordinary command in the East, but the appointment at the same time of a new governor of Syria, Cn. Piso, was thought by many, including (apparently) Piso himself, to be designed to keep a check on Germanicus. It was not long before the two quarrelled openly, and when Germanicus succumbed to a mysterious illness, he was convinced that he had been poisoned by Piso, and before he died, he made an impassioned death-bed plea for vengeance against his alleged murderer. His death was greeted with deep sorrow in Syria and the neighbouring provinces and territories, and Tacitus records that there were those who regarded him as the equal, or even the superior, of Alexander the Great. At Rome news of his illness was received with dismay, and on his death manifold honours were decreed to perpetuate his memory. The Germanicus theme continues into Book III, the first eighteen chapters of which describe his funeral at Rome and the trial and suicide of Piso.

Both the space allotted to Germanicus and the colourful language in which his actions are so often described make it abundantly clear how much his personality had engaged Tacitus' interest. At the beginning and end of his appearances in the *Annals* he is accorded a speech in *oratio recta*—the first (1.42–3) is the first long direct speech and is one of the two longest speeches in the work; when he decides to send his wife and baby son away from the mutinous legions, the language and rhythms are chosen to emphasise the pathos of the situation (1.40.4); his visit to the site of the defeat of Varus and his legions and the burial of the bones of their fallen or butchered comrades is a scene of high emotion, vividly described (1.61–2); a battle against the German leader, Arminius, is preceded by a dream with auspicious omens, a speech of encouragement to his troops (this time in *oratio obliqua*) and the appearance of eight eagles, 'birds of Rome, the legions' own deities'; and when the transport fleet suffered heavy losses in a storm, the storm is depicted in highly coloured vocabulary and poetical tones, while the description of Germanicus bemoaning the loss of so many of his men on the rocky promontories reflects more of Tacitus' imagination than the geographical features of the Dutch coastline (2.23–4).

The stylistic brilliance that is found in incidents involving Germanicus enhances the implied contrast between emperor and adopted son. At times the contrast is made explicitly; so in 1.33.2, 'the young man had an unassuming nature and a remarkable friendliness, quite unlike the haughty and secretive conversation of Tiberius'. And there are numerous references to Tiberius' suspicious resentment of Germanicus' popularity and, as a consequence, Germanicus' efforts to be self-effacing. But the attraction that Germanicus exerted on Tacitus does not entirely blind him to the young man's shortcomings, and in a number of the most colourful episodes Germanicus is shown in a far from favourable light. At 2.8.2 Tacitus roundly declares that Germanicus made a blunder in not transporting his army further up the river Ems. Elsewhere Tacitus leaves the reader to supply the criticism, as when Germanicus attempts to placate the mutineers by a letter purporting to come from the emperor, the obvious forgery of which only exacerbated their demands (1.36.3). So too the reduction in the period of enlistment, which Germanicus had to grant to appease the mutineers, receives no comment at the time from Tacitus; it is only later, when the concessions are reversed (1.78.2) that Tacitus describes them as 'ill-considered measures' (*male consulta*).

Though Tacitus seeks in a series of incidents to show the emperor's hostility and envy of Germanicus, a close reading of the text suggests that on matters of policy Tiberius acted wisely. So, when people at Rome heard of the mutinies in Germany and Pannonia, and asked why Tiberius did not go in person to quell them, Tacitus imagines the thoughts that led the emperor not to leave the capital; with mutinies on two fronts it was prudent to send one son to each of the scenes, without compromising the imperial dignity. Those thoughts reveal calculated good sense. And when, later (at 2.5.1), Tacitus says that troubles in the East were not unwelcome to Tiberius, because it offered him a pretext (*species*) for withdrawing Germanicus from Germany, where his popularity with the legions was a source of worry to the emperor, Tiberius' reason for refusing Germanicus' request to be allowed a further year's campaigning to complete the subjugation of the Germans is again marked by a wisdom that came from experience: in the many campaigns that he, Tiberius, had served in Germany, he had achieved more by diplomacy than by force (*se . . . plura consilio quam ui perfecisse*; 2.26.3).

It is clear that when Tiberius was succeeded by Germanicus' son, Gaius (Caligula), there was a good deal of history (or what passed for it) written, in which eulogy of Germanicus was matched by denigration of Tiberius. In a thoroughly Tacitean chapter (1.52) Tiberius reacts to the news that Germanicus has quelled the mutiny of the German legions; public profession of gratitude to Germanicus is matched by private suspicion of him. Almost all of this occurs in Dio too (57.6.2-4). Since the material probably reached Tacitus and Dio from a common source, it is a timely reminder that the dissembling Tiberius is not a Tacitean invention. It is not surprising that, in spite of a natural bent towards scepticism, Tacitus accepted from the written tradition at his disposal much that seemed to emphasise or illustrate Tiberius' deviousness. What is really surprising is the amount of evidence he records that makes it possible for us to come to a more balanced judgment on Tiberius.

The last ten chapters of Book I, which return the reader to Rome, mark both the end of the Book and the end of a year (AD 15). Because of this Tacitus organizes his material with special care. In the annalistic tradition it was a common practice to accumulate at the year's end a number of items, which might not separately have justified inclusion, but which, assembled in a group, attained a collective impressiveness; religious celebration, political appointments and other *notabilia* affecting the leading families would figure prominently. Chapter 72 begins in this manner, 'There were decreed in that year the triumphal insignia to . . .', and a number of similar items—the measures taken to deal with the flooding of the Tiber, the steps taken to control violence in the theatre, the transfer of two senatorial provinces to Tiberius, the granting of permission to the Spaniards to build a temple to Augustus, the extension of a provincial governorship—are dealt with in the succeeding chapters.

Senatorial debates and decisions are among the items recorded, but though occasionally Tiberius takes no part in them, the senatorial matter of these chapters usually involves the emperor, and mention of Tiberius in senatorial contexts leads on to other items where his authority is paramount or absolute. The second sentence of c. 72 begins as though it were simply going to continue the catalogue of annalistic items: 'Tiberius rejected the title of *pater patriae* ('father of the fatherland') that the people sought time and again to thrust on him'. He also refused to allow an oath of loyalty to his enactments to be taken. But, Tacitus continues, he did not thereby create a belief that he was an egalitarian (*non tamen ideo faciebat fidem ciuilis animi*),[21] for he revived the law of treason.

The charge of *maiestas* (i.e. *maiestas laesa*, lèse-majesté) was to become the scourge of imperial politics, and it is proper that a historian should underline its importance at its first appearance. But the two cases Tacitus selects to illustrate it are remarkable, for Tiberius made it clear that he regarded the charges against two Roman knights as frivolous, while in the more substantial case against the governor of Bithynia the defendant was acquitted on the charge of treason and the charge of extortion referred to a board of assessors. It is not until the following year, with the trial of Libo Drusus (2.27 ff.), that the *maiestas* law claimed its first victim—Libo committed suicide, when it was already clear that he would be found guilty. The emphasis placed on the theme of treason trials in 1.73-4 shows an important function of these final ten chapters of Book I; themes and persons are mentioned who will be prominent in later years of the emperor's reign. In addition to the three men to whom triumphal insignia had been granted for their successes under Germanicus in Germany (A. Caecina, L. Apronius, C. Silius), six other senators are mentioned who will figure prominently. Of these Cn. Piso, Asinius Gallus and L. Arruntius had already appeared in c. 13 where their future deaths were predicted, while Ateius Capito and Poppaeus Sabinus are later accorded the rare honour of an obituary (3.75 and 6.39 respectively). The last named is quoted as an example of Tiberius' policy of prolonging provincial governorships and army commands. With stricter application of judicial remedies for cases of extortion or exploitation Tiberius' policy—in this, as in so much else, he followed the precedent of Augustus—helped to raise the standard of provincial administration. Tacitus does not mention this, but wonders why Tiberius adopted such a policy. Various reasons, he says, are recorded—natural conservatism, a desire to restrict the number of men who should receive such an honour, the feeling that there was safety in mediocrity.

Through these final chapters there runs a leitmotiv whose significance becomes apparent only with the very last words of the Book. The keyword is *libertas*, which in this context means approximately the freedom of a senator to speak his mind. Two of the passages cause no difficulty—one involves Cn. Piso (1.74.5), the second Asinius Gallus (1.77.3; for both men see above). A third passage (1.75.1) is perhaps more revealing than Tacitus intended it to be. After mentioning Tiberius' attendance at judicial sittings of the senate, Tacitus adds that he 'sat in' on the praetor's court, where his presence frequently acted as a safeguard against the attempts of the powerful to influence the verdict. According to Tacitus this 'aided truth and justice, but destroyed freedom'. 'Freedom' to pervert the course of justice! But, of course, that had been the practice and prerogative of the republican aristocrat.

The last chapter of the Book discusses the conduct of consular elections under Tiberius. Tacitus confesses himself puzzled by the diversity of views that he found not only in earlier historians (*auctores*) but also in the speeches of Tiberius himself (*in ipsius orationibus*). Unless Tacitus is to be regarded as unduly deceitful, the statement should be taken at its face value—Tacitus had access to, and consulted, the actual speeches of Tiberius. The perplexity concerns the manner and extent of Tiberius' interference with the list of candidates. Whatever the doubts, Tacitus says that the method most often used by Tiberius was to say that only those whose names he had passed to the consuls (as presiding officers for the election) had in fact put forward their names, adding the remark that anyone else who had sufficient confidence in his own merit or influence might put his name forward. The Book ends with Tacitus' comment: what Tiberius said sounded fine, but in practice was meaningless or misleading; 'the greater the show of freedom in which it was cloaked, the more oppressive the slavery in which it would issue.' Almost every word in the sentence is loaded— *speciosa* ('specious'), *subdola* ('deceitful'), the contrast between *uerbis* and *re* (what was said contrasted with the reality) and between the show of freedom (*libertatis imagine*—again the keyword *libertas*) and *seruitium*. The last word of the whole book is *seruitium*, 'slavery'; the sombre colour of Tiberius' reign cannot be more emphatically stressed.

The second book of the *Annals* is dominated by the theme of Germanicus—his final campaign in Germany, his recall and appointment to a command in the East, his activities there, his illness and death, and its aftermath. But within the sphere of domestic events two topics are enlarged upon, the treason trial and senatorial debate. In the course of the latter Tiberius is given his first speech in *oratio recta*, a forceful rejection of an appeal for financial assistance from an impoverished senator (2.38). The senatorial debates are preceded (cc. 27–32) by a detailed account of the trial on a charge of high treason of a young nobleman, M. Scribonius Libo Drusus. Tacitus announces that he will deal with the trial in detail because of its great importance. The indictment accused him of plotting revolution (*moliri res nouas*), and the Fasti Amiternini speak of Libo's 'criminal designs against the emperor Tiberius and his family'. Tacitus speaks of him as a foolish young man, inclined to dabble in astrology. Is Tacitus trying to play down what was in fact a serious conspiracy, and so discredit the official version of the affair? Probability favours Tacitus' version. It is wholly unlikely that Libo Drusus had the competence to plot effectively against the emperor, though that does not mean that he did not toy with half-baked schemes that could be construed as treasonable.

But Tacitus' real purpose is not to demonstrate the triviality of Libo's offence. Quite explicitly it is to give an account of practices that were to become widespread under the principate, particularly the incitement to treasonable speech by seeming friends, and the accumulation of sycophantic proposals of senators after the condemnation of one of their number. The case was brought before the senate in its judicial capacity, and apart from an ingenious suggestion that would have made the evidence of Libo's slaves available to the court Tiberius studiously refused to interfere with the process of justice. Only after Libo's suicide and subsequent condemnation did Tiberius say that he would have intervened to beg for Libo's life, had he not committed suicide. It is possible to argue that the 'correctness' of Tiberius' behaviour was a charade, performed in the full knowledge that, without his intervention, the senate would arrive at the verdict he desired. A parenthetical remark that at an earlier stage Tiberius had concealed his resentment of Libo (28.2) may support this interpretation, but that is all. The principal blame attaches to the senate; it is only later in his reign that Tiberius actively encourages *delatio*.

In the next case of *maiestas* that Tacitus records (that of Appuleia Varilla, a niece of Augustus' sister; *Ann.* 2.50) Tiberius does in fact intervene, but it is to direct that the charges of adultery and treason (the latter an alleged blasphemy against Augustus) should be considered separately; and after an adjournment he causes the count of *maiestas* to be dropped. The incident is wholly to the credit of Tiberius, but Tacitus continues to try to prejudice the reader against him by introducing the episode with the words, 'the law of *maiestas* was growing apace' (*adolescebat interea lex maiestatis*). In spite of the outcome of this particular case Tacitus insists that this is a growing malady that has yet to reach its climax.

Whereas home affairs for the year 16 are allowed sufficient space for some considerable detail to be given first to the trial of Libo Drusus and then to a series of senatorial debates, in the rest of the Book they are dealt with in much more summary fashion. At two points items rebounding to the emperor's credit are listed. First in cc. 47–8, without any adverse comment, a list is given of public and private benefactions—we are reminded of Tacitus' statement in 1.75.2 that, even after he had discarded all other good qualities, Tiberius still retained an eagerness for spending money on worthy objects. Then in c. 87, at the end of a series of brief annalistic items, we are told that, after intervening to stabilise the price of corn, he once again declined the offer of the title of *pater patriae*. Moreover he sharply rebuked those who spoke of his 'sacred duties' and called him 'master'. But lest the last word in the Book about Tiberius should be wholly favourable, Tacitus appends the comment that speech was restricted and rendered dangerous, when the emperor feared freedom and hated flattery (*unde angusta et lubrica oratio sub principe, qui libertatem metuebat, adulationem oderat*).

Book III begins by continuing to exploit the aftermath of the death of Germanicus. Three threads, all begun in the closing chapters of the previous Book, intertwine—the public grief, the reaction of Tiberius, the behaviour of Cn. Piso and the events leading up to his trial. When there was popular grumbling because Germanicus had not been buried with the pomp and ceremony due to his position, an explanatory decree from the emperor proclaimed the duty of imperial persons and people to show firmness in adversity; 'rulers die, the state lives for ever'. Four years later Tiberius will show the same brave and dignified bearing when his son Drusus dies (4.8). Neither on that occasion nor on this does Tacitus say anything that might diminish the reader's admiration for the emperor's behaviour. But when the earlier speech is read in the context of Germanicus' death, a different picture emerges. The spontaneous displays of grief of all sections of society are contrasted with the aloofness of Tiberius and his mother. There was no element of flattery in the popular demonstrations, '*for everyone knew that Tiberius had great difficulty in hiding his pleasure at Germanicus' death*'. The next chapter (3.3.1) begins: 'Tiberius and Augusta (=Livia) did not appear in public, thinking it inconsistent with their royal dignity, if they were to show their grief openly, or perhaps out of fear that, with the eyes of all upon them, their insincerity be revealed.' The less creditable explanation is given, in typically Tacitean fashion, in the more emphatic second place, and though Tacitus does not, in this sentence, state his own preference, the previous sentence leaves the reader in no doubt. Moreover, after saying (3.3.2) that his scrutiny of other authors and the daily gazette[22] reveals no mention of Germanicus' mother, Antonia, taking any part in the funeral ceremony, he mentions two straightforward possibilities (ill-health or grief may have prevented her attendance) only to reject them in favour of his own preferred explanation—Tiberius and Livia kept her in the palace to make their own absence from the funeral seem more natural. In these chapters, as clearly as anywhere, one can see how Tacitus operates. Facts are given and explanations offered. No attempt is made to detract from the forcefulness of Tiberius' own claim, but the alternative, often emotionally conveyed as oblique reportage, is made, by implication and the occasional remark from Tacitus himself, to seem the preferred view.

In the account that follows of the trial of Piso (3.10–18) it is similarly necessary to distinguish between fact and impression.[23] Tiberius declined to hear the case under his own personal jurisdiction and referred it to the senate. There the emperor told his audience to put from them any thought of the personal issues and keep separate the two questions of fact—had Piso poisoned Germanicus and had his relationship with the armed forces in Syria been treasonable? On the latter charge Piso could offer no defence, for he had tried to re-enter the province by force. The charge of poisoning failed, though many retained a suspicion that Germanicus had not died a natural death. When he saw that there was no prospect of the emperor intervening on his behalf, Piso asked for an adjournment and, after writing to Tiberius, committed suicide. The letter, which asked that his sons should not suffer for their father's errors, was read to the senate by Tiberius, and in the upshot he mitigated the sentences passed on them by the senate. Piso's wife, Plancina, was also spared; she was a friend of Livia.

Nothing in the above account is, or is made to sound as if it were, to Tiberius' discredit. But Tacitus has already affirmed Tiberius' dislike of Germanicus and recorded the suggestion that Piso's appointment as governor of Syria was intended to serve as a check on Germanicus. Against this background Tiberius' studied impartiality during the trial can be seen as a refusal either to support his own nominee or to seek retribution for his dead nephew and adoptive son. Moreover there are passages where Tacitus shows his hand. One such is when, after describing Piso's suicide, he records some information that he himself had heard from his elders (3.16.1). Piso, it was said, was often seen carrying what his friends said were Tiberius' instructions to him about Germanicus. It had been his intention to confront Tiberius with them in the senate, but Sejanus hoodwinked him into keeping quiet. But even if some such communication existed, nothing that Tiberius could have said to Piso could condone his treasonable action in trying to make a forcible re-entry into Syria. The most he could have hoped to do would be to embarrass the emperor in public. Tacitus' purpose in recording the oral tradition can only have been to suggest a discreditable collusion between Tiberius and Piso against Germanicus. Perhaps Tacitus shows his own uneasiness, when he concludes the whole episode thus:

> That was the end of avenging Germanicus' death, a subject on which varying rumours circulated not only among contemporaries, but also in succeeding ages. So uncertain are events of the greatest importance, for some take any sort of hearsay as established fact, while others twist truth into falsehood, and both sorts of errors increase with the passage of time. (3.19.2)

The end of the Germanicus theme leaves Tacitus with three-quarters of a book to be filled with the events of three years (the rest of AD 20 plus 21 and 22).[24] A very large number of items is included, so that Tacitus' reader can have the impression that he is reading an old-fashioned annalistic account. But the items are cunningly chosen and arranged, and added emphasis is given to those items that are treated at length by virtue of the fact that they occur in the midst of so much that is more briefly annotated. A long digression on the origin and development of Roman law (3.25 fin.–28) arises from a proposal to abate the provisions of the *Lex Papia Poppaea*, which was part of Augustus' legislation to encourage a higher birth rate among the upper classes. The digression, written in a Sallustian manner and showing that author's brevity and tartness, has as its ostensible theme the proposition that laws are most numerous where government is most corrupt. The proposition is supported by a rapid and highly selective survey of Roman history, in which what is included and what is omitted is highly idiosyncratic. Legislation designed to preserve freedom and social harmony terminated with the *decemviri* (middle of the fifth century BC). Thereafter— though no event or person is mentioned to justify the statement for the next three centuries—law was an instrument of class warfare (*dissensio ordinum*). Beginning with the Gracchi a number of names are mentioned. In more recent times two only are singled out—Pompey and Caesar Augustus. Pompey, appointed consul for the third time in 52 BC to restore the moral order (*corrigendis moribus*), passed his own laws and broke them (*suarum legum auctor idem ac subuersor*). The next twenty years are described as a period of unbroken strife, in which neither moral standards nor law existed—so much for Julius Caesar and his legislative programme! Augustus, of whom Tacitus has already said (3.24.2) that he exceeded the provisions of his own laws, gave the world

peace and a *princeps*. The result was a further tightening of restraints
and a universal terror. On this occasion, at least, Tiberius was on the
side of the angels, for he appointed a senatorial commission to mitigate
the rigours of the law.

As well as containing the first excursus in the *Annals*, this section also
contains the first instance since 1.53 of a formal obituary.[25] Such
notices might customarily be found in annalistic writers among those
items that are briefly catalogued at the end of a year's narrative, and it
is at the year's end (3.30; the year is AD 20) that Tacitus places the
present obituary. It is indeed a double obituary, a procedure that gives
Tacitus additional scope for point and antithesis. The first of the two
dead men, L. Volusius Saturninus, was an estimable senator, who had
been consul (the first of his family to achieve the distinction) and
proconsul of both Africa and Asia. Tacitus mentions neither pro-
consulship, nor does Volusius figure anywhere else in his pages.[26] He
appears principally to point the contrast with C. Sallustius Crispus,
adopted son of the historian Sallust. Crispus had followed Maecenas in
three respects. He had declined to become a senator and pursue a
traditional political career; his luxuriously extravagant life-style was in
marked contrast to a shrewd intellect; and, like Maecenas, he had been
the emperor's closest confidant. But, Tacitus adds, he shared one other
point with Maecenas; his influence with the emperor waned as he grew
older. Therein lies a moral: exceptional power rarely lasts for ever, or
perhaps emperor and minister grow tired, the one of giving, the other
of wishing to receive.

The years 21 and 22 were uneventful, and for much of the time
Tiberius was away from Rome in Campania. More than ever Tacitus
is free to select his material to suit his own purposes. Persons, incidents
and themes are mostly chosen because they link up with what has gone
before or because they point to the future. Drusus, the emperor's son,
comes into greater prominence, and the conferment on him, at
Tiberius' request, of *tribunicia potestas* marks him out as his intended
successor (3.56). There are briefer mentions of Sejanus, and *his* power is
alluded to (3.66.3); that power cannot attain its goal as long as Drusus
lives. And, of course, though absent from Rome, Tiberius is never for
long absent from Tacitus' comments. Though he is still the target for
pejorative innuendo, much of what he says and does during this period
is marked by good sense, and is accepted as such by Tacitus. Even
when he seems set to criticise, he may end by giving his approval.
When rumours of the revolts of Julius Florus and Julius Sacrovir in

Gaul filtered through, Tiberius was the object of severe criticism at Rome. The emperor remained unmoved; he was, says Tacitus, only showing his normal reserve—or perhaps he had better intelligence, and knew that the reports were greatly exaggerated (3.44.4).

Two themes are particularly prominent in these chapters, the continuing growth of the operation of the *maiestas* law and of senatorial *adulatio*. Flattery had become so much a part of the senatorial way of life that when Tiberius refused to allow a treason charge to be proceeded with, Ateius Capito (shortly to receive an equivocal obituary notice), with a show of outspokenness (*quasi per libertatem*), protested that the emperor should not deprive the senate of its right to prosecute and convict (3.70.2). Tacitus declares his own feeling in a famous and much-quoted sentence (3.65):

> I have made it my aim not to go through in detail every motion, but only those that are signalised by their integrity or a conspicuous shamefulness; for I regard it as the special task of history to see that virtues should not be passed by in silence, and that base words and deeds should fear the obloquy of posterity.
>
> exsequi sententias haud institui nisi insignes per honestum aut notabili dedecore, quod praecipuum munus annalium reor, ne uirtutes sileantur utque prauis dictis factisque ex posteritate et infamia metus sit.

He goes on to say that it is recorded that Tiberius was in the habit of saying (in Greek), whenever he left the senate house, 'Bah! Men fit to be slaves!' (*o homines ad seruitutem paratos*).

More revealing than a mere list of the items selected for inclusion in these two years is a closer look at those incidents that are given extended treatment and also the manner in which Tacitus rounds off each of the two years. The first item is a senatorial debate on whether provincial governors should be accompanied by their wives during their tour of duty. Both sides of the case are given, in reported speech. Caecina Severus, who had been one of Germanicus' generals in Germany, argued the case for prohibition. He is answered in a speech full of rhetorical questions; a few words added by Drusus clinched the issue: governors' wives should be allowed to accompany their husbands.

The final two items for AD 21 are an obituary notice and a long account of the trial, possibly on a charge of treason, of a Roman knight, Clutorius Priscus. Three things stand out in Tacitus' account of this trial—the nature of the charge, a plea for clemency delivered in *oratio recta* by Marcus Lepidus, and Tiberius' reaction to the condemnation and execution of the defendant. Priscus had been rewarded by Tiberius for a eulogistic poem he had written on the death of Germanicus. When Drusus had fallen ill, he had composed a similar poem on him. Had Drusus died, Priscus might have hoped to be similarly rewarded. But Drusus recovered! The speech of Marcus Lepidus allows us for the first time to linger over a man who is a key figure for the understanding of Tacitus' own political *credo*. When he dies in 33, Tacitus studiously avoids giving him an extended obituary: 'I have said enough', he writes, 'about his moderation and good sense in the preceding books.' The earnestness of his speech on this occasion (3.50) is shown by its literary treatment. Style and content both owe a great deal to the speech that Sallust puts in the mouth of Julius Caesar, when he argued that the interests of the state would be better served by not executing the Catilinarian conspirators, however manifest their guilt. Lepidus' plea, like Caesar's, was unavailing. Clutorius Priscus was condemned and hurriedly dragged off to execution. To this outcome Tiberius' reaction is a masterpiece of ambiguity. He praised the zeal of the senate in avenging the insult to his imperial person, but deplored the haste with which the sentence had been carried out. As a result the senate resolved that an interval of ten days should pass before the decree should take effect. The essence of the foregoing is also in Dio Cassius (57.20.3-4), but the comment that follows is only in Tacitus: 'but this did not give the senate freedom to change its mind, and the interval never softened Tiberius' heart.'

The opening sentence for events in AD 22 begins almost in formulaic manner with the names of the consuls, then a dichotomy into events abroad ('it was a year without disturbances') and home affairs: 'at home there was apprehension of strict measures against the excessive extravagance that had broken out.'

This latter theme occupies the first four chapters of the year and allows room for an extended pronouncement (3.53-4) by Tiberius (as he was not in Rome the communication came as a letter to the senate) and a sociological excursus by Tacitus. Once more Tiberius' remarks are shrewd and full of good sense, and Tacitus makes no attempt to denigrate them. While acknowledging the existence of the evil he again insists that legislation is no cure for it; moreover if there are those who wish to make a name for themselves by attacking vice, knowing that any odium arising from attempts to check it would fall on the emperor, Tiberius declares that he is no more eager than they to provoke animosities.

In the next chapter (3.55) Tacitus proceeds to look at the spread of luxury in its historical context, and comes to a conclusion that will surprise those who regard him as an incorrigible pessimist. Conspicuous expenditure was (he says) a feature of the hundred years between the battle of Actium and the reign of Galba (31 BC-AD 69), but thereafter gradually went out of fashion. Tacitus speculates on the causes of the change. The old aristocratic families, who had sought political advancement through conspicuous display and patronage, had died out (or been wiped out) or come to realise that there was no place for such display under the empire, while many of the new senatorial aristocracy—as was the case with Tacitus himself—came from the provinces and brought with them a much simpler way of life. Above all the example set by Vespasian was decisive; he showed an old-fashioned strictness in dress and table. Perhaps habits and morals, like the seasons, follow a cyclical pattern. Certainly it is not the case that everything was better in the good old days: some things change for the better, and his own age too can offer examples to imitate. Does something of the real Tacitus peep through here?

The end of Book III not only brings the year 22 to an end, but completes the first half of Tacitus' account of Tiberius' reign. It is to be expected that Tacitus will choose with particular care the material that is to close the first triad. A double obituary fills c. 75; but it is not quite what it seems. The real contrast is not between the two deceased, Asinius Saloninus and Ateius Capito, one of the leading jurists of the age—but between Capito and another jurist, Antistius Labeo. Capito has already appeared in Tacitus' pages; he was guilty of an unnecessary piece of adulation (3.70). Labeo appears only here in Tacitus; unswerving adherence to the principles of *libertas* kept him from the consulship, but his reputation outshone that of Capito, whose obsequiousness to his rulers won him the consulship and people's hostility.

But the Book does not end with Capito and Labeo. That honour is reserved for another personage, Junia, half-sister of Marcus Brutus, and once the wife of C. Cassius, who died in this year, the sixty-fourth after the battle of Philippi—she must by now have been at least in her eighties. Birth and alliance proclaimed her republicanism; the fact that she did not include Tiberius in her will emphasised it. Tiberius took the slight graciously, and made no attempt to prevent the delivery at the Rostra of the traditional funeral oration. In the procession the busts of twenty famous families were carried. 'But Cassius and Brutus outshone them by the very fact that their busts were nowhere to be seen' (*sed praefulgebant Cassius atque Brutus, eo ipso quod effigies eorum non uisebantur*; 3.76.2). The reader may first be struck by the epigrammatic 'conspicuous by their absence', and an epigram is no bad way to give a decisive end to the first triad. But Tacitus rarely seeks only stylistic ends. The next Book will open with Sejanus. Before long Brutus and Cassius will recur (4.34.1); with Sejanus sure of the emperor's ear, mention of their name can mean death.

The opening sentence of Book IV affirms that in the year 23 the reign of Tiberius took a perceptible turn for the worse; the next sentence ascribes the change to the influence that Sejanus now began to exert on the emperor. As Germanicus serves as a foil to the emperor until his death at the end of Book II, so Sejanus acts as a counterweight to Tiberius in the second triad until *his* death at the end of (the missing) Book V. Moreover, as the first part of Book III deals with the aftermath of Germanicus' death, so the opening chapters of Book VI deal with the aftermath of Sejanus' death. The structural parallelism is palpable: but the differences are equally striking. Once Germanicus' loyalty to Tiberius was assured (and for Tacitus that loyalty was as absolute as it was undeserved), Germanicus could exert no direct influence on Tiberius; he can serve only as the reverse of the coin on whose obverse the image of the emperor is stamped. By contrast the influence that Sejanus exerts on Tiberius is immediate and direct, and the structure of Book IV (presumably the same must have been true of Book V) reflects the manner in which the actions and decisions of the two are intertwined.

In the fabric of Book IV there are four main strands—Tiberius, Sejanus, the senate, members of the imperial family. The strands are interwoven to develop a series of relationships, each of which involves either Tiberius or Sejanus or both—between emperor and minister,[27] between emperor or minister and senate, between Tiberius or Sejanus and members of the imperial family, especially those (Drusus, the sons of Agrippina) who stood between Sejanus and his ambition of succeeding Tiberius. For the most part senators are involved either as exemplifying sycophantic flattery or as the instigators or victims of political trials. But the trials, which form the principal subject matter of events during AD 24 and much of 25, give Tacitus the opportunity, by way of comment on the conduct of Marcus Lepidus and Cremutius Cordus,[28] to reveal his thoughts on two subjects that were of particular interest to him and his generation, namely what rôle could be played

under an autocracy by politicians and historians of integrity. Further
political comment was possible by the shrewd use of the obituary
notice, while military campaigns in Africa (4.23–6) and Thrace (4.46–
51) gave scope for colourful writing that would relieve the monotony
and gloom of trial after trial at Rome.

Tacitus' account of events during 23 occupies the first sixteen
chapters of Book IV. The last four chapters consist largely of 'annalistic'
items—the hearing of petitions from the provinces, the banishment of
actors from Italy, discussion about the appointment of a new *flamen
Dialis* (priest of Jupiter). The preceding chapters are built round the
theme of Sejanus' increasing influence over Tiberius, and this in turn is
based on two acts, the concentration of the praetorian guard (the basis
of Sejanus' power) in a single camp adjoining the city wall, and the
elimination, apparently by poison,[29] of the emperor's son, Drusus, who
was the first obstacle between Sejanus and his goal of becoming
Tiberius' successor. But within this framework there are two important
excursuses. In the first of these Tacitus reviews the military strength,
the civil administration, and the state of the economy of the empire.
Tacitus' excuse for including the survey here—this was the point at
which things began to change for the worse—is a little specious, but the
survey itself is of great interest. An introductory survey of the Roman
army's disposition in 69 at the beginning of the *Histories*[30] had followed
a clockwise spiral starting with Spain and ending in Rome. Here, after
mentioning the two Italian fleets, the survey moves to Germany and
traces an anti-clockwise path along the frontiers, returning eventually
via Pannonia, Moesia and Dalmatia to Italy and Rome with its three
urban and nine praetorian cohorts.

More interesting is what Tacitus has to say about the civil
administration, for the impression he gives is that, the law of *maiestas*
excepted, it was a period of good government. This seems to conflict
with what he has said in the earlier books, where he says that Tiberius
allowed only the *simulacra* of liberty to the senate. But even in the
present passage, when Tacitus speaks of Tiberius making appointments on the basis of merit, the clear implication is that the ultimate
power is autocratic; the machinery of constitutional government is
operated by Tiberius. As regards the populace of Rome, Tiberius did
all he could to mitigate the hardship caused by the high price of corn,
while at least in theory provincial government was purged of its worst
physical and financial abuses. Nor had the imperial household yet
acquired a massive bureaucracy of freedmen. Perhaps Tacitus feels

that he has said too much to Tiberius' credit, for he begins the next chapter by saying that though Tiberius retained all these practices until the death of Drusus, he showed no graciousness in doing so, but a roughness that often gave cause for alarm.

The death of Drusus in September 23 after a long illness resulted from the administration of poison at the instigation of Sejanus and with the connivance of Drusus' wife Livia or Livilla. So at least was the accredited version that established itself when, after the overthrow of Sejanus eight years later, his former wife Apicata revealed the facts to Tiberius before her own suicide.[31] There was, however, another version of the poisoning of Drusus that Tacitus discusses at some length. According to this version Sejanus arranged for *Tiberius'* cup to be poisoned, and then secretly informed the emperor that Drusus had poisoned the cup in order to kill Tiberius. Consequently, when Drusus offered his father the cup, Tiberius passed the cup to his son, who unsuspectingly drank the draught and so was poisoned. Tacitus is at pains to reject the tale as utterly implausible. His arguments are three. It is inconsistent with the calculating character of Tiberius that he should so precipitately have taken an irrevocable step; the wickedness of Sejanus was such that fictitious crimes were invented to blacken his character; lastly, a detailed account of the truth was subsequently given by Apicata and confirmed by the evidence, given under torture, of Drusus' doctor and his eunuch. Tacitus concludes by explaining that his detailed scrutiny of the rumour is paradeigmatic; from it the reader should learn not to prefer the gossip eagerly swallowed by the man in the street to the sober truth.

The death of Drusus removed the most immediate threat to Sejanus' plans for his own advancement. There remained a more considerable hurdle, the male issue of the house of Germanicus, whose interests were jealously and vigorously guarded by his widow, Agrippina. Two sons, Nero and Drusus, born in AD 6 and 7 respectively, had already been commended to the senate by the emperor; a third, the future emperor Gaius, was only eleven, and had not yet caught the public eye. The popularity that still attached to the memory of Germanicus was used by Sejanus as a means to increase Tiberius' suspicion against the family, for if Germanicus himself had never given Tiberius reason to believe that he sought the succession for himself, Agrippina's behaviour had been less discreet, and she seems to have made little attempt to conceal the ambitions she cherished for her sons.

The subsequent banishment of Agrippina and her elder son, Nero, and the death of the latter were contained in the missing part of Book V, but the deaths of Agrippina herself and of her son Drusus in AD 33 are described briefly, but with pathetic incident, in 6.23 and 6.25. The fact that their deaths occurred two years after the fall of Sejanus raises the question whether Tacitus is right in making Sejanus the prime mover in engineering their overthrow. Suetonius, at least, says that the cruelty the emperor continued to show after Sejanus' death indicates that Sejanus was rather Tiberius' aider and abetter than the instigator in cruelty.

The loss of almost all of Book V of the *Annals* prevents us from following the later stages of the relationship between Tiberius and Sejanus, but already in 25 there was a temporary setback in Sejanus' plans. A written request to be allowed to marry Livia, the widow of Drusus, received from the emperor a long and dusty answer. The request was not turned down, and hints were made that further advancement was in store for Sejanus, but the tone of the letter left no doubt of the emperor's displeasure. Conscious that his success had generated envy and hostility, Sejanus now began to urge the emperor to withdraw from Rome. By forfeiting some of its trappings Sejanus' real power would be increased (*sublatis inanibus ueram potentiam augeri*; 4.41.2). By now the emperor was nearing seventy, and in the following year Sejanus' advice bore fruit, when the emperor retired first to Campania and then, in the following year, to Capreae (Capri). Astrologers foretold that he would never again return to Rome, and their predictions were borne out in fact, though many people unwisely and erroneously inferred that his reign would soon end. Tacitus, who has so far unquestioningly ascribed Tiberius' retirement to the persuasions of Sejanus, at this point (4.57.1) pauses to speculate whether the explanation is sound, or whether Tiberius' own wish to secure privacy for his cruelty and lust was not the prime motive. The momentary setback in Sejanus' fortunes seemed now to have been redressed, and when Sejanus saved the emperor's life by shielding him from a rock fall in a cave with his own body, the demonstration of his courage and loyalty cemented still further the friendship between minister and emperor.

At the point where our manuscripts break off at the beginning of Book V Tiberius is about to take action against Agrippina and Nero; the death of Livia, widow of Augustus, had removed the one person whose influence with Tiberius could still safeguard the family of Germanicus. Within the next year Agrippina's second son, Drusus, had been incarcerated in Rome, and when Sejanus was designated as consul along with Tiberius for 31, his power was at its height. We cannot say with certainty at what point Tiberius began to have his suspicions of Sejanus, nor are all the details of his downfall clear, but the loyalty of the new prefect of the praetorian guard had been secured in advance, and when a long letter from Tiberius was read in the senate denouncing Sejanus, no hand was raised to prevent his arrest and execution. When our manuscripts resume, we are in the middle of the persecution of his family, friends and followers.

Since the relevant portions of the text are missing, it would be idle to ask what answer Tacitus gave to the question whether Sejanus was guilty of a treasonable conspiracy against Tiberius, but three points are to be noted. First, Tiberius' own assertion (recorded in Suetonius, *Tiberius* 61.1) that he had punished Sejanus for his feud against the children of Germanicus is, as Suetonius says, belied by Tiberius' own treatment of them. Secondly, among those who perished as supporters of Sejanus there is a conspicuous absence of military commanders[32] apart from Sejanus' uncle, Iunius Blaesus. Sejanus may have intended a *coup d'état*; he had scarcely made adequate provision to ensure its success. Lastly, the position of Gaius (the future emperor) throughout these events is somewhat obscure. By the time of Sejanus' death he was already nineteen and must, like his brothers Nero and Drusus, have been another obstacle between Sejanus and his ambition of succeeding Tiberius. A later remark of Tacitus (6.3.4) implies that Sejanus plotted against Gaius also—and this we should have expected—but there is no mention of it in the narrative up to the beginning of AD 29. Towards the end of the following year Gaius was summoned to Capreae, and from this time he was out of Sejanus' reach.

Since the characters of Sejanus and Tiberius are so closely intertwined, it is inevitable that Sejanus should figure prominently in Book IV (as he presumably did in Book V), but it is still the figure of Tiberius that dominates. As often in Tacitus the author's emphasis shows itself in the invented speech in *oratio recta*. There are four such speeches in *Annals* IV, three of them by Tiberius; the fourth is delivered by the historian Cremutius Cordus. After the death of his son Drusus Tiberius first defends himself (in *oratio obliqua*) for continuing to attend meetings of the senate; he was well aware that others might prefer to hide their grief: he preferred the more resolute remedy of immersing himself in public business. He then asked for the two elder sons of Germanicus and Agrippina to be brought into the senate, and commended them to the senate's protection. The speech (4.8.4-5) is brief, but the words are moving, and there is no hint in Tacitus of irony or cynicism, though ten years later both young men would be dead, condemned as public enemies by the emperor's wishes.

Two longer speeches come close together. In the first of these (4.37-38) Tiberius rejects, in a powerful and dignified speech, the request of the province of Further Spain to be allowed to erect a temple to Tiberius and his mother. Conscious of his own mortality, he prayed only to deserve to be remembered with affection and gratitude. It is not easy to be sure what Tacitus himself thought of Tiberius' arguments. He records that when the emperor persisted in his refusal of divine honours during his lifetime, there were different reactions among the people. Some put it down to modesty, many to diffidence; there were those who regarded it as indicative of a mean spirit. This last group was the most vociferous. It does not follow that Tacitus agreed with them.

The second 'speech' is the long letter which Tiberius sent in reply to Sejanus' request for permission to marry Drusus' widow, Livia. Tacitus has already said (4.1.2) that Tiberius was Sejanus' superior in shrewdness. The present letter (4.40) is a masterpiece of concealment. Professing to speak frankly because of their close friendship, Tiberius explains that the emperor cannot, as do others, think only of his own personal inclination; interests of state too must be weighed. Sejanus' request was neither granted nor refused, but it was clear that the emperor had been alerted to Sejanus' far-reaching ambition. How far this may have contributed to Tiberius' ultimate distrust of his minister the loss of *Annals* v makes it impossible to say.

The one other substantial area in which Tiberius and Sejanus can be seen operating is in their dealings with the senate. One theme predominates, the growing tide of prosecutions, mostly involving charges of treason (*maiestas*). In his treatment of this theme Tacitus emphasises three elements, while a fourth is left for the alert reader to note for himself. First there are several striking affirmations in general terms about the malaise: 'the year saw such an unbroken series of accusations' (4.36.1), 'a larger and daily more savage force of prosecutors walked abroad' (4.66.1), 'there lay a vast horde of dead of every sex, age and social condition' (6.19.2). Suetonius (*Tiberius* 61.4) more prosaically notes that as many as twenty victims in a single day were executed and dragged off to the Tiber.

Next, as Tacitus handles the individual cases, certain prosecutions are singled out for a more elaborate treatment, and it is possible to discern in them a mounting scale of anger or repugnance in Tacitus' reaction to them. In 4.28.1 we have 'a horrible instance of wretchedness and cruelty, a father as defendant, the accuser his son'; shortly after Cremutius Cordus is arraigned on a charge, unprecedented and never before heard of—in his history he had praised Brutus and called Cassius 'last of the Romans'. The case of Titius Sabinus was remarkable less for the person of the defendant (he was a knight) than for the way in which the incriminating evidence against him was gained. One of the accusers, all senators and all Sejanus' supporters, acted as *agent provocateur*, and invited their victim to his house where the other accusers were concealed between the roof and the ceiling, 'a hiding place as disgraceful as the deception was abominable' (4.69.1). The reason for the prosecution was that the defendant had been a friend of Germanicus and had continued to show the same friendship towards his widow and children; that was enough to make him a target for Sejanus' attack. Here is the third element that appears in many of the trials in Books IV and VI. Supporters of Sejanus appear in Book IV as prosecutors (often of those who remained loyal to Agrippina) and in VI, after Sejanus' overthrow, as defendants.

The part played by Tiberius in the treason trials is, naturally, less obtrusive. Domitian is said to have asserted that 'an emperor who does not check prosecutors encourages them': it is clear that many of the prosecutions during the years of Sejanus' ascendancy were brought with the connivance and tacit support of the emperor. Two instances make this particularly clear. C. Silius, who had been governor of Upper Germany at the time of Germanicus' German campaigns, had continued his friendship with Germanicus' widow. When prosecuted by Visellius Varro, one of the consuls for 24, acting as an agent for Sejanus, he asked for a postponement until Varro had laid down his office. Tiberius refused the request, saying that there must be no diminution of the power of the consul, on whose watchfulness lay the responsibility of seeing that the state came to no harm (4.19.2).[33] On another occasion, when a defendant had committed suicide before a verdict had been returned, the senate was on the point of passing a proposal that in such cases the prosecutors should not receive the rewards normally given in the case of a successful prosecution, when Tiberius—much against his normal practice—openly intervened to oppose the motion: 'better abolish the laws than their defenders' (4.30.2). In such a way, Tacitus adds, were *delatores* encouraged through financial incentives.

Though Tacitus lays great stress on the prosecution mania and pays particular attention to cases that show novel features or are in some way more than usually outrageous, he also records, though mostly with less acclaim, cases where the tables are turned on the *delator*.[34] There are also cases where Tiberius intervenes to exercise his powers of clemency (cf. 4.31. 1–2), and there are occasions, most of which receive little comment from Tacitus, where the part played by Tiberius is by no means discreditable. After he has described how Tiberius encouraged the *delatores* (4.30 fin.), Tacitus in the next chapter quotes three further cases, none of which supports the general statement he has just made. In the first he shows his clemency—and is praised by Tacitus for it—in the second Tacitus admits that Tiberius' insistence that P. Suillius should be banished to an island was justified by subsequent events; in the last case Tiberius admittedly intervenes to save the *delator* Catus Firmius from exile, but he allows him to be expelled from the senate.

Similarly, after his striking assertion that the year (AD 25) witnessed an unbroken series of prosecutions, three instances are given (4.36). In the first it is the prosecutor who is exiled, in the second the city of Cyzicus is justly deprived of its independence, while the third case sees the acquittal of the defendant, the proconsul of Asia. Even in the years after the execution of Sejanus there are instances of prosecutors being punished, but it is true of the years 32–37 that prosecutions in which the defendants are convicted or commit suicide become the order of the day, and Tacitus' statement (6.29.1) that there was 'ceaseless bloodshed at Rome' comes close to the truth. It must be remembered that the majority of the victims came from the comparatively small number of prominent senatorial families, and it is such families that would most interest the senatorial historian and his readers.

The recurring theme of political trials might, Tacitus realised, become monotonous, but by skilful manipulation the threat of boredom in the reader could be circumvented. There are two passages in Book IV, the second of considerable importance, where Tacitus puts to good account the reader's natural desire for some interruption. When C. Silius committed suicide to forestall condemnation on charges of extortion and treason, his wife was exiled and a proposal made that half her estate should be confiscated. M. Lepidus, to whom Tacitus has already accorded the rare honour of an extended speech in *oratio recta* (3.50), proposed instead that only a quarter of the estate, apparently the legally required minimum, should be sequestered to reward the prosecutors. Tacitus takes the opportunity to pay a direct tribute, in markedly Sallustian language, to this remarkable man, who, even at this stage in Tiberius' reign, was able to find a middle way between flattery and obduracy (4.20. 2-3). Only rarely does Tacitus express himself so unequivocally; there can be no doubt that he so greatly admired Lepidus, because he exemplified that ideal of political conduct that he himself upheld.

The second interruption in the series of political trials is more striking. The narrative for the year 25 begins with the trial of the historian, Cremutius Cordus, whose outspokenness and republican sentiments had provoked the anger of Sejanus. The last two chapters of the previous year's narrative are given over to an excursus (marked as such by its final words, *nunc ad inceptum redeo*, 'now I return to my theme'), in which Tacitus first laments the triviality of his subject matter compared with that of historians of the Republic, and then goes on to claim some usefulness for his own history. We need not take too seriously his profession of humility; what matters is his diagnosis. The subject matter of history varies according as the constitution about which the historian writes is democracy, oligarchy, or monarchy (autocracy). Although history under the latter is necessarily mono- tonous—'cruel orders, incessant prosecutions, treacherous friendships, the destruction of the innocent, always the same reasons for doom, with a palpable repetition and monotony' (4.33.3)—its study can still be useful by helping the reader to distinguish what is honourable and advantageous from their opposites.

The relevance of the excursus to Tacitus' own situation is unmistak- able, and the position he chooses for it, immediately before the trial of Cremutius Cordus, is significant. Cremutius too was a historian, who had written fearlessly about events that seemed to have a particular relevance for *his* contemporaries. The reader is left to apply the moral as he will, Cremutius' outspokenness had cost him his life. Perhaps Tacitus, while asking the reader to admire his own outspokenness, is paying a deft compliment to his own times when such freedom of speech need not bring with it the fate of a Cremutius Cordus.

The monotony that Tacitus affects to fear in Book IV threatens to become a reality in Book VI. Six years are covered in just over fifty chapters, and apart from the interminable series of political trials Tacitus seems to be gravelled for matter, until the aged emperor's inconclusive deliberations about a successor set the scene for his last moments and Tacitus' final pronouncement on him. It is probably not without significance that for the events of these years the resemblance between Tacitus and Dio is especially close; much of the material they have in common probably derives from the same source.[35] With the old emperor now irremovably settled at Capri, domestic policy hung fire, while Tiberius' experience as a general had long since convinced him that more could be accomplished by diplomacy than by the sword. Foreign affairs and wars would require little attention; there would be no imperial expansion.

The historian, then, was obliged to eke out his material with digressions and minor matters. The obituary notice of L. Piso (6.10.3), for long an admirable Prefect of the City of Rome, allows Tacitus to discourse on the history of that post. There is a senatorial debate about an alleged Sibylline Book.[36] A corn shortage nearly leads to a riot; an attempt to deal with high interest rates by government legislation almost causes money to disappear from circulation, until a handsome injection of cash by the emperor revives the flow. An account of how the astrologer Thrasyllus had gained Tiberius' confidence leads to a Tacitean digression on freewill and determinism; the appearance in Egypt of the phoenix leads to a digression on the bird, while a fire in Rome in 37 gives Tacitus the opportunity to pay a belated tribute to Tiberius' generosity. Roman military intervention in the affairs of Armenia and Parthia—Tacitus joins the events of two campaigns together, in order, he says, that the reader's mind may have a respite from troubles at home—is succeeded by a diplomatic settlement; a revolt in Cappadocia is crushed. The account of domestic events for the years 34–36 is especially jejune. Tacitus may have been glad that he could fall back on the obituary notice, which, while challenging his powers of concision, could allow him to look outside the unrewarding year about which he was writing.

Obituary notices begin to occur regularly only in Book III, after the death of Germanicus. Their favoured, but not invariable, position is at the year end (*fine anni*), and several notices deal with two personages, a device that allows Tacitus to employ his favourite weapon of contrast.[37] Why obituaries begin to appear regularly only in Book III cannot be explained with certainty, but there is no plausibility in the suggestion that Tacitus had at that point changed to a source that included obituaries. A simpler explanation may come closer to the truth: Tacitus begins to include regular obituaries, as soon as the deaths occur of men whose life had some importance or relevance for Tiberius' reign. It is this reason that gives additional significance to the obituaries of Book VI. Each of the four persons selected[38] for Tacitus' *elogium* was a notable consular and had survived to the end of Tiberius' reign without self-effacement or abasement. That in itself might seem sufficient cause for their selection. Moreover in two of the cases Tacitus' praise is unequivocal—that is a rarity. Lucius Piso, pontifex and Prefect of the City, never initiated a servile proposal, and when need arose sagaciously moderated those of others (*sapienter moderans*); Marcus Lepidus, who had already been singled out for praise at 4.20, is also praised for his *moderatio* and *sapientia*. These are the qualities that Tacitus admires, and which might bring a man safely through the perils of a tyrannical reign.

The case of Aelius Lamia, whose obituary is conjoined with that of Lepidus, is slightly different, though he too was a man whom Tacitus clearly thought worthy of commemoration. For many years he had been titular governor of Syria, but had not been allowed by Tiberius to leave Rome; no discredit, certainly, to Lamia. At the end of his life he had succeeded Piso as Prefect of the City. Around the fourth recipient of an obituary notice there is some air of damning with faint praise. Poppaeus Sabinus had no exceptional talent; he was up to the job, but not above it. A *nouus homo*, he had won the friendship and confidence of both Augustus and Tiberius; this had brought him the consulship and a series of provincial governorships. From Tiberius' view he was a safe man. Perhaps, though, Tacitus' obituary is a little ungenerous: the successful Thracian campaign of 26, for which he was awarded the triumphal insignia, is described by Tacitus with something approaching enthusiasm.[39]

It is fitting that Book VI should end with an obituary notice of the emperor himself: 'thus Tiberius ended,[40] in the seventy-eighth year of his life.' To a dozen lines of biographical detail are appended eight more, in which his character is analysed; one mask after another is stripped off, until at the end the portrait is revealed of an imperial Dorian Gray.

The picture is forceful and memorable: but is it true? An answer to that question cannot be given without consideration of another question: is the explanation of the obituary notice compatible with the view expounded in 4.1 and 2, that the deterioration in Tiberius' character was caused by the malevolent influence that Sejanus exercised upon him? Sejanus, it may be noted, also appears in the explanation given in the obituary notice; he is the last person who could exercise a restraining influence on the emperor.

The appearance of Sejanus at the beginning of Book IV in memorable language, with its heavy indebtedness to Sallust,[41] is a conscious structural device, designed to emphasise the division of the narrative of Tiberius' reign into two halves, each of three books. But though Sejanus' part is underplayed in the first three books, so that he may make a greater impact at 4.1, his growing power and importance are not concealed from the attentive reader of the earlier books.[42] At 1.24.2 we are told of his 'considerable influence (*auctoritas*) with Tiberius', and at 3.66.3 of his *potentia* (*de facto* political power).[43] Nevertheless, from the beginning of Book IV the space devoted to Sejanus is in sharp contrast to the brief mention he receives in the earlier books. Two interlinked strands carry the main weight of the narrative, the extension of Sejanus' own influence and his intrigue to eliminate first Drusus, then Agrippina and her children by Germanicus. Though the details of the latter element may owe some of their colour to the fact that Tacitus drew on the memoirs of Agrippina's daughter of the same name (mother of the emperor Nero), there can be little doubt of their essential truth; their elimination was a necessary part of Sejanus' strategy, if he was to become Tiberius' partner and possible successor.

As for the other strand, Sejanus' advancement is shown by a series of incidents, some of them described at considerable length—the concentration of the praetorian guard in a single camp abutting the city wall in 23 or a little earlier, the steady promotion in both civil and military spheres of his supporters, coupled with the subversion of friends of the dead Germanicus, the persuasion of Tiberius to leave Rome for Capri, leaving Sejanus as his vicegerent in the capital. In 30 Tiberius asked that Sejanus be elected consul for the following year along with himself. Only one more honour was needed to establish Sejanus as co-regent, the conferment of tribunician power. Sejanus hoped that that would come to him during his year as consul: instead, with a sudden and dramatic reversal of fortune, he was denounced in a letter from the emperor and executed.[44]

If the narrative seems substantially to bear out the enhanced importance that Tacitus gives to Sejanus from the beginning of Book IV, the same is not true of the stages of Tiberius' moral deterioration recorded in the obituary notice of 6.51.3. The first stage antedates the starting point of the *Annals* and need not concern us. The second period, to the deaths of Germanicus in 19 and Drusus in 23, is covered in Books I to III. Though tradition spoke of Tiberius' fear at the outset of his reign that Germanicus might use the eight German legions under his command to claim supreme power for himself, there is no indication in Tacitus or anywhere else that Tiberius' behaviour was motivated by regard or fear of either Germanicus or Drusus.

There is a real difficulty about the third and fourth stages. The clear implication is that the third stage lasts from the death of Drusus in 23 to the death of Livia in 29, and that it is only after the latter date that the influence of Sejanus becomes paramount. This is doubly misleading: it gives too much influence to Livia, too little to Sejanus. Livia would be eighty or more at the time of Drusus' death, and such influence as she still had must have been confined to family matters—that she did have such influence is indicated by the fact that it is only after her death that Sejanus begins to make open moves against Agrippina and her children. But the implication that Sejanus only begins to exercise decisive influence upon Tiberius after Livia's death is contrary to the assertions of 4.1 and 2, and is belied by the whole narrative of events between 23 and 29.

Except in the sphere of family matters it is better to regard the fourth stage—that in which Tiberius either loved or feared Sejanus—as extending from the death of Drusus in 23 to that of Sejanus himself in 31. At what point Tiberius ceased to love Sejanus and began to fear him is not clear. It might go as far back as AD 25, when Tiberius refused Sejanus permission to marry Drusus' widow; it was clear to the emperor that such a match must have had dynastic consequences. More probably, however, the period of fear comes later, perhaps in the years 30–31, for which Tacitus' narrative is missing.

The fifth period of Tiberius' life (31–37), in which, after Sejanus' death, 'he threw himself into crime and vice alike', can also be divided into two. Convictions and executions of Sejanus' supporters continued until a final bloodbath in 33 (*Ann.* 6.19). Though there were further judicial condemnations and executions in the remaining four years of Tiberius' life, there is no systematic persecution such as had followed Sejanus' downfall.

During these years, with the emperor permanently absent from Rome, communication between emperor and senate may well have been meagre. Because of this Tacitus really does seem to be stuck for matter, and close resemblances between his account and that of Dio Cassius suggest that for considerable portions of his narrative he is content to draw closely on the source common to them both. In the absence of those matters that most interested a senatorial historian

Tacitus had to deal with much that was mere tittle-tattle—it is, for example, impossible to estimate what residue of truth there is in the lurid tales of sexual excess that Tiberius is said to have practised in the obscurity of Capri.

The stages listed in the obituary notice of Tiberius, then, correspond less well to Tacitus' own narrative than does the alternative explanation of a single, crucial turning point in AD 23. But about that explanation too Tacitus came to have doubts: 'following the majority of writers I have referred his (sc. Tiberius') departure from Rome to the scheming of Sejanus, but since he continued in the same solitude for six years after Sejanus' execution, I am on the whole inclined to ascribe it rather to his own nature . . .' (*plerumque permoueor num ad ipsum referri uerius sit*; 4.57.1). To that extent, despite its over-schematised framework and outmoded psychology, the obituary notice comes nearer to penetrating the truth, for it seeks an answer within Tiberius' own character. How was it that a man who till his mid-fifties had been 'excellent in both achievement and reputation' became at the end a cruel tyrant and licentious recluse?

For an answer to that question we must look at *Annals* I-VI as a whole. Confronted with the opposing facets of Tiberius' character, Suetonius was content to gather the good and bad points of his reign into two separate bundles. Tacitus sought to come to grips with the evidence that faced him and to give a coherent explanation of it. His essential honesty as a historian is nowhere more evident than in his handling of Tiberius' speeches. Though he was free, according to the canons of ancient historiography, to put his own words into the emperor's mouth, what he offers is not an expression of studied insincerity, but an effective mixture of blunt common sense and shrewd political judgment. Tiberius declines to impose sumptuary controls or exercise a moral censorship over political appointments and rejects the silly offer of an armed senatorial bodyguard with sarcasm (3.53–54; 3.69; 6.2.4). The fortitude with which he faced the deaths of Germanicus and Drusus is epitomised by his assertion that 'emperors are mortal, the state lasts for ever' (*principes mortales, rem publicam aeternam esse*; 3.6.3), and in refusing the people of Spain permission to erect a temple to himself and Livia he affirmed that he would be satisfied if, after his death, he were remembered with gratitude for his services to the state (4.38.3). Only in the long letter in which he refuses Sejanus permission to marry Drusus' widow (4.40) is a strong element of dissimulation manifest.

That element in Tiberius' character already stood in the historical tradition. It accorded well with what senators had learned during the reign of Domitian, when it could be perilous to reveal what one thought. After Domitian's murder, when other senators were carried away by euphoria, Tacitus (to judge by his writings) retained a keen awareness of the gulf between motive and profession. That suggested a way in which the enigma of Tiberius' reign might be explained. The true Tiberius was there from the start, but hidden; progressively the veneer of virtue and civility wore off. But why? Neither the deaths of members of the imperial family nor the rise and fall of Sejanus give a satisfactory explanation. Perhaps the truth, implicit throughout the narrative of the reign, comes out in the words of Lucius Arruntius before he committed suicide a short time before the death of Tiberius. There was nothing to be hoped for, he said, by prolonging life into the new reign of a vicious youth, when he reflected that Tiberius, despite his considerable experience of affairs, 'had been undermined and altered by the force of absolute power' (*ui dominationis conuulsus et mutatus*; 6.48.2). The suicide of Arruntius is also in Dio (58.27.4), as is his statement that he was unwilling to live to see Gaius as emperor: 'I cannot in old age become the slave of a new master.' But it is only Tacitus who has the remark that it was the force of despotic power that subverted the character of Tiberius. Absolute power corrupts absolutely.

# VI

## THE *ANNALS* · CLAUDIUS

The surviving portion of Tacitus' account of the reign of Claudius begins in the middle of a sentence in the middle of his reign in the middle of Book XI. It is unlikely that the earlier years were patterned on the model of Tiberius, showing an early period of good government, after which an inevitable decline would set in, for the senatorial tradition was hostile to Claudius from the outset. There was good ground for their hostility, for on the murder of his predecessor, when the senate was deliberating whether to restore the republic or put forward its own nominee as *princeps*, Claudius, dragged from behind a curtain, had been proclaimed by the praetorian guard as its own choice. After a brief attempt to assert its authority the senate bowed to the will of the soldiery. According to Suetonius, reflecting the senatorial tradition, Claudius was wholly under the thumb of his wives and freedmen, who dictated imperial policy. It is clear that Tacitus worked within the framework of the same tradition. The first sentence of Book XI has as its subject 'she' (sc. Messalina, his wife) and the Book ends with her death, while Book XII begins with the contest between the imperial freedmen to provide the emperor with a new wife, and ends with Claudius' death at the hands of that new wife, Agrippina.

An incident during the reign of Tiberius, when the name of Claudius was added to those of other members of the imperial family only as an afterthought, had already given Tacitus the opportunity to make his own comment on the future emperor:

> As I extend my reflections on present and past events, I am the more struck by the mockery that everywhere attends human affairs. For no-one was less marked out for supreme power by public opinion, expectation and regard than the man whom fortune was keeping in reserve as the future emperor. (3.18.4)

Yet the tradition also contained elements that might have produced a different picture of the emperor. Most revealing are some remarks of

Augustus, recorded by Suetonius from letters sent by Augustus to his wife, Livia. That the young Claudius was a physical embarrassment with his limp, slobber, stammer and nervous twitch[1] is abundantly clear; but Augustus also saw in him a certain nobility of spirit, when he turned his mind to serious matters, and a surprising gift for effective public speaking.[2]

How far, we must ask, was Tacitus aware of these two sides to Claudius' character? The way in which *Annals* XI ends and the following Book both begins and ends suggests that, in the main, Tacitus accepts the hostile senatorial tradition. Much, too, of the detail that Tacitus gives is critical of, or hostile to, Claudius. But that is not the whole picture. A number of items in Book XI[3] show aspects of Claudius' interests and character that are at variance with the picture of him as a bumbling fool or the tool of his wife and freedmen. It is true that most of these items are set within a framework designed to remind the reader that the emperor is being cuckolded by his wife,[4] but the items can stand on their own feet.

The first of these items, treated at some length, is the report of a senatorial debate on whether advocates should be permitted to claim a fee for their services—the theory, established by the *lex Cincia* of 204 BC, was that fees were illegal; but in practice the law was commonly circumvented. Those who had opposed the strict enforcement of the 'no payment' rule included two of the most powerful, and notorious, speakers of the day, P. Suillius Rufus[5] and Cossutianus Capito, later the accuser of Thrasea Paetus. Tacitus describes their arguments as *minus decora* ('undignified'), but Claudius felt that they had some point and proposed a sensible compromise solution: payment should be permitted, but a comparatively modest maximum figure was set. Though there is no doubt of Tacitus' antagonism towards Suillius and Cossutianus, and though his final comment seems to convey disapproval of Claudius' solution, that solution did not favour the grand *delator* such as Suillius or Cossutianus, for whom a fee of 10,000 sesterces would be very small beer.

After a brief interlude on the Eastern Question (cc. 8–10) Tacitus reverts to Rome and the celebration of the *ludi saeculares*.[6] Tacitus, apart from an allusion to himself (he had taken part in their celebration under Domitian in 88), observes that they marked the first occasion on which the public was able to show warmer support for Agrippina's young son, the later emperor Nero, than for Britannicus, the son of Claudius and Messalina. The latter might well have sought

Agrippina's downfall, Tacitus says, had she not at this time become obsessed with her infatuation for C. Silius.

The next chapter (c. 13) gives, in jejune annalistic style, a number of measures taken by Claudius as censor. These include three of some interest—the passing of a law prohibiting the lending of money at interest to young men against their fathers' death, the introduction into the city of a new water supply, and the addition of three new letters to the Latin alphabet. The first two were salutary measures that might well have been placed in a larger context—for the latter see Suetonius c. 20 on Claudius' public works, which were 'substantial and necessary rather than numerous': but it is to the introduction of the three new letters that Tacitus gives his chief attention. His digression in c. 14 on the origin and development of the alphabet is nicely suited both to his own and to Claudius' antiquarian interests, but Tacitus' comment at the end of the digression reveals what he thought of the experiment: the letters were used while Claudius was emperor, and then forgotten. The disproportion between the space allotted to the 'three letters' and the two foregoing items may reasonably be interpreted as indicating that Tacitus was reluctant to take seriously important aspects of Claudius' policy, but was prepared to emphasise the emperor's penchant for scholarly pedantry. The following chapter underlines that same quality in Claudius, for he got the senate to decree that a college of *haruspices*[7] should be founded, to ensure that the ancient art should be preserved. The speech that the emperor delivered in support of his motion is reported, albeit briefly, by Tacitus; as one of the *quindecimuiri sacris faciundis* Tacitus had a special interest in those foreign cults that the Roman state had accepted.

At the end of the narrative for AD 47 two items are recorded (c. 22), an attempted assassination of the emperor and a senatorial motion that gladiatorial games should be given annually by those elected to the quaestorship, a post that gave automatic entry to the senate. To the latter item Tacitus appends a short history of the office that has some remarkable features. It contains more than one statement that at best can be regarded as half truths, while one assertion—that the function of the two quaestors originally appointed was to serve the consuls while on campaign, while urban duties began only with the creation of two further quaestors—expressly contradicts what is given by all other authorities. Since there is some evidence that Claudius himself delighted in expounding historical views that ran contrary to those generally accepted, there is some attraction in the suggestion[8] that Tacitus' excursus on the quaestorship derives ultimately from Claudius himself.

The Claudian items that have so far come under discussion have it in common that in every case Tacitus seems to play them down, either by the brevity of his treatment or by unfavourable comment or by the context in which he places them.[9] The treatment he gives to the next item is accordingly all the more surprising.

The year 48 begins with the discussion in the emperor's privy council of an issue about which passions ran high: should the aristocracy of Gaul, who already held Roman citizenship, be allowed to seek office and entry to the senate at Rome? The arguments against the proposal were powerful and predictable: appeal to ancient custom (*prisci mores*) and contemporary examples of valour and renown (*uirtus* and *gloria*) among present-day Italians. No need, therefore, to call in foreign blood—much less that of Rome's former bitterest enemies—to fill the senatorial rôle or high office. Claudius took the opposite view, and when he (apparently) failed to convince his *consilium*, he took the matter to the senate, where his speech carried the day. Tacitus gives his version of that speech in *oratio recta*, the only direct speech ascribed to Claudius in the surviving books. The speech is important for another reason. Here alone in the whole of Tacitus there is extant a substantial part of the speech that Claudius actually delivered on this occasion, for a copy of it was inscribed on a bronze tablet at Lyons (Lugdunum), the emperor's birthplace, and recovered in 1528. Comparison of the speech actually delivered and Tacitus' version has given rise to a lively debate.[10]

Claudius' speech of eighty lines[11] begins with an appeal to the senate not to be frightened of constitutional innovation, for that, he says, has been a continuing feature of Rome's history. He then treats the senate to two historical lectures (lines 8–24 and 24–37). In the first of these he explains how during the monarchy the succession, far from being always hereditary, frequently passed to outsiders, some of whom were men of lowly birth. Then, when Rome became a republic, constitutional change saw many innovations (including the creation of the tribunate of the plebs), until finally the plebeians were allowed to hold both magistracies and priesthoods. So far the argument, though not explicitly stated, is clear: the lesson of Rome's history is one of willingness to open high office to new sections of the community. At this point Claudius (not for the last time) interposes a personal note.

147

The history of Rome's warfare similarly shows a constant broadening of the theatre of war. Then, with a brief allusion to his conquest of Britain (39–40), he breaks off to return to his theme. Now, however, he concentrates on the extension of membership of the senate. First he quotes the precedents of Augustus and Tiberius, who had recruited the flower of the chartered towns of Italy,[12] 'men of true hearts and substantial wealth' and promises by implication that his current census will preserve Italian dominance in the senate, while making provision for those provincials who can give it adornment. He now passes beyond Italy and points out that for some time the *colonia* of Vienne in Narbonese Gaul has supplied senators. Mention of Vienne sidetracks him momentarily. He refers to two of its citizens, a distinguished knight, in whose sons' future at Rome he expresses warm interest, and the former consul Valerius Asiaticus, who had been condemned to death for treason in the previous year.[13] Once more Claudius calls himself back to the matter in hand—this time by means of a self-apostrophe: 'It is time now, Tiberius Caesar Germanicus (= Claudius), to reveal your drift to the conscript fathers; for already you have reached the utmost limits of Narbonese Gaul.'

However, instead of now disclosing the purpose of his speech, Claudius seems deliberately to blur the argument and employ a dubious analogy. No-one regrets the presence in the Roman senate of 'distinguished young men' (sc. from the Allobroges of Narbonese Gaul, in whose territory the *colonia* of Vienne stands); *ergo* there is no reason why the senate should not admit members from that part of Gaul in which another *colonia*, Lugdunum (Lyons—incidentally, Claudius' own birthplace), stands. The fact that Vienne and Lyons lay, respectively, in the provinces of *Gallia Narbonensis* and *Gallia Comata* has no constitutional relevance for the other inhabitants of those provinces. Citizens of a *colonia* were automatically eligible for membership of the Roman senate: for other inhabitants of the same province what counted was the degree of their political and social Romanisation. That was something that Narbonese Gaul had achieved in considerable measure: *Gallia Comata* had not.

Claudius counters the objection that for ten years the peoples of Gallia Comata had fought a bitter war against Julius Caesar by pointing to the fact that for the subsequent hundred years they had maintained unbroken and loyal peace, even when the Romans had trouble on their hands in neighbouring Germany—one such occasion was when his father Drusus had been called from conducting a census in Gaul in 12 BC to undertake the first of four campaigns against the Germans. Mention of Drusus' census of the Gauls allows Claudius to end his speech with a personal (but scarcely relevant) reference to the onerous nature of his own task in conducting a census.

The speech shows those personal characteristics that figure in Suetonius—a tendency to digress, a penchant for historical homily, a vein of cruelty, and flashes of self-satisfaction. But it is not a foolish speech; very much the reverse. What then of Tacitus' version? First, though there is no significant verbal echo of the emperor's speech, though the points that are taken from him are differently organized in the historian's version, and though each makes important points that the other does not, there is no doubt that Tacitus was familiar with the emperor's oration.[14] His own version was more concise, it was more antithetical, and it ended with a ringing phrase ('Everything that is now regarded as ancient was once new. . . . This practice too will become ancient, and what today we defend by precedents will itself become a precedent.'), clearly taken from the opening sentence of Claudius' speech. There is, of course, no trace of the gauche and the bizarre that feature in Claudius' own words, but Tacitus has given a Claudian touch more subtly than by direct borrowing. The Lyons tablet shows in both style and substance the influence of the speech that Livy puts in the mouth of the tribune Canuleius, when he pleaded for the right of intermarriage between plebeians and patricians. Tacitus' Claudius is characterised by palpable borrowings from that same speech in Livy; the first borrowing comes in the first sentence—'My ancestors, of whom the most ancient, the Sabine Clausus, was admitted at the same time into Roman citizenship and the patrician order, urge me to apply the same principle in governing the state by transferring to Rome all that is excellent, wherever it may be'[15] (cf. Livy 4.3.14).

The speech that Tacitus puts in the mouth of the emperor is neither transcript nor paraphrase. But it is clearly designed to answer the objections that had been raised within the privy council as given by Tacitus in 11.23.2-4. Now it is quite improbable that Tacitus could have any way of knowing what actually transpired in the emperor's *consilium* on that occasion, but two of the points that are made in 11.23 clearly derive from the answers that the real Claudius gave in his speech to the senate. The first point is the fear that senatorial recruitment from Italy will be prejudiced by the admission of provincials; to this point the Lyons tablet replies in lines 45-48. The second point is the bitterly contested struggle between the Gauls and the deified Julius (Tac. 23.4 :: Lyons Tablet 72 ff.).

Once it is realised both that the Tacitean version of Claudius' speech is part of a political argument, the other side of which is given in c. 23, and that both chapters derive from the material contained in the speech actually delivered in the senate by Claudius, it is possible to see what Tacitus intends his reader to make of his 'Claudian' oration. In the face of strong opposition within the ranks of his closest advisers the emperor, who is traditionally depicted as the dupe of his women and his freedmen, is seen to take a clear stand on the side of the progressive cause. Had Tacitus followed up the implications of the situation he has just depicted, he might have gone on to ask some further questions. Why did Claudius take this particular stand? Is it not likely that an emperor who could take such an independent line on one matter of high policy may have done so on other occasions also? But Tacitus did not ask these questions, and quickly reverts to acceptance of that dominant tradition that saw Claudius largely as a manipulated puppet. Further details of Claudius' activity as censor are given without comment in annalistic fashion. The jejuneness of the language is deliberate: it throws into greater relief the highly-coloured account of the scandalous behaviour of Messalina, the emperor's wife, which provides in a continuous narrative of thirteen chapters (26–38) the climax and conclusion of Book XI.

Modern historians are agreed that Tacitus gives undue prominence and importance to the last excesses of Messalina. Indeed Tacitus himself feels it necessary to apologise in advance ('I am not unaware that it will seem pure fiction (*fabulosum*) . . .' 11.27.1) for the bizarre tale he is going to tell, but the opportunities that it afforded were too good to be missed by one writing in the tradition of rhetorical historiography.[16] Messalina's behaviour is by turns sensational, melodramatic and, finally, pathetic; for each mood Tacitus has an appropriate language. But amid the fine writing he pursues a more serious purpose. The sexual excesses of the empress begin to interest the historian only when she sought to put the seal on her liaison with the consul-designate, the handsome Gaius Silius, by a publicly witnessed celebration of the marriage ceremony with him. For Messalina the attraction seems to have been the outrageous gesture itself: for Silius there was clearly an ulterior political motive—he would replace Claudius not only as husband, but also as emperor.

But Tacitus' main interest is not in Silius—neither his arrest nor his execution is described—but in the part played by the imperial freedmen, above all by Narcissus, in convincing the emperor of the seriousness of the situation and in securing the execution of Messalina. The theme accords well with the traditional picture of Claudius; oblivious of what was going on around him, he could be manipulated through fear to act against his wife, provided only that no chance was given for his addiction to the pleasures of table and bed to soften his resolve. The 'wedding' of Messalina and Silius was celebrated while the emperor was absent at Ostia, and it was while he was still at Ostia that Narcissus broke the news to him: 'Do you know of your divorce? For the wedding with Silius has been seen by the people, the senate and the army. If you don't act quickly, the city is in the hands of her husband' (11.30 fin.).

An emergency meeting of the emperor's *consilium* was called, and it was decided that Claudius should return to Rome and ensure the support of the praetorian guard. But since the loyalty of one of the praetorian prefects was suspect and two of the emperor's closest friends were thought likely to try to undermine his determination to punish Messalina, the freedman Narcissus successfully urged that supreme military authority should be vested in him for that one day. As the day wore on, only Messalina of those who had been implicated in the affair remained unpunished. By now Claudius had returned to the palace, where food and drink had begun to mellow him; the poor woman (*miserae*), he said, should appear next day to defend herself. Hearing this, Narcissus left the emperor's presence and ordered the duty officers to carry out her execution, affirming that such was the emperor's command. The news of her death was received by Claudius without any sign of emotion. Publicly the incident was closed by senatorial decrees ordering the removal of Messalina's name and statues from public places, and by the conferment on Narcissus of a quaestor's insignia.

The death of Messalina makes a suitable point for Tacitus to end Book XI, but it marks neither a year end (AD 49 begins at c. 5 of the next book) nor the end of the theme of Claudius, his freedmen, and his wife. For no sooner was Messalina removed than discussion and intrigue developed to provide the emperor with a new wife; a bachelor's life was not for him (*caelibis uitae intoleranti*). Each of the three leading imperial freedmen urged the merits of his own candidate,[17] but it was Pallas, financial secretary (*a rationibus*), not Narcissus, who supported the winning candidate. This was the emperor's niece Agrippina, daughter of his renowned brother, Germanicus. Only one obstacle stood in the

151

way; marriage of uncle and niece was unheard of at Rome, and commonly regarded as incestuous.

Early in the new year L. Vitellius, who had shared the censorship with Claudius, asked leave to introduce a special motion in the senate; there was a matter of great import to the state that needed debating— the emperor needed a wife. Tacitus chooses to give the substance of Vitellius' speech, in *oratio obliqua*. To her own merits of high birth, fecundity and chastity the foresight of the gods had ensured that she was a widow, available for marriage to an emperor who confined his desires to the marriage bed. A scholiast to Juvenal suggests that Agrippina had got rid of her previous husband by poisoning him, while Claudius' sexual morals, though far superior to those of his predecessor, were not spotless. Tacitus expects his reader to be aware of the irony that attaches to what Vitellius says. There is irony too in the manner in which he makes Vitellius end his oration. After refuting the objection that marriage with a niece is unprecedented among Romans with the argument that such marriages are practised elsewhere, Vitellius concludes with the statement that fashions change and that this too will soon become common practice. Here Vitellius is surely aping the words with which Claudius (in Tacitus' version) concluded his own speech urging the admission of Gallic notables into the Roman senate (11.24.7). The enabling decree was quickly passed, but the habit of marrying a niece was less catching than Vitellius had predicted: 'only one person was found desirous of such a marriage' (12.7.2). He was a Roman knight, who (most people said) was motivated by a wish to please Agrippina.

Her marriage to Claudius marked a turning point in the reign; in place of the uncontrolled passions of Messalina Agrippina employed a steely resolve, worthy of a man; there was no sexual looseness—unless it helped to advance her political control. The first fruits of her activity were the recall from exile of Seneca to act as tutor to her son Domitius (later the emperor Nero) and the betrothal of Domitius to Claudius' daughter, Octavia. The remaining chapters of Book XII cover a period of almost six years, up to the death of Claudius, and during that period the dominant domestic theme is how Agrippina progressively establishes the ascendancy of her son over the emperor's own son, Britannicus.

Yet, though Agrippina's continuing efforts to promote her son's advancement provide a vital leitmotiv for the rest of Book XII, it is only in the final chapters when, according to Tacitus (in common with almost all other authorities), Agrippina secured Claudius' death by poisoning, that the theme provides a substantial continuous section of narrative (cc. 64–69; see below). For the rest Tacitus relies on the traditional annalistic scheme of dividing events under the two heads of *domi* and *militiae*. The latter include long sections on affairs in the East and in Britain, as well as a shorter German section. In fact for each of the years 49, 50 and 51 foreign affairs provide more than half the year's narrative.

The loss of the early books of Claudius' reign makes it impossible to say whether Tacitus comprehended the shift in attitude that Claudius brought to the conduct of Rome's foreign policy; the annexation of Mauretania and the decision to invade Britain (both belonging to the first years of the reign) are only the most obvious indications that, unlike Tiberius, Claudius did not intend to abide by Augustus' advice (*Ann.* 1.11.4) not to extend the boundaries of the empire.[16]

In the surviving portions of Tacitus' narrative there are three areas of foreign affairs to which he gives particular attention, the East (11.8–10; 12.10–21 and 44–51), Germany (11.16–21; 12.27–30), and Britain (12.31–40). Only in Britain is a continuous policy of advance followed: in dealing with the Rhine frontier and in the relationship between Rome and Parthia other considerations prevailed, for Claudius was not prepared to commit large-scale resources where the use of force could not guarantee long-term success. In the East, accordingly, it was necessary for Rome to strike a *modus vivendi* with the Parthian empire, and that in turn was directly affected by the internal politics of both Parthia and its western neighbour, Armenia. Rome might (and did) encourage internal intrigue and disaffection, but beyond that, during Claudius' reign, she preferred to extemporise, as the situation in the East fluctuated.

The short section on Eastern affairs in Book XI (cc. 8–10) does little more than bring the reader up to date about the dynastic position in both Armenia and Parthia, and, though nominally recorded under the events of 47, in fact summarises what has happened from the beginning of Claudius' reign to the year 49, at which point Tacitus picks up the narrative in Book XII. By now the Iberian Mithridates,[19] the Roman nominee, was firmly established as king of Armenia, while Parthia was under the firm, but oppressive rule of Gotarzes. As a result the Parthians had sent an embassy to Rome, requesting that the grandson of Phraates IV, Meherdates, should be sent to replace Gotarzes. The Parthian request and Claudius' answer are given in *oratio obliqua*. The emperor urges Meherdates to rule according to the principles of constitutional government; clemency and justice should be his watchwords. If the reader does not observe at once how incongruous such ideals are for a race of barbarians, it will soon be brought to his notice. After Meherdates had been escorted to the banks of the Euphrates by the governor of Syria,[20] he failed to pursue his campaign with any urgency. Treachery and disillusionment among his supporters got to work, and in the ensuing battle he was defeated and captured by Gotarzes, who spared his captive's life and contented himself with cutting off his ears—to display *his* clemency[21] and bring humiliation on the Romans.[22] Such was the outcome of Claudius' intervention in Parthian affairs. Gotarzes died soon after, and in 51 or 52 (recorded under the year 49 by Tacitus) the throne passed to Vologeses, with whose accession relations between Rome and Parthia were to enter a new phase.[23]

The following chapters (15-21) describe the unsuccessful attempt of the Bosporan Mithridates to recover the kingdom from which he had been removed by Claudius. What most interests Tacitus is the discussion at Rome, apparently in the emperor's *consilium*, in which it was debated whether or not to accept his offer of surrender. Some argued that he should be crushed by force: the arguments of those who advocated the milder course are reported in *oratio obliqua* and in colourful language, with marked Sallustian borrowings. Accepting the arguments of this latter group, Claudius wrote offering to spare Mithridates' life and reaffirming Rome's traditional policy of relentless effort against an enemy, matched by a kindly generosity towards suppliants.[24] On this occasion at least Tacitus seeks neither to question the good sense of the decision nor to minimise the part played by Claudius.

The final section on Eastern affairs in Book XII reverts to Armenia. Two incidents receive particular prominence: the revolting treachery by which Mithridates' brother and nephew engineer his murder, and the romantically pathetic account of the fate of Zenobia, wife of Mithridates' nephew. The treachery against Mithridates is compounded by Roman action or inaction, and it is against these, rather than against predictable oriental perfidy, that Tacitus uses his lash. Even the governor of Syria does not escape his censure. He summons a *consilium* of advisers and accepts the majority view that Rome's interests will be best served by leaving the foreigners to cut each other's throats.

154

In the short section on German affairs in Book XI (cc. 16–21) it is on Domitius Corbulo, later to distinguish himself in the East at the beginning of Nero's reign, that Tacitus' main interest centres. Newly appointed as governor of Lower Germany,[25] Corbulo quickly repulsed marauding raids of the Chauci, restored discipline in his own army, received the submission of the Frisii, and had already advanced into the territory of the Chauci, when he received a despatch from the emperor ordering him to pull back to the western bank of the Rhine. His comment, 'Fortunate the Roman commanders of old!' *beatos quondam duces Romanos*; 11.20.1), is given *verbatim* by Dio also (60.30.5). But more important than Corbulo's resigned comment are the reasons that Tacitus ascribes to Claudius for ordering the withdrawal. Typically they are put into the mouths of certain undefined persons (*quosdam*), who argue that, while failure would recoil on the state, a successful general would be dangerous to an unmilitary emperor. Then, at the end of the episode, Tacitus adds his own comment: the emperor granted Corbulo triumphal decorations, though he had denied him war. Here Tacitus seems to be doing no more than airing his (or his source's) prejudice against Claudius, whose German policy can only be understood in the light of his strategy as a whole; the emperor who had ordered the invasion of Britain cannot fairly be described as a coward or stick-in-the-mud (*ignauo principi*; 11.19.3).

By contrast a more balanced judgment appears in the short German section in Book XII (27–30). After a transition from domestic events by way of Agrippina to the colony established in the town of her birthplace (modern Cologne) in 50, Tacitus turns to the success of the governor of Upper Germany against the marauding raids of the Chatti. After Roman auxiliaries had inflicted losses on them and recovered much of the plunder they had taken, the Chatti, faced with the prospect of a battle against legionary troops in the Mount Taunus region, preferred to send an embassy to Rome to ask for peace. Like Corbulo Pomponius Secundus was awarded the triumphal insignia, but this time there is no hint of criticism by Tacitus of the fact that Pomponius neither sought nor, presumably, would have been permitted to carry the war to the enemy.[26] Nor is there adverse comment of Claudius, when, despite frequent requests to intervene, he instructs the governor of Pannonia not to interfere in dynastic struggles among the Suebi, but to safeguard the line of the Danube and offer a safe refuge to king Vannius, if (as happened) he should be driven from his throne. On any prudent estimate this was a more sensible policy than that which found voice in the jingoistic objections to the order to Corbulo to pull back across the Rhine.

If Roman policy along the Rhine and Danube frontiers was essentially defensive, and in the East sought to maintain the balance of power by fostering the internal dissensions of the enemy, the Claudian invasion of Britain completely belies the picture of a timorous emperor. In view of the particular interest that the conquest of Britain had for Tacitus, it is unfortunate that his account of the invasion and the initial campaigns under Aulus Plautius does not survive. Though the emperor's sixteen-day visit to the front and his subsequent triumph might be discounted as instruments of propaganda, the determined and systematic advance during the years of Plautius' governorship was a theme that must have delighted Tacitus. In the *Agricola* (14.1) he is described as 'distinguished in war': the same praise is given to his successor, Ostorius Scapula, whose governorship (47–52) forms the subject matter of *Annals* 12.31–40.[27]

The British chapters in *Annals* XII reveal clearly both the merits and deficiencies of Tacitus as a historian. The uneasy military situation that met Ostorius on his arrival and the vigour with which he demonstrated his determined control of the situation are briefly described, and the initial aim of his strategy is given; he would first ensure the safety of all that lay to the south east of the Trent and Severn. To do so necessitated the disarming of natives; the Iceni in East Anglia resisted and were subdued. Only now was it safe to move further north-west. His first move took him through Flintshire towards the Irish Sea, but he had to pull back because of unrest among the Brigantes in the north of England. But the real enemy lay in Wales, where Caratacus, leader of the Silures in S. Wales, fearing that he could not withstand the Roman advance there, moved north to the territory of the Ordovices and prepared in the mountain region of Snowdonia to give battle to the Romans on a site of his own choosing. The description of the terrain, the speeches of the opposing generals, the battle itself are vividly described, in language that astutely combines rhetorical generalisations and details peculiar to the specific engagement. The British are defeated, Caratacus' family taken prisoner, while he himself escapes to the Brigantes, whose queen hands him over to the Romans.

The bold resistance of Caratacus clearly captured the Roman imagination. For whatever reason his life was spared. Tacitus underlines the occasion by giving him a short oration in direct speech

(12.37.1–3), which gains prominence from the fact that it is the only *oratio recta* speech in *Annals* XII. Though the speech is, of course, Tacitus' own invention, and the smoothness and point of its rhetoric part of the stock-in-trade of the Roman historian, the substance of the appeal underlines Tacitus' assessment of the moral values appropriate to the situation; if his life is spared (Caratacus asserts) he will be an everlasting example of Claudius' clemency. Clemency (*clementia*), it will be remembered, was one of the most highly prized and publicised imperial virtues.

The capture of Caratacus by no means ended the resistance of the Welsh tribes, and both under Ostorius and his successor, Didius Gallus, the Silures in particular continued to inflict losses on the Romans, while in the North there was armed conflict between Cartimandua, queen of the Brigantes, and her former husband. The Romans were reluctantly forced to take a hand in the fighting, since they had an obligation to Cartimandua, who had handed over Caratacus to them. It is on this inconclusive note that Tacitus concludes the present British section.

Although it is likely that the biographer and son-in-law of Agricola had much more detailed knowledge of Britain than his account discloses, his main concern is to gain and keep his reader's interest. To do this he concentrates on those persons and incidents that afford the maximum opportunity for colourful writing. So in Book XII, within the context of the governorship of Ostorius Scapula, the narrative builds up to a climax that centres on Caratacus. Similarly the next British section (14.29–39; see pp. 173–5) confines itself to the governorship of Suetonius Paullinus (AD 58–61), and within that period concentrates on the dramatic and horrific details of the rebellion of Boudicca (= Boadicea). All that happened in the years between Ostorius' death and the great rebellion is cursorily dismissed in a few lines. Such is the convention of rhetorical history-writing, especially when it is dealing with foreign affairs. For the modern reader the repeated failure to consider events within a broader strategic and political framework is annoying and, at times, misleading. One would like to know what was Ostorius' aim, after ensuring the safety of all that lay behind the Severn-Trent line, in pushing further north-westwards; and it is difficult to believe that the real motive for Didius Gallus' failure to continue the aggressive policy of his predecessor was simply the inertia of old age.

The placing within the structure of Book XII of the sections on foreign affairs is carefully chosen. Within a given year the alternation between domestic and foreign matters corresponds to the traditional annalistic division, and when domestic events are drab or gloomy, the scope that the sphere of *militiae* allows for colourful and dramatic writing affords a welcome contrast. But in *Annals* XII Tacitus places his overseas material with even greater than usual care, for the British section on his own admission, and the Eastern sections on internal evidence, contain the narrative of more than one year, and could have been introduced under different years, if he had so chosen.

The reasons that led Tacitus to distribute his foreign material in the way he has are not hard to discern. In each of the years 49, 50 and 51 there is a section (two for AD 50) on foreign affairs, occupying more than half of the year's narrative. For the remaining three years of Claudius' reign foreign affairs disappear almost completely. To some extent it may be true that in the last years of his reign the sixty-year-old emperor had ceased to take initiatives abroad, but the more important fact is that Tacitus now wishes to concentrate on domestic narrative. It is to be observed that each of the six year beginnings that occur in Book XII has as its first item, after the announcement of the names of the consuls, a reference either to Agrippina or to the advancement of her son (Nero) or the impending death of Claudius, while in the last year (54) the whole narrative is taken up with Agrippina's plans, resulting in the emperor's murder, although that does not take place till the middle of October.

However, until that last year events at Rome are not exclusively concerned with Agrippina and her scheme to ensure the succession for her son. At the end of the narrative for AD 49 (cc. 23–4) four items are briefly listed. The last two are matters of antiquarian interest, the renewal of the Augury of Safety after an interval of 25(?) years and the extension by Claudius of the augural boundary of the city (*pomerium*) as a sign that he, for the first time since Augustus, had extended the boundaries of the Roman empire. Chapter 24, in an excursus of uncertain origin and accuracy, then gives a short account of the history of the *pomerium* during the regal period. For the details of Claudius' extension the reader is referred to the public records.[28]

Under the year 51 the section on events at home (which here precedes that on foreign affairs) ends with a chapter (c. 43) in which a number of prodigies are listed,[29] while a shortage of grain (itself commonly regarded as a prodigy) so concerned the people that they jostled and buffeted the emperor in public. Tacitus takes the opportunity to lament that Italy, which once exported corn, is now forced to import it from Africa and Egypt, but makes no mention of the steps taken by Claudius to safeguard and encourage the shipment of grain to Rome; for these details we have to turn to Suetonius (*Claudius* 18.2).

The narrative for 53 (12.58) begins with Nero's marriage to Claudius' daughter, Octavia, and then passes to senatorial business, in which, for the last time in Tacitus' account, the emperor appears in his own right—in the following year he is treated simply as Agrippina's victim. The granting of exemption from tax to Cos and remission of tribute for five years to Byzantium is the formal sort of business that often occupied the senate's time. On Byzantium Tacitus adds a brief geographical description, expressed in the style of Sallust. In the case of Cos the concession was granted as a favour to his personal physician, Xenophon, a native of that community. Tacitus leaves the reader to observe the irony of the situation; in the following year Xenophon was employed by Agrippina to poison the emperor.[30]

As the narrative enters AD 54 (at c. 64) it concentrates exclusively on Agrippina's dynastic plans. But since Agrippina's aim was not merely to secure Nero's succession, but to ensure that she herself should have undivided influence over him, she first secured the conviction of Nero's aunt, Domitia Lepida, who had looked after Nero as a young boy during his mother's exile. Ties of birth and marriage—she was also mother of Messalina—made her a potential danger to Agrippina. It is interesting that Tacitus omits a detail given by Suetonius (*Nero* 7.1); Nero acted as a witness for the prosecution against his aunt. Tacitus does not wish to give Nero any individuality at this point; all initiative issues from his mother.

Domitia's condemnation had been bitterly opposed by the imperial freedman, Narcissus—he had earlier opposed Claudius' marriage to Agrippina. He saw clearly what Agrippina was aiming at, and sought to urge Britannicus' claim to succeed Claudius.[31] There was now urgent need for Agrippina to eliminate Claudius, and Narcissus' absence from Rome on a health cure gave her an opportunity that was too good to miss.[32]

With the exception of the Jewish historian Josephus, who speaks only of a rumour that Claudius was poisoned, the ancient tradition is unanimous that Claudius was murdered by poison, administered by, or on the orders of, Agrippina. Even though there is dispute about some of the details, the tradition is also agreed that the poison was given along with a dish of mushrooms. So many items intermesh that it is probable that Claudius *was* poisoned, but it is not entirely impossible that he died a natural death, perhaps accelerated by his own intemperance. Whatever the truth, Agrippina acted quickly to ensure the succession for her son. Three years earlier she had secured the post of prefect of the praetorian guard for Afranius Burrus, and he now came out with Nero to the cohort on guard duty. Nero was then escorted to the praetorian camp, where, after a suitable speech (written, Dio tells us by Seneca) and the promise of a donative, he was proclaimed emperor (*imperator*); the senate quickly endorsed the soldiers' choice.

At this point Book XII might have been expected to end; or, at most, an obituary notice of the emperor might have been added. But Tacitus chooses differently. Anticipating by some days an event that properly belongs to the beginning of Nero's reign (and is duly noted there) he records that divine honours were decreed to Claudius; in the funeral that was to be given to the husband whom (according to Tacitus) she had murdered Agrippina was not prepared to be outdone by the widow of Augustus. In one respect, however, there was a difference. Claudius' will was not read aloud; it would have been invidious to remind the public that the stepson (Nero) had been preferred to the son (Britannicus).[33] Tacitus' account of Claudius' reign thus ends with neither obituary nor retrospect. Instead it looks forward to the new reign and the part that Agrippina would seek to play in it.

If we look back at Tacitus' portrait of Claudius as a whole, it is clear that for the most part he followed, as did Suetonius and Dio, a tradition that is generally uncomprehending of, or actively hostile to, this unusual man. But the defects and faults attributed to Claudius are not all the invention of that hostile tradition. The important rôle ascribed to the leading imperial freedmen is too well attested; nor is it to be doubted that he was unduly susceptible to the pressure that his wives (he was married four times) could put on him—and that, at least in the case of Agrippina, this pressure was not confined to personal matters. It is possible, too, that his mental powers had begun to decline during the period covered by the extant portions of Tacitus' narrative.

Nevertheless, the reign of Claudius as a whole bears the stamp of a man who followed a most individual approach to the problem of reconciling the needs of desirable innovation with the observance of established tradition. That quality comes out clearly in his speech to the senate on the admission of Gallic nobles to the Roman senate, and here Tacitus has done the emperor justice. But mostly he has taken a different line. In his narrative of foreign affairs he has sought to emphasise the colourful incident or personality, the instances of moral excellence or turpitude; there is little room for Claudius here. As for home affairs, though many of the emperor's acts, political, constitutional and religious, are recorded, they are frequently given in the brief, unemotional style of annalistic writing, or at most are made the subject of antiquarian comment. Thereby they make a more effective contrast both with the narrative of foreign affairs and with those sections that deal with palace intrigues. But they do so at the cost of omitting any attempt to see the continuous thread that runs through the reign. But that continuous thread is the product of Claudius' own personality, and Tacitus was committed to the acceptance of a tradition in which Claudius was the tool of others. Even that area which normally most interests Tacitus, and which is to become perhaps the most important thread in the later Neronian books—the relationship between emperor and senate—dwindles almost into insignificance in *Annals* XII.

By contrast palace politics and intrigue assume an ever increasing importance, and it is on them that Tacitus lavishes all his literary skill. A modern historian of the reign of Claudius writes: 'It is hardly necessary to add that Messalina and Agrippina and their like will appear but in the dim background of this essay. . . . In spite of all that has been said to the contrary, they had no influence upon the history of the Empire, save through the single external circumstance that one of them caused Nero and not Britannicus to be Claudius' successor.'[34] Rightly or wrongly Tacitus took a different view. In his eyes—writing in an age when it seemed a self-evident truth—political power lay effectively with the central organ of government. Claudius, according to the tradition that Tacitus accepted, was a political cipher; *ergo* the centre of power lay elsewhere. At the end of the reign (Tacitus was sure) it lay with Agrippina. The most important task of the historian, therefore, was to trace how she engineered the transfer of power to her son. The next chapter would show how she was deceived in her belief that it was she who would control her son.

# VII

## THE *ANNALS* · NERO

*Prima nouo principatu mors*, 'The first death in the new reign . . .': the opening words of Book XIII are powerful and ominous—a new reign begins, and it is signalised by a political murder. But more than that: the reader is reminded of the words with which the principate of Tiberius began (1.6.1), 'the first deed of the new reign . . .' (*primum facinus noui principatus*). There the victim was Agrippa Postumus, grandson of Augustus, here it is a great-great-grandson of Augustus, M. Iunius Silanus; and in both cases an emperor is involved who, in Tacitus' opinion, had come to the throne through the scheming of his mother. The parallelism in language[1] is designed to focus the reader's attention. But the differences between the two situations are no less important than their similarity. In the case of Tiberius the act is the first act *of* the principate; responsibility firmly attaches to the *princeps* himself. In the case of Nero Tacitus speaks of the first death *in* the new reign, and goes on to say that the murder was engineered without Nero's knowledge (*ignaro Nerone*) by his mother Agrippina. Nero, after all, at the time of his accession was not quite seventeen: Tiberius had been in his middle fifties. From this difference in the relationship between mother and son consequences flow, which determine the content of the opening chapters of Book XIII, which in turn foreshadow the main framework of the account that Tacitus gives of Nero's reign.

Before the themes of these chapters are considered, one seemingly peripheral question deserves attention. The structure of the *Annals* to this point has been markedly hexadic—six books for the reign of Tiberius, a further six for the reigns of Gaius (Caligula) and Claudius. Did the hexadic structure hold for the reign of Nero? When our manuscripts break off, at c. 35 of Book XVI, we are in 66 (the year's narrative had begun at 16.14). A hexadic structure would imply a further two and a half books for the events of only two years (Nero committed suicide on 9 June 68). Even if Tacitus continued his narrative to the end of the year to link up with the nominal starting

point of the *Histories*,[2] this would imply an expansiveness of treatment
that is found nowhere else in the *Annals*. The last four years of the reigns
of Tiberius and Claudius are despatched in 24 and 28 chapters
respectively. Though the ground that Tacitus had still to cover in
Nero's reign was considerable, it could probably have been accommodated in the lost second half of Book XVI.[3]

We should not look for—for we shall not find—a hexadic structure
or a Tiberian pattern in the Neronian books of the *Annals*. Instead,
continuity is achieved, and the reader's attention sustained, by what
are basically much simpler means. First, much of the narrative
proceeds in long, self-contained units, within which interest concentrates on one person or theme. At the same time the traditional
annalistic framework, with its subdivision into the spheres of *domi* ('at
home') and *foris* ('abroad') or *militiae* ('in the field'), allows scope for
writing that is varied, vivid, and exciting. So the dramatic interest of
palace intrigue and murder (Britannicus, Agrippina, Octavia) can
alternate with the graphic account of Boudicca's revolt in Britain
(14.29-39) or Rome's rapidly changing fortunes in dealing with the
Armenian question.

But the most striking organizational feature of the whole of Nero's
reign is the construction of Book XIV, which begins with the murder of
the emperor's mother and culminates three years later in the murder of
his wife. Yet, though Book XIV has a palpably organized structure,
artistic unity is not its main objective. Rather, by seeking to give
coherence to a chain of events, Tacitus is expressing a view of the
history of the period. He rejects the easy solution of looking for a single
point in time when Nero's reign took the conventionally expected turn
for the worse. Instead he sees the dynastic murders of Agrippina and
Octavia as part—albeit an important and sensational part—of a nexus
of events that involved a significant shift of power within the imperial
household and in the emperor's relations with the senatorial class,
whose authority he had pledged himself in his initial address to respect.

The emperor Trajan is reputed to have spoken in terms of warm
praise of a *quinquennium Neronis*. If, as is probable, he was referring to the
initial five years of the reign, there is a seeming paradox, for the period
begins with two political murders. But responsibility for them rested
with his mother who, having engineered the succession of her son,
clearly intended herself to direct the main lines of government policy.
In that she was thwarted by the combined efforts of Afranius Burrus,
commander of the praetorian guard, and the philosopher Seneca,

163

who had acted as tutor to the young Nero and now served as his political adviser. For the moment Agrippina was treated with deference and granted signal honours.[4] But these were no more than the trappings of power: determination of policy was another matter, and here public pronouncement showed a strong senatorial bias.

The oration that Nero delivered on the occasion of Claudius' funeral was written, Tacitus tells us, by Seneca: it can be assumed that Nero's first speech to the senate also comes from the hand of Seneca. Some topics were required by tradition—respect for the senate's authority, praise of the army's loyalty. But the speech also included specific promises to remove abuses of the preceding reign, particularly the determination of judicial cases within the privacy of the palace, where the emperor was peculiarly susceptible to the influence of imperial freedmen and his mother.

The arrival at Rome, shortly after Nero's accession, of news that the Parthians had decided to operate a more decisive policy of intervention in Armenia allows Tacitus to give preliminary attention to a theme that will figure prominently in the narrative of Nero's reign. Nero, following the advice of Burrus and Seneca, responded quickly and firmly, and the Parthian king, faced also by unrest at home, withdrew. This success, achieved without military engagement, was hailed at Rome with great acclaim. Extravagant honours were proposed for Nero. But in addition to this 'customary flattery' (*sueta adulatio*) there was genuine pleasure, because Nero had appointed Domitius Corbulo, a general of proven ability, to take charge of operations. The Eastern Question was to occupy the Romans for almost a decade of Nero's reign, and throughout that time it was the figure of Corbulo that dominated Roman military action.

Of the themes enunciated by Tacitus in the opening chapters of Book XIII the relationship between Agrippina and Nero and his political advisers claims first attention; for on its resolution the whole tenor of the reign depended. Accordingly the narrative of AD 55 (cc. 11-24), which is given up entirely to home affairs, concentrates almost exclusively on that relationship. But the year begins with a short chapter, in which the optimistic note on which the previous year ended is sustained. After recalling from exile the senator, Plautius Lateranus,[5] Nero graced the occasion with a speech, in which he bound himself to continue the policy of *clementia* ('clemency') that this act typified. *Clementia* is a keyword of imperial ideology, for he who has the power to forgive can also condemn; the nuances of the word would not

be lost on Tacitus' contemporaries. This speech, too, was composed by
Seneca; it may be recalled that in this year or the next Seneca
dedicated to the emperor a treatise entitled *De clementia*.

To wean Nero from his mother's influence Seneca and his followers
encouraged the young emperor, already estranged from his wife,
Octavia, in a liaison with a freedwoman, Acte; it was a kinsman of
Seneca who kept the first stages of the emperor's involvement secret.
Shortly afterwards the freedman Pallas, who from the first had been
Agrippina's strongest supporter, was removed from his post as
financial secretary (*a rationibus*). Tacitus, never slow to criticise
imperial freedmen, remarks that Nero sarcastically declared that
Pallas was formally going to lay down his magistracy.[6]

Agrippina's next move was to begin to support Britannicus, who,
though younger than Nero, might be regarded as having a more direct
claim to the succession as Claudius' son. Nero, thoroughly alarmed,
arranged that his rival should be poisoned at an imperial banquet. The
description of the scene is a brilliant cameo that gives a foretaste of the
more extended description of the murder of Agrippina. As the
fourteen-year-old boy fell to the ground, those around him betrayed
their panic: those who were shrewder kept their eyes on Nero. The
emperor kept his place, saying that Britannicus was suffering from an
epileptic fit (the detail is in Suetonius). Trained though she was to
conceal her feelings, Agrippina could not prevent it being seen that her
terror was genuine; she realised that a precedent for her own murder
was before her eyes (13.16.4).

The aftermath of Britannicus' death was twofold. On his closest
friends—these must have included Seneca—Nero bestowed lavish
gifts. The recipients were criticised by some: others saw that acceptance
was inescapable, and that the emperor's consciousness of guilt was
assuaged by involving others in the consequences. Agrippina's reaction was very different. Favouring Octavia helped neither herself
nor her daughter-in-law, and was no more than a minor irritant to
Nero. But her determined accumulation of financial resources,
coupled with the attempt to court the favour of officers of the guard
and her open praise of the merits of descendants of the republican
nobility, suggested that she had a more directly political aim in view.
Nero countered by removing her military bodyguard and requiring his
mother to live away from him, in the house of Antonia. His own visits
to her were brief and his attitude aloof.

Agrippina had her enemies, and one of these, Iunia Silana, judged that the time had come to pay off old scores. An accusation was laid that Agrippina planned to marry Rubellius Plautus, who as great-great-grandson of Tiberius might claim adoptive descent from Augustus. Agrippina was interrogated by Burrus in the presence of Seneca and a number of imperial freedmen. Tacitus gives her spirited reply in *oratio recta* (13.21)—it is significant that it is she, not Nero, who is given the first major speech in *oratio recta* in the Neronian books. At its end she couples her assertion of her innocence on the charges levelled against her with the admission that she *was* guilty of 'charges of which no-one but her son could acquit her'—the reference is to the murder of Claudius, which had put Nero on the throne. Then, moving over to the offensive, she demanded to see her son, from whom she gained 'vengeance against those who had accused her and rewards for her friends'.

The rewards and punishments are detailed in the next chapter (22). Two important and prestigious prefectures went to her supporters; the corn supply was put in the hands of Faenius Rufus, the prefecture of Egypt fell to Balbillus. More important still, the governorship of Syria, with its powerful legions, was earmarked for another of her protégés, Publius Anteius. But, for whatever reason, Anteius was never allowed to take up his appointment; possibly it was felt too risky to allow one of Agrippina's supporters to have control of so large a legionary army. The punishment of those who had unsuccessfully tried to undo Agrippina included the exile of Silana; 'Rubellius Plautus was passed over in silence for the time being'—the remark is a sure sign of his ultimate destruction.[7]

It might have been expected that Agrippina would now endeavour to tilt the balance still further in her own favour. But here Tacitus surprises us. For three further years (56–58) Agrippina disappears totally from view; her name is not even mentioned. Only in 59, at the beginning of Book XIV, does she return, and from that point onwards she dominates the narrative until she is murdered. It is inconceivable that during the intervening years Agrippina was entirely inactive. Clearly it is a deliberate decision on the part of Tacitus to keep her off the stage until a time when her re-appearance can make the maximum impact. Nowhere in the whole of his domestic narrative does Tacitus more conspicuously arrange his material to reveal only what he regards as significant.[8]

The absence of Agrippina for a period of three years during the remaining thirty-five chapters of Book XIII leaves Tacitus with room to develop other themes. In due course (under AD 58) Corbulo and the Armenian Question will come back into the picture and allow Tacitus once more the opportunity of writing a continuous section on a single theme (cc. 34.2–41). But before then the narrative concentrates exclusively on events at Rome, and no single issue occupies more than two chapters. Though the emperor's intervention, actual or anticipated, is never far away, most of the business is senatorial. A debate on how the ingratitude of freedmen towards their former masters might be checked clearly roused passions, and there was strong support for the idea that the former master should have the legal right to revoke the grant of freedom in cases where the freedman did not sufficiently honour his obligations towards his patron. The consuls refused to put the motion formally, but informed the emperor of the senatorial consensus.

The issue was now discussed in the *consilium principis*, the emperor's Privy Council. Tacitus retails the arguments for and against in *oratio obliqua* (13.26–27), and it is the milder view-point that prevails. It is unlikely that Tacitus had any means of knowing what arguments were used on that occasion; what we read is his own invention. When, therefore, the arguments he ascribes to the winning side show palpable speciousness, this may well be his way of showing that he did not agree with the decision of the imperial *consilium*. If that is so, his implied criticism may touch Seneca, whose writings suggest that he would have urged the more clement view.[9]

There now follows a series of senatorial matters that fall into the traditional mould of republican politics and the year ends with a double obituary notice (13.30.2). The first of the pair, Caninius Rebilus, a jurist and man of great wealth, is included mainly to heighten the contrast with L. Volusius, who had lived to the ripe old age of ninety-three, a friend of successive emperors and a rich man, but with an unblemished reputation.[10] Though the brevity of an obituary notice excuses any mention of his earlier political career, it is astonishing that no mention is made of the fact that for over fifteen years, right up to the time of his death, he had held the post of Prefect of the City, *praefectus urbi*.[11]

Book XIII ends with the narrative of events in 58. Unlike the two preceding years[12] that year is treated at length, and unlike them it contains sections on events abroad as well as at home. The two areas that attract Tacitus' attention are the Near East (continuing the narrative of 13.6–9) and Germany. In both cases the events recorded

167

cover more than a single year, and the grouping of details and the
location of the sections consequently represent an act of choice on the
part of the historian. Between the Armenian and German sections
there stands an important section of events, mostly but not exclusively
senatorial, at Rome (42–52).

The first episode in the domestic section (42 ff.) involves Seneca, and
contains the first overt criticism against him. His critic, P. Suillius
Rufus, had won notoriety as a prosecutor during Claudius' reign.
Although Suillius' attacks recoiled on himself and resulted in his
banishment to the Balearic Isles, there was some substance in his
charge that Seneca, having become wealthy through the emperor's
generosity, had exploited and extended that wealth with a shrewdness
that ill became a philosopher who preached contentment with a
humble lot.[13] It is interesting to note that Tacitus allows his reader to
be reminded of the allegations, but puts them in the mouth of a
notorious *delator*. That does not necessarily invalidate them.[14]

The next episode that Tacitus retails is a sensational *crime passionelle*,
the murder by the tribune Octavius Sagitta of his well-born mistress.
The incident had clearly caught Tacitus' eye, for he had already
briefly referred to it in *Histories* 4.44.2. But apart from its intrinsic
interest Tacitus has another reason for its inclusion here: it leads on to
another equally scandalous episode, which was to have far-reaching
consequences. 'In that year a scandal of equal notoriety proved the
start of great misfortunes for the state' (45.1). With these words we are
introduced to Poppaea, who was to become first Nero's mistress, then
his wife, and who, according to Tacitus, was to drive the emperor to
murder his mother and his wife. The manner in which Tacitus
introduces this remarkable woman is striking. For the first time in the
Neronian books Tacitus draws heavily on Sallust, as he had, for
example, done at the beginning of *Annals* IV to characterise Sejanus. In
his *Catiline* Sallust tells how Catiline was able to win for his conspiracy
the support of a number of women of distinguished families. To one of
these, Sempronia, he accords a full-length character sketch ( c. 25). She
was as beautiful as she was unprincipled; it is in her mould that Tacitus
sees Poppaea. However, in one important respect the two women are
treated differently by their respective historians. After receiving a
character sketch that matches that of Catiline himself, Sempronia,
apart from one passing allusion, disappears completely. Tacitus works
differently; Poppaea is given this extended introduction because of the
importance of the part she is to play in future events.

One further point requires note. Like Octavius Sagitta in the previous chapter, Poppaea has already appeared in the pages of Tacitus' *Histories*. But there is a significant difference between the two. In the *Annals* Tacitus merely gives in greater detail the story of Sagitta that he had already mentioned in *Histories*. In the case of Poppaea the *Annals* version, without so much as a hint that Tacitus has already given a different account, gives a radically different motivation. According to the version given in the *Histories*—a version shared by Plutarch, Suetonius and Dio—Poppaea was already Nero's mistress when Otho agreed to marry her to act as a cover for the emperor's liaison. In the *Annals* Poppaea, who is already Otho's wife before she is introduced by him to Nero, schemes to achieve the position of imperial mistress; she is the prime mover and Nero little more than the tool of her passion. The new version harmonises with the respective rôles that Tacitus gives to mistress and emperor in Book XIV, whereas the earlier version, in which Nero seems to take the initiative, does not.

Next (cc. 48–9) there appear two consulars who deeply interested Tacitus. C. Cassius Longinus had a reputation for strict military discipline and judicial severity—the latter quality will be strikingly exemplified in Book XIV, when Tacitus puts in his mouth a long speech in *oratio recta* advocating the execution of all the slaves of the murdered Prefect of the City. Thrasea Paetus,[15] who in a few years' time is to become the most prominent figure among the intellectual opposition to Nero, now appears for the first time in the *Annals* as extant. In fact, two years earlier, while *consul suffectus*, he had helped to secure the conviction of Cossutianus Capito in a political trial of the first magnitude. That fact is revealed only at 16.21.3. Tacitus, it seems, has deliberately omitted mention of it under the events of 56, so that Thrasea's first appearance in the *Annals* can be in a situation where his intervention on a trivial matter can be open to some criticism.[16]

The section on German affairs, which, but for a single sentence (c. 58), concludes the account of events in 58, both balances and contrasts with those chapters that dealt with the Armenian problem. Those chapters had been dominated by Corbulo and the vigour with which he had strengthened discipline in the Roman army and pressed on to capture the capital of Armenia. By contrast events in Germany begin (53.1) with the sentence 'Up to that point things had been quiet in Germany, as a result of the disposition of its commanders, who . . . hoped for greater renown by the continuance of peace'. Events in Germany continue to fascinate the author of the *Germania*, but it is interesting to note how he ends the German section in this Book; an extraordinary account of the method by which salt is produced is followed by the description of a curious method of fire-fighting near Cologne.[17] A modern reader looks in vain in Tacitus for some mention of the strategic considerations that made the retention of the *status quo* along the Rhine at this time an important element in Rome's foreign policy.

'In the consulship of Gaius Vipstanus and Gaius Fonteius Nero postponed no longer a crime he had long contemplated. . . .' The crime is the murder of his mother, and the first thirteen chapters of Book XIV give without interruption a vivid and dramatic account of the circumstances leading up to her murder, the murder itself, and the reaction to it of Nero and his subjects. That the crime should have been 'long contemplated' is inherently probable, but it is unlikely that there could have been any evidence available to a historian to prove that it was so. Whether that is the case or not, Tacitus has studiously avoided any mention of Agrippina since the end of 55, three years previously. Her re-entry on the scene is dramatic—and contrived.

A question-mark must similarly be placed against the rôle that Tacitus ascribes to Nero's mistress, Poppaea. It is she who, according to Tacitus, triggered off Nero's decision to get Agrippina out of the way, since it was Agrippina who stood in the way of her goal, to get Nero to divorce Octavia and marry Poppaea. The fact that three years elapsed between Agrippina's murder and Poppaea's marriage to Nero (Octavia had been divorced only twelve days earlier) must at least cast doubt on the part Tacitus assigns to Poppaea in motivating Agrippina's murder. Moreover the manner in which Poppaea works on Nero's feelings, conveyed in *oratio obliqua*, is Tacitus' own construction, and is exactly paralleled by her *oratio obliqua* appeal in 14.61 to Nero to get rid of Octavia. In both speeches she draws attention in rhetorical questions to her own physical charms and her wish to bear Nero's child, stresses the political danger of letting her rival go unchecked, and taunts Nero with the prospect of taking Octavia back. When there is added the further fact that Poppaea appears only on these two occasions in the whole of Book XIV, the conclusion is inescapable that the structure of Book XIV is deliberately contrived by Tacitus to bring out the parallelism of the two actions of Poppaea.

The means by which Agrippina's death was to be secured gave Nero pause for thought. Finally the imperial freedman Anicetus, who was in charge of the fleet at Misenum, suggested a stratagem; a boat could be constructed which would collapse, when required, as though by accident. Hypocrisy could be added to crime: Nero, he suggested, could build a temple to his mother along with other marks of filial respect (*cetera ostentandae pietati*; 14.3.3). *Pietas* was a much-vaunted imperial virtue! Before the stratagem could be put into effect, Nero had first to effect a pretended reconciliation with his mother. That was not difficult, since (Tacitus says) women are ready to believe what pleases them (*facili feminarum credulitate ad gaudia*)! The plan however misfired. Agrippina was thrown into the water, and managed to swim to safety, but not before she had seen her companion battered to death and had herself been wounded on the shoulder.

Fully aware that she had been the object of her son's murderous attack Agrippina at the same time recognised that her only hope of survival was to pretend to believe that she had had a miraculous escape from an accident; a message to this effect was sent to Nero. Before the messenger arrived, Nero had already heard of his mother's escape and, in terror that she would rally military support to her cause, had turned to Burrus and Seneca for advice. The degree of their complicity is open to question. Dio, who throughout shows hostility towards the philosopher Seneca, affirms—on the evidence of 'many reliable authorities'—that Seneca had from the outset encouraged Nero to get rid of his mother. For Tacitus the only doubt is whether they were, or were not, aware in advance of what was afoot: the manner of their involvement at this point is carefully itemised by him. To a question of Seneca Burrus replied that the praetorian guard would not lift a hand against the daughter of Germanicus; it was up to Anicetus to conclude the business he had begun, when he had suggested the device of a collapsible boat.

But before Anicetus and his assassins could reach the villa where Agrippina was staying, there occurred an incident that is found only in Tacitus, and is in all probability included to afford a moment of dramatic retardation before the expected climax is achieved. News of Agrippina's escape from drowning had got about the neighbourhood, and people began to flock to her villa to offer congratulations. They were quickly removed by the arrival of Anicetus and his military detachment, who surrounded the villa in menacing fashion. The scene within the villa is brilliantly described—the desolation, the flickering half-light, Agrippina's reproach, as the last of her maids deserts her; then, confronted by Anicetus and the two officers who accompanied him, the baring of her belly and her defiant 'Strike here!' (8.5).

The murder of Agrippina offered a theme that no historian trained in a rhetorical tradition could resist, and Dio, though preserved here only in epitome, makes the most of the sensational aspects of the episode. For much of the detail and in the general organization his narrative closely matches, though it does not exactly follow, that of Tacitus. Even the shorter account of Suetonius (*Nero* 34.2-4) has sufficient material in common with Tacitus to make it certain that all three authors drew upon a common source. What that implies for Tacitus' method of writing and historical reconstruction is discussed in a later chapter, but the extent of the resemblance over a sustained part of the narrative is greater than in any earlier part of the *Annals*, and approaches the degree of parallelism that exists between Tacitus' account of the reigns of Galba and Otho and Plutarch's lives of the two emperors.

Even with his mother's death Nero still needed reassurance that his position was secure. The visions and sounds that were reported to have troubled his guilty conscience can be ignored as rhetorical embellishment; there were more real anxieties facing him. But Burrus was able to demonstrate the praetorian guard's continuing loyalty to him, and a letter to the senate (written, Tacitus tells us, by Seneca), in which much play was made of Agrippina's past political ambitions, so inimical to the senate's authority and good government, met with the predictable reaction; it decreed general thanksgiving and condemnation of the memory of Agrippina. Only Paetus Thrasea took a contrary course. Hitherto he had ignored, or given perfunctory assent, to senatorial adulation. Now he chose to walk out of the senate.[18] His action, Tacitus says, brought danger to Thrasea without achieving any corresponding extension of freedom for others. There follows the sardonic observation that numerous prodigies occurred, which might have been believed to portend the imminent end of the matricide's reign; in fact the indifference of the gods was such that Nero was to continue his reign and his crimes for many years to come.

The year ends (c. 19) with an obituary notice, which records the deaths of two eminent consulars, and compares and contrasts their lives and characters. Both were renowned for their eloquence, but whereas Domitius Afer's ability had been compromised by his doubtful integrity, Servilius Nonianus had added to his renown as an advocate the reputation of being a distinguished historian with a fastidiousness of character that set him apart from Afer. Distinction as an orator and as a historian, and fastidiousness of character; these are qualities that Tacitus might well lay claim to for himself.

After the sensational events of 59 the narrative of the succeeding year is cast in a relatively minor key. Between two short Rome-centred sections Tacitus continues his account of Corbulo's advance in Armenia, but though his capture of Tigranocerta marked a further Roman military success, a change in the home government's policy denied him the chance to impose a military solution. Tigranes was sent as Roman nominee to occupy the throne, and Corbulo retired to Syria, whose previous governor had recently died. The 'Tigranes' solution was to be short-lived, and Corbulo was soon once more to be actively engaged (See 15.1 ff.). The events related in 14.23–26, apparently covering the years 59 and 60, are separated from what is to follow, since Tacitus sees them as a self-contained, and abortive interlude.

The year 61 begins with the announcement of the theme that is to dominate the next eleven chapters, the revolt in Britain of Queen Boudicca (conventionally known as Boadicea) during the governorship of C. Suetonius Paullinus. Tacitus gives no hint in his narrative that the events he describes must surely have extended over more than one year. Given that Suetonius was superseded in 61, the prudent assumption must be that Boudicca's rebellion began in the previous year. The reason why Tacitus concentrated on the last two years of Paullinus' governorship[19] is not far to seek. We are to be given what is almost an epic *aristeia*, set off by graphic writing in which the horrendous and the pathetic, the heroic and the cowardly all play their part. In addition there is a strong note of moral judgment, of condemnation of the exploitation and injustice that stirred the revolt of Boudicca, and of praise for the gallantry and steadfastness of the Roman army in the field.

At its end a further judgment, both moral and political, emerges. Against Suetonius' determination to stamp out rebellion by ruthless military action the emperor's newly appointed financial agent urged that a policy of clemency was likely to achieve more. An imperial freedman, Polyclitus, was sent out to assess the situation, and reported back to Nero in a manner that suggested that, while there should be no open criticism of Suetonius, an early opportunity should be taken to replace him. The occasion soon presented itself, and Suetonius was succeeded by Petronius Turpilianus, of whom Tacitus says that he cloaked indolent inaction with the honourable name of peace (*honestum pacis nomen segni otio imposuit*; 39.3). Clearly to Tacitus the recall of

Suetonius was only too like that of his father-in-law, Agricola, who had similarly—in Tacitus' judgment—been denied the opportunity to reap the fruits of military success.

What the modern reader is likely to miss is any attempt to relate events in Britain to a strategic policy emanating from Rome; or, rather, a policy *is* implied by the moralising judgments that Tacitus makes—sensible military policy is undermined first in the province by the rapacity and insensibility of the civil administration, then by a governmental decision inspired by a financial official's jealousy of the governor's military success. Yet it is possible to discern a rational policy behind the sequence of events. Suetonius Paullinus' predecessor, Veranius, who died within a year of taking up his post, is brusquely dismissed by Tacitus as a man who forfeited a reputation for severity[20] by his obsequiousness towards Nero in his will, which he coupled with the boast that he would have completed the conquest of the province in a further two years. In fact Veranius, like Paullinus, had won a considerable reputation for his skill in operating against hill tribes in difficult country. The successive appointment of two such men at a time when the British campaign was faced with the mountainous terrain of North Wales seems a clear indication of an aggressive policy on the part of Nero and his ministers. The rebellion of Boudicca and its aftermath clearly required a reconsideration of that policy, and the replacement of Paullinus was a necessary consequence.

If Tacitus' account of Boudicca's rebellion shows a lack of historical perspective and a pronounced prejudice against those who sought to promote the pacification of Britain by non-military means, the narrative of the rebellion itself has a sustained brilliance[21] that can easily blind the reader to the solid substructure of fact on which it is based; it should be remembered that Tacitus' father-in-law, Agricola, had served as a young man of twenty on the headquarters staff of Suetonius Paullinus at the time of the rebellion. Although indications of date or time are almost totally lacking, and names of places and persons do not overload the account, all that is crucial to the impact that Tacitus seeks to make is given: Anglesey (Mona), Colchester (Camulodunum), London (Londinium) and St Albans (Verulamium); on the British side Prasutagus, king of the Iceni, his widow Boudicca, and the Trinovantes, in whose territory Colchester stood; on the Roman side, in addition to Paullinus, Petilius Cerialis, commander of the ninth legion, and Poenius Postumus, the ill-starred prefect of the camp of the second legion—we are not told where this or any of the other three legions in Britain were stationed—and, of the non-military men, the procurators Catus and Classicianus, and Nero's freedman Polyclitus. Such are the necessary *dramatis personae*; any addition would be superfluous to Tacitus' purpose. Some of the detail shows literary embellishment, and the respective speeches (both in *oratio obliqua*) with which Boudicca and Paullinus address their troops are rhetorical invention,[22] but the basic framework of events is firmly and surely organized. Rhetoric is used to emphasise what actually happened, not—as in Dio's long-winded and sensational account—as a substitute for it.

The rest of *Annals* XIV concentrates on domestic events during the rest of 61 and part of the following year, but the character of the chapters until the end of 61 differs markedly from what follows; the former section (to c. 47) is almost exclusively senatorial, what follows centres on Nero and those about him. At some time in 61 the *praefectus urbi* (prefect of the city) was killed by one of his slaves. Roman law required that all slaves under the victim's roof should be put to death along with the one guilty of his murder. In the present case four hundred slaves were at risk, and a public outcry against the severity of the law found some echo within the senate. It is at this point that Tacitus gives his first extended senatorial speech in *oratio recta* in the reign of Nero (14.43-4). Speaker, theme, and style all deserve attention. Both as a military man and jurist C. Cassius Longinus was an upholder of the old standards of strictness and severity.[23] On the present occasion he reasserts his support of 'ancient customs and laws' (*instituta et leges maiorum*) with such vigour that after him no one dare speak openly in favour of a more clement course.[24] Did Tacitus approve of the course that Cassius advocated? It has been argued that the historian would have favoured a more humane course of action. That, to say the least, is dubious.

The final chapter of the year includes the obituary notice of P. Memmius Regulus (47.1). This is the last formal obituary in the *Annals* as extant. It is uncertain why Tacitus makes no further use of a convention so strongly reminiscent of the Roman annalistic tradition. Perhaps the explanation is simple. The formal obituary implies an ordered state, in which men of note die in their beds. The next year (62) sees the beginning of that period of Nero's reign when a normal life— and death—became increasingly difficult for a prominent senator. If that is the case, the nature of Memmius' obituary takes on a particular relevance. Noted alike for *auctoritas*, *constantia* and *fama* ('his personal authority, steadfastness and good name') he none the less avoided incurring the emperor's hostility; he was the last man of such eminence in Nero's reign to do so. His obituary not only testifies to political qualities of which Tacitus approves; it marks the end of an era when such qualities could survive in public life.

The reintroduction of the *lex maiestatis* ('law of treason'; 14.48.2) bodes ill for the future, but for the moment it seems to give an opportunity for a display of senatorial independence. When the praetor Antistius was accused of having written scurrilous poems about the emperor, a proposal that he should be executed by the traditional form of punishment, by scourging, was countered by a proposal from Thrasea Paetus that it would be more in keeping with the tone of the reign, if Antistius were exiled. The exercise of clemency was virtually an imperial prerogative, and Nero was gravely offended that the senate should have effectively pre-empted his right to exercise it. However, what interests Tacitus here is clearly the behaviour of Thrasea, not that of the emperor.

This is perhaps the most appropriate point at which to consider Tacitus' attitude to this man. In the *Agricola* (42.4) Tacitus had spoken contemptuously of those opponents of imperial tyranny who had sought the publicity of a martyr's death without contributing to the common weal; in contrast to such men were those who, like his father-in-law and Tacitus himself, had continued to try to serve the state, even under evil emperors, with diligence and loyalty. Unless he were false to his own past, it is unlikely that Tacitus radically altered the view he had expressed in the *Agricola*.

Is Thrasea, then, to be placed among those who sought an ostentatious death without profit to the state?[25] In the complex of chapters (from 16.21) leading up to Thrasea's enforced suicide there is, of course, no note of censure; Tacitus does not detract anything from those who knew how to die nobly. But judgment of a man's political worth is to be made on how he lived, not on how he died. Before his death Thrasea appears twice more in Tacitus. In the same year (62) Thrasea once more delivered a powerful speech in the senate (15.20. 3–21). An influential Cretan had boasted that it lay in his hands whether or not a departing governor should receive a vote of thanks. In supporting the motion of his condemnation Thrasea went further and proposed that the practice of allowing such congratulatory motions should be stopped, thus eliminating a fertile source of corruption. The speech is rich in Sallustian phrases—a sure sign that Tacitus' interest is engaged—and Thrasea's proposal was received with great acclaim. However, the consuls, recalling how a previous proposal of Thrasea (14.48-9; see p. 176 above) had caused great embarrassment between senate and emperor, declined to put the motion until Nero could be consulted. The emperor warmly approved the motion and allowed it to be moved in his name.

But early in the next year, when a child was born to Nero and Poppaea and the senate flocked to Antium to offer congratulations on the happy event, Thrasea alone was denied admittance; Nero presumably remembered how Thrasea had reacted to Agrippina's murder. The snub was a clear indication of future danger for Thrasea *praenuntiam imminentis caedis contumeliam*; 15.23.4), though that danger was not to materialise for a further four years. If, as Tacitus later reveals (16.22.1), Thrasea now ceased to attend the senate, it is hard to believe that his conduct, in view of Nero's declared enmity, amounted to that ostentatious pursuit of martyrdom that Tacitus condemned.[26]

The death of Burrus in 62 opened the way for the appointment to joint command of the praetorian guard of Tigellinus and weakened the position of Seneca. Conscious of a rising swell of allegations against him Seneca sought an audience of the emperor, offered to surrender to him a large part of his wealth—much of it had come from Nero in the first place—and sought permission to retire from public life. After thanking Seneca for having taught him how to make an extemporaneous reply Nero declined his request in a speech of studied insincerity. Only here (14.53-6) in the whole of the *Annals* does Tacitus allow himself the luxury of giving in *oratio recta* the *pro* and *contra* of an argument. There is intended irony in the fact that the device, so loved of rhetorical historians, is used by Tacitus only when the artificiality of the occasion is apparent; *ars est non celare artem*.

With Seneca's effective power weakened, Tigellinus saw the opportunity to advance his own influence over Nero. He began to play upon Nero's fears of two men he had already banished as possible dynastic rivals, Cornelius Sulla and Rubellius Plautus; both men, he alleged, were dangerous, Sulla because he assumed a guise of indolence, Rubellius Plautus because he was an upholder of the subversive tenets of the Stoics. Nero gave orders for the execution of them both. Only when he had received confirmation of their deaths, did Nero write to inform the senate that both men were a threat to the state; the fact that they were already dead was not mentioned. The senate responded by voting to remove them from the senate—the

177

mockery, Tacitus adds, being more grievous than the crimes (*grauioribus iam ludibriis quam malis*; 14.59.4).

Nero now turned to a plan that, according to Tacitus, had lain in abeyance for three years, his divorce from Octavia and marriage to Poppaea. If Poppaea had really been as insistent as Tacitus makes her out to be at the beginning of Book XIV, it is improbable that she would have let three years elapse before gaining her end. Whatever was Poppaea's rôle in 62, the part given to her at the beginning of Book XIV should be discounted. A simpler explanation of the sequence of events offers. The continuance of Nero's nominal marriage to Octavia was politically desirable. Herself the daughter of an emperor, she enjoyed the affection and sympathy of the people, while (according to Dio) she had in Burrus a strong supporter. But with the death of the latter an obstacle to the divorce was removed. Another, more pressing factor, is likely to have weighed with the emperor. At the time of his divorce, which preceded his marriage to Poppaea by only twelve days, Poppaea was already pregnant with the child that was to be born the following January. That there may have been a popular uprising in favour of Octavia is by no means impossible, and on this occasion it is more than likely that Poppaea's apprehension expressed itself. The *oratio obliqua* that Tacitus puts in her mouth at 61.2–4 is accordingly an acceptable fiction. Events moved quickly. Octavia was banished to Pandateria; within a few weeks she was murdered on the emperor's order.

The pathos of Octavia's fate was to inspire a contemporary to write a verse tragedy entitled *Octauia* in the style of Seneca. For once Tacitus cannot restrain his indignation at the obsequious adulation with which the senate greeted her death:

> What limit will there be to my recording that gifts were decreed to temples for such atrocities? Anyone who reads, in my pages or another's, the events of those times must take it for granted that, whenever the emperor ordered exile or death, thanks were offered to the gods, and that what were once the marks of prosperity were then the signs of public disaster. Yet I shall not remain silent if any decree of the senate breaks new ground in flattery or exceeds the previous limit of submissiveness. (14.64.3)

But though the death of Octavia marks a pathetic climax, it is only one link in a chain of events that sees Nero emancipated from the restraints that had formerly been laid upon him. Henceforth he will need to consult nobody's interests but his own.

A puzzling sentence ends the Book. Seneca had to refute an accusation that he was a *socius* of Gaius Piso, who, in terror at finding his name linked to that of Seneca, embarked on his ill-fated conspiracy against Nero. The word *socius* normally implies some concerted action, often of a political nature. But the Pisonian conspiracy belongs to 65, and is specifically stated by Tacitus (15.48.1) to have originated in that year. There seems no possibility that Piso had already begun to entertain treasonable designs in 62; it is even more unlikely that there could have been any reason to accuse him of such complicity at that date.

The structural unity of *Annals* XIV is incontestable. In what remains of the *Annals* (Book XV and half of XVI) it is not possible to discern any organized relationship between Book and political development. Instead a number of substantial themes are developed, and it is convenient to deal with them separately. There are four such themes, the fourth following naturally, almost inevitably, upon the third. The four themes are the settlement of the Eastern Question, a series of domestic events (mostly, but not exclusively concerning Nero, and including the Great Fire of Rome and the consequent persecution of the Christians), the Pisonian Conspiracy, and lastly an unbroken series of executions or forced suicides of a number of prominent men, mostly senators, culminating in the deaths of Thrasea Paetus and Barea Soranus.

Tacitus' narrative deals with the Eastern Question—essentially the problem of the balance of power between Rome and Parthia and the manner in which the kingship of Armenia should be decided—in five separate sections and under the events of five separate years: 13.6–9 (AD 54); 13.34–41 (58); 14.23–6 (60); 15.1–17 (62); 15.24–31 (63); for, although each section may contain events of more than one year, Tacitus seeks to preserve the illusion of an annalistic structure and, within the year-by-year account, an appropriate balance between events at home and abroad. It is more instructive to consider the Eastern narrative as a whole, for by so doing it is possible to discern a deliberate Neronian policy, whereas in Tacitus' narrative the handling of the Eastern problem is almost (though not quite) exclusively an account of the generalship of Corbulo.

Since experience had taught both Rome and Parthia that neither could annex and hold Armenia against determined opposition from the other, each of the two great powers employed diplomacy and arms to ensure that the occupant of the Armenian throne was favourable, or at least not hostile, to it. During the dozen years from the accession of a vigorous king, Vologeses I (from about 51), Parthia and Rome in turn sought to impose their own nominee without reference to the other. For a time Roman successes under Domitius Corbulo did indeed enable Nero to place the Cappadocian Tigranes on the throne. Soon, however, Tigranes was once more under attack from Vologeses, and when Corbulo, now transferred to the governorship of Syria, wrote to Nero that the defence of Armenia required a separate command, the appointment went to one of the consuls of 61, Caesennius Paetus. After some initial success he was forced to conclude a humiliating agreement with the Parthian king to evacuate Armenia. When news of this reverse reached Rome, it was decided that Corbulo should once more be put in charge of the Armenian campaign, and that to ensure success he should be granted *imperium maius*, a power overriding that of neighbouring governors and client kings.

Corbulo quickly convinced Vologeses to accept a compromise solution, whereby the Parthian nominee, Vologeses' brother, Tiridates, should go to Rome to receive the crown of Armenia as the gift of Nero. Although it was to be three more years before Tiridates came to Rome, the Armenian problem was settled for half a century. Tacitus ends his account with a striking phrase. When it had been agreed that Tiridates should go to Rome to receive the diadem from Nero, Vologeses had written requesting that his brother should be subjected to no humiliation, but should at least receive the deference accorded to consuls; 'being accustomed (Tacitus writes) to foreign pomp, he was unaware of the Roman practice, which values effective power in an empire, and ignores vain show' (15.31). There is not a hint of irony in Tacitus' aphorism, yet in the present case it is Tiridates who has secured the real power, Nero the vain show.

For the most part Tacitus' narrative of Eastern affairs is shaped to produce a sustained panegyric of Corbulo. The point need not be laboured, but it is particularly clear in the manner in which Corbulo is introduced in 54, though four years were to pass before his army was ready to move effectively into Armenia, and in the dramatic contrast that is made between the supineness of Caesennius Paetus and the resoluteness of Corbulo. In 15.16.1 Tacitus expressly names Corbulo as a source for one of his details. It is hard to resist the conclusion that for much of the eulogistic matter and tone the same source was responsible.

It is therefore surprising that during that phase of Armenian affairs when Tigranes, the Roman puppet, was on the throne, and subsequently when Caesennius Paetus was in charge of Roman troops there, Tacitus describes Corbulo's behaviour with some equivocation.

When Tigranes' own rashness had brought Parthian arms against him, Corbulo despatched two legions to his assistance but gave instructions to their commanders that they should act with circumspection rather than haste 'because he (Corbulo) preferred to have a war on his hands rather than fight it' (15.3.1). The phrase is inordinately cryptic, but it is certainly intended to be unflattering to Corbulo. Later when Caesennius Paetus was hard pressed by Vologeses and wrote to Corbulo for help, Tacitus suggests a remarkable reason for the lack of urgency with which Corbulo responded to Paetus' request—he felt that if the danger to Paetus were allowed to mount, the glory that would accrue to his rescue act would be the greater; the allegation is gratuitous, and must surely derive from a source hostile to Corbulo.

How then are we to explain the one or two jarring notes that obtrude into the otherwise eulogistic account of Corbulo's handling of the 'Armenian problem'? At the outset there had been friction between him and the governor of Syria, Ummidius Quadratus. Later he had made no attempt to conceal his contempt for Caesennius Paetus. But Paetus, despite his disgrace in Armenia, was himself to become governor of Syria during the reign of Vespasian. It is not difficult to imagine that among his supporters there were those who, at the time or subsequently, sought to disparage the rôle played by Corbulo in Armenia and Syria. They are probably the source of those criticisms of Corbulo that Tacitus has accommodated within his narrative, without effectively trying to assess where the balance of truth lay.

The second and third phases of the Armenian Question provide almost all the material for the first third of Book xv—but not quite. Five chapters of domestic events (cc. 18–22) conclude the narrative of 62, while for 63 single chapters of domestic news at the beginning and the end of the year frame the final Armenian section. Much of the domestic material is pitched in a low key, but two incidents, one at the end of 62, the other at the beginning of 63, are treated more extensively; significantly both concern Thrasea Paetus and the emperor.

The narrative of the next year (64) is occupied exclusively with domestic events whose main theme is the degrading behaviour of Nero. It is to the description of Nero's unnatural marriage to a eunuch (it was the eunuch who played the part of the husband) that Tacitus appends a famous episode, introduced by the words *sequitur clades* ('There follows a disaster' (15.38.1)). The disaster is the Great Fire of Rome. According to Suetonius (*Nero* 38) and Dio (62.16.1ff.) Nero was responsible for the fire: he ordered it, whether to rebuild a better Rome (Suetonius) or just for the pleasure of seeing it burn (Dio)! Tacitus, alone of surviving ancient writers, is more guarded: 'it is uncertain whether it was accidental or criminally contrived by the emperor (for both versions have been recorded by authorities)'. He makes no overt attempt to discriminate between the alternatives, but leaves the reader to make up his own mind from a careful reading of his narrative. At the time of the outbreak of the fire, which broke out in the crowded shopping centre of the Circus, Nero was away from Rome and did not return until his own property was threatened by the fire. Up to this point it is wholly improbable that Nero had had anything to do with the fire. Indeed he took active steps to succour the homeless and destitute—even though the popularity that this act might otherwise have gained for him was nipped in the bud when the rumour got about that, as the fire was raging, he had enacted a dramatic version of the Fall of Troy.

On the sixth day the fire had apparently been brought under control, when a new outbreak occurred on the property of Tigellinus. This fact, which is mentioned by neither Suetonius nor Dio, caused many to believe that it was a deliberate act, designed to clear the ground for Nero's subsequent rebuilding of Rome. Among Nero's plans was a grandiose project to build a palace in keeping with his idea of his own greatness: 'he did not seek to arouse admiration by the use of jewels and gold, which had become a vulgar commonplace, but by fields and lakes, with woods on one side emphasising wildness, and on the other side open spaces and broad vistas' (15.42.1). But all this would cost money, and contributions were exacted not only from the whole of Italy, but also from the provinces. Whatever people might think of the new architecture, they resented having to pay for it.[27]

One important feature of Tacitus' account of the Great Fire is found in no other ancient author. He asserts that Nero, conscious that he had so far failed to allay the suspicion that he himself was responsible for the fire, sought to put the blame on Christians, who were crucified, torn to bits, or set alight as a public spectacle. That some Christians were executed in Rome during Nero's reign is not in doubt; Suetonius (16.2) indeed seems to commend it as a salutary measure designed to preserve law and order. The surprising thing is that no early Christian writer[28] used this example to blacken Nero's character as a persecutor of the faith. Yet Tacitus' account (15.44.2-5) is so circumstantial that its general veracity must be accepted, as must the explicit connection he makes with the fire; *ergo abolendo rumori* . . . ('accordingly, to scotch the rumour . . .') he executed Christians as scapegoats.

The whole of this passage, which is the earliest pagan testimony to the execution of Christ (*Christus*), the founder of the sect of *Christiani*, by the procurator Pontius Pilate during the reign of Tiberius, is riddled with vexatious problems. These, however, do not affect an understanding of Tacitus' attitude to the whole affair. As an ex-consul and former governor he shared the belief of his contemporary Pliny the Younger that Christianity was a subversive foreign belief not deserving of that general tolerance that Rome showed to other religions. But execution of Christians on a trumped up charge could not be justified. Even the ordinary man, though he regarded the accused Christians as guilty (presumably of arson) and as deserving any punishment they got, felt some sympathy for men who so obviously were being put to death to gorge the emperor's sadism.[29]

The narrative for the year (64) ends with a number of brief annalistic items and the statement that 'at the end of the year there was much talk of omens presaging imminent disasters' (15.47). The scene is set for the continuous account of the Pisonian conspiracy, which fills the remaining third of the Book. The year begins with a studied variant on the normal consular formula: 'Then Silius Nerva and Atticus Vestinus entered on their consulship, during which there was initiated and developed a conspiracy to which senators, knights, soldiers, even women vied in giving their allegiance' (15.48.1). No less diverse than the social position of the participants were their motives, which ranged from personal pique to disinterested love of their country.

Tacitus' narrative of the plot and its unmasking is brilliantly and— remarkably so for him—straightforwardly told. If it has one leitmotiv it is a note of moral paradox: the greatest courage and loyalty was shown by those whose social standing was the lowest. Equal courage was shown by two senators whose previous dissoluteness and effeminacy made such a quality least expected: by contrast others of their class informed on each other and perished tamely. The same contrast obtained among the military; Subrius Flavus, tribune of the praetorian cohort, and the centurion Sulpicius Asper died bravely—Tacitus makes a point of quoting the last words of them both ('the blunt and powerful words of a soldier are no less deserving of remembrance')— whereas their commander Faenius Rufus 'did not show equal resolve, but even continued his lamentations in his will' (15.68.1).

Amid the series of suicides and executions two in particular caught

Tacitus' imagination. A freedwoman, Epicharis,[30] endeavoured to win supporters for the plot among the fleet at Misenum. When betrayed and arrested, she refused to reveal anything she knew, even in the face of severe and protracted torture. The aristocratic Tacitus pays fitting and ample tribute to her heroism. The other death on which Tacitus bestows particular attention is that of Seneca. The apparent contradictions in Seneca's character attracted the comment of his contemporaries and puzzled historians of the next two generations. His advocacy, as a philosopher, of a simple and austere life was in marked contrast with his position as the emperor's tutor and—for many years—closest adviser, a position that brought him not only power but exceptional wealth. The conflicting views about him find some echo in Tacitus, but as far as the chapters (60.2-65) dealing with his suicide are concerned, another factor operates. Whatever a person's life had been, Tacitus judges the manner of his death on its own merits; fortitude in the face of death deserved, and gained from the historian's pen, its own tribute. The picture that Tacitus paints of Seneca's last hours is, accordingly, composed to emphasise the calmness of the Stoic philosopher, when commanded by the emperor to die.

There is a stylised, almost histrionic element about his final gesture. Having failed to find a quick death by opening his veins, when a dose of hemlock also had no effect, he entered a hot bath, sprinkling those about him with the water, and saying that he was pouring a libation to Jupiter the Liberator (*Ioui Liberatori*). Exactly the same words were to be used later by Thrasea Paetus, as he opened his veins and sprinkled his blood on the ground. Even if there was an element of the theatrical in the deaths of Seneca and Thrasea, the seriousness and authenticity of their last words should not be doubted.

The aftermath of the conspiracy was predictable. A further number of citizens were banished—Tacitus, who normally eschews lists, gives over twenty names in c. 71—informers were rewarded and the praetorian guard given a cash and corn largesse. Finally the senate was summoned, and obsequious decrees of gratitude were passed for the discovery and suppression of the conspiracy.

The Book end is carefully chosen to mark off the aftermath of the Pisonian conspiracy from the other events of the same year. These constitute a miscellaneous group, almost wholly domestic, and occupy the first thirteen chapters of Book XVI. They form an immediate contrast in tempo with the long, continuous sections that both precede and succeed. The initial incidents are trivial and without political significance. But at c. 7 a different note is struck. Nero forbade the distinguished jurist and consular, C. Cassius, to attend Poppaea's funeral—in a fit of temper Nero had kicked his pregnant wife—and, shortly after, wrote to the senate to procure his exile; the exact charge is not clear from Tacitus, but Cassius had continued to honour the memory of his ancestor, the tyrannicide.

About the same time the widow and father-in-law of Rubellius Plautus, murdered in 62 as one of the first victims of Tigellinus, committed suicide together, after they had ascertained that a criminal prosecution in the senate, with the certainty of a guilty verdict, threatened the father-in-law. In spite of their death the trial was carried through, and when the senate had voted that they should be punished *more maiorum* (viz. execution by scourging), Nero intervened to propose that the condemned be allowed their choice of death. Tacitus' comment ('such mockery was added to the murders that had already been carried out') recalls the comment he had made on the senatorial decree ordering the expulsion of Rubellius Plautus, when he too had already been murdered.[31]

The incomplete narrative for the year 66 (16.14–35) consists of an unbroken series of enforced suicides among the senatorial and equestrian classes. In most cases the threat of a trial, with condemnation a foregone conclusion, was enough to cause the victim to open his veins. The account culminates in a long and detailed description of the circumstances leading to the deaths of Thrasea Paetus and Barea Soranus. The highly dramatic account that Tacitus gives reflects the importance he attaches to these chapters; the lives and deaths of those who did not demean the aristocratic code of conduct deserve a lasting memorial in the pages of history.

First, though, Tacitus turns his attention to a man of a very different sort, who, nevertheless, by his manner of dying, seemed deserving of commemoration. Titus (or Gaius—the *praenomen* is uncertain) Petronius, though not previously mentioned by Tacitus, had, by his tasteful extravagance, established himself in Nero's circle as the dictator of elegance (*arbiter elegantiae*). Falling foul of the jealousy of Tigellinus, he too received the imperial command to die. Tacitus takes an obvious delight in telling how he studiously avoided the sort of end that philosophers and men of high principle cultivated. Instead there was a banquet with light-hearted conversation and versifying. But his will was devoid of the flattery of Nero and Tigellinus that some other suicides thought it prudent to include. Instead he sent Nero a letter listing every name and detail of the emperor's lubricious private life. Then, when the letter had been sealed, he broke the signet, so that it could not be used to imperil the lives of others (16.19 fin.).[32] Tacitus could have had no sympathy with the life of such a man, but he could not withhold his admiration from the manner of his death; it had style and an aristocratic touch.

Tacitus now goes on to describe the deaths of Thrasea Paetus and Barea Soranus. The section begins at c. 21 with a memorable phrase: 'After the butchery of so many notable men Nero finally conceived the desire to root out virtue itself by the murder of Thrasea Paetus and Barea Soranus' (*trucidatis tot insignibus uiris ad postremum Nero uirtutem ipsam exscindere concupiuit interfecto Thrasea Paeto et Barea Sorano*).[33] Tacitus' writing here needs virtually no comment; the organization of the material and the language employed mark this section as a sustained passage of fine writing. First Thrasea is accused in private to Nero by Cossutianus Capito (we learn now for the first time the reason for his hostility towards Thrasea: Thrasea had earlier helped to secure his conviction for extortion). The speech begins in *oratio obliqua*, but, as it warms up, switches to *oratio recta* (it is the last piece of sustained direct speech in the *Annals* as they have come down to us). After Thrasea had decided not to expose his fellow senators to the odium of being compelled to denounce him to his face, the scene moves to the senate where the arguments of Capito, supported by Eprius Marcellus in a vivid and bitter denunciation, secured his condemnation—typically enough, Tacitus leaves the reader to infer the fact.[34] Later in the same day the consul's quaestor was sent to Thrasea to impart the senate's verdict to him. Accompanied by his son-in-law, Helvidius Priscus, and the Cynic philosopher, Demetrius, with whom he had been discussing the immortality of the soul (just as Socrates had done, according to the account given in Plato's *Phaedo*), Thrasea went inside and, after his veins had been opened, sprinkling blood on the ground, he called the quaestor to him and said: 'We pour a libation to Jupiter, the Liberator. Mark it, young man; and though I pray the gods will avert the omen, yet you are born into an age when it pays to fortify your spirit with brave examples' (16.35.1).

The opening words are the same as those uttered by Seneca.[35] In both cases they are intended to recall the Stoic adage that (through death) the path to freedom is always open,[36] but in Thrasea's case the fact that they are spoken in the presence of the young quaestor underlines the political nature of the occasion. The antithesis of *libertas* and *seruitium* ('freedom and slavery') had ended the first Book of the *Annals*. But for the first time, during his account of the reign of Nero, Tacitus delimits the sphere of *libertas* by the adjective *senatoria* ('senatorial; cf. 13.49.2). Behind the phrase lurks a sinister implication. During the Republic one could speak of the freedom of an individual or of the Roman people (*libertas populi Romani*); but within the rule of law one could not (and did not) specify a freedom that was peculiar to the senate. The concept of senatorial freedom begins to be formed only when it is threatened by a despotic emperor.[37]

In what remained to be narrated before Nero's death[38] there is opportunity, both in the Jewish revolt and in Nero's tour of Greece, for Tacitus to write in a colourful and telling manner, but senatorial politics had virtually ceased by the year 66. There is, accordingly, an appropriateness in the fact that our manuscripts break off in the middle of the description of Thrasea's death.[39] In his earliest work, the *Agricola*, Tacitus had castigated those who had ostentatiously provoked the emperor's displeasure, and had suggested that a policy of 'keeping a low profile' (to use the current jargon)—the policy that he and his father-in-law had pursued—was a better alternative. Closer study had shown him that the latter alternative was not possible for a senator in the final years of Nero's reign. Industry and indolence, probity and turpitude alike might incur imperial displeasure. In such a society the most that lay within a man's power was to be true to himself and his ideals; and, when no other alternative offered, he could still die with dignity. At this point the tenets of Stoicism and the creed of the Roman aristocracy coincided, and it is because he died faithful to that tradition that Thrasea Paetus' death is recorded with such warmth by Tacitus.

The traditional pattern of an emperor's reign was of an initial period of good government, followed by a decline, gradual or sudden, into tyranny. In the case of Nero ancient testimony, it seems (see p. 163), spoke of an initial prosperous quinquennium, after which extravagance, vice and megalomania began to gather momentum, until, at the end, Nero was proclaimed a public enemy and forced to commit suicide. The final moments are graphically described in Suetonius (*Nero* 49.1; *qualis artifex pereo*, 'What an artist dies in me!'), and there is no reason to doubt that Tacitus' account was equally colourful.[40] But the loss of the last two years of Nero's life make it difficult to guess whether Tacitus was able to form a rounded view of the reign as a whole, as he had attempted to do in the case of Tiberius.[41] But the construction of *Annals* XIV offers an important clue. Beginning with the names of the consuls for the year (it is the only Neronian book so to begin), it clearly marks off what has gone before from what follows. Now what precedes, narrated in a single book (*Annals* XIII), is the narrative of the initial quinquennium (AD 54–58), a period of comparatively good government. That must surely be the traditional *quinquennium Neronis*. Book XIV itself is a deliberately shaped, self-contained unit,[42] beginning with the murder of the emperor's mother in AD 59 and ending with the murder of his wife three years later. The removal by death in the same year (AD 62) of the restraining hand of the praetorian prefect, Afranius Burrus, and the appointment in his place of the odious Ofonius Tigellinus might have been regarded as the point at which Nero's reign took a decisive turn for the worse, just as the rise of another praetorian prefect, Aelius Sejanus, had marked the critical turning point in the reign of Tiberius. But whereas Sejanus' rise is underlined by its appearance at a structurally significant point (see p. 106f.) at the beginning of *Annals* IV, the promotion of Tigellinus is given no such structural prominence; it is only one of a number of events between 59 and 62 that mark the emperor's emancipation from restraint upon his personal desires.

From AD 62 there is still no indication that Nero tried to exercise any continuous influence on matters of policy; in that sphere he remained passive, and susceptible to the promptings of such men as Tigellinus. This corresponds so closely to the tradition that we find in Suetonius and Dio that we may reasonably assume that the same general picture obtained in the missing portions of Tacitus' narrative for the end of Nero's reign. There would be plenty of opportunity for colourful writing—the reception in Rome of an oriental monarch (Tiridates), Nero's triumphal tour of Greece, the bitter fighting against the Jews, and, lastly, the whole nexus of events that led up to the revolt against Nero of provincial governors in the West and the senate's proclamation of him as *hostis*, 'public enemy'. But nowhere in this sequence is there material that is likely to have given Tacitus occasion to probe more deeply than other historians had done. The main lines of the imperial portrait were too well established, the rôle played by the senate too restricted. All that was left to Tacitus (one may hazard the guess) was to paint the traditional portrait and the events that framed it with greater brilliance than that of other writers.

# VIII

## THE SOURCES · *HISTORIES*

The first task of the historian today is clear: he must master the evidence. To do this he must not only know the evidence, but be able to assess its value and its interrelationship with other pieces of evidence. But it has to be remembered that this approach to the writing and study of history is little more than a hundred years old. For the ancient world it was different. Cicero might write (*De oratore* 2.62) 'Who does not know that it is the first law of history that it should not venture to write anything that is false', and it must have been self-evident to the Roman mind with its legal flair that witnesses were liable to give different accounts, of different reliability, of the same events: but the need to seek out all the evidence and subject it to systematic scrutiny was neither practised by Roman historians nor expected of them.[1]

The attempt to discover how Tacitus handled *his* sources faces the almost insuperable difficulty that no substantial portion of any of them survives. The difficulty is increased by the fact that Tacitus, in conformity with the normal practice of ancient historians, does not generally cite his authorities by name. In the extant books of the *Histories* only two authorities[2] are named. At 3.25.2 Vipstanus Messalla is given as Tacitus' authority for a gruesome incident in the second battle of Cremona, in which a son killed his father. Three chapters later (3.28) Messalla is again named, this time along with Pliny the Elder. That is all.

In a much larger number of cases Tacitus refers to unnamed written sources. Apart from cases where he mentions 'writers' (*scriptores*) or 'authorities' (*auctores*),[3] more general expressions, such as 'many have recorded' (3.59.3; cf. 3.54.3), certainly reproduce written accounts, while others (e.g. *sic accepimus*, 'we have received the following account' (3.38.1), or 'it is disputed whether' (3.71.4), or 'it is believed/said that' (many examples)) may, and often clearly do, refer to written sources. This still does not take us very far. Indeed, the fact that many of these examples appear where an event of particular note or notoriety occurs, such as the last moments of an emperor who dies violently,[4] may at least suggest that it is only for such moments that Tacitus consults different authorities; elsewhere (it might be assumed) he is content to follow whatever is, for the time being, his main source. That suspicion is perhaps increased by the extended sequence in 1.41, where Galba's death is described. Parallel versions in Plutarch and Suetonius indicate that in all probability the variants for Galba's last words and for the name of his killer already existed in their common source.[5] That raises doubts about the degree of independence with which Tacitus consulted and evaluated the sources available to him.

The question can be made more general. For substantial sections of Books I and II (to the death of Otho) resemblances between Tacitus and the account given by his contemporary, Plutarch, in his *Lives of Galba and Otho* are so close that dependence of the one on the other, or of both on a common source is inescapable.[6] That neither used the other as his main source is evident from a number of details that one, but not the other, includes.[7] It is best to accept that each used the same source, drawing on it not only for its general narrative, but also for a number of individual turns of phrase. Plutarch also wrote a life of Vitellius, and though that is lost, parallels between *Histories* III and Suetonius' *Life of Vitellius* suggest that the same common source was used by all three (Tacitus, Plutarch, and Suetonius) for Vitellius too.

Modern source criticism begins with Mommsen's attempt[8] to show that Tacitus' source for the early books of the *Histories* was the consular historian, Cluvius Rufus. Seven years earlier H. Nissen[9] had demonstrated that for his account of Eastern affairs in Books 31–45 Livy used Polybius as his main source, drawing on him in such a way that what he writes is often little more than a transcription, somewhat Romanised, of his Greek model.[10] Mommsen argued that 'Nissen's law' held good for Tacitus' *Histories*. If this were true, it would mean that Tacitus' rôle was in essence confined to transmuting into Tacitean Latin a pre-existing narrative.

Though scholars have not generally accepted Mommsen's identification of Cluvius Rufus as Tacitus' main source—Pliny the Elder has had more advocates[11]—there has been a general willingness to believe that 'Nissen's law' could be substantially applied to the *Histories* of Tacitus. A note of caution needs to be sounded. That Tacitus drew on the common source to a degree that would be unacceptable in a modern historian is undeniable. But the idea that he unwaveringly followed a single source is belied by the facts. The overall structure of the narrative is of his own devising, and sources other than the common source are used by him to contribute to that structure. Nevertheless it is with those elements that derive from the common source that any study of Tacitus' sources must begin. For by seeing how he has used and adapted that source we can learn much about the nature of Tacitus' historical writing.

The manner in which Tacitus handles his material can be illustrated by his treatment of three incidents during the period leading up to the first battle of Cremona on 14 April 69. Four points need to be borne in mind. First, as the parallel narrative of Plutarch (not to mention parallels in Suetonius' life of Otho and the excerpted narrative of Dio Cassius) amply demonstrates, Tacitus drew heavily on an anonymous narrative, no longer extant. Secondly he is prepared to take whole phrases, even sentences, from that earlier source and use them in a context different from that which (to judge from Plutarch) they occupied in the lost source. Thirdly, Tacitus uses additional material from sources other than that which he has in common with Plutarch. Lastly, though Tacitus' account is much the most detailed we possess, his primary aim is not to give a complete factual narrative of events.

To take the last point first. There is no firm date in the whole of the section under consideration,[12] and phrases such as *isdem diebus* ('about the same time'; 2.23.3) and *interea* ('meanwhile'; 2.24.1) leave uncertain even which of two sets of events came first. We are not told when the Vitellian troops occupied Cremona, though its seizure determined where the decisive battle of the war should take place. Uncertainty attaches to the exact location at the relevant times of the legionary troops moving to the aid of Otho from the East. Yet judgment whether it was more prudent to seek an immediate confrontation with the Vitellian armies (for Valens had now joined Caecina), as Otho himself wished, or await the substantial addition to their forces that might be expected from the East—the policy advocated by Suetonius Paullinus and supported by Marius Celsus and Annius Gallus—depends crucially on such considerations.

Fortunately, it is possible, without too great a margin of error, to reconstruct a timetable of events, based on fairly well established norms for the speed of travel of infantry, cavalry, and express courier.[13] When this is done, the Tacitean narrative, in spite of its maddening omissions, can be seen to cohere.[14] One instance may illustrate the point. According to Plutarch the appointment of Otho's brother, Titianus, to command the Othonian forces is the direct result of the failure of Suetonius Paullinus to push home the advantage gained against the enemy in the engagement *ad Castores*. This took place (probably) on 5 April. Titianus was able to come from Rome to take part in the council of war that preceded the battle of Cremona, which itself took place on 14 April. It is impossible for an express courier to have ridden from the Po and for Titianus to have got from Rome to Bedriacum, a distance of over 350 miles, between 5 and 12 April. Plutarch's causal chain cannot stand. Tacitus, like Plutarch, records the troops' dissatisfaction with Suetonius' generalship at the battle of *ad Castores*, but he deliberately separates from it Otho's appointment of his brother to the supreme command. As often, Tacitus does not make entirely clear the point at which Otho decided to transfer the command of his brother, but it is certainly earlier than the *ad Castores* engagement.

The counterpart to Tacitus' indifference to supplying details that a reader needs to know, if he is to form a complete picture of what happened, is his readiness to dwell on incidents that, for one reason or another, particularly interested him. The rhetorical nature of the 'common source' provided much material that had already been worked up to emphasise dramatic or moral highlights—the events leading up to Otho's suicide and the historian's final judgment on the emperor's life and death afford an obvious example. But Tacitus not only uses, and transmutes, this material. He extends it both by his own comment and by material clearly derived from different sources. The detailed account of the battle *ad Castores* (2.24) illustrates this well.

Plutarch's account (*Otho* 7) is straightforward and intelligible; but, in fact, it is too simple. The tale of the would-be ambushers being themselves ambushed is devoid of all particularising detail, and might appear almost anywhere at any time in the pages of Livy. Moreover Plutarch's version implies that the Othonian camp was close at hand, and that the infantry were held in reserve there, until such time as Celsus should summon them. This inherently improbable arrangement is disproved by Tacitus' detailed and circumstantial account of the engagement.

There are three significant features in Tacitus' account. First it does not consist of the generalised commonplaces of a rhetorical historian; the ultimate source of information was someone who had first-hand knowledge of what happened. That does not necessarily mean that the account is accurate, but it represents the version of someone who was there. The second point is that the detailed information is confined to details about the Othonian side. The last point is the attention that is given to Suetonius Paullinus. The suggestion presents itself that it is from him that the details of the engagement emanate. It would not be surprising if Tacitus took a particular interest in the version supplied by one who, like Tacitus' father-in-law, had been governor of Britain. That would obtain, even if Tacitus himself never met Suetonius, who may have died in the early seventies, before Tacitus came to manhood. But if Suetonius is the ultimate source of the details that Tacitus gives in this section, Tacitus has not accepted his version unquestioningly.

Tacitus' account, then, is an amalgam. Here too he utilises the common source, but he both extends and alters it by the use of material from another source, probably Suetonius Paullinus. The additional material of which Tacitus makes use leads him to produce a significantly altered version of what happened, and (as a result) material he derives from the common source is often given a different location or a different relevance. Lastly, upon the account that he has so constructed Tacitus is prepared to make his own judgment, whether explicitly or implicitly. Suetonius *was* guilty of delay in giving the signal for battle, and this *did* allow a number of Vitellian troops to escape. But the delay did not prevent the engagement from being a considerable success (*Paulini et Celsi ductu res egregie gestae*; 2.24.1) nor was it the delay that saved Caecina and his army from annihilation. That originated from a second act of Suetonius, his decision to call a halt to the action. For that decision Suetonius had a very good reason; that (Tacitus adds) might commend itself to the thinking few, but—as the version from the common source made abundantly clear—it did not convince the majority.

The same technique is shown in Tacitus' handling of an earlier episode, the defence of Placentia by Vestricius Spurinna (2.20 fin.-22). Spurinna was to live right through the Flavian dynasty and hold a third consulate in the reign of Trajan. He was a person to whom Tacitus must have spoken; his second consulship fell in 98, a year after that of Tacitus. There is sufficient common material in Plutarch and Tacitus to show that the latter drew on the same source (our putative common source) as Plutarch—the near-mutiny of Spurinna's over-confident troops, including the threat of physical violence to their general, the accusations of treachery which they levelled against him, and during the siege itself the Vitellian taunts against the Othonian troops (especially the praetorians) as being more used to being spectators at games than to fighting. But once again Plutarch's version

(*Otho* 6) is over-simplified and over-dramatised. According to him, it is the enemy taunts, made during the initial stages of the siege, that cause Spurinna's troops to discard their earlier insubordination and beg him to reassert discipline and authority over them; this is scarcely the way troops behave in real life. Tacitus has a much more detailed account. Two features distinguish his account of the siege from that of Plutarch. First the siege extended over two days, a fact which makes the determination of the attackers and the heroism of the defenders all the more notable. Secondly, from the outset Spurinna's men are resolute; when their opponents taunt them with being spineless and addicted to the circus and theatre, they give as good as they get. There is no question of it being the taunts that restored discipline among them; that had already been achieved by the earlier route march, described by Tacitus (2.18–19), but omitted by Plutarch.

The amount of detail that Tacitus gives to these events seems almost certainly to reflect Spurinna's pride in his achievement. For Tacitus those details had a twofold importance. They enabled him to amplify and correct the version that was available in the common source; and at the same time they gave him an opportunity to elaborate on congenial themes, on military morale and discipline, and on moral values such as *pudor* (a sense of shame as a spur to action) and *gloria* (renown won by valorous action). In so doing he was willing to incorporate material from the common source, but it had to be fitted into the narrative framework which his greater knowledge of detail here enabled him to provide. There can be little doubt that—due allowance having been made for Spurinna's understandable exaggeration of the importance of the incident—Tacitus' account comes much closer to what actually happened than does that of Plutarch.

A third illustration of how Tacitus handles his source material has already been considered,[15] but may merit a brief recapitulation because of its striking nature. Immediately after his description of the Othonian council of war at Bedriacum (*Otho* 8) Plutarch speaks of other reasons, which, according to various writers, influenced the speakers. There was (it was alleged) an inclination among both armies to come to an agreement and select one of their generals (or, failing that, leave it to the senate to do so) as emperor in place of Otho or Vitellius. Plutarch (apparently giving his own opinion) comments that it was indeed probable that many experienced soldiers, conscious of the sufferings caused by the civil wars between Sulla and Marius, and between Caesar and Pompey, did entertain such thoughts. Tacitus uses the same material, but in a different place and with a different interpretation (2.37). He dismisses with scorn the possibility that in an age riddled with corruption (*corruptissimo saeculo*) the ordinary soldier would have been willing to exchange war for peace, and from this point he develops, as a digression, a more general theme of Actonian reflection: love of power not only corrupts, but also increases with the extension of empire. Using the same historical examples as Plutarch, Tacitus comes to a more pessimistic and more realistic conclusion; as the citizen armies at the end of the Republic were unwilling to settle the issue other than by force of arms, *a fortiori* the armies of Otho and Vitellius would not do so. Thus Tacitus uses material borrowed from the common source to controvert that source.

In the last chapter of Book II Tacitus writes of the treacherous compact of Caecina and Lucilius Bassus to desert the Vitellian cause:

> Contemporary writers, who have written an account of the war during the period when the Flavian dynasty ruled, ascribed to them (sc. Caecina and Bassus) motives of patriotism and a concern for peace. . . . My own view . . . is that they were motivated by jealousy, because they feared that others might outstrip them in Vitellius' favour. (2.101)

Among the historians whom Tacitus is criticising may be the pro-Flavian Jew, Flavius Josephus. According to Josephus Vespasian yielded reluctantly to the overwhelming demands of his troops to assume the purple. They in turn are portrayed as being moved by resentment at the behaviour of Vitellius and his troops in Rome—a chronological impossibility, since Vitellius cannot have reached Rome till the very end of June or early July, while Vespasian's own proclamation was made in Egypt on 1 July. Further, the part of Mucianus is played down in Josephus, the proclamation of Vespasian by Tiberius Alexander in Egypt is deliberately postdated to make it appear to result from the spontaneous proclamation of Vespasian by his own troops, and the rôle of Vespasian's son, Titus, is 'whitewashed', his return from Greece on receipt of news of Galba's assassination being ascribed to a 'divine impulse', while the main narrative suppresses any hint that he had earlier been engaged as a go-between between Vespasian and Mucianus, and thus privy to earlier discussions of the possibility of a concerted revolt by the troops in the East.

In Tacitus the events are very differently narrated and causally connected. Titus' function as an intermediary is suitably stressed, the reasons for his return from Greece are discussed in terms of political advantage, and the possibility is there mentioned of Vespasian making a bid for power; the rôle of Mucianus as 'kingmaker' is heavily underlined (including a speech in *oratio recta*; 2.76–77); lastly, the sequence of events is made abundantly clear—first proclamation in Egypt on 1 July, then by Vespasian's own troops two days later, and then, by the middle of the month, throughout Syria.

The assessment one makes of Tacitus' handling of his sources during the civil war of 68–69 depends in large measure on the estimate one makes of his relationship to the common source on which Plutarch, Suetonius (and Dio Cassius) also drew. But with the death of Vitellius at the end of Book III Tacitus' narrative enters a new phase. For the first time since the beginning of the *Histories* an emperor is in uncontested control of the Roman world. The changed emphasis, which is marked by a reversion to the traditional structure of Roman historical writing, with its alternation between events at home and abroad, brings with it a different attitude to the use of available sources. For affairs at home Tacitus concentrates almost entirely on senatorial events and relations between emperor and senate. There is little doubt that the information about senatorial business and debate ultimately comes from the *acta senatus*.[16]

The main thread that runs through these chapters (4.3.3 ff. the debate on 21 December; 4. 39 ff. the meeting of the senate on 1 January 70 (and an unspecified number of subsequent meetings)) is clear. Two themes predominate: the attempt of individual senators to settle old scores with other members of their order, especially powerful *delatores* such as Eprius Marcellus, Vibius Crispus and Aquilius Regulus; and, secondly, the attempt of some senators to reassert the independence of the order, before the new régime had fully established itself, and while Vespasian himself was still absent from Rome—he was to arrive in Rome only in the summer of 70. The two themes unite in the person of the designate praetor, Helvidius Priscus, who both sought to pursue a personal vendetta against Eprius Marcellus, and was the author of two abortive proposals (9.1) that would have asserted the authority of the senate above that of Vespasian. Tacitus introduces Helvidius at some length (4.5.1–6.1), adding biographical details that certainly did not come from the *acta senatus*; and to both Helvidius and Eprius Marcellus he accords (in reported speech) opposing speeches of some length and importance. It is typical of Tacitus' ambivalence that in spite of the moral superiority he allows to Helvidius, it is to Eprius Marcellus that he gives the more telling, and more successful speech (cc. 7 and 8 respectively).

Conversely, when Tacitus gives the only speech in Book IV in *oratio recta* (4.42.3-6) to the estimable senator Curtius Montanus, the speaker's splendid oratory is deliberately emphasised by Tacitus to point the contrast with the realities of the situation. Since the arrival in Rome during the last week of December of Mucianus, Vespasian's chosen vicegerent, it was with him that real power resided (*uis penes Mucianum erat*; 4.39.2): eloquent debate could achieve nothing.[17]

The extensive coverage that Tacitus gives in Books IV and V to the revolt of the Batavian, Iulius Civilis, and the ensuing insurrection in Germany and Gaul betrays both Tacitus' interest in the Rhine frontier and the use of a source or sources that provided much detailed information. Pliny the Elder is known to have served for most of a decade in Germany, and his writings include a work in twenty books on 'all the wars we have waged with the Germans'.[18] The Elder Pliny was an indefatigable compiler—according to his nephew he never read any book without making notes from it—and it is inconceivable that Tacitus did not make use of this work here, as he certainly did in writing *Annals* I, where the Elder Pliny is named (1.69.2). Some of the qualities of his writing may be gathered from his *Natural History*, whose thirty-seven books survive. A work of immense, but ill-digested learning, it is thorough and pedestrian.

The greatest merit of Tacitus' account is its awareness of the complexity of the situation. Civilis' personal ambition and resentment against the Romans, the differing motives actuating the Batavians (especially the irksomeness of the levy), the Germans beyond the Rhine (mainly plunder), and the Gauls (only patchy and belated support under the unrealistic banner of an *imperium Galliarum*), the crucial accession to Civilis' military strength of the Batavian cohorts from near Mainz, the initial encouragement of Civilis by Antonius Primus and Hordeonius Flaccus—all are clearly brought out as contributory elements to the course and nature of the revolt; and no less clearly does Tacitus emphasise that neither among the tribes of German stock nor amongst the Gauls was there anything like universal support for the cause of rebellion—on the contrary the Romans continued to receive aid, including military support, from some Gallic tribes, while the colony of Cologne went to some considerable lengths to preserve its pro-Roman stance. Tacitus' account, then, is of a complex defection from Roman rule; in that movement nationalism was an important factor in encouraging the revolt from Rome, but the desire to throw off a yoke that had come to be felt particularly oppressive is not to be taken (nor is it so taken by Tacitus) as proof of a realistic desire to set up an alternative *imperium* of Gaul or Germany or both in its place.

Tacitus' version is refreshingly free from the pro-Flavian bias that vitiates the account of Josephus. He applauds bravery and stigmatises cowardice, wherever they occur; the cancerous dissension between troops and officers on the Roman side is repeatedly stressed, while neither Dillius Vocula's bravery nor Petilius Cerialis' military success stop Tacitus from criticising the former's tactical inadequacies and the latter's imprudence. If there was any pro-Flavian bias in Pliny's account,[19] there is nothing of it in Tacitus.

Three conclusions may be drawn for Tacitus' account of affairs in and near Germany at this time. Pliny may well have been a substantial source, but cannot have been the sole source for Tacitus. Next, if any pro-Flavian bias was shown by Pliny in this part of his work, Tacitus was able to correct it. Lastly, whatever the source or sources from which he has gathered his material, Tacitus has imposed on it his own over-view of the events, their causes, and their interrelationship. Moreover, the treatment of the whole section bears his own unmistakable imprint, in which moral judgment and dramatic impact unite to give a peculiarly Tacitean emphasis and profile to the narrative. In the last resort, here too as elsewhere, it is this that counts rather than trying to put a name or names to the sources he has employed.[20]

# IX

## THE SOURCES · *ANNALS*

### 1 · TIBERIUS

The loss of all the *Histories* after AD 70 deprives us of the opportunity of observing how Tacitus handled his material as he moved into the period when he himself had taken an active part in politics. Even had he wished to adopt some other writer's account as the basis of his own, no one had as yet imposed his version of history on the reigns of Vespasian, Titus and Domitian; Tacitus must have sought and sifted his own material. Whether that enabled him to take a more detached view of Domitian than that he gives in the *Agricola*[1] is uncertain; probably not.

When he came to write the *Annals*, the main lineaments of portraits of the Julio-Claudian emperors had already been firmly established. The first chapter of the *Annals* reveals Tacitus conscious that the history of an emperor's reign was inevitably falsified—by flattery during his life-time, by hatred after his demise. How then was Tacitus to attempt to strike a truthful and impartial balance between those two extremes? The beginning of Tiberius' reign lay a century away, and Tacitus had necessarily to rely on the written record of authorities whose bias he was aware of, but not always able to control.

As in the *Histories* Tacitus gives us virtually no indication in the Tiberian hexad of the *Annals* who his authorities were. Pliny the Elder is named at *Ann.* 1.69.2 for a detail concerning the elder Agrippina, wife of Germanicus. Tacitus names Pliny as *Germanicorum bellorum scriptor* ('writer of the German Wars'). The manner in which he is cited suggests that he is being named as the authority for an additional detail rather than as his main source. The only other person named as a source by Tacitus in the Tiberian books is the Younger Agrippina (mother of Nero), whose memoirs (*commentarii*) are quoted as the authority for a detail about her mother, which (Tacitus says) is not recorded by the writers of history (*scriptores annalium*; 4.53.2). That is all.[2]

There are also a number of references to anonymous authorities, 'some record/have recorded' (*quidam tradunt/tradidere* etc.). In most of these cases, scarcely totalling a dozen for the whole of *Annals* I-VI, the words introduce an additional fact for which there is *some* authority,[3] or a variant on the version already stated. So at 1.13.3 after mentioning the names of three senators Tacitus writes: 'There is agreement about the two former names: in place of Arruntius some authorities have given the name of Cn. Piso';[4] or, in the case of the appearance in the senate for his trial of Libo Drusus (2.29.2) 'he was carried to the doors of the senate-house, sick with fear and ill, or, as some have recorded, pretending to be ill . . .'. At 1.29.4 the differing versions are made explicit, *tradunt plerique . . . alii* ('the majority report . . . some (sc. say)'), while at 1.80.2 there are three versions.

Somewhat more specific, though still without mention of names, are cases where *scriptores* or *auctores* ('writers', 'authorities') are mentioned. In 1.81.1 Tacitus confesses his inability to find out the truth about the conduct of consular elections in Tiberius' reign—'so varied are the accounts not only in historians but also in Tiberius' own speeches'. For this point, at least, Tacitus' words guarantee that he has consulted a number of historians and the primary authority of the emperor's speeches. Where did he find the speeches of Tiberius? Possibly in the *acta senatus*,[5] but not necessarily so; it is possible that they were published separately.[6] In any case Tacitus did not believe that consulting the emperor's *ipse dixit* necessarily revealed the truth.

On one or two occasions (in *Annals* I-VI) Tacitus himself interposes to supplement or correct what he has found in earlier writers. According to most authorities Tiberius' retirement to Capri had been engineered by Sejanus. Tacitus first gives that account (4.57.1), 'following the majority of writers', but then expresses his own doubts: if that had been the case, why did Tiberius continue to live at Capri after Sejanus' exposure and death? A more likely explanation, Tacitus suggests, was that Tiberius found the privacy of life on the island the ideal way of concealing his cruelty and lusts.[7] In the same way at 4.53.2 he mentions a detail not recorded by the writers of history (*scriptores annalium*) which he has found for himself in the memoirs of the Younger Agrippina. Two other passages deserve attention. Tacitus gives an account of the death of Tiberius' son, Drusus, which he says is that given by the majority of writers; he then records at some length a persistent rumour that gave a different, and more sensational account of what had happened (4.10–11). On this occasion Tacitus accepts the 'standard' version, and goes to some pains to discredit the rumour.

In 3.3.2, writing of the funeral of Germanicus, Tacitus notes that neither in any historian nor in the 'daily gazette' (*non apud auctores rerum, non diurna actorum scriptura*) could he find any mention that Germanicus' mother had taken a prominent part in the funeral. The notice has a double interest. First, it shows that at least on occasion Tacitus would consult both historians and public documents. And, secondly, it reminds us of the existence of the 'daily gazette' (usu. *acta diurna*), which was instituted by Julius Caesar, along with the *acta senatus*, for the editing of which an editor had been appointed by Tiberius (5.4.1). Though it is uncertain how much detail the latter contained, they must have contained a list of all motions proposed— whether successful or not—the names of the chief speakers and at least some others. They may also have contained the main heads of the arguments advanced by the protagonists; but it is unclear whether they contained any of the speeches in full, or whether references to speeches delivered in the senate derive from their separate publication after the event—it is clear from Pliny (*Ep.* 5.8.6) that this was not an unusual practice.

The existence of such non-literary evidence does not guarantee that Tacitus made regular use of it. But a letter of the Younger Pliny to Tacitus, in which Pliny writes of the part he has taken in an important political trial, says that the incident will not have escaped the historian's watchful eye, 'since it is in the public records' (*cum sit in publicis actis*; 7.33.3). This, on the face of it, implies that Tacitus would customarily look at such archival material.[8] But that he did not always do so is suggested by another passage (2.88.1): 'I find in the writers and senators[9] of those times (he is talking of AD 19) that a letter from the chief of the Chatti was read in the senate, promising the death of Arminius by poison . . .? Was this item not to be found in the *acta senatus*?[10] The failure to mention the *acta senatus* at 1.81.1 (see p. 2 above) might seem to result from the same *modus operandi* by Tacitus, but on that occasion it is unlikely that a matter that was deliberately kept obscure by Tiberius could have been cleared up by reference to the *acta*; if they said anything, they are likely only to have compounded the obscurity.

If to the sources already mentioned there are added biographies, autobiographies, the occasional consultation of inscriptions, and some orally transmitted information, the main sources available to Tacitus will have been covered. But their enumeration helps but little towards understanding what part each of them played as sources for Tacitus. Nevertheless, the passages quoted in the preceding pages suggest (as do those still to be mentioned in dealing with the sources for the later books of the *Annals*) that Tacitus drew on the writings of earlier historians to a greater extent than would be expected or permitted of a modern historian. So three questions remain to be looked at. What histories of the period were available to him, which of them did he use, and what use did he make of them?

Even to the first of those questions there is no very satisfactory answer. It is ironical that the only work which substantially survives, that of Velleius Paterculus, written immediately before the downfall of Sejanus, is so adulatory of both Tiberius and his first minister that it was ignored by all subsequent Roman historians.[11] Two historians, whose work does not survive, wrote of Tiberius' reign (at least) and are included in the brief list of Roman historians whom, along with Sallust and Livy, Quintilian mentions as worthy to be compared with Greek historians. The two are Servilius Nonianus and Aufidius Bassus. Servilius was consul in AD 35 and figures in a double obituary in 59 (*Ann.* 14.19), where Tacitus pays tribute to his moral qualities and his fame as a historian; like Tacitus himself he had earlier made a name as an orator. Quintilian speaks well of him, but says that he was less concise than the dignity of history requires.

From that fault he exempts Aufidius Bassus, though he adds that his work did not always sustain the same standard. He was the author both of a history of 'the German war', whatever period that may have covered,[12] and a historical work of such note that the Elder Pliny could describe his own history (in thirty-one books) as its continuation (*a fine Aufidi Bassi*). Neither starting point nor finishing point of Aufidius' history is known. The only surviving fragment of his writing is an account of Cicero's death (43 BC), but there is no certainty that that comes from the history. Its terminal point has been variously surmised, with most scholars favouring a date close to AD 50. There is no indication that he was a senator, or indeed took any part in public life—a stance fully in keeping with the fact that he was an Epicurean.[13]

Since the enumeration of names is so unrewarding, the approach already followed for the *Histories* again recommends itself. For though there is no parallel account for the reign of Tiberius of such closeness as that which exists between Tacitus and Plutarch for Galba and Otho, a direct comparison is possible both for the beginning and the end of his reign with the history of Cassius Dio (here complete), as well as with information contained in Suetonius' life of Tiberius.[14]

The first point at which close comparison becomes possible is in the account given by the three writers of the death of Augustus and the accession of Tiberius. Problems begin with events immediately before Augustus' death. Did Augustus visit the banished Agrippa Postumus on the island of Planasia? Next, Augustus' death. Was it from natural causes, or was he murdered? Was he still alive, or already dead, when Tiberius reached him at Nola? And was the announcement of his death deliberately delayed by Livia?[15]

It is notable that throughout Dio takes the view most unfavourable to Tiberius and Livia, Suetonius the most favourable, while Tacitus generally gives both alternatives. So Dio states as fact that Augustus sailed secretly to see Agrippa Postumus, and was thought likely to be reconciled with him. Because of this, 'so they say' (the Greek equivalent to *tradidere quidam*) Livia, to safeguard Tiberius' succession, poisoned Augustus with some figs—though even Dio expresses some doubt about the allegation of poisoning. Suetonius has no mention of a visit to Agrippa and no mention of a suspicion that Livia may have poisoned Augustus. In Tacitus the more opprobrious version is introduced by 'and some suspect a criminal act on the part of his wife. For a rumour had got about that a few months previously . . . Augustus had sailed to Planasia to see Agrippa' (1.5.1).

Similarly, on the question of whether Tiberius reached Augustus' bedside before he died, Suetonius' version—surely, in view of the amount of circumstantial detail, the correct one—states quite clearly that Augustus and Tiberius talked together at some length. According to Dio the majority and more trustworthy witnesses record that Augustus was already dead when Tiberius arrived; though he notes that some authorities say that Tiberius was present to receive some last instructions from Augustus. Tacitus leaves open the question whether Tiberius found Augustus alive or dead. Shortly after, a close verbal similarity (*Ann.* 1.6.3 in. = Suet. *Tib.* 22 fin.) makes it overwhelmingly probable that Tacitus and Suetonius are using a common source here.

The same is true of the parallels between *Ann.* 1.12 and Dio 57.2.5-7, in which the exchange in the senate between Asinius Gallus and Tiberius contains a number of very close verbal similarities.[16] But there are points in each writer (more in Tacitus) that the other writer does not have; more important, there are points at which the two writers give disparate versions (esp. over the exact nature of Tiberius' reply). Dio cannot, therefore, have used Tacitus exclusively, though he may have used Tacitus, or the same source as Tacitus, for much of his narrative. At the very least Tacitus or Dio must have used one source not shared with the other.

One particularly revealing instance is the appearance in both Tacitus and Dio of a wholly improbable suggestion that Augustus' choice of Tiberius to succeed him was dictated by the desire to enhance his own reputation in people's eyes when they compared him with the unattractive Tiberius (*Ann.* 1.10.7 = Dio 56.45.3). Suetonius, too, knows the 'invidious comparison', but spends some time in arguing against its probability (*Tib.* 21.2 fin.-7). It has been suggested that Suetonius is here explicitly trying to controvert Tacitus (the fact that he does not mention Tacitus' name is of no matter, since, as we have seen, Latin historians tend not to name authorities). But Suetonius speaks of a 'general belief' (*uulgo persuasum*), and Tacitus and Dio give it, not as their own belief, but either as that of critics hostile to Augustus (so Tacitus) or as the suspicions entertained by 'some' unnamed persons (so Dio).

Yet, though Tacitus draws—at times heavily—on the same source as Suetonius and Dio, it is not difficult to see that, in spite of the fact that he writes impressionistically rather than explicitly, he not only supplies a good deal more factual detail, but also has a much clearer picture than Suetonius and Dio of the underlying chronological and causal sequence of events. Without allowing the reader the luxury of precise dates, he distinguishes clearly between the sessions of the senate, at the first of which only the will of Augustus was read and the arrangements made for his funeral; and because he had a sure grasp of the chronology, he avoids the nonsensical idea, stated explicitly by Dio (57.7.1) and flirted with by Suetonius (*Tib.* 25), that Tiberius put off accepting a formal conferment of power until he could be sure that Germanicus was not minded to use the German legions, which he commanded, to claim the purple for himself.[17]

It has been a vexed question of scholarship whether the common source thus inferred was responsible for the main features of the portrait of Tiberius that is visible in all our written authorities, and, if so, when that portrait was first drawn. The theory of Eduard Schwartz[18] that an unknown annalist of great talent, probably writing soon after Tiberius' death, was responsible for giving shape to that portrait, has many adherents. It is the simplest theory that will account for the many common elements that exist in subsequent writers (especially Tacitus, Suetonius, and Dio), and when we look at some of the events covered in *Annals* VI and the corresponding parts of Dio's narrative, it will become still clearer that there was a literary source that provided not only incidents but also turns of phrase that were taken over by later writers.[19]

It is important neither to exaggerate nor to minimise the influence of the common source on Tacitus. Since Dio survives only in brief excerpts from AD 17 to 31, direct comparison is possible only for the beginning of Tiberius' reign and its last six years. For the earlier period some indication has already been given of the closeness of Tacitus and Dio (and, in parts, Suetonius). But even for the years 15 and 16 (to *Ann.* 2.41) the differences are far more noticeable than the resemblances, and it is difficult to believe that, had Dio survived complete, he would have shown the same structure as Tacitus—to take a single example, the fact that Tacitus' narrative for AD 18 concentrates exclusively upon Germanicus in the East must be the result of deliberate choice by Tacitus.

In the closing years of Tiberius' reign similarities between Tacitus and Dio abound. The parallelism is particularly close in their narratives for the years 34 and 35 (*Ann.* 6.28-39 :: Dio 58.24-26.4):

| TACITUS | DIO |
|---|---|
| **28** Appearance of phoenix in Egypt; its nature | The appearance of the phoenix is recorded in 27.1 (A.D. 36), where it is one of a number of events thought to presage the death of Tiberius; no information is given about the nature of the bird |
| **29** Suicides of Pomponius Labeo and Mamercus Scaurus | **24.3-5** Suicides of Pomponius Labeo and Mamercus Scaurus |
| **31-38.1** Eastern affairs, centring on Artabanus of Parthia | **26.1-4** Eastern affairs, involving Artabanus of Parthia |
| **38.2-3** Suicide of Fulcinius Trio | **25.2-3** Suicide of Fulcinius Trio |
| **39.3** Death of Poppaeus Sabinus; his obituary | **25.4** Death of Poppaeus Sabinus |

It is not, perhaps, surprising that during the last years of Tiberius' life, when he was away from Rome, historians found themselves at a loss for matter that was both interesting and important, but it cannot be mere coincidence that Tacitus and Dio have so many items in common. Apart from the fact that for the year 35 Tacitus has the order

'Eastern affairs/home affairs' whereas Dio has the reverse order, two points of detail need noting. The first is that the two historians give different dates for the appearance of the phoenix in Egypt. The second point is that Dio records (at 25.1) the appearance of a false Drusus (son of Germanicus) in 34, whereas Tacitus has it under the year 31. Though these are in themselves minor points, they help to show that the relationship of the two authors to their sources is neither simple nor uniform. For whereas Dio's information about the phoenix might, apart from the date, derive from Tacitus,[20] the two accounts of the false Drusus are irreconcilable. There are other items too in the sequence of events given by the two writers for 34 and 35—a sequence which at first sight seems to have so much in common—where the versions of the two writers are in conflict (e.g. the responsibility for the death of Mamercus Scaurus (Macer or Tiberius himself?), and the accounts of the death of Poppaeus Sabinus).

The influence of the unknown annalist on Tacitus is undeniable. He may even have been responsible for drawing what became the definitive portrait of Tiberius' character, with its traits of dissembling and rancorous tyranny. But for more than a decade at the beginning of Tiberius' reign Rome was the centre of political life, and all roads led to Tiberius. What we can deduce from the common elements in Tacitus and Dio suggests that their common source was fond of the dramatic and the rhetorical. These elements are not lacking in Tacitus, but the core of his portrait of Tiberius depends on his attempt to come to grips with the person of the emperor himself and of relations between him and the senate until his final departure from Rome in AD 26. That necessitated a deeper knowledge of his actions and pronouncements and of the senate's behaviour than was likely to have been available in the pages of the unknown annalist.

Much of the material was to be found in the *acta senatus*, while the speeches of Tiberius, whether they appeared in the *acta* or not, were available and were studied by the historian. But it is going too far when Syme writes of the sources of *Annals* I-VI that 'the straight path of enquiry leads to the archives of the senate. That is the only "single source"' (p. 278) and 'it is not rash to conclude that Tacitus . . . decided to build up much of the first hexad on a steady and conscientious employment of the primary material' (p. 286). That, at best, is true only of parts such as the extensive domestic sections of Book III, where the structure he had chosen for the first half of Tiberius' reign would necessarily lead him to copious consultation of the *acta senatus*.

But there is nothing to prove that he examined the *acta* with the same thoroughness for the whole of Tiberius' reign; indeed, after the fall of Sejanus in 31, with the emperor continuously absent from Rome, it is likely that the *acta* could have offered little that would serve Tacitus' needs.

## 2 · CLAUDIUS

The question of Tacitus' sources for what survives of the reign of Claudius can be dealt with more briefly than adequately. No source is named in the one and a half books that remain, and references to anonymous writers are infrequent, though that may be an accident. Predictably, it is on the circumstances surrounding the death of Claudius, allegedly by poison, that the most explicit reference to *temporum illorum scriptores* ('writers of those times' 12.67.1) occurs.

But some observations can be made. Our manuscripts of the later books of the *Annals* resume in the year 47 with the trial of Valerius Asiaticus. Dio's version (60.29.4–6) differs markedly from Tacitus'. It is a reasonable conjecture that they followed different sources. Shortly afterwards the two authors give virtually identical accounts of Corbulo's recall from Germany, both authors presumably now following the same source. Not too much should be built upon that hypothesis. Unless one believes that both Tacitus and Dio followed a single source through thick and thin, there is no reason why domestic and foreign affairs should have come from the same source.[21]

Two further points may be noted. The speech made by Claudius in the senate in favour of admitting Gallic nobles to the Roman senate (11.24) is Tacitus' own composition, but it clearly shows acquaintance with the speech that was actually delivered.[22] That may have come from a separate publication of the emperor's speeches or—if they contained such detail—the *acta senatus*. Use of the *acta senatus* for other sections of the domestic narrative of Claudius' reign is self-evident.

## 3 · NERO

The literary tradition of the reign of Nero was, like that of Claudius, sufficiently uniform for it to cause no surprise that the portrait drawn by Tacitus and Dio is substantially the same. That is not invalidated by the fact that in one significant area, the treatment of Seneca, the two historians take palpably different lines, Dio consistently taking a hostile view, Tacitus remaining more impartial, or at worst ambivalent. But resemblances between the two writers (with many further parallels in Suetonius too) are sufficiently numerous and detailed to make it certain that they were able to draw independently on a common source. In Tacitus there are also, as there were in *Annals* I-VI, a number of anonymous references, e.g. 13.17.2 'the majority of writers of those times record' (*tradunt plerique eorum temporum scriptores*), 14.9.1 (of the report that Nero viewed and praised his murdered mother's body—stated as a fact by Dio 61.14.2; cf. Suetonius *Nero* 34) 'some have affirmed it, others deny it', 15.54.3 'as the majority have reported'.

But an additional factor of importance is introduced by two passages, in 13.20 and 14.2 respectively. In the earlier passage, after reporting that an unsuccessful attempt to convict Agrippina of treason threatened also to cause the removal from his post as prefect of the praetorian guard of Afranius Burrus, Tacitus continues:

> Fabius Rusticus states that a letter of credentials was sent to Caecina Tuscus, conferring on him command of the praetorian cohorts, but that the efforts of Seneca kept the post for Burrus: Pliny and Cluvius make no mention of doubt being entertained about Burrus' reliability. And, of course, Fabius tends to sing Seneca's praises—he owed his position to Seneca's patronage. But it is my intention to follow my sources, where they are unanimous: but where they have given different reports, I will record them under their names.

This is a remarkable promise, quite unlike anything that has occurred in the earlier books of the *Annals* (or *Histories*, for that matter). The passage carries no implication for events where documentary evidence was available, such as the *acta senatus* for senatorial business. But for the present nexus of incidents, where there was no documentary evidence to which Tacitus could refer, his testimony is explicit: he is dependent on three named literary sources—no more.[23]

At the beginning of Book XIV a similar passage occurs. 'Cluvius records' that Agrippina sought to restore her waning influence with her son by offering him an incestuous relationship. Fabius Rusticus says that the initiative came from Nero, not from Agrippina. But, says Tacitus, Cluvius' version was supported by the remaining authorities, and it was intrinsically more in keeping with Agrippina's character that she should take the initiative. Two points call for comment. First, Tacitus has gone back, to some extent, on his promise to name all his

authorities when they give divergent accounts.[24] Secondly, since the
plural *ceteri quoque auctores* implies at least two authorities, that with the
addition of the two named writers, Fabius and Cluvius, means that for
the present incident Tacitus must have consulted at least *four*
authorities. That contrasts with 13.20, where (on the normal interpretation) only three authorities existed. Doubtless the spiciness of the
incident attracted additional writers!

In the rest of the *Annals* there is no further mention of Cluvius Rufus.
Fabius Rusticus is cited by name once more, at 15.61.3, for an
additional detail concerning Seneca; Pliny is mentioned by name at
15.53.3 for a detail that Tacitus roundly dismisses as absurd, and is
alluded to in uncomplimentary terms at 13.31.1. Otherwise Tacitus
reverts to his practice of referring to variants anonymously. The
contrast between what he had promised at 13.20 (and partly observed
at 14.2) and later cases where alternatives are mentioned is stark and
not to be explained away.[25] One must (it seems) assume that Tacitus
changed his mind during the process of composition. There is nothing
remarkable about that, but it is scarcely in keeping with that 'steady
and conscientious employment of the primary material' which Syme[26]
believes to have been Tacitus' method of work in the first hexad.

Whatever the reason for Tacitus' abandonment of the promise he
had made at 13.20 to name the authors responsible for variant
versions, there is in the same book one notorious case where variant
versions existed, yet Tacitus makes no mention of the fact. At 13.46
Tacitus tells how Poppaea, already the wife of the later emperor, Otho,
set out to capture the affections of Nero. No mention is made of the fact
that at *Hist*. 1.13 he had given a different version, one that is found also
in Plutarch, Suetonius and Dio. According to that version Poppaea
was already Nero's mistress when he got Otho to marry her as a cloak
for his own liaison. One can only presume that Tacitus was reluctant to
refer to a version which he himself had once accepted, but now
believed to be false.

If there are sections of the narrative of Nero's reign—especially those
involving the emperor and his family—where Tacitus seems to have
worked directly from literary sources, it does not necessarily follow that
he did so, when documentary evidence was available. The only
explicit reference in the *Annals* to the use of the *acta senatus* occurs in the
Neronian reign (at 15.74.3), and it is preceded (in 15.71) by a list of
persons banished after the failure of the Pisonian conspiracy that itself
probably comes from the *acta*. But did Tacitus begin with primary

sources (here principally the *acta*) or did he refer to documentary sources to supplement a basic narrative derived from pre-existing literary sources? There is no easy answer. But if we take Tacitus' narrative of the Pisonian conspiracy (15.48–74), a long continuous section that includes the reference just mentioned to the *acta senatus*, there are between Tacitus and Dio such close resemblances[27] that the existence of a literary source, on which both writers drew heavily, must be assumed.

Yet it is clear that Tacitus looked for information beyond that supplied by men such as Cluvius, Pliny and Fabius Rusticus. For German affairs during the reigns of Claudius and Nero the more detailed information given by the *bella Germaniae* of the Elder Pliny was available, for Eastern affairs the memoirs of Corbulo, who is expressly cited for an item at 15.16.1. But even if a great deal of Tacitus' Eastern narrative derives from Corbulo himself, there must have been some other source as well to account for the note of criticism that is found in parts of the Eastern narrative.[28] For British affairs it is possible that Tacitus would have had access, directly or indirectly, to Suetonius Paullinus' account for the period of his governorship. But here, as elsewhere, comparison with Dio's account in the opening chapters of Book LXII suggests that Tacitus and he drew on a common literary source. Even if Suetonius wrote about his campaigns in Britain (and that is not certain), he was not that common source.

For the Pisonian conspiracy and its aftermath there was available to Tacitus a number of biographical writings, some of them frankly tendentious. The Younger Pliny's friend and correspondent, the equestrian Titinius Capito, wrote accounts of the deaths of famous men[29] and the genre was fashionable. More important was a biography of Paetus Thrasea, alluded to in *Agricola* 2.1, written by Arulenus Rusticus, who was tribune of the plebs in the year of Thrasea's death, and had offered to interpose his veto against the senate's decree condemning Thrasea. The eulogistic tone accorded to Thrasea in *Annals* XVI and much of the detail probably derives from Arulenus, whose biography of Thrasea was to result in his own death during the Domitianic persecution a quarter of a century later.

Lastly, it must be remembered that with the reign of Nero we move into Tacitus' own lifetime. Even forty years after Nero's death there survived some of those who had played a part in the political and military life of the times. From them or their sons it is likely that

Tacitus was able to gain much oral information to supplement the results of his reading; but he did not necessarily believe all he was told. An incident might be dismissed as being inherently implausible or because it conflicted with a better attested version.

It is clear, then, that Tacitus read widely and that the idea that he was an uncritical follower of a single source is quite untenable. But the evidence does not support the view that before writing he marshalled all the evidence available, and then applied to it the technique and critical skills of a modern scholar. Tacitus' manner of operation has been, and is likely to continue to be, a matter for lively dispute. But the following view seems consistent with the evidence.

The overall structure of each reign (and, within the reign, each Book of the *Annals*) is the result of a deliberate act of choice by Tacitus. Within that structure he accommodated the traditional divisions of events at home and abroad—the former now often sub-divided to admit the new sphere of palace affairs—to bring out his interpretation of the individual emperor's reign. After forming a clear picture of the articulation he intended to give to the whole, he would turn to procuring the evidence for each of the sections within that whole. Where he found a pre-existing literary narrative that satisfied him (see pp. 209—210), he would use that as a basis *for that section*,[30] supplementing it, where necessary, with material from other sources including archival material, especially items drawn from the *acta senatus*. And where a pre-existing narrative did not supply his needs, he would go elsewhere; so for the short narrative of the year 57 (three chapters in all, 13.31-3) it is probable that he drew exclusively on the *acta senatus*. As he moved from one section to another, he would keep to the same source or move to another, as it suited his purpose. The variety of sources already mentioned suggests a willingness to change rather than the reverse.

Two final points are worth discussing. First, do the references to differing versions (except for 13.20, 14.2 and one or two minor examples, almost always recorded anonymously) indicate that Tacitus consistently looked for such variants in all the sources he was using? His statement at 13.20 that he would follow the 'consensus of authors' seems to imply that he knew where such a consensus existed. That in turn would imply that he had continuous knowledge of what existed in each of the authorities he was using. If, as 13.20 seems to indicate,[31] his main literary sources were three only in number, that is not an unlikely procedure. As for archival material there is not enough evidence to prove whether he consulted such sources continuously or only when he had some particular reason for so doing. The only specific mention in the *Annals* of the *acta senatus* (15.74.3) occurs in a section where internal evidence[32] suggests that Tacitus is making consecutive use of them, while the *acta diurna* are mentioned (along with *auctores*, 'historians') only to prove a negative, namely that Germanicus' mother was not present at his funeral (3.3.2). Since it is quite improbable that Tacitus read all issues of the *acta diurna*—that *would* turn him into a diligent researcher on the modern model—why should he have looked into them here? In the previous sentence he notes that Tiberius and Livia did not attend the funeral. That item may well have come from Tacitus' written source (Dio exists only in excerpts here, but 57.18.6 describes Tiberius' and Livia's reaction to Germanicus' death in terms similar to Tacitus), and it may have been the common source's mention of the absence of Tiberius and Livia from the funeral that sent him looking in the *acta*. By so doing he was able to verify (as he expressly states) that all the imperial family (even Claudius!) were there with the exception of Tiberius, Livia, and Germanicus' mother, Antonia. On this occasion, therefore, he has (it seems) consulted other authors and archival material to prove (or disprove) a point suggested to him by his written source. That may well be his normal method of operation.

The last point to be considered is how Tacitus decided between differing versions. We have already seen how at 13.20 he rejects a version particularly favourable to Seneca, because it was given by Fabius Rusticus, whose pro-Senecan sympathies were well known. At 14.2 Tacitus discusses the alleged incest between Nero and Agrippina. According to Cluvius Rufus it was Agrippina who initiated the attempt, while Fabius Rusticus says that the initiative was Nero's. Tacitus explains why he thinks that Cluvius' version is the true one; it is the version followed by 'the other authorities' and it is supported by popular belief (such seems the force of *fama* here), whether that belief corresponds to the truth, or whether Agrippina's past reputation made it the more plausible. Tacitus' conclusion is drawn on the basis of probability and common sense.

The grounds on which Tacitus dismisses the unlikely rumour that Sejanus manoeuvred Tiberius into poisoning his son, Drusus,[33] are similar; the rumour is inconsistent with a proper understanding of Tiberius' character. That the proof is psychological does not render it invalid; but it should warn us not to see in one who interprets history in this way the makings of a modern historian. Tacitus operates within the canons of ancient historiography. It is enough that he does so with a penetration that rivals Thucydides and a pungency unequalled by any writer, Greek or Roman.

# STYLE

'To the new age, so often sceptical, tentative, and self-conscious in its
exploration of hidden motives, a new style was necessary, a style that
could express the mind as it was in movement, could record the
thought at the moment it arose in the mind. The amplification and
formal figures of Elizabethan rhetoric were as unsuitable for their
purpose as the roundness of the Ciceronian period wheeling its way to a
long foreseen conclusion.' The adjective 'Elizabethan' gives the game
away; without it the passage neatly expresses the situation which faced
Tacitus as he came to write history. In England the new style is the
Senecan amble.[1] In Rome too anti-Ciceronian reaction culminated,
almost a century after Cicero's death, in the modish popularity of
Senecan prose. The Senecan vogue did not long outlive his death, and
within a generation Quintilian would be advocating a return to
Cicero. Neither Cicero nor Seneca could provide a style suited to
Tacitus' needs, and he was obliged to forge a new instrument. Only
Sallust among his predecessors contributed substantially,[2] and Sallust,
it should be remembered, was anti-Ciceronian. So paradoxically, the
best way to understand what Tacitus' style is, is to begin by seeing what
it is not.

Three qualities of Cicero's oratory deserve particular note: a fullness
of expression (*copia uerborum*) that sounds excessive to modern ears; a
symmetry or balance (*concinnitas*) in construction of phrase, clause and
sentence, often emphasised by rhetorical figures, especially assonance
and antithesis; a periodic sentence structure, in which an anticipated
rounding off of the sentence duly occurs as the sentence closes.[3] The
relevance of Cicero's style to the most striking features of Tacitus' style
is immediately apparent, for the most obvious qualities of Tacitus'
style are, first, brevity (contrast Cicero's *copia uerborum*), and, secondly,
a studied avoidance of symmetry in sentence structure (contrast
Cicero's *concinnitas*).[4] To these two qualities a third must be added, the

use of choice or colourful words[5] to lend emphasis to, or heighten the tone of, a passage. Here too the contrast with Cicero is marked, though this is a feature that Tacitus shares with other historians. It is scarcely possible to illustrate this quality by English examples, for whereas words like 'forebears' 'anent' 'governance' tend in English to sound affected, quaint or pretentious, *prosapia* (in Sallust and Suetonius, Tacitus' contemporary, but not used by Tacitus himself), *super* as a preposition with the ablative (= *de*, 'concerning'), or *claritudo* ('renown': Cicero uses only the alternative form *claritas*) are available to lend enhancement to the language of a Roman historian.

Tacitus' style is the medium through which are expressed certain qualities of mind that make him unique among Latin prose writers. Two of these qualities are particularly noteworthy. First is his fastidiousness. Tacitus has an aristocratic cast of mind which not only distances him from other social classes, but separates him also from the more tolerant and easy-going of his social and political equals. Secondly, Tacitus has an acute sensitivity for the disparity between men's professions and their actions, and still more between their professed and their real motives. Under the empire some concealment in public life of the thoughts of the inner man was a necessary condition of political survival and a tolerable social existence, and, as far as we can tell, Tacitus' public actions conformed to the prescription. But in his historical writings he shows an unremitting awareness of the gap between the two spheres of human existence. Because of it he shows an interest in psychology that was as rare in the ancient world as it is commonplace with us. Because of it, too, his sentence repeatedly breaks out of the classical mould, avoiding the rounded period and displacing the centre of gravity from a syntactical predicate that states the action to an appended phrase or clause in which cause or purpose is emphasised.

Brevity, then, is the first quality of style that attracts attention in Tacitus.[6] A tendency to brevity may be a general feature of an author's style, reflecting his habitual cast of mind, or brevity may be deliberately employed in a given context for a specific purpose. Tacitus' brevity is more of the latter kind. It can be used to give pace or urgency to narrative, emphasis to description, and point to moral statement; but it is also employed to give an impression of antique simplicity to a list of prodigies. Each of these uses may be illustrated.

Tacitus describes the initial stages of the revolt of Boudicca (Boadicea) thus:

et cetera quidem impetu direpta aut incensa sunt: templum, in quo se miles conglobauerat, biduo obsessum expugnatumque. et uictor Britannus, Petilio Ceriali, legato legionis nonae, in subsidium aduentanti obuius, fudit legionem, et quod peditum interfecit: Cerialis cum equitibus euasit in castra et munimentis defensus est. qua clade et odiis prouinciae, quam auaritia eius in bellum egerat, trepidus procurator Catus in Galliam transiit.

Everywhere else (sc. in Colchester) was plundered or burnt at the first assault: the temple, where the armed Romans had banded together, was besieged for two days and carried by storm. And as Petilius Cerialis, commander of the ninth legion, came up in support, the victorious British met him and routed the legion, massacring the infantry: Cerialis escaped with the cavalry to the camp and took refuge behind its defences. As a result of this disaster and the hatred of a province, which his greed had driven to war, the financial agent Catus crossed in panic to Gaul. (*Ann.* 14.32.3)

The lightning initial successes of the British and the stark military reality that faced the Romans is fittingly conveyed by rapid narrative, but Tacitus has also chosen brevity to make more effective the contrast with the measured and resolute reaction to the situation of Britain's military governor, Suetonius Paullinus (cc. 33 ff.). Narrative shades into description in another British scene. The military climax of Agricola's governorship was his overwhelming defeat of the British at Mons Graupius. At a critical moment in the action the Roman cavalry turned the British rear and the enemy was routed. The scene that met the eye is vividly described:

tum uero patentibus locis grande et atrox spectaculum: sequi uulnerare capere, atque eosdem oblatis aliis trucidare. iam hostium, prout cuique ingenium erat, cateruae armatorum paucioribus terga praestare, quidam inermes ultro ruere ac se morti offerre. passim arma et corpora et laceri artus et cruenta humus; et aliquando etiam uictis ira uirtusque . . .

Then on the open plains there was a great and terrible scene; pursuit, wounding, prisoners taken, then murdered, as others offered. Now, as each was inclined, armed masses of the enemy turned tail before smaller numbers, while some charged unarmed against the Romans and offered themselves up to death. Everywhere arms and bodies and mangled limbs, and the ground soaked in blood; and at times even among the vanquished fury and valour. (*Agricola* 37.2–3)

The passage is additionally interesting, because it shows Tacitus at the outset of his career as a writer drawing directly on Sallust:

tum spectaculum horribile in campis patentibus: sequi fugere occidi capi; equi atque uiri adflicti, ac multi uolneribus acceptis neque fugere posse neque quietem pati; niti modo ac statim concidere; postremo omnia qua uisus erat constrata telis, armis cadaueribus, et inter ea humus infecta sanguine.

Then a dreadful sight was to be seen on the open plains; pursuit, flight, slaughter, capture; horses and men cut down, and many with wounds unable to escape or remain still, now struggling to get to their feet, now falling back again; in short, as far as the eye could see, everywhere strewn with weapons, arms, corpses, and between them the ground stained with blood. (Sallust, *Jugurtha* 101.11)

In both Sallust and Tacitus vivid description is used to bring out the pathos of the scene, but there is in Tacitus a greater interest in the psychology of the participants, both victors and vanquished—the greed of the former leading them to kill the prisoners they had already taken, as more came their way, and the final acts of defiance by the defeated enemy.

The use of brevity in the description of scene is matched by its use in the description of character. But here the emphasis is on moral qualities rather than physical description, and point and antithesis are used to bring them out. The first character sketch in the *Histories* (1.10) gives a telling portrait of Licinius Mucianus:

> Syriam et quattuor legiones obtinebat Licinius Mucianus, uir secundis aduersisque iuxta famosus. insignes amicitias iuuenis ambitiose coluerat; mox adtritis opibus, lubrico statu, suspecta etiam Claudii iracundia, in secretum Asiae sepositus tam prope ab exule fuit quam postea a principe. luxuria industria, comitate adrogantia, malis bonisque artibus mixtus: nimiae uoluptates, cum uacaret; quotiens expedierat, magnae uirtutes. palam laudares, secreta male audiebant: sed apud subiectos, apud proximos, apud collegas uariis inlecebris potens, et cui expeditius fuerit tradere imperium quam obtinere.

> Syria and its four legions were controlled by Licinius Mucianus, who was equally notorious in success and failure. As a young man he had cultivated friendship with the great as a means of self-advancement; soon after, with his wealth exhausted, his position insecure, and the suspicion even of having incurred Claudius' wrath, he was removed to the remoteness of Asia, and came as close to exile as he later did to the throne. Extravagance, application, affability, aloofness, he was a mixture of bad and good qualities: pleasures to excess, when he was idle; when he was on active service, immense talents. His public career might win your praise, his private life had an evil reputation. But with those under him, with friends, with colleagues he gained power by various enticements; he was, in short, a man for whom it proved easier to be king-maker than king.

If there is something a little artificial in the extended series of antitheses here, the technique has been refined and pared down in a double obituary notice in *Annals* (14.19):

> sequuntur uirorum illustrium mortes, Domitii Afri et M. Servilii, qui summis honoribus et multa eloquentia uiguerant, ille orando causas,

217

Seruilius diu foro, mox tradendis rebus Romanis celebris et elegantia uitae, quam clariorem effecit, ut par ingenio, ita morum diuersus.

There follow the deaths of two distinguished men, Domitius Afer and Marcus Servilius, whose careers had prospered with the holding of high office and the display of great eloquence, Afer winning renown as an advocate, Servilius after a long career at the bar by writing history and a fastidious life-style, to which he gave greater distinction by equalling Afer in talent, while being his complete opposite in moral probity.

The obituary is placed at the very end of events for the year (59), where by the tradition of Roman historiography such events are commonly recorded. Another item that tends to gravitate to the same position is the record of prodigies and the like. It is in this way that Tacitus ends his account of AD 64. (*Ann* 15.47). But whereas his obituaries are written with studied art, the style in which prodigies are recorded is affectedly jejune:

At the end of the year there was much talk of prodigies that foreshadowed coming disasters. Lightning occurred with unparalleled frequency, and there was a comet, an event that was always appeased by the shedding of blood in high places; two-headed births of humans and beasts were exposed to public view or discovered in sacrifices where pregnant victims are sacrificed. Near Placentia a calf was born beside the road with its head attached to its leg; the public seers gave the explanation that a new head of human affairs was in the course of preparation, but that it would lack strength and not remain concealed, because it had been stunted in the womb and born by the wayside.

But brevity in the sense of shortness of phrase or sentence is by no means a universal trait of Tacitus' style, for it is equally characteristic of Tacitus to employ extended units of thought. These are marked by a density of texture and compactness of thought, so that Tacitus' style is better described as sinewy than as characterised by brevity:

ac primum legio gradu immota et angustias loci pro munimento retinens, postquam in propius suggressos hostis certo iactu tela exhauserat, uelut cuneo erupit. idem auxiliarium impetus; et eques protentis hastis perfringit quod obuium et ualidum erat. ceteri terga praebuere, difficili effugio, quia circumiecta uehicula saepserant abitus. et miles ne mulierum quidem neci temperabat, confixaque telis etiam iumenta corporum cumulum auxerant. clara et antiquis uictoriis par ea die laus parta: quippe sunt qui paulo minus quam octoginta milia Britannorum cecidisse tradant, militum quadringentis ferme interfectis nec multo amplius uulneratis. Boudicca uitam ueneno finiuit. et Poenius Postumus, praefectus castrorum secundae legionis, cognitis quartadecimanorum uicesimanorumque prosperis rebus, quioa pari gloria legionem suam fraudauerat abnueratque contra ritum militiae iussa ducis, se ipse gladio transegit.

At first the legion stood its ground and used the enclosed terrain as a defence; then, after it had discharged its javelins with unerring aim at the enemy, as they drew closer, it burst forth in wedge formation. The auxiliaries attacked in like fashion, and the cavalry, with spears thrust before them, broke the stoutest resistance. The rest of the enemy turned tail, finding it difficult to escape, since the circle of their wagons blocked their escape routes. The Roman army did not spare even the women, and baggage animals, run through with spears, added to the pile of dead. It was a glorious victory that was won that day, and one that matched the victories of yore. For it is reported that almost eighty thousand Britons fell, while about four hundred of our troops were killed and not many more wounded. Boudicca ended her life by poison. And Poenius Postumus, camp prefect of the second legion, on learning of the success of the men of the fourteenth and twentieth legions, ran himself through with his sword, because he had cheated his legion of a share in the glory and had, contrary to army tradition, disobeyed his general's orders. (*Annals* 14.37)

The pace and vividness of the passage is clear. The centre of interest is transferred from one group or person to another with nervous energy. Within this dynamic whole sentence length is regulated to achieve an intended effect. The first sentence is of some length, and expresses the initial calm of the legionaries in a long phrase that contrasts with the final lightning burst into action (three words only in Latin—*uelut cuneo erupit*). The penultimate sentence (four words—*Boudicca uitam ueneno finiuit*) is also deliberately abrupt. Boudicca had already proclaimed her intention—victory or death (c. 35 fin.). Her reaction to defeat is swift and uncompromising. The last sentence, by far the longest of the whole passage, contrasts strikingly with the previous one. The Roman victory left the prefect of the second legion also with no choice. But he is a Roman, and Tacitus is prepared to linger, in order to convey some of the unfortunate man's thoughts before he takes the only honourable course open to him, death by his own sword. In this passage brevity is only one element among many that contribute to the total effect.

Under the rubric of brevity there is one other feature in Tacitus' writing that requires note—his use of the epigram. Tacitus shares with other writers of the Latin Silver Age a penchant for this form of expression. But the detachable epigram is more a feature of his earliest work, the *Agricola*, than it is of the *Histories* or *Annals*. So *omne ignotum pro magnifico* ('What is unknown always arouses wonder') and *ubi solitudinem faciunt, pacem appellant* ('Where they make a wilderness they call it peace'), both spoken of Roman imperialism by the British general Calgacus in *Agricola* 30; or (42.3) *proprium humani ingenii est odisse quem laeseris* ('It is characteristic of human nature to hate someone you have harmed'). In the *Histories* there is a tendency for an epigram to round off a chapter or a speech. The first three chapters of the first Book end as follows: *rara temporum felicitate, ubi sentire quae uelis et quae sentias dicere licet* ('in these times of rare happiness when you can think what you want, and say what you think'); *et quibus deerat inimicus, per amicos oppressi* ('and those who lacked an enemy were brought down by their friends'); 'Never was it demonstrated by more terrible disasters to the Roman people or by more convincing proofs that the gods are not concerned for our safety, but only for our punishment' ( . . . *non esse curae deis securitatem, esse ultionem*).

By the time he came to write the *Annals*, Tacitus had pared down his style still further, and the self-standing epigram has been virtually discarded. Perhaps a vestige remains in the fact that the last sentence in each of the first three books of *Annals* finishes in an epigram, but for the most part, where epigrams occur, they are integral to the context in which they occur. And even so the majority of them seem to occur in the first six Books:

> facta arguebantur, dicta impune erant (1.72.2)
> 'Deeds only were prosecuted: words went unpunished.'
> deorum iniurias dis curae (1.73.4)
> 'The gods could look after themselves' (lit. 'offences against the gods were the gods' concern').
> principes mortales, rem publicam aeternam esse (3.6.3)
> 'Emperors die, the state is immortal.'
> (Both this and the preceding example are statements made by Tiberius.)
> neque femina, amissa pudicitia, alia abnuerit (4.3.3)
> 'And a woman who has yielded her virtue will not refuse anything else.'
> facili feminarum credulitate ad gaudia (14.4.1)
> 'with a woman's readiness to believe what gives her pleasure.'[7]

The second feature of Tacitus' style—his studied avoidance of syntactical balance and the pursuit of asymmetry (*variatio*)—offers a direct insight into the working of his mind. At its simplest it focuses attention on a word in a phrase; so, when he writes 'the words of the edict (sc. of Tiberius) were few and *in a modest tone*' (*uerba edicti fuere pauca et sensu permodesto*; *Annals* 1.7.4), the substitution of a descriptive ablative (*sensu permodesto*) for an adjective coordinate with 'few' throws emphasis on the striking and loaded word *permodesto* ('completely self-effacing'). But *variatio* is repeatedly, and most significantly, employed where the question of alternative motives arises. An example occurs in the same chapter (1.7.3):

For Tiberius initiated all business through the consuls, as though the Republic still stood and he himself were diffident about ruling.

nam Tiberius cuncta per consules incipiebat, tamquam uetere re publica et ambiguus imperandi.

The single word *tamquam* ('as though') already warns the reader that what follows is alleged motive. But what gives the sentence its bite is the final three-word phrase. The switch from the ablative absolute (*uetere re publica*) to the nominative adjective *ambiguus*, agreeing with *Tiberius*, drives home the point that a deliberate act of deception by Tiberius is involved.

If it is the *variatio*, the syntactical asymmetry, that first catches the eye in this sentence, there is another feature that is still more significant for Tacitus' style. The sentence consists of a statement ('For Tiberius initiated all business through the consuls, — in the Latin it ends with the finite verb *incipiebat*)' to which there are appended comments. These comments typically analyse motives, either of the subject of the sentence or of those who react to, or are affected by, the subject's action. In a periodic sentence in classical Latin prose the syntactically subordinate elements normally precede the verb of the main clause.[8] Such is the nature of the vast majority of complex narrative sentences in Caesar, and though Livy makes more use than Caesar of appended elements, his long narrative sentences—and some of them are enormously long—tend to follow the same pattern. Though Tacitus too writes periodic sentences of this kind (though rarely very extended ones), he makes use, far more than any other Latin writer, of sentences in which the main clause is completed early and the centre of gravity is displaced to appended, syntactically subordinate, elements. But the restructuring of the sentence is not simply a mannered anti-classical reaction; rather it reflects a different attitude towards history. It was not enough for Tacitus to try to record what actually happened; he was even more interested to try to understand why it had so happened. The sentence with appended elements exactly reflects this interest. The most important (though not the only) function of *variatio* is ·to emphasise by syntactical means the difference in men's motives or reactions to events; because Tacitus sees more clearly than any other Roman writer that men's motives are rarely simple and their reactions to events seldom uniform, *variatio* is repeatedly used to emphasise these divergences.

Two examples, one each from the reigns of Tiberius and Nero, may illustrate the point. According to Tacitus the death of Germanicus,

Tiberius' nephew and adopted son, was not unwelcome to the emperor. Germanicus had been immensely popular with the Roman crowds, and when his widow returned from Antioch with his ashes, the display of public grief at Rome knew no bounds. How then were Tiberius and Livia, his mother, to comport themselves? According to Tacitus (*Annals* 3.3.1),

> Tiberius and Livia did not appear in public, thinking it beneath their imperial dignity if they were to mourn openly, or perhaps for fear that with the eyes of everyone fixed on their features their insincerity would be realised.

> Tiberius atque Augusta publico abstinuere, inferius maiestate sua rati si palam lamentarentur, an ne omnium oculis uultum eorum scrutantibus falsi intellegerentur.

Here the main clause is completed after five words of the Latin sentence. What follows is Tacitus' suggestion of alternative motives that may have led to their failure to appear in public. The first motive is introduced by a participle (*rati*, 'thinking'—equivalent to a causal clause, 'because they thought'), the second depends on the subordinating conjunction *ne*, 'lest' 'fearing that', and the disparity between the two suggestions,[9] the first wholly honourable, the second discreditable, is emphasised by the difference in syntactical expression. It will be noted too that Tacitus reserves the final position for his innuendo (for it can be nothing but that). Tacitus does not attempt to tell his reader which alternative to believe, but he is well aware that the final suggestion is most likely to linger in the reader's mind; an accumulation of such suggestions may produce a portrait that is irresistible.

During the reign of Nero, when the praetor Antistius was accused of treason, the senate uncharacteristically allowed itself to be swayed by the outspokenness of one of its members, Thrasea Paetus, to vote that exile rather than death should be the penalty imposed on the defendant. To have come to a decision without consulting the emperor was a sure way to provoke imperial displeasure, and the consuls refused to ratify the decision, until they had ascertained Nero's opinion. Nero's reply left the senate to make its own decision, but at the same time made clear how deeply offended he was. Tacitus goes on:

> in spite of the emperor's manifest displeasure the consuls did not alter the terms of the motion, nor did Thrasea drop his proposal, nor did the other senators abandon what they had already voted for—some of them fearing that they might seem to put the emperor in a bad light, the majority seeking safety in numbers, while Thrasea acted with his customary resolve and to avoid damage to his good name.

offensione manifesta non ideo aut consules mutauere relationem aut Thrasea decessit sententia ceteriue quae probauerant deseruere, pars ne principem obiecisse inuidiae uiderentur, plures numero tuti, Thrasea sueta firmitudine animi et ne gloria intercideret. (*Annals* 14.49.3)

The subject of the sentence is divided into three—consuls, Thrasea, the rest—and the main clauses end at *quae probauerant deseruere* ('abandon what they had already voted for'). Then Tacitus lists the reasons that motivated them. Three groups (not quite the same as those that constituted the subjects of the three main verbs) are mentioned. The motive of the first group is expressed by a subordinate clause introduced by *ne* ('lest' 'fearing that'), the second by an adjective *tuti* ('safe'), having the force of a participle; lastly for Thrasea two motives are suggested, the first expressed by an ablative of cause, the second introduced by the conjunction *ne*. Even when people do the same thing, their motives may be different, and varying syntactical means underline this. In the case of Thrasea the suggested motives are not exclusive (Tacitus' usual pattern), but complementary. Public esteem was perhaps the most highly prized aristocratic virtue among the Romans, and Tacitus indicates that private and public motives, though of a different nature, here reinforce each other.

Tacitus' use of the 'appendix' type of sentence structure, with or without syntactical *variatio*, results from looking at events and their surrounding circumstances in a way different from that of the writers of orthodox classical prose. The third conspicuous feature of Tacitus' style, his use of choice or colourful vocabulary, is one he shares with other Roman historians; for theorists of historiography, including Cicero and Quintilian, accepted that it was open to historians to seek to give distinction to their style by the use of words that were normally excluded from the vocabulary of the classical orator. Words with a mild flavour of archaism could add dignity, while the tonal quality of the narrative might be enhanced by words which, though not confined to poetry, were favoured by poets of the higher literary genres such as epic. Only Latin quotation and extended comment can do justice to this aspect of his work, but an example will perhaps give some hint of what is meant.

In his campaign against the Germans in the year AD 15 Germanicus had pushed far East beyond the Ems, but had been unable to bring the campaign to a decisive conclusion. His own legions were evacuated by the fleet, but his lieutenant, Caecina, was left the difficult task of extricating himself from enemy territory by land. Tacitus graphically describes how, surrounded by the enemy, the Romans spent an anxious night in camp, while to Caecina himself there appeared in his sleep a vision of Quintilius Varus, the Roman general who, six years earlier, had been defeated by the Germans with the complete destruction of all three legions serving under him:

> nox per diuersa inquies, cum barbari festis epulis, laeto cantu aut truci sonore subiecta uallium ac resultantis saltus complerent, apud Romanos inualidi ignes, interruptae uoces, atque ipsi passim adiacerent uallo, oberrarent tentoriis, insomnes magis quam peruigiles. ducemque terruit dira quies: nam Quintilium Varum sanguine oblitum et paludibus emersum cernere et audire uisus est uelut uocantem, non tamen obsecutus et manum intendentis reppulisse.

> The night was *restless* for different reasons, the barbarians, as they revelled, filling the valleys below and the *echoing woods* with joyful song or *fierce war chant*, while the Romans, around flickering fires, talked intermittently, lying down here and there behind the defences or *wandering* from tent to tent, *sleepless* rather than *fully on guard*. Their general too was frightened by a *terrible dream*; for he seemed to see and hear Quintilius Varus, covered with blood and *rising from the marshes*, summoning him, while he himself refused the call and thrust aside the beckoning hand. (*Ann.* 1.65.1-2)

All the underlined words have in Latin a quality that elevates them above the tone of normal prose;[10] they are chosen deliberately to enhance what is clearly intended to be a piece of fine writing. The appearance of the dead and defeated Varus also follows a pattern that belongs to poetry and imaginative prose. There is no reason to think that Tacitus had any evidence that Caecina had such a dream, but the tradition of Roman historiography tolerated, or indeed welcomed, such invention.

Within the sphere of domestic politics there is little scope for fine writing. Instead Tacitus' literary skill is directed to a more important end, the understanding and interpretation of political history. One area where this skill is particularly apparent, the invented speech, will be considered later, but within the narrative portion of his work there are two ways in which literary technique is conspicuously employed to influence the reader's judgment. Both work by implication rather than overt assertion. Tacitus, the trained orator, was well aware that insinuation is often the most effective means of persuasion. The first category concerns words or phrases of Tacitus' own selection, the second class—one far more difficult for us to come to terms with as a legitimate device of the historian—is the adaptation from earlier writers, above all Sallust, of phrases that are meant to import into the

Tacitean passage something (but not all) of their original context.

An example of the former category was given in illustrating Tacitus' use of syntactical *variatio*: 'the words of the edict (sc. by which Tiberius summoned the senate after the death of Augustus) were few and couched in a self-effacing tone'. The Latin adjective here translated as 'self-effacing' is *permodestus* (lit. 'exceedingly modest'). It is a low-key word deliberately chosen to echo Tiberius' profession of *moderatio* as an imperial virtue. But edge is given to the word from its context. The *words* of the edict were of this nature, but the *reality* was different: from the moment of Augustus' death Tiberius had acted, above all in dealing with the army, as emperor (*ut imperator . . . tamquam adepto principatu*). The contrast between appearance and reality is one that Tacitus repeatedly makes. Another Tiberian example concludes the first book of the *Annals*. Tiberius asserted that others than those whose names he had passed on to the consuls might stand as candidates for the consulship. The assertion, says Tacitus, was fair-sounding (*speciosa uerbis*) but in fact (*re*) devoid of substance or actually misleading (1.81.2). *Specie* ('in appearance') . . . *re* ('in fact') form a favourite antithesis in Tacitus. The Tiberian virtue of *moderatio* is again subverted in c. 8 of Book I. The offer of the senators themselves to carry the body of Augustus to the funeral pyre was declined by Tiberius 'with condescending moderation' (*adroganti moderatione*);[11] the adjective *adrogans* renders the imperial virtue offensive and reminds the reader of Tacitus' earlier statement (c. 4) that while Tiberius' military record marked him out as Augustus' most likely successor, people remembered that he possessed the ingrained arrogance of the *gens Claudia*.

The second device that Tacitus uses to influence his reader's judgment is to draw on his predecessors for words or phrases that will lend emphasis to persons or situations that particularly engage his interest. In the *Annals*, partly because of the nature of its subject matter, partly as the result of personal predilection, it is on Sallust above all that he draws. The character sketches of Poppaea, Nero's mistress and later wife, and Petronius—both equally elegant and notorious—are drawn in heavily Sallustian language, and some Sallustian tone occurs when Tacitus speaks of two military commanders, of whom on the whole he approved, Suetonius Paullinus and Domitius Corbulo.

But it is in the second triad of the *Annals* (Books IV-VI) that Sallustian resonances are most directly involved in matters of historical judgment.

At the beginning of Book IV, in the character sketch of Sejanus, and at the end of Book VI, in the obituary of Tiberius, the harmonics are enriched, in the first case by adding overtones from Sallust's description of Catiline, whose desperate enterprise so nearly brought the undoing of the Roman state, while in the case of Tiberius the moral decay of the last period of his life is given added importance by applying to it language that Sallust had used to describe the moral and political collapse of the Roman Republic. When too in the fourth Book Tacitus makes one of his very few unqualified statements of approval of a Roman politician and statesman (4.20 on M. Aemilius Lepidus), he endorses Lepidus' character by an unmistakable Sallustian reminiscence.[12]

The features of Tacitean style that have been discussed serve as the vehicle of a certain intellectual approach to the history of events and persons. So Tacitus turns his back on classical periodic sentence structure, not simply because of an antipathy towards Ciceronian balance, but because a different mould was generally necessary to express his train of thought. It is all the more remarkable, therefore, when one of his sentences significantly exceeds his normal length. One such sentence occurs at the outset of the *Annals*. Since it is unique in the whole of Tacitus' writing, it will repay closer study. Though the *Annals* formally begin with the reign of Tiberius, Tacitus has promised at the end of the first chapter to say a few words about Augustus. Chapter 2 begins with the following massive sentence:

When, after Brutus and Cassius had been cut down, there remained no army under the control of the state, and Sextus Pompeius had been crushed in Sicily, and, with Lepidus discarded and Antony killed, even the Julian party was without any leader but Caesar (i.e. Octavian, the later Augustus), laying aside the name of Triumvir and proclaiming himself as consul and satisfied with tribunician authority for defending the people, after he had allured the soldiery by gifts, the people by the distribution of corn, and everybody with the attractions of peace, *he gradually increased his stature and gathered into his own hand the functions of senate, magistrates and laws*, opposed by nobody, since his fiercest opponents had fallen in battle or through proscription, while the rest of the nobility were elevated by wealth or office in proportion to their readiness for servitude, and, as beneficiaries of revolution, preferred a safe present to the dangerous past.[13]

Postquam Bruto et Cassio caesis nulla iam publica arma, Pompeius apud Siciliam oppressus exutoque Lepido, interfecto Antonio ne Iulianis quidem partibus nisi Caesar dux reliquus, posito triumuiri nomine consulem se ferens et ad tuendam plebem tribunicio iure contentum, ubi militem donis, populum annona, cunctos dulcedine otii pellexit, *insurgere paulatim, munia senatus magistratuum legum in se trahere*, nullo aduersante, cum ferocissimi per acies aut proscriptione cecidissent, ceteri nobilium, quanto quis seruitio promptior, opibus et honoribus extollerentur ac nouis ex rebus aucti tuta et praesentia quam uetera et periculosa mallent.

In translating I have deliberately kept the one-sentence syntax of the original,[14] since even in Latin it neither reads nor is intended to read smoothly. Its structure, with ablative absolutes inserted within a series of temporal clauses, followed by a further ablative absolute, participle, and temporal clause, before two parallel main clauses of very different length (underlined in the translation above) reflects in the complexity of its organization the multiplicity of obstacles that had to be overcome by Octavian before he could achieve sole power, while all that follows the main clause is an extended appendix explaining why he met with no opposition: those who dared to try were liquidated, while the others were paid for their subservience.

But this colossal sentence not only mirrors the magnitude of the task that Octavian had set himself; the means—bribery—by which he attained his end, and the nature of his goal—autocracy veiled by the manipulation of republican institutions—are clearly described. The whole is a masterly epitome of Tacitus' verdict on the true nature of the Augustan principate. The sentence impressed Gibbon, for a memorable paragraph at the beginning of his *Decline and Fall* is in essence no more than an adaptation and paraphrase of Tacitus:

Every barrier of the Roman constitution had been levelled by the vast ambition of the dictator; every fence had been extirpated by the cruel hand of the Triumvir. After the victory of Actium, the fate of the Roman world depended on the will of Octavianus, surnamed Caesar, by his uncle's adoption, and afterwards Augustus, by the flattery of the senate. The conqueror was at the head of forty-four veteran legions, conscious of their own strength, and of the weakness of the constitution, habituated, during twenty years' civil war, to every act of blood and violence, and passionately devoted to the house of Caesar, from whence alone they had received, and expected, the most lavish rewards. The provinces, long oppressed by the ministers of the republic, sighed for the government of a single person, who would be the master, not the accomplice, of those petty tyrants. The people of Rome, viewing, with secret pleasure, the humiliation of the aristocracy, demanded only bread and public shows; and were supplied with both by the liberal hand of Augustus. The rich and polite Italians, who had almost universally embraced the philosophy of Epicurus, enjoyed the present blessings of ease and tranquillity, and suffered not the pleasing dream to be interrupted by the memory of their old tumultuous freedom. With its

227

power, the senate had lost its dignity; many of the most noble families were extinct. The republicans of spirit and ability had perished in the field of battle, or in the proscription.[15]

Nowhere else does Tacitus feel the need to write a sentence of such length, in which the main clauses are reached after subordination of such complexity, but there are a number, perhaps not more than half a dozen, of other long sentences, organized in a more typically Tacitean fashion. Such a one is the first sentence of Book XIII, with which the reign of Nero begins:

> The first death in the new reign, that of Iulius Silanus, proconsul of Asia, was prepared, without Nero's knowledge, through the scheming of Agrippina, not because he had provoked his destruction by any natural wildness—for he was indolent and regarded during other reigns with such disdain that the emperor Gaius used to call him the golden sheep—but Agrippina, having engineered the murder of his brother, Lucius Silanus, feared his vengeance, there being much popular talk that there should be preferred to Nero, who had scarcely passed the years of boyhood and had gained the throne through crime, a man of mature years, guiltless, of noble birth, and, what then counted for much, a descendant of the imperial line; for Silanus too was a great-grandson of Augustus.

> Prima nouo principatu mors Iunii Silani proconsulis Asiae ignaro Nerone per dolum Agrippinae *paratur*, non quia ingenii uiolentia exitium inritauerat, segnis et dominationibus aliis fastiditus, adeo ut C. Caesar pecudem auream eum appellare solitus sit: uerum Agrippina fratri eius L. Silano necem molita ultorem metuebat, crebra uulgi fama anteponendum esse uixdum pueritiam egresso Neroni et imperium per scelus adepto uirum aetate composita, insontem, nobilem et, quod tunc spectaretur, e Caesarum posteris; quippe et Silanus diui Augusti abnepos erat.

The main clause ends at *paratur* (line 2; after 'Agrippina', line 3, in the translation); everything that follows discusses the motive for Agrippina's action. One motive, introduced by *quia* ('because') is rejected: the real motive, no longer contained in a subordinate causal clause, but stated as an independent main clause, has attached to it an appendix in the form of an ablative absolute (with dependent indirect statement), which further explains the reason for her action. A sentence that begins as a conscious reminiscence of a similar statement at the beginning of Tiberius' reign (1.6.1) develops a new direction of its own. The reign begins, as does that of Tiberius, with a murder, but the responsibility is not the young emperor's, but his mother's; it is she who will hold the stage during the early months of the new reign. The breaking of her power becomes the first objective of Nero's advisers. The manner in which this was done is told in c. 12, which consists of

228

two sentences (the second a long one of over fifty words), both consisting of a main clause followed by a lengthy appendix of some complexity. The situation is one of underhand action and secret plotting; the involved sentence structure nicely conveys the web of intrigue that lay behind the action.

There is one further device of style, of which Tacitus makes effective use in *Annals* I-VI. On a number of occasions Tiberius acts in a manner that, interpreted on its own, would seem creditable—the adjective or adverb *ciuilis* or *ciuiliter*, 'acting like an ordinary citizen', is sometimes applied to such conduct. If the merit of the action cannot be discredited by ascribing it to Tiberian dissembling, *dissimulatio*, the bloom may be taken off the act by the immediate juxtaposition of some other less creditable piece of behaviour by the emperor. A particularly striking example occurs towards the end of *Annals* I:

> Tiberius refused to accept the title of 'father of the fatherland' that the people sought repeatedly to thrust upon him; nor, though the senate voted for the proposal, would he allow the oath to be taken to his deeds, saying that life was full of uncertainty, and that the more he gained, the more perilous was his position. *Yet he did not thereby convince people that he was moved by republican sentiments, for he had reintroduced the law of high treason (non tamen ideo faciebat fidem ciuilis animi; nam legem maiestatis reduxerat).* 1.72.1-2.

After the death of his son Drusus he asked that the two eldest children of the dead Germanicus be brought into the senate-house. When this was done, he begged the senate to regard itself as guardian to the two boys. His request was warmly received and

> if he had set a limit to his speech, he would have filled his listeners' hearts with compassion and admiration; but by turning once more to ridiculous talk about restoring the Republic he robbed a genuine and noble request of all credibility. (4.9.1)

When Tiberius acceded to the request of a senator to spare his brother, who had been convicted of writing libellous verses about him, Tacitus comments

> this makes it all the more remarkable that with full knowledge of the better alternative and the good name that followed the exercise of clemency he nevertheless preferred harsher courses. (4.31.1-2)

In AD 27, when a disastrous fire swept the Caelian Mount, the emperor's financial generosity to those who had suffered loss won praise from both senate and people. But, Tacitus continues,

> though the emperor's gifts brought relief to those who had suffered loss, there was no relief against the prosecutors, who went about their business with ever increasing strength and virulence. (4.66.1)

Elsewhere a similar effect is obtained more simply by emphasising how rare it was for such good qualities to be shown by Tiberius. So, when he prudently declines an extension of his powers of moral censorship, the popularity of his decision is 'all the more welcome in proportion to its rarity' (3.69.5), and when he again shows his generosity in meeting the financial losses caused by a fire on the Aventine in AD 36, his munificence was greeted 'all the more warmly as he had shown so little inclination to encourage building both private and public' (6.45.1).

One whole area of Tacitus' writing has not yet been touched upon, that of the invented speech. One of its problems Tacitus shared with other historians. Important speeches, both forensic and political, were normally of considerable length. Whatever the scale of his work, the historian has to convey the sense of the occasion in a few hundred words. For Tacitus the task was still more difficult, since the canvas on which he worked made a speech of forty or fifty lines quite exceptional. Within that space he has both to give an impression of oratorical breadth and balance and to maintain a style that does not openly contradict the anti-Ciceronianism of his narrative style. Because of the restricted compass there are necessarily abrupt changes in direction and obvious abridgment in the argument; there is also a tendency, which Tacitus shares with most Silver Latin writers, to favour the telling epigram. But the quality that first strikes one is the balanced sentence structure and the use of rhetorical figures. Indeed, when Germanicus quells a mutiny of his troops (*Annals* 1.42–3), the careful balance of his phrases, some of which have a Livian ring about them, approaches the style of classical oratory, and it is only an occasional word that betrays its author. More often a series of small points of vocabulary or syntax gives a speech an unmistakably Tacitean quality; in the speech that Otho makes before his suicide (*Histories* 2.47) Tacitus' signature is evident in almost every phrase.

The marked difference in style between the two speeches illustrates an important feature of Tacitus' invented speeches, a feature in which he breaks away from the convention of his predecessors. In them, though circumstances cause some differentiation of style, there is an overall uniformity that makes Hannibal speak like a Roman general and a fifth-century tribune of the plebs like a Ciceronian senator. Not all Tacitus' speeches are varied to suit the speaker, but in a significant number of cases the style has a palpable individuality. At the one extreme there is a single speech (unique in the whole of Tacitus' writing) in which in both vocabulary and rhythms there is a sustained

Ciceronian tone (the speech of Curtius Montanus in *Hist*. 4.42);[16] at the other there are two or three speeches by eminent senators that have a marked Sallustian quality. In addition the speeches of Tiberius and an important oration of Claudius are given an individuality of their own. At least to the extent that it is practised by Tacitus such an adaptation of style to speaker is original among Roman historians. Since we have seen in the narrative portions of his work that stylistic qualities are rarely displayed solely for their own sake, it is reasonable to look for some ulterior purpose in these individualised speeches.

In *Histories* 4.42 it is not difficult to see an intended contrast between the heady attractions of Ciceronian oratory and the political reality, in which first Domitian, then Mucianus, acting with Vespasian's authority, put an end to the brief flowering of free speech. The speech in which Marcus Lepidus pleads for a milder penalty than death for a Roman knight, Clutorius Priscus (*Ann.* 3.50), also fails of its purpose, for Priscus is condemned and executed. But here Tacitus' intention is not to illustrate the ineffectuality of the speech. On the contrary it is clear from one of the few unequivocal assertions that Tacitus makes about any of the historical personages he depicts that Lepidus' conduct won his unqualified admiration (*Annals* 4.20). The language in which that assertion is made is palpably Sallustian, and a strong Sallustian flavour is also present in Lepidus' defence of Clutorius Priscus. It is reasonable therefore to assume that Tacitus expects a similar reaction from his reader, when two speeches of Paetus Thrasea[17] are similarly couched in Sallustian language (14.48—this speech is in reported speech—and 15.20-21). The Sallustian tone is a linguistic device designed to alert the reader. But it is more than that. The language is solemn and slightly old-fashioned: so too were the political attitudes of both men. The reader need not be surprised that Lepidus' speech is unsuccessful, while those of Thrasea, though partly successful, also marked steps towards an estrangement between Thrasea and the emperor.

Some comment has already been made on the speeches of Tiberius and Claudius. The speeches and letters of Tiberius play an important part in *Annals* I-VI. Tacitus was fascinated by the public pronouncements of a man whose natural tendency to conceal his thoughts from the public gaze had been cultivated during a long life to a point where the truth became impenetrably opaque. What Tacitus offers us is a nicely calculated blend of old-fashioned phrasing and shrewd political assessment. Whether the mild archaisms and unusual words that Tacitus' Tiberius uses were actually taken from the emperor's writings, or represent what a writer of three generations later regarded as typical of the language a man of Tiberius' time might use is unclear.[18] But the individualised style that Tacitus gives to Tiberius' utterances is the historian's own creation. The fact that neither Claudius nor Nero is similarly individualised indicates the fascination that the character of Tiberius exercised upon him.

In the extant portions of the reign of Claudius only one substantial speech by the emperor occurs. It has a double importance. First it shows Claudius opposing senatorial conservatism over the question of opening the highest magistracies in Rome to the chieftains of Gallia Comata. Secondly, the speech is unique in that for a considerable part of its subject matter there survives, inscribed on a bronze tablet at Lyons, a copy of the speech that Claudius actually delivered on this occasion. Here we are able to see at first hand how Tacitus handled his source. The original, at times diffuse, rambling, pedantic has a very personal quality about it. Tacitus' version is necessarily more compressed, but it is also better organized and more cogent; and it ends with a pointed phrase ('what we today defend by precedents will itself become a precedent'), where Claudius' own oration dwindles away with a grumble about the arduousness of conducting a census.

The style of the speech, then, is deliberately non-Claudian, but there is more to it than that. Claudius had studied under Livy, and it is not surprising that on the Lyons tablet there is a clear reminiscence of the argument that Livy puts in the mouth of the tribune Canuleius to support his proposal that plebeians should be allowed the right to intermarriage with patricians. Though Tacitus takes over no significant word or phrase from Claudius, he too draws on Canuleius' speech (*Ann.* 11.24.4 *aduenae in nos regnauerunt* :: Livy.4.3.13 *cum maiores nostri aduenas reges non fastidierint*). Claudius' speech can thus be alluded to, but in the more acceptable style of Livy.[19]

Of Nero Tacitus says that he was the first emperor to require the services of a ghost writer (13.3.2 *primum ex iis qui rerum potiti essent Neronem alienae facundiae eguisse*). Tacitus accords him no public oration in direct speech. It was Seneca who made good the young emperor's deficiencies, and it is with deliberate irony that Tacitus gives (*Ann.* 14.53–6) in *oratio recta* the private exchange between the two, in which Seneca sought, and Nero refused him, permission to retire from public life. The speeches match each other in their studied insincerity.

The style of the set speeches in Tacitus differs, then, from that of the narrative, and from speech to speech. All display Tacitus' rhetorical skill, and some of them are given an individual characterisation. But literary virtuosity is not an end in itself. All the speeches occur at significant points in the narrative, and are designed to underline character, motive, or situation—not infrequently emphasising a contrast between what was said and what was done. But the extended speech in *oratio recta* is only one aspect of Tacitus' use of dramatic speech. Short passages of quoted words, often no more than a single sentence, and frequently in the mouths of minor characters, are used to signalise or give point to a climax. In doing this Tacitus was following a practice long established in the tradition of rhetorical history.

Much more important for him is the widespread use of reported speech. Indeed, though individual passages of reported speech never extend to the lengths of some of the set speeches in *oratio recta*, reported speech accounts for almost twice as much space as does direct speech. Unlike its use in English, where in historical narrative its use is severely limited, representing a somewhat abridged and depersonalised report of what was said, or alleged to have been said, *oratio obliqua* has a wide range in Latin, and Tacitus uses its potential to the full. Since the impact of the formal speech in *oratio recta* would be diminished by too frequent use, the extended reported speech provides a useful substitute. As such it can span the same range of tone and emotion as *oratio recta*— the tearful appeals of Poppaea to Nero to divorce Octavia so that he can marry her, the malicious attack of Eprius Marcellus on Paetus Thrasea, Thrasea's own intervention to secure clemency for the praetor Antistius—but it is also available to reflect the measured language of a diplomatic embassy or a minister's advice to his emperor.

In a society accustomed to forensic and deliberative debate both sides of any discussion were assured of a ready audience, but to record them both in *oratio recta* might unduly emphasise the artificiality of the convention of the invented speech, and in the *Annals* its use in recording a private interview between Seneca and Nero only serves to emphasise the insincerity of the exchange. But no such restriction lay on reported speech, and it is employed to give both sides of a senatorial debate on the position of freedmen (13.26–27) or the pre-battle harangues of opposing generals.[20] Reported speech is also used both for characters such as Tiberius who appear frequently—to reduce the number of set speeches in *oratio recta*—and for characters of lesser importance—to avoid giving them more prominence than they deserve.

There are also two other spheres in which extended *oratio obliqua* is particularly useful for Tacitus' purposes; to summarise the words or thoughts of groups of people and to convey popular rumour (particularly unfavourable rumour).[21] But *oratio obliqua* is also used frequently (perhaps more so in Tacitus than in any other Latin author) in very short passages that amplify or justify assertions. In such cases the narrative is scarcely interrupted, but the impression is given that the statements of the narrative are endorsed by the words of the participants. After the murder of Agrippina Nero was uncertain what sort of a reception he would get if he went to Rome. He was assured by his toadies that

> the name of Agrippina was hated and popular enthusiasm had been fired by her death; let him go (sc. to Rome) without fear, and find out for himself how the people revered him (*Ann.* 14.13.1).

The second part of the sentence (from 'let him go . . .') seems to give an air of authenticity to the assurances of the toadies. In fact the whole sentence is Tacitus' own invention. It is entirely probable that Nero did need some reassurance, and that this was given by his friends; it is unlikely that Tacitus had any evidence that such assurances were in fact given, much less that they were given in the specific words he records.

'The style of an author', according to Gibbon, 'should be the image of his mind.' The analysis of individual elements in Tacitus' style can show the reader, particularly the reader of Tacitus in translation, in what direction to look, if he wishes to understand why Tacitus is the greatest of all Roman historians, and in the preceding pages I have tried to show how stylistic features reflect or correspond to qualities of mind. 'Sublimity', in the words of the author of the treatise *On the Sublime*, 'is the echo of a noble mind.' Before Tacitus turned to writing history 'elevation' is the quality that his friend and contemporary Pliny singled out in his oratory. To history Tacitus brought both passion and aloofness. Because of this his style is both gripping and austere. Though he invented for the telling of both domestic and foreign affairs an original and unique narrative technique, it is clearly built on foundations firmly established by his predecessors. But the quality that sets him apart from other Roman historians is his ability, while living within, and actively serving, the Principate, to look at the history of the past hundred years with the eye of a Republican writer. He accepts the necessity of the rule of one man, and he accepts the necessity of seeking a *modus vivendi* between senate and emperor; but, opposed to the tendency towards absolutism in the one and sycophantic abasement in the other, he sought, as a historian, to diagnose the causes and trace the process.

His solution, which may not seem very startling to a sceptical age like our own, but required a penetrating eye in a successful politician at the beginning of that 'period in the history of the world, during which the condition of the human race was most happy and prosperous', assumed the simultaneous interplay of two sets of opposites: of action and reaction in the public domain between ruler and ruled, and in the individual a tension between public profession and private motive. Because senators, whose class had been the effective ruler of the Republic, were now in the ambivalent position of being both rulers and ruled, it was they who were most strained by the tension between pretext and reality. Tacitus' literary inventiveness devised a sentence structure that reflected the interplay of these opposites, while his fastidiousness in the choice of words produced phrases of striking originality, telling, compact, and often acerbic. But into this mould, whose framework is intellectual, strong feelings from time to time force their way, when actions arouse his detestation or, less often, his admiration. His claim to write without anger or favour is not always borne out, for he stands firmly in the Roman tradition in believing that actions call for strong moral condemnation or approval; the warmth of his language is an indication that emotion sometimes gets the better of reason. Tacitus believes that he has found an explanation of the events about which he writes in the conflict of opposing forces. What gives his writing continuing interest is the fact that he himself too is affected by a variety of tensions, above all by the conflicting claims of objectivity and the desire to write vividly and forcefully. The marvel of Tacitus' style is that it is so often able to encompass both aims.

# XI

# POSTSCRIPT

The flourishing state of Tacitean studies today[1] might seem to bear out Pliny's prophecy to Tacitus that his histories would be immortal. In fact, the descent of so considerable a proportion of what he wrote[2] has been by the most tenuous of threads. Even in the immediately succeeding generations there is little evidence that he was much read; serious history (Polybius' *pragmatike historia*) became unfashionable, giving way to imperial biography and panegyric. The emperor Tacitus (d. 276), who claimed descent from the historian, is said to have given instructions for copies of his works to be made, 'lest he perish through the indifference of readers' (*SHA* 10.3: *ne lectorum incuria deperiret*); that suggests that Tacitus' writings were already in danger of being forgotten and lost. A century later Ammianus Marcellinus, a Greek writing in Latin, saw his history[3] as a continuation of Tacitus; and in the middle of the fifth century two references in the letters of Sidonius Apollinaris (4.14.1; 4.22.2) show that Tacitus still had readers among the cultivated noblemen of Gaul. But early in the sixth century the reference of Cassiodorus (*Var.* 5.2) to 'a certain Cornelius' to explain the origin of amber—the reference is to *Germania* 45.4-5— suggests a somewhat shadowy figure. Among Christian writers— Tertullian (who accused him of mendacity), Sulpicius Severus, and Orosius—it is mostly his account of the Jews in the *Histories* that attracts their attention.

During the Carolingian Renaissance, in addition to the perfection *c.*780 of the clear and elegant script which we know as Caroline minuscule, an imperial mandate to the abbot of Fulda, Baugulf (in or a little after 794), the so-called *De litteris colendis*,[4] encouraged the study of classical Latin literature as a necessary preliminary to the full understanding of Christian texts. The contribution that this age made to the preservation and transmission of our Latin classics is immense,[5] but it is remarkable that Tacitus should have been among those copied, for the difficulty of his Latin meant that he could have little use for the educational aims that Alcuin sought to implement for Charlemagne.[6] Nevertheless, it is in the ninth century, and in Fulda, that knowledge of Tacitus re-emerges; Rudolphus of Fulda quotes from the *Germania* and seems to show some knowledge of the early books of the *Annals*. From the neighbouring (and sister) monastery of Hersfeld comes the ninth-century manuscript of a substantial part of the *Agricola*,[7] while the unique manuscript (M 1, the first Medicean) of *Annals* I-VI, also written in the ninth century, may well have come from Fulda.[8] The third and last strand, that which gives us *Annals* XI-XVI and the surviving portions of the *Histories*, is a Beneventan manuscript (M 2, the second Medicean), written in Benedict's own monastery of Monte Cassino in the second half of the eleventh century. Since close links existed between Fulda and Monte Cassino, it is possible—though no more than a hypothesis—that all that survives of Tacitus goes back to a copy or copies made in Fulda in the ninth century.[9] Whether that is true or not, the tripartite division of the manuscript tradition had already been effected in the ninth century, and the fortunes of the three strands (*Opera Minora; Annals* I-VI; *Annals* XI-XVI and *Histories* I-V) are best now considered separately. Only the transmission of the *Opera Minora* requires more than the briefest description.[10]

By 1425 it was known among Italian scholars that the monastery of Hersfeld had among its manuscripts 'some unknown works of Cornelius Tacitus'.[11] Though it was to be a generation before efforts to secure this manuscript succeeded, a list and description of its contents quickly became available. In 1426 a letter of Panormita lists *Germania*, *Agricola*, 'a dialogue about the orator' (*quidam dyalogus de oratore*), which Panormita conjectured to be by 'Cornelius Tacitus'. A list drawn up five years later by Niccolò Niccoli adds that the *Germania* consisted of twelve leaves, the *Agricola* of fourteen, and the *Dialogus de oratoribus* of eighteen. A quarter of a century later, in 1455, Pier Candido Decembrio saw at Rome what must be the same *codex*.[12] If that identification is right, there is a further point of some consequence. Whereas Poggio and Niccoli had stated nothing about the authorship of the *Dialogus*, and Panormita had ascribed it to Tacitus only by conjecture (*est, ut coniectamus, Cor. Taciti*), Decembrio states categorically 'Cornelii taciti dialogus de oratoribus incipit'. That gives a strong presumption that the Hersfeld *codex* gave Tacitus as the author.[13]

Within three years of its arrival in Rome the Hersfeld *codex* was in poor shape and had lost the leaves containing the *Agricola*; from this time the history of the manuscript text of the *Agricola* is separate from

237

that of the *Germania* and *Dialogus*. After copies of the two latter works had been made, that portion of the *codex Hersfeldensis* was discarded (a common practice in the fifteenth century) and passed into oblivion. The same fate seemed to have befallen the part of the Hersfeld *codex* that contained the *Agricola*, but in 1902 a quire of the ninth-century *codex* was discovered embedded in a fifteenth-century manuscript of the *Agricola* and *Germania*.[14]

By the second half of the 1460s numerous manuscripts were in existence that contained both *Germania* and *Dialogus*, and when the *editio princeps* of Tacitus was printed (by de Spira in Venice) *c.* 1470, it contained these works as well as *Annals* XI-XVI and *Histories* I-V. For the two latter the sole manuscript source[15] is the second Medicean (M 2), a Beneventan manuscript of the eleventh century, which was known to Boccaccio before 1360.[16] The elegance of the script of this manuscript is not matched by its legibility,[17] and when the *editio princeps* was printed, it was taken from one of the copies which had begun to be made from just before 1450. It would be over a hundred years before an editor made a sustained, direct use of the second Medicean.

The *Agricola*, whose ninth-century archetype had been separated from the other *Opera Minora* between 1455 and 1458, was first printed in Puteolanus' edition of 1476(?), which contained all Tacitus' works except the as yet unknown *Annals* I-VI. As in the other cases, the first printed *Agricola* was dependent, not on the Carolingian *codex Hersfeldensis*, but on a fifteenth-century copy.[18]

The text of *Annals* I-VI derives from the first Medicean, which was brought from Corvey to Rome about 1508.[19] There it was acquired by Pope Leo X, and it was by his commission that it was published in 1515 by the younger Beroaldus. Thus, alone of all the works of Tacitus that have survived, the text of *Annals* I-VI was printed directly from its primary authority. Almost a century was to pass before Pichena's edition of 1607 gave a text that was founded directly on *both* Medicean manuscripts.[20] In the intervening years much was to be done for the text of Tacitus—and from a little before 1580 his influence on the political thought of Europe began to be of great importance—but it was done on a vulgate text (*textus receptus*) far removed from that available in the two Medicean manuscripts. That makes the editions of Rhenanus (1533) and Lipsius (first edition 1574) all the more remarkable.[21] It lies outside the purpose of this chapter to examine the contribution of subsequent scholars to the establishment of a sounder text of Tacitus.[22] Textual emendation is subject to the law of diminishing returns, and the number of certain or highly probable corrections suggested by scholars of the twentieth century is inevitably very small indeed.

Allusion has already been made to the fact that from about 1580 there was an immense upsurge in interest in Tacitus. For about a century the influence he exercised on European thought and politics was such that one can justly speak of an era of 'Tacitism'.[23] Even crude statistics are sufficiently indicative of the phenomenon.[24] Until 1550 the number of editions of Tacitus place him at the bottom of the list of all Roman historians. Interest begins to quicken in the second half of the sixteenth century, when he is placed sixth. But during the next fifty years (1600-49) there are more editions of Tacitus than any other Greek or Roman historian. The number of commentaries and translations shows a similar trend.

But the genesis of the movement goes back earlier in the sixteenth century. In applying the concept of 'reason of state' to contemporary politics Machiavelli had drawn extensively on illustrations from Roman history. But though he had some knowledge of Tacitus,[25] it was to Livy and Roman republican history that he turned in his *Discourses on the First Decade of Livy* (1516-19?). As the Tiberian books of the *Annals* began to be known with the publication of Beroaldus' edition in 1515, the greater relevance of that subject matter and its treatment by Tacitus soon became apparent. Machiavelli's younger contemporary, Guicciardini, makes the point succinctly: 'Cornelius Tacitus teaches those who live under tyrants how to live and act prudently, just as he teaches tyrants how to establish tyranny.'[26] Already by 1533 Beatus Rhenanus, in the Preface to his edition, was affirming Tacitus' superiority to Livy, not on the ground of style, but because his narrative of events showed how men must and should live under 'those who have the power to destroy by a mere nod of the head.'

Tacitism was to have many strands,[27] but, from the beginning, text, commentary and relevance to contemporary politics were closely intertwined. Two years before Lipsius published his first edition of Tacitus (Plantin, Antwerp; 1574), he was lecturing on Tacitus at Jena. There, as the Netherlands had begun their revolt against King Philip of Spain, he drew an exact parallel between the king's governor, the Duke of Alba, and the Tacitean Tiberius. Lipsius' interest in contemporary politics[28] was underlined by the publication, in 1589, of his *Six Books on Politics*, which (as Burke points out) went through fifteen Latin editions by the end of the century.

239

Lipsius was foremost, too, in advocating Tacitus' claims as a stylist. That, for him, was a question of Latin. But towards the end of the sixteenth century the times were conducive to a change in style in the vernacular literature of England and France, away from Ciceronian amplitude to something less diffuse. Tacitus was by no means the only classical influence in that change—Senecan sententiousness was suited better to the essays of Bacon and Montaigne—but his example of concise expression and pregnant thought was an important factor in the anti-Ciceronian movement.

In the field of drama Burke (op. cit. 158–60) singles out Ben Jonson's *Sejanus* and Racine's *Britannicus* as striking examples of Tacitism. In both plays the subject matter alone would have made the influence of Tacitus clear. But that influence is explicitly recognised in both cases, in Jonson's play by the marginal notes that Jonson himself added in the quarto edition, and in Racine's case by the second preface, prefixed to the 1676 edition of *Britannicus*. There Racine declares: 'I have copied my characters from the greatest painter of antiquity (*le plus grand peintre de l'antiquité*), I mean from Tacitus.'

Though the rise of Tacitism was due to a combination of factors—political, religious, cultural and literary—its core lay in its rejection of one classical model, the Ciceronian, for another, the Tacitean. The decline of Tacitism during the last third of the seventeenth century is similarly due to a complex chain of circumstances, but one factor, itself the by-product of several others, is the decline in the estimation in which classical literature came to be held in comparison with vernacular literatures. The lessening of interest in Tacitus was only part of that general decline. One aspect of it is shown by the foundation of the Royal Society whose aim, the 'Improving of Natural Knowledge', favoured a plainer prose style—'the language of artisans, countrymen and merchants before that of wits and scholars'. Swift's *Battle of the Books* (1697), echoing the *Querelle des Anciens et des Modernes* in France, marks the end of an era when the superiority of ancient literature would be automatically conceded.

The reputation that Tacitus enjoys today is the outcome of a process that began in the early nineteenth century,[29] when German scholars, following the example of Niebuhr, began to apply the new technique of source criticism to the study of ancient history. Their predecessors had not been unaware that the reliability of earlier historians varied immensely, but for the most part ancient history meant essentially a narrative based on the best surviving literary sources. Niebuhr sought to discover what primary sources, contemporary with the period that was being narrated, lay behind Livy's narrative of the early history of Rome, and though his conclusions about those primary sources are unconvincing, the clear distinction between primary and secondary sources is henceforth a cornerstone of historical criticism. The investigative technique that was now developed can fairly be described as 'scientific'.

The technique could more readily be applied to recent history, where contemporary documents were often available in great numbers, than to ancient history.[30] But the secondary nature of the evidence afforded by Livy could be clearly demonstrated,[31] and (seemingly) the same might be true for the early books of Tacitus' *Histories*. By the 1860s a clear dichotomy had begun to develop in Tacitean scholarship, and this split was to dominate the approach to Tacitus for more than half a century. As a historian Tacitus' reputation declined; he was derivative and rhetorical. But as a stylist he continued to be acclaimed. Almost at the identical time that Mommsen was destroying his reputation as a historian, a series of articles—themselves no less systematic in method than Mommsen's—was opening up a new approach to the study of the language of Tacitus. In an age that had become accustomed (more or less) to the concept of evolution, Wölfflin showed[32] that Tacitus' style followed an evolutionary curve. Not all Wölfflin's arguments are valid, and the stylistic evolution turns out to be much less fundamental than was at one time supposed, but the work gave an important impetus to the study of Tacitus as a literary artist, which in turn was pursued to compensate, as it were, for the loss of esteem that he had suffered as a historian.

Though their method of investigation was 'scientific', neither Ranke nor Mommsen would have subscribed to Bury's aphorism that history is 'a science, no less and no more', but by the turn of the century that was a commonly held view. A new factor was needed to bring that view into question and to pave the way for a resolution of the division between Tacitus as an historian and as a literary artist. Two world wars and three major revolutions[33]—in Russia, Italy and Germany—have shattered the pervasive optimism of the late nineteenth and early twentieth century. The dark tones of Tacitus' writing accord well with the present age, which is more willing to accept the possibility of political wickedness—and its justification by 'reasons of state'.

But that does not bridge the gap between the two Tacituses. The most notable contribution to Tacitean studies since the war, Sir

241

Ronald Syme's monumental *Tacitus*, has as its implicit, but fundamental aim to demonstrate that historian and stylist are one. To prove
his point he comes close to arguing that Tacitus operated essentially in
the way prescribed by the nineteenth-century German school. Such a
claim is (or would be) anachronistic and exaggerated. But within
certain limits it is—or so it seems to me—valid. Tacitus was not
dealing, as was Livy in his early books, with a remote period of
antiquity, but with a period (or, rather, two periods, one in *Histories*,
one in *Annals*) not too distant from his own, and for which substantial
documentary evidence existed. That he did not consistently consult all
such evidence is overwhelmingly probable, and that he at times draws
too liberally on pre-existent literary sources is clear. But for much of
the time the extent of his 'research' (to use the modern word) is
concealed by the fact that he has put before us an impressionistic
portrait. The impressionism is the product of literary skill. Sometimes
the rhetorical and dramatic façade may be a substitute for a rigorous
attempt to get at the facts. But Tacitus can rarely be detected in
falsehood, and by the standards of the ancient world he is careful and
conscientious in his search for the truth. To that extent the dichotomy
between the two sides of the man is false.

That Tacitus has his shortcomings is obvious; many of them have
been noted in earlier chapters.[34] He is partial in both senses of the
word—prejudiced by class, temperament and tradition, and incomplete in his field of vision. The latter defect he shares with all Greek
and Roman historians. As for the former, the profession to write
impartially is a historian's commonplace of dubious validity. Mommsen
knew that when he echoed—and contradicted—Tacitus in the
following words: 'Those who have lived through historical events, as I
have, begin to see that history is neither written nor made without
love or hate.'[35] Bury, too, who in 1903 had pronounced history to be a
science, wrote very differently after the end of the first World War: 'I
do not think that freedom from bias is possible, and I do not think it is
desirable . . . the most effective histories have usually been partial and
biassed, like those of Tacitus, Gibbon, Macaulay,[36] and Mommsen.'

Few people today believe that history repeats itself, nor do many see
its purpose as narrowly didactic; but the attempt to understand the
past is an enlargement of the human spirit. Tacitus stood at a
watershed in Roman, and European, history. Political stability and
the survival of civilisation depended on an effective autocracy. That
had, in fact, been true since the time of Augustus, but it was only with

the accession of Trajan that the truth was accepted by the senatorial class as a whole. Though he took a prominent part in a society well organized to control its public face, Tacitus had the ability to see, and the courage to describe the gulf between public profession and private motive. From his contemporaries he was distinguished by a combination of three qualities: a temperamental affinity with republican values, a concern as a historian to prove how the change from republic to autocracy had come about,[37] and, lastly, a unique gift for communicating his thoughts in language that is pungently memorable. At his best—and that is for much of the time—those qualities are integrated; then there is no dichotomy between Tacitus the historian and Tacitus the writer.

# NOTES

It is not possible to do justice to the Roman historiographical tradition within the compass of a short chapter, and I have concentrated on those aspects and writers who have the most direct relevance for Tacitus. For historians prior to Sallust E. Badian's chapter in *Latin Historians* (ed. Dorey, T. A., London, 1966), 1–38 is incomparably the best brief survey. In the same volume F. W. Walbank's chapter on Polybius and P. G. Walsh's chapter on Livy are excellent, the latter distilling much of the essence of his *Livy* (Cambridge, 1961) in just over twenty pages. For Sallust see R. Syme, *Sallust* (Berkeley and Los Angeles, 1964). There is no satisfactory account of the fragmentary historians between Livy and Tacitus; for Velleius Paterculus, however, see A. J. Woodman (reference in n. 30).

1. The Greek Timaeus, writing at Athens, had already included Italy in his history earlier in the third century.
2. H. B. Mattingly sounds a note of scepticism in *LCM* 1 (1976), 3–7; he argues that Q. Fabius Pictor 'was not the envoy of 216—rather the praetor of 189—and he wrote in Latin and not in Greek'.
3. Cf. J. E. A. Crake, 'The Annals of the Pontifex Maximus' in *C.Ph.* 35 (1940), 375–86, and OCD *tabula pontificum*. The capture of Rome by the Gauls (390 or 387 BC) may have destroyed many of the earliest records, but it is likely that these were quickly reconstituted, though opportunities for falsification in the interests of individual aristocratic families were clearly available and utilised.
4. Not unnaturally it is they rather than fifth-century historians, such as Thucydides, who mainly influenced the Romans; compare the same phenomenon in Comedy, where it is the New Comedy of the fourth and third centuries, not the Old Comedy of Aristophanes, that served as the model for Plautus and Terence.
5. Though he is classed as one of the canonical Ten Attic Orators, he did not in fact speak in public; his fame depends on his teaching as a rhetorician and educationist.
6. In addition to numerous references in Livy see Cicero's *De senectute* and the biographies by Cornelius Nepos and Plutarch. See now A. E. Astin, *Cato the Censor* (Oxford, 1978).
7. See OCD *novus homo*.

8. See, for instance, Tacitus, *Annals* 2.33 and 3.52 ff. on proposed sumptuary legislation.

9. Hence his cognomen *Frugi* ('honest').

10. See n. 3 above.

11. For both these men see OCD.

12. For these points see fragments 1 and 2, which are preserved in Aulus Gellius 5.18.8 and 9.

13. Even if, behind the constitutional façade, thuggery and violence, as typified by the gangs of Clodius and Milo, became increasingly common.

14. Cf. OCD *optimates, populares*.

15. In addition to Badian (see Bibliography) see P. G. Walsh, *Livy* (C.U.P., 1961) 115 ff. and A. H. McDonald in *JRS* 47 (1957), 155 ff., who makes an extended comparison of two striking episodes in which Livy is directly indebted to Quadrigarius.

16. See pp. 12 ff. in R. M. Ogilvie's Commentary on Livy I–V (Oxford, 1965).

17. Though, perhaps surprisingly, what Cicero had suggested unsuccessfully to Lucceius is carried out, but from a very different political standpoint, by Sallust in his *Catilinarian Conspiracy*. In that work the desire to impose on events a particular dramatic structure leads Sallust to neglect chronology and clarity of exposition.

18. Though only fragments of the *Histories* survive, it seems that in them Sallust reverted to annalistic history, with its subdivision of *res . . . militiae et domi gestas* (roughly 'foreign and home affairs'). However, he still treated Roman history *carptim*, for the work appears to have been restricted to the twelve years from Sulla's death.

19. See 4.3 *de Catilinae coniuratione*; the manuscripts seem to indicate *bellum Catilinarium* as the title of their archetype.

20. So, after a prologue, explaining his reasons for writing about Catiline, and a character sketch of Catiline himself, but before starting the narrative of events, Sallust gives a sketch of Roman history ( cc. 6–13; it totals about 150 lines, roughly one tenth of the whole work) with a strong moral bias: Rome grew great through the *uirtus* (see next note) of her citizens; but when she had acquired an empire and defeated her greatest rival, Carthage, greed and ambition subverted integrity and every other virtue (10.4).

21. For this aristocratic concept of 'doing the state some service' see D. C. Earl, *The Political Thought of Sallust* (1961) and *The Moral and Political Tradition of Rome* (1967).

22. As Ciceronian 'balance' is described by *concinnitas*, the imbalance of Sallust is *inconcinnitas*; for the same feature in Tacitus (more often described as *variatio*) see the chapter on Style, p. 220 f.

23. See, above all, his character sketch of Catiline in c. 5, and for Tacitus' 'borrowings' pp. 225–6. The same quality appears in his prologues and in some of his excursuses, e.g. in a 'Thucydidean' paragraph at *Cat.*38.3, ending 'under the pretext of the public good they all (sc. politicians of 'left' and 'right' alike) strove to obtain power for themselves'.

24. That is a fault that Tacitus, when he comes to write similar passages in the Sallustian mould, avoids.

245

25. Several long speeches (or letters) survive from the otherwise fragmentary *Histories*. These are printed in Ernout's Budé edition (Paris, 1946); for short fragments one must still have recourse to Maurenbrecher (Teubner, 1891–3).

26. Especially those of Caesar and Cato ·(*Cat.* 51 and 52), Marius (*Jug.* 85), and in the *Histories*, e.g. Licinius Macer (see p. 18 above).

27. cf. 8.7.16 *disciplinam militarem, qua stetit ad hanc diem Romana res*, 'military discipline, through which to this day the Roman state has stood firm'; 26.41.12 *stetit una integra et immobilis uirtus populi Romani*, 'the valour of the Roman people alone stood immovable and unimpaired'.

28. For Livian influence on Tacitus' version of Claudius' speech urging admission of Gallic nobles to the senate see pp. 149 and 232.

29. Certainly so in his independence of political judgment—the emperor Augustus called him 'a supporter of Pompey' (*Pompeianum*).

30. For different reasons the surviving works of three writers can be ignored. Valerius Maximus produced a book of memorable historical examples, Curtius Rufus a history of Alexander. Velleius Paterculus, writing just before the downfall of Sejanus in AD 31, is something of a problem. Beginning as a very brief summary of (Greek and) Roman history, his work becomes more expansive as it nears his own day. As it does so, it more and more succumbs to its author's weakness for overblown rhetoric. Beneath the turgidity lies much historical information, but neither does Velleius claim that his work deserves the name 'history', nor did any of his countrymen regard it as such. For a recent survey see A. J. Woodman, 'Questions of date, genre and style in Velleius' in *CQ* 25 (1975), 272–306.

31. See also Pliny, *Ep.* 1.13.3 and Quintilian 10.1.102.

32. Cf. Pliny, *Ep.* 3.5.6; Seneca, *Ep.* 30 (for his death), Tacitus, *Dialogus* 23.2, Quintillian 10.1.103. See also Syme, Index and Appendix 38.

33. See G. B. Townend, *Hermes* 88 (1960), 98–120 and *Hermes* 89 (1961), 227–48.

34. A Fabius Rusticus is named in the will of Dasumius in AD 108.

35. Not always: see, for instance, *Ann.* 1.65 with Goodyear's notes thereon.


**II** · TACITUS AND THE CONTEMPORARY SCENE   *pages 26–38*

1. Gaius according to Sidonius Apollinaris (*Epp.* 4.14.1 and 22.2) in the fifth century, P. (Publius) according to the ninth century manuscript of *Annals* I-VI.

2. There is inscriptional evidence for the rare cognomen *Tacitus* from Narbonensis; see Syme 622 n.3.

3. For another view (consul in 78) see A. R. Birley in *Essays in honour of C. E. Stevens* (1975), 139–54.

4. Titus died in autumn 81, but it is possible that the quaestors for the following year had already been appointed.

5. Inscriptional evidence for the date is in *Inscr. Ital.* xiii, 1, p. 62 f.

6. A few high fliers might become praetor before the age of 31 or 32, but many aspirants would have to wait till their later 30s.

7. The others were the *pontifices*, augurs, and the *epulones*.

8. See A. N. Sherwin-White on Pliny 4.8.1; also Syme 66 n.4 and Appendix 22.

9. A civilian post, such as that of prefect of the military treasury (*aerarium militare*), held by the Younger Pliny after his praetorship, might be equally conducive to further advancement.

10. See Syme 68 n.4.

11. The two consuls who took office on 1 January of each year were *consules ordinarii*. At some time during the year it became the custom under the Empire to replace them with a pair of *consules suffecti*, who in turn might be replaced by a further pair of suffect consuls. During Tacitus' lifetime there were normally six or more consuls each year; the total would not fall very far short of the total number of legionary legates who lived long enough after that post to have a normal expectation of a consulship.

12. See *Agric.* 9.1; Agricola probably became governor of Aquitania in AD 74 and suffect consul in 77 (or 78, see n. 3) at the age of 37.

13. Pliny reached that goal at the age of 38 or 39; his exceptional merit was in the financial sphere. Tenure in succession of the prefecture of the military treasury and of the Treasury of Saturn brought him to the consulship not more than seven years after his praetorship; nine or ten years would be a more normal gap.

14. No English word quite hits off the Greek adverb *semnōs*, which Pliny here uses to describe Tacitus' style—clearly Pliny felt that no Latin word would do either; the general idea is 'with majesty, stateliness'.

15. The post was generally, though not exclusively, held by those who had not gone after the consulship to command of an imperial province. It would have been unusual, therefore, if Agricola had gone on to be proconsul of Asia after serving an extended term as military governor of Britain; in the upshot (if Tacitus is to be believed) he was persuaded to request Domitian to be allowed *not* to stand for the post (*Ag.* 42.1-2).

16. Professor Goodyear's note on *exin . . . patescit* (2.61.2) concludes that (i) *mare rubrum* means our Red Sea; (ii) the expansion referred to is the annexation of Arabia Petraea in AD 106; (iii) 'Trajan's Parthian campaigns are still in the future'. I agree.

17. A parallel has been thought to exist between the accessions of Tiberius and Hadrian, both of whom came to power (it was believed) by the scheming of the former emperor's widow. The same year also saw the execution of four eminent ex-consuls on a charge of treasonable conspiracy; for possible correspondences (not always convincing) see Syme 465 ff.

18. A. N. Sherwin-White, *The Letters of Pliny* (Oxford, 1966) 100.

19. See the list in Syme, Appendix 12.

20. The same would presumably be true in the *Histories*, if the portions more concerned with domestic politics had not been lost.

21. See Pliny, *Ep.* 4.22.4-6.

22. Pliny was one of his prosecutors; it is about this trial that he writes to Tacitus in *Ep.* 7.33 in the hope that Tacitus will include some account of it in his *Histories* (see p. 30 above).

247

23. That is, the ideal achieved during the reign of Tiberius by Marcus Lepidus; see *Ann.* 4.20 and Index.

24. The emphasis must be on 'primarily', since even those whose career was mainly in the civilian sphere normally spent some time in a legionary post, though that need not involve active military service.

25. See Pliny *Epp.* 4.3 and 8.18 respectively.

26. A third in 100 is now guaranteed by the *Fasti Ostienses*.

27. He was, however, to be executed by Hadrian in 136 as part of the intrigue for the succession at the end of Hadrian's reign.

28. See Pliny 7.6.10 and A. N. Sherwin-White ad loc.

29. See Syme *s.vv.* and c. XLIV (especially pp. 603–6).

30. Not always rated as low as it is nowadays; it impressed Dante and Chaucer.

31. For Tacitus' reaction to this in the Dialogus see p. 61.

32. Even so, in his programmatic first satire Juvenal thought it prudent to refrain from attacking living persons; see 1.170–1.

33. The last letter of Pliny referring to Tacitus (9.23, probably to be dated between AD 106 and 108) still seems to imply that Tacitus' fame depended on his oratory; see Sherwin-White on *studiis* (9.23.2).


**III** · THE LESSER WORKS   *pages 39–66*

1. See, however, p. 17.

2. In the present instance Tacitus seems to be recalling both the opening words of the *Origines* (*clarorum uirorum atque magnorum*, 'great and famous men') and another phrase from the same work, *clarorum uirorum laudes atque uirtutes* (note again the use of the word *uirtus*).

3. In case there should be any doubt about this, language and style deliberately recall Sallust, especially the following phrases: (1) 'he was present everywhere on the march'; *multus in agmine* reproduces Sallust's description of Sulla in *Jugurtha* 96.3, *in agmine . . . multus adesse*; (2) 'he gave the enemy no rest'; *nihil . . . quietum pati* follows Sallust, *Jug.* 66.1 *nihil intactum neque quietum pati*.

4. For its plausible identification with Bennachie, 3½ miles SW. of Durno ('the largest camp known N. of the Antonine Wall') see J. K. St Joseph in *JRS* 67 (1977), 141 ff.

5. Similar digressions designed to mark off sections of the narrative occur also in Sallust and Livy.

6. So in Livy XXI we are given speeches of the opposing generals, Scipio and Hannibal, before the Battle of Ticinum in 218 BC.

7. It is a paradox that in his later, purely historical works he seems to have entertained doubts about the convention, at least to the extent of generally avoiding pairs of speeches, both written in direct speech (*oratio recta*); see p. 177.

8. See Ogilvie-Richmond ad loc.

9. Cf. OCD.

10. Especially by the preservation and display of the portrait masks of ancestors; cf. OCD *imagines*.

11. The manuscript reading *obruet* (future) is defended by Ogilvie-Richmond ad loc.: Haupt's conjecture *obruit* ('has buried') gives a more obvious antithesis, but *difficilior lectio potior*.

12. It begins with the phrase 'the geography and peoples of Britain'; cf. Sallust, *Jug.* 17.1 'My subject seems to demand a brief account of the geography and of those nations. . .' and Livy, *per.* 104 'The first part of the book contains a description of the geography of Germany and of the ways of its people' (*situm Germaniae moresque*). This (lost) book of Livy's history may well have been laid under contribution by Tacitus for his *Germania*, whose full and correct title was (it seems) *de origine et situ Germanorum*, 'On the origins and geography of the Germans'.

13. The transition to the second half at 27.2 is marked with the words: 'This is the account we have received in general about the Germans as a whole: now I will explain the customs and practices of the individual tribes. . . .'

14. For the ambiguity attached to the name see n. 22 below.

15. The better attested reading is *pariendum* ('she must give birth'), not *pereundum* ('she must die'). The idea of 'giving birth' comes naturally into the next sentence, but the parallelism of the sentence 'so she must live, so she must . . .' guarantees that the sentence refers to what has just been said, not what is about to be said. In that context the antithesis of 'life and death' is more appropriate.

16. The most conspicuous feature, which survives in translation, is the repetition at the beginning of parallel phrases or clauses of the same word.

17. The statement that the bride gave a sword to her husband seems to be in conflict with Tacitus' earlier statement (6.1) that few Germans use swords; nor is there later evidence for the practice that Tacitus here mentions.

18. For the latter see Herodotus 1.133.3–4.

19. Tacitus is more than normally vague about where they lived, but they are said to be neighbours of the Suiones (= Swedes).

20. See OCD *agri decumates*. The paragraph may be a late insertion into material drawn by Tacitus from an earlier source, for it breaks the geographical progression from the Mattiaci in c. 29 to the Chatti in c. 30. That earlier source may well be the Elder Pliny, who had served for a decade on the Rhine until the late 50s, and wrote an account of the wars in Germany in twenty books.

21. See Syme 127–8.

22. Their organization into the two provinces of Upper and Lower Germany dates to about AD 90, in the reign of Domitian; even then their financial administration remained with the procurator of Gallia Belgica.

23. R. Much, *Die Germania des Tacitus*, 3rd edition, revised by W. Lange, with the assistance of H. Jankuhn, 1967; the excellent English edition by J.G.C. Anderson (1938) is briefer, but still occupies nearly three hundred pages.

24. Vipstanus Messalla and Iulius Secundus are attested outside the *Dialogus* (for the former, who is mentioned several times in the *Histories*, see p. 87), Curiatius Maternus may be (see n. 37): Marcus Aper is known only from the *Dialogus*. For the last three see Syme, Appendixes 90 and 91.

25. See p. 237.

26. Both Rhenanus and Lipsius in the sixteenth century believed that Tacitus could not be the author.
27. See p. 39.
28. For alternative suggestions, none of them convincing, see Syme 670 nn. 2–4.
29. There are two problems here, the exact meaning of *statio* in 17.3 and the fact that the arithmetic contained in 17.2 and 3 gives a date two or three years later.
30. For their feud and a character sketch of Priscus see *Hist.* 4.4.5.
31. The name of the new play will be *Thyestes*. A play of that name by Seneca survives. The theme of dynastic murder and revenge might seem more than pertinent in view of the murders of Claudius, Britannicus and Agrippina.
32. Quintilian also wrote a lost work on 'the causes for the decline in eloquence', *de causis corruptae eloquentiae.*
33. In so doing, of course, Maternus neither contests Cicero's supremacy as an orator nor the superiority of the broad-based Ciceronian education over the contemporary concentration on rhetorical exercises.
34. In Cicero's *De oratore* (2.40) Antonius admits to having played such a rôle. There are very close parallels between the *Dialogus* and the *De oratore* (see below), but nowhere does Aper concede that he is putting forward a view in which he does not believe.
35. Both names are significant; they figure in Tacitus' *Histories* as immensely powerful and unsavoury. Both held the consulship more than once (Marcellus for the second time in 74, Crispus for the third time c. 83). But Tacitus' readers would know one further fact; in the last year of Vespasian's reign Marcellus was accused of conspiracy and executed.
36. The victory is not explicitly conceded, but seems to be tacitly accepted by the participants—with the possible exception of Aper.
37. That depends on the identification of Tacitus' Maternus with the 'sophist' Maternus, about whom Dio Cassius records under the year 91 that Domitian put him to death, because he spoke against tyrants 'in a practice speech'. The date and other details perhaps tip the scales against the identification.
38. See c.xi, n. 12.
39. The closest parallel is in Longinus' treatise 'On the Sublime', where reference is made (c. 44) to the common view that 'democracy is a good nurse of talent; great writers flourished with democracy and died with it'. For some other post-Augustan discussions of the problem of literary decline cf. Velleius Paterculus 1.16–18; (elder) Seneca, *contr.* 1 *praef.* 6–10; (younger) Seneca, *Ep.* 114.1–2.
40. To take examples only from his first and last works, cf. *Agric.* 42.4 (of Agricola) and *Ann.* 4.20.2–3 (of Marcus Lepidus).
41. Colour is lent to the suggestion by the fact that history was acknowledged to have close stylistic affinities with poetry; cf. Quintilian 10.1.31 *historia . . . est proxima poetis, et quodam modo carmen solutum est,* 'History is very close to poetry; it is, so to speak, poetry free from the restrictions of verse.'
42. So, in the Preface to the *Histories* (1.2.3) Tacitus says: 'refusal and

acceptance of office were both regarded as grounds for accusation', *omissi gestique honores pro crimine*.

# IV · THE *HISTORIES* *pages 67–103*

1. *Ag.* 3.3; see Ogilvie-Richmond ad loc.
2. The figure depends on the estimate for the total for the *Annals*. Together *Histories* and *Annals* totalled thirty books (Jerome, *Comm. ad Zach.* 3.14).
3. He is accorded a character sketch, in typically Tacitean style, in c. 10; see p. 217.
4. Galba's speech, the first in the *Histories*, has as its central argument the claim that adoption produces better rulers than hereditary succession: *optimum quemque adoptio inueniet* ('adoption will find the best man'; 1.16.1 fin.). Many scholars have seen in Galba's speech a graceful tribute to the reigning emperor, Trajan, who had himself been adopted by the elderly Nerva. But though Galba's language is noble and fine-sounding, when he speaks of himself as called to assume imperial power by the unanimous will of gods and men, or when he asserts that the adoption of Piso will remove the only charge against him—that he is old—his claims are at odds with the facts. Nor would it be any compliment to Trajan to imply that his adoption by Nerva might be equated with that of the ill-starred Piso by Galba. Yet, though Galba's speech is not to be regarded as an oration *à clef*, many contemporaries would readily apply to Trajan such phrases as 'adoption will find the best man'. We may doubt whether that is Tacitus' message. Galba's speech is to be taken neither as praise nor as condemnation of Trajan. If it has a contemporary lesson, it is that adoption is not to be regarded as a panacea.
5. *Hist.* 1.49.3 *pecuniae alienae non adpetens, suae parcus, publicae auarus* :: Sallust, *Cat.* 5.4 *alieni adpetens, sui profusus*. As in many of Tacitus' 'borrowings' from Sallust, the differences are no less important than the similarities.
6. 1.71; Tacitus seems to show a marked partiality towards Celsus. Was he among Tacitus' sources? See Syme, Appendix 32.
7. Plutarch, *Otho* 3 :: Tacitus, *Hist.* 1.81.1.
8. In the upshot their main forces did not arrive in time to influence the decisive battle, but Tacitus' assertion that over-confidence caused them to travel slowly is disputed by modern scholars, who are inclined rather to praise the speed with which they moved into north Italy; see section 8 (The Arrival of the Balkan Legions) in Wellesley's article in *JRS* 61 (1971), 28 ff.
9. 2.18–9. The Spurinna episode is found also in Plutarch (*Otho* 5); comparison between the two authors is instructive, and overwhelmingly in Tacitus' favour (see pp. 193–4. Spurinna himself is a person of some interest; see p. 193).
10. This is an article of faith, held by almost all scholars; it is based more on probability than demonstrable fact. Such evidence as there is supports the thesis: Tacitus seems repeatedly to re-locate and reorganize transmitted material, Plutarch does not.
11. The prominence that Tacitus gives to Paullinus suggests the use of a source favourable to that general.

12. Plutarch gives greater prominence to Celsus than to Suetonius Paullinus, Tacitus the reverse—see n. 11.

13. It is usually so called, though in fact it took place much nearer Cremona.

14. Another view of the digression and its memorable language is possible; Mr. Wellesley writes to me: 'I find this purple patch of Tacitus mere rant.'

15. Dio, however, after making the general observation quoted above, goes on to make the same specific contrast as Tacitus: 'having seized the empire most villainously (sc. by the murder of Galba) he quit it most excellently.' The references for the preceding quotations are: Plutarch, *Otho* 18; Suetonius, *Otho* 12.2 fin.; Dio 63.15.2$^2$; Tacitus, *Hist.* 2.50.1.

16. The date of 18 July, given by Tacitus at 2.91.1, seems to refer to an incident soon after Vitellius' arrival in Rome, but does not fix that date; *maturis frugibus* (2.87.2)—the corn was already ripe, but not gathered—probably suits a later date better than an early one; so Heubner 290-1. K. Wellesley (*The Long Year* 101) prefers a date late in June, and this fits in with Josephus' account (B.I.4.585 ff.). But even if this is so, it scarcely allows time for news of Vitellius' behaviour in Rome to reach Vespasian soon enough to be the cause of his proclamation as emperor at the beginning of July. See now Chilver's Commentary on 2.87.1 and pp. 161-2.

17. K. Wellesley, *The Histories, Book III* (Sydney, 1972), p. 19.

18. See especially K. Wellesley in *Tacitus* (ed. T. A. Dorey; Routledge & Kegan Paul, 1969) 92-5.

19. Also Dio 65.17.1 ff.

20. This corresponds with the second of Vitellius' attempts to abdicate in Suetonius' version. The first attempt, unlike the second and third, was quite informal. If it ever happened (and that is not certain) Tacitus may simply have omitted it; see K. Wellesley, *The Long Year* 166-7 and 188 ff.

21. The details, including his attempt to surrender his dagger, the symbol of his power of life and death over citizens, are in essence those given by Tacitus for the abortive abdication on the previous day.

22. Some of the powers conferred on Vespasian can be read on the fragmentary bronze tablet (= *Inscriptiones Latinae Selectae* 244), commonly referred to as the *Lex de Imperio Vespasiani*; see Wellesley, *The Long Year* pp. 207 ff. and Plate 12.

23. A warning is perhaps necessary about the term 'Stoic opposition'. Many of the people here referred to happened to be Stoics, and doubtless their Stoicism coloured their republican sentiments; but Stoicism did not, as a matter of principle, preach opposition to monarchic rule—witness Seneca.

24. *Libertas* is here used primarily in the sense of freedom of speech and action for the senate. For the concept of *libertas senatoria* cf. p. 187.

25. To some extent this may only reflect the use of an excellent source or sources. The Elder Pliny, who wrote a history of the times and had firsthand acquaintance with the area, is a likely candidate; but the idea that Tacitus merely transcribed what he found will not hold water; see p. 198.

26. See previous note.

27. 4.57.3; *flagitium* is one of the strongest words of moral condemnation in the Latin language.

28. It is probable that another pair of balancing speeches occurred in Book V, for where our manuscripts break off Civilis and Cerialis face each other across a gap in a broken bridge, and Civilis has just embarked on a speech defending his conduct; it is almost certain that there would be an answering speech from Cerialis.

29. The peroration closely follows the words that Livy puts in the mouth of the consul, Sp. Postumius, who had been in charge of the humiliating Roman surrender at the Caudine Forks; see Livy 9.8.8 f.

30. The evidence is given by the author in *JRS* 57 (1967), 109–14.

## V · THE *ANNALS* – TIBERIUS  *pages 104–143*

1. See pp. 162–3.

2. The Roman numerals are added for the reader's convenience. The relevant dates are (i) death of Augustus, AD 14, (ii) deaths of Germanicus and Drusus, 19 and 23 respectively, (iii) death of Livia, AD 29, (iv) death of Sejanus, AD 31.

3. And others who wrote of Tiberius.

4. '*postquam remoto* pudore et *metu*' (*Ann.*6.51.3) :: *postquam remoto metu Punico* (Sallust, *Hist.*1.12M).

5. So it is to Tiberius that Tacitus applies *subdolus* and the concepts of *simulatio* and *dissimulatio*; see, for instance, *occultum ac subdolum fingendis uirtutibus* ('given to concealment and an artful simulator of virtues') in stage (ii) of Tiberius' obituary notice.

6. See (ii) in the passage quoted on p. 105.

7. Compare the same phrase at *Hist.*1.11.3, which similarly marks off the first eleven chapters of the *Histories* as a self-contained unit.

8. See the chapter on Style, pp. 226–7.

9. There is a strong probability that Livia is cast in the rôle of the emperor's murdering wife on the analogy of Agrippina, who may very well have murdered her husband, the emperor Claudius. If this is the case, the rumour could not have attached itself to the Augustan situation till after AD 54, the date of Claudius' death. The episode has been much discussed by scholars; for a balanced survey cf. pp. 125–9 of F.R.D. Goodyear's edition of *Annals* I (cc. 1–54).

10. 'Merely corroborative detail, intended to give artistic verisimilitude to an otherwise bald and unconvincing narrative' (Pooh-Bah in the *Mikado*).

11. Compare the description of Domitian's behaviour in *Agricola* 45.2.

12. That does not mean that people did not talk and think in this way. Dio Cassius has the same motif, probably independently of Tacitus; if so, Tacitus is utilising, not inventing, a rumour.

13. Cf. Dio 57.3.1–2; 4.1 and Suetonius, *Tib.*25.

14. The whole of the section (*Res Gestae* 34) is relevant to the two chapters of Tacitus under discussion here; 'In my sixth and seventh consulships (28–7 BC), after I had blotted out civil wars, gaining complete control of affairs with the consent of all, I transferred the state from my own power to the jurisdiction of the senate and Roman people. In return for this service I was called Augustus by decree of the senate . . . and a golden shield was set

in the Curia Iulia, which, as its inscription testified, the senate and Roman people gave me for my valour, clemency, justice and piety. After this time I excelled all in personal authority, though I possessed no more constitutional power than the others who were my colleagues in the various magistracies.'

15. Contrast Augustus' own claim in the opening words of the *Res Gestae*: 'At the age of nineteen on my own initiative and at my own expense I raised an army, with which I reasserted the freedom of the republic, which had been oppressed by the tyranny (*dominatio*) of a faction.'

16. This, rather than 'hesitant', seems to be the sense required here for *suspensa*, 'held in the balance'.

17. For this man see Index.

18. The death of Augustus at Nola on 19 August and the date on which the senate voted for his deification (17 September) are guaranteed by the *fasti* (official calendars). The cortège would take roughly a fortnight to make its way from Nola to Rome, so a date early in September is probable for the first meeting of the senate, at which Augustus' will was read and the funeral arrangements made. The date of the funeral may be put about a week later. At the meeting of the senate on 17 September the constitutional position of Tiberius was settled, and a grant of *imperium proconsulare* conferred on Germanicus. For a different (and controversial) view see K. Wellesley ('The *dies imperii* of Tiberius', *JRS* 57 (1967), 23–30) and the discussion (with select bibliography) in F. R. D. Goodyear's edition of *Annals* I. 1–54 (pp. 169–76).

19. The subject matter of cc. 46–7 may be regarded as *foris*; they describe the reaction at Rome to the two mutinies.

20. The six chapters (2.53–58) for AD 18 deal exclusively with Germanicus abroad. Did nothing happen at home? The *acta senatus* can scarcely have been a blank.

21. *ciuilis animus* implies the attitude of being no more than a *ciuis*, a citizen equal before the law.

22. See p. 201.

23. For a detailed study of the contrast between factual and non-factual material see B. Walker, *The Annals of Tacitus*, cc. 4, 6 and 7.

24. The overall structure, with its two triads for the reign of Tiberius, dictates that Book IV shall begin with the year 23, which sees the beginning of the rise of Sejanus.

25. That too is a double obituary, but is distinguished from all subsequent ones by the fact that the first of the pair is a woman and the daughter of Augustus.

26. Two things seem to have caught Tacitus' eye. He it was who founded the great wealth of the family; and his homonymous son appears in a double obituary at the end of AD 56—they are the only father and son to receive obituaries in the extant books of the *Annals*.

27. Until 31, the year of his downfall, Sejanus' only formal appointment was as prefect of the praetorian guard, but the word 'minister', in its sense of 'servant of the ruler', can conveniently be applied to him.

28. See p. 137 below.

29. See p. 131.
30. See p. 70.
31. Tiberius and Tacitus believed Apicata's word: not all modern scholars are persuaded. One may ask how Apicata, whom Sejanus had divorced after his seduction of Livilla and before the murder, knew the 'facts'. The 'proofs' that Tiberius later obtained are not above suspicion either.
32. But it might not be easy or politic to try to bring military commanders to trial; see what is said in 6.30 of Lentulus Gaetulicus, governor of Upper Germany.
33. These last are the words used by the senate to proclaim a state of emergency.
34. E.g. 4.21.3 (Cassius Severus), 6.4.1 (Latiaris), 6.10.2, 6.30.1 ('Yet, wherever opportunity offered, prosecutors were punished'—examples follow).
35. See p. 205 f.
36. The matter was referred to the *quindecimuiri* ('college of fifteen'); Tacitus was a *quindecimuir* himself half a century later.
37. One notice (4.44) covers three people.
38. The second of the three notices gives a double obituary.
39. See Syme 729.
40. The Latin, *sic Tiberius finiuit*, is as strikingly original as the English.
41. See p. 106 f.
42. Books I and III; Sejanus does not figure in Book II.
43. See also 1.69.5; 3.16.1; 3.29.4; 3.35.2; 3.72.3.
44. Many modern historians regard the whole Sejanus affair with scepticism— did he really poison Drusus, did he scheme to succeed Tiberius? Two points seem incontrovertible. The details of the narrative of these years show Sejanus determined to establish himself as the most powerful man after the emperor; the extreme caution and secretiveness with which Tiberius arranged his overthrow indicates that here was a man whom the emperor feared.

**VI** · THE *ANNALS* - CLAUDIUS   *pages 144–161*

1. The details are from Suetonius, *Claudius* 30.
2. *Ibid.* 4.5–6.
3. The last of these is in c. 25, since from c. 26 Tacitus is concerned, in a continuous narrative, with the remarkable series of events that led up to the death of Messalina.
4. 11.13.1 'But Claudius, ignorant of the state of his marriage and busy with the duties of a censor . . .'; 11.25.5 'That was the end of his unawareness of what was going on in his own house. . . .'
5. His future success and infamy is singled out for comment by Tacitus during the reign of Tiberius (4.31.3); during the reign of Nero he crossed swords with Seneca (see 13.42–43 and p. 168).
6. A *saeculum* was variously calculated as being of 100 or 110 years duration. The games had been celebrated by Augustus in 17 BC. Claudius, using the

100 year cycle, marked the 800th anniversary of the traditional date of Rome's founding.

7. Diviners, of Etruscan origin, who inspected and interpreted entrails (also portents and prodigies); cf. OCD.

8. Cf. Syme, Appendix 40, esp. pp. 704–5.

9. Or by divorcing them from a meaningful context—so the failure to look at the quaestorship in the total context of Claudius' administrative reforms.

10. For opposing views cf. K. Wellesley, 'Can You trust Tacitus?' (*Greece and Rome* N.S. I (1954), 13 ff.) and N. P. Miller, 'The Claudian Tablet and Tacitus: a Reconsideration' (*Rheinisches Museum* 99 (1956), 304 ff.). Wellesley defends the good sense of Claudius' speech and condemns Tacitus' version for its futility and artificiality: Miss Miller argues that Tacitus 'while re-writing the speech into the elaborate and conventional literary form . . . has preserved for us correctly the speaker, the occasion and the main arguments'.

11. The top of the tablet is broken, giving what I take to be a short lacuna at the beginning and in the middle of the speech.

12. Such I take to be the meaning of *omnem florem ubique coloniarum et municipiorum*, though Italy is not specifically mentioned.

13. Though Valerius Asiaticus is not mentioned by name, the reference to 'that brigand's accursed name and that squirming monstrosity of hatefulness' (*dirum nomen latronis . . . et odi illud palaestricum prodigium*) is clinched by the mention of his consulship.

14. See n. 10.

15. The Tacitean Claudius adds further historical parallels to demonstrate the success of the Roman policy of non-exclusiveness, and he mentions that there is historical precedent for allowing the sons of freedmen to hold office. This latter remark we know from Suetonius (*Claudius* 24.1) to have been made by the historical Claudius on a different occasion, and it is interesting to speculate (for it can only be speculation) why Tacitus should have inserted the detail here. Clearly, however, it is a stroke of the pen that helps to identify the speaker as Claudius.

16. See too Dio 60.31.1–5; much of the material is also found in one place or another in Suetonius—see especially *Claudius* 29.3.

17. Tacitus is clearly contemptuous of the fact that on a matter of such importance it is the opinion of his freedmen that Claudius seeks, for the language he uses is, ironically, that which describes the summoning of an imperial privy council (12.1.2 fin.).

18. None of the early emperors took greater pleasure in being saluted as *imperator* by the army. He was so acclaimed twenty-seven times in his reign of fourteen years.

19. To be distinguished from Mithridates, king of Bosporus, who is the subject of 12.15–21.

20. C. Cassius Longinus. Cassius is to figure prominently in Tacitus' account of Nero's reign. He is here (12.12.1) accorded a character sketch, couched in Sallustian language and style, that underlines his determination to uphold ancient standards (*priscus mos*), as far as contemporary circum-

stances would allow. He is clearly one of those historical personages who particularly engaged Tacitus' interest.

21. See Claudius' use of the same word two pages earlier.
22. *ostentui clementiae suae et in nos dehonestamento*; 12.14.3. The last word is a 'choice' noun, whose use is confined almost exclusively to Sallust and Tacitus, in neither of whom is it common. Standing alongside the imperial virtue of *clementia* it strongly emphasises the sarcasm intended by Gotarzes' gesture.
23. See pp. 179 ff.
24. *ita maioribus placitum, quanta peruicacia in hostem, tanta beneficentia aduersus supplices utendum*; 12.20.2. The same ideal is epitomised in Virgil's 'spare the vanquished, and fight the arrogant to the end', *parcere subiectis et debellare superbos* (*Aen.* 6.853).
25. The appointment will have been noted in the earlier, missing part of Claudius' reign; Corbulo is mentioned by that single name, an indication that he had already been spoken of.
26. There is, however, a curious coda; the triumphal insignia, according to Tacitus, pale into insignificance in comparison with Pomponius' renown as a poet. In the traditional scale of Roman values, to which Tacitus normally subscribes, poetry does not rank above military prowess.
27. In fact c. 40 deals with the governorship of his successor, Didius Gallus; but Gallus is rapidly dismissed—he was an old man, rich in honours, who was content to keep the enemy at bay. Tacitus notes at the end of the chapter that he has departed from the annalistic structure in this section; in fact, though recorded at the end of his account of AD 50, the British chapters here cover the period 47-57.
28. The exact meaning of *publica acta* is uncertain.
29. This is the first time that prodigies have figured prominently in the *Annals*; for further examples see esp. 12.64.1 and 15.47.1. It has been argued that Tacitus has now turned to a source, perhaps Pliny the Elder, that had a particular interest in such matters. There is not enough evidence to prove or disprove the hypothesis.
30. Tacitus, however, is the only authority to implicate Xenophon in Claudius' murder; some scepticism is perhaps advisable.
31. Tacitus builds up the dramatic tension by a piece of palpable invention. Narcissus, he says, embraced Britannicus and, calling on the gods, urged him to grow up quickly, so that he might scatter his father's enemies and take vengeance on his mother's murderers. Since it was Narcissus himself who had given the order for Messalina's murder (11.37.2), such an appeal to Britannicus is incredible. Moreover, Suetonius (*Claud.* 43) describes the same scene, but with Claudius, not Narcissus, embracing Britannicus. That at least seems possible. Tacitus has apparently transferred the detail to Narcissus to heighten the tension.
32. The attested absence of Narcissus from Rome at the time of Claudius' death may have helped to give credence to the belief that the emperor had been poisoned.
33. The contents of the will are uncertain. Suetonius (*Claud.* 44.1) might imply that the will placed Britannicus before Nero, while Tacitus (12.69.3) could

257

imply the reverse. Possibly Nero's name was mentioned first simply because he was the elder. For Agrippina and her supporters any mention of Britannicus was undesirable, and that may have been cause enough for the suppression of the will.

34. A. Momigliano, *Claudius: the Emperor and his Achievement* (1934; 2nd edition 1961).

**VII** · THE *ANNALS* - NERO    *pages 162-188*

1. It is underlined by further parallels between 1.5.4 and 12.68.3.
2. 1 January AD 69; but the opening chapters include some backward glances at events of the preceding six months.
3. It would have included the state visit to Rome of Tiridates, Nero's own visit to Greece and his triumphal return to Rome, as well as the outbreak and first stages of the Jewish revolt and the rebellions of Vindex in Gaul and Galba in Spain. Others have argued that Nero's reign occupied six books; see especially Syme 263-66 and Appendix 35 ('The Total of Books'). On that assumption the *Annals* totalled eighteen books, the *Histories* twelve.
4. Numismatic evidence supports the literary testimony, for at the start of Nero's reign the head of Agrippina appears opposite Nero's on the obverse of coins.
5. He had been exiled for his adultery with Messalina, penultimate wife of Claudius.
6. The sarcasm lies in the fact that a freedman could not hold a magistracy, his relationship to Nero being a personal one without any constitutional basis.
7. See p. 177.
8. The same technique is used elsewhere, but less blatantly, e.g. in the way in which the appearances of Thrasea Paetus are organised; see p. 169.
9. For the whole of this passage cf. Miriam T. Griffin, *Seneca, a Philosopher in Politics* (Oxford, 1976), 281 ff.
10. 13.30.2; his father was the recipient of a formal obituary in 3.30.
11. He was further accorded a public funeral and other honours, as can be seen from a recently discovered inscription, published by Joyce Reynolds in *JRS* 61 (1971), 143.
12. The narrative of AD 56 had occupied only six chapters. That of 57 is still briefer, and its three chapters consist of events drawn exclusively from the realm of home affairs. Tacitus' affirmation that little worthy of note occurred, unless one wishes to fill volumes with an account of the building operations concerning the construction of Nero's amphitheatre in the Campus Martius, is almost certainly a dig against the Elder Pliny, whose *Natural History* (16.200) has just this sort of detail. What Tacitus himself offers for this year is jejune enough.
13. The picture of Seneca as capitalist and usurer figures prominently in Dio Cassius, who shows a marked hostility towards the philosopher.
14. See p. 94 on Eprius Marcellus.
15. His full name is Publius Clodius Thrasea Paetus, but he is commonly

referred to by the last two names, which are often inverted (Paetus Thrasea).

16. For Tacitus' attitude to Thrasea see 176 f., 186 f.

-17. The source of one (possibly both) of these incidents is Pliny the Elder, to whom Tacitus seems to have alluded so recently ( c. 31) in unflattering terms.

18. 12.1; Tacitus' attitude towards Thrasea at this time seems to be ambivalent.

19. His appointment to the province is probably to be put early in AD 58.

20. 14.29.1.

21. Some of the graphic qualities of the writing are discussed in the chapter on Style (c. 10); see pp. 218-9.

22. The effectiveness of Tacitus' invention is clearly seen by comparing the lengthy and turgid speech Dio gives to Boudicca (62.3-5) with the taut and telling words (14.35—less than half a page) that Tacitus puts in her mouth. The forcefulness of her closing words loses nothing from the fact that they bear the imprint of a skilled Roman rhetorician—'in that battle they must conquer or die. That was the resolve that she, a woman, had already made: let men live, and be slaves' (*uincendum illa acie uel cadendum esse. id mulieri destinatum: uiuerent uiri et seruirent*): rhetoric here underlines the desperate resolve of the British, and by punctuating the narrative marks the fact that the climax is at hand.

23. For the former quality cf. 12.12.1: for the latter 13.48.

24. His speech begins and ends with Sallustian phrases, the first recalling a phrase in the speech of the younger Cato (*Cat.* 52.7), in which he had argued for the execution of the Catilinarian conspirators, the latter underlining his point by a reference to the salutary military practice of decimation.

25. That interpretation has been widely held, and support for it has been claimed from Tacitus' comment (14.49.3) that Thrasea persisted in his motion about Antistius 'with his customary resolution and to avoid tarnishing his reputation' (see pp. 222-3 for a discussion of the passage). But this misinterprets the Latin; *gloria* does not here mean that Thrasea was moved by a spirit of vainglory, but by the desire to be seen remaining true to the principles that had already won him renown. Such an aim was wholly within the realm of public Roman virtues.

26. Since, however, attendance at meetings of the senate was normally obligatory, it might be construed as treasonable by Thrasea's enemies.

27. See A. Boethius, *The Golden House of Nero* (1960) and OCD *domus aurea*.

28. Tertullian, *Apologeticum* 16 criticises only Tacitus' lies about the Jews in *Histories* V.

29. This interpretation takes *sontes et nouissima exempla meritos* ('guilty and deserving the most extreme punishment') as representing the attitude of the people towards the Christians. As far as the Latin goes, it might be a statement of Tacitus' own view; but although he regarded Christianity as a 'pernicious superstition' (*exitiabilis superstitio*), he clearly did not regard them as guilty of arson, and it is doubtful whether he would feel that 'the most extreme punishment' was deserved on some more general charge,

such as the 'hatred of the human race' (*odium humani generis*), to which he makes reference in the previous paragraph.

The bibliography on this chapter is immense; among the sample of works quoted by Koestermann in his Commentary (1968) J. Beaujeu, 'L'incendie de Rome en 64 et les Chrétiens', *Latomus* 19 (1960), 65–80 and 219–311 is a useful starting point.

30. Tacitus expresses ignorance of the reason for her involvement in the plot; a later authority, not necessarily reliable, indicates a connection with the family of Seneca.

31. 14.59.4 :: 16.11.3. Use of the same word *ludibria* ('mockery') in both passages emphasises their parallelism.

32. Though the identity is not certain, it is not hard to believe that this was the Petronius who wrote the picaresque *Satyricon* (sc. *libri*).

33. The similarity of Dio 62.26.1 suggests that Tacitus' memorable phrase may have been inspired by their common source.

34. The same senatorial sitting saw the trial and condemnation of Barea Soranus.

35. See p. 184 above.

36. Cf. Seneca, *De ira* 3.15.3: *in omni seruitute apertam libertati uiam*, 'in slavery the path to freedom is always open'.

37. In such a context 'senatorial freedom' means primarily the right of a senator to speak his mind; no one any longer believed that a senator could have, or should have, an unrestricted right to control events—that power ultimately lay with the *princeps*.

38. It is uncertain whether the *Annals* ended with Nero's death in June 68, or continued to the end of the year, thus joining up with the starting point of the *Histories*, 1 January 69.

39. In fact, they break off in the middle of a sentence, just as Thrasea, in great pain and on the point of death, turns towards the philosopher, Demetrius.

40. Tacitus' superiority is evident from a comparison of his account of the death of Vitellius (*Hist.* 3.84.4–85) with that of Suetonius (*Vitellius* 16–17).

41. The fact that scholars cannot agree whether the rest of the reign was completed in a further half book, or required two and a half books more (see p. 162–3 and n. 3) is some indication of the uncertainty that attends the issue.

42. For the evidence see pp. 170 ff.

## VIII · THE SOURCES — *HISTORIES*   pages 189–198

1. Pliny, *Ep.* 5.8.12 explains his reason for shying away from writing (past) history: *parata inquisitio, sed onerosa collatio*, 'the material is to hand, but the task of comparing the different accounts is a burden'; cf. Cicero, *ad Att.* 2.6.1 for a similar attitude.

2. At 3.51 Sisenna is named as the authority for a particularly heinous incident 150 years earlier.

3. E.g. 2.37.1, 101.1; 3.29.2, 51.1; 4.83.1; 5.3.1.

4. E.g. 1.41 (Galba), 3.84–5 (Vitellius); for other conspicuous moments signalised by variants cf. 1.42–3; 3.29.2, 51.1.

5. See also Plutarch, *Otho* 3in. ('Cluvius Rufus says') and Suetonius, *Otho* 7.1 (*ut quidam tradiderunt*, 'as some have recorded'), which strongly suggest that the reference (sc. to Cluvius Rufus) already stood in the common source. Though Tacitus omits this incident (Otho's use of the name 'Nero' on documents dispatched to Spain—Suetonius simply says 'some provincial governors'), he makes a similar point at 1.78.2 fin., on which now see Chilver's Commentary.

6. The evidence may most conveniently be consulted in E. G. Hardy, *Studies in Roman History* (First Series) 294–333 or in the Introduction to his edition of Plutarch's *Lives of Galba and Otho* (1890).

7. See note 6.

8. *Hermes* 4 (1870), 295 ff.

9. *Kritische Untersuchungen über die Quellen der 4. und 5. Dekade des Livius* (1863).

10. See P. G. Walsh, *Livy* (Cambridge, 1967), 141 ff.

11. For the whole question see Syme, Appendix 29.

12. From 2.55.1 we can infer that Otho's death was reported in Rome on April 19th.

13. See K. Wellesley, *JRS* 61 (1971), 28–51 (esp. p. 41), and Appendix in his edition of *Histories* III.

14. See, for example, the interrelationship of events concerning Flavius Sabinus, Vitellius and Antonius Primus at the end of Book III, for which see pp. 90–1.

15. See pp. 81–2.

16. For the present series of debates see Syme 186–8.

17. Documentary evidence for Mucianus' almost autocratic powers exists in the *Lex de imperio Vespasiani* (see c. IV n. 22): Tacitus chooses to make the reality apparent through a vividly dramatic episode.

18. Pliny (the Younger), *Ep.*3.5: 'all the wars' may not extend beyond AD 47, the year when Claudius recalled Corbulo from Germany.

19. His instruction that his history should not be published till after his death was motivated by his desire to escape accusations that he was seeking to ingratiate himself with the ruling household; cf. *N.H. praef.* 20.

20. At the end of Book IV (4.82 ff.) there is an excursus on the origin and nature of the worship of the god Serapis, whose shrine Vespasian visited while waiting at Alexandria for favourable sailing conditions to take him to Italy. Tacitus writes: 'the god's origin has not yet been made generally known by Roman writers.' There is no reason for not taking Tacitus' statement at its face value; any attempt to find a *Latin* source for the information he gives is misguided. But it would be equally misguided to expect that Tacitus had conducted his own researches into these questions; he is likely to have consulted a Greek author familiar with the Egyptian scene. Such a one is Manetho, an Egyptian priest associated with the worship of Serapis, who wrote a history of Egypt in Greek in the third century BC. Tacitus may have consulted him at first hand or through an intermediary.

The excursus at the beginning of Book V on the origins, customs, religion, geography and history of the Jews is a mish-mash of fact and fiction. It has generated a great volume of literature; for a brief selection

261

see pp. 305–6 of K. Wellesley's Penguin translation of the *Histories*, and add E. M. Smallwood, *The Jews under Romen rule: from Pompey to Diocletian* (1976).

**IX** · THE SOURCES – *ANNALS    pages 199–213*

1. The references to Domitian in the surviving books of the *Histories* do not suggest that his views had changed.
2. It is interesting that the only named citations both refer to the Elder Agrippina. That Pliny should take an interest in her is not surprising; his nephew claims that he was inspired to write his account of the German Wars by a vision in a dream of her father-in-law, Drusus (Tiberius' brother), who had campaigned in Germany and died there after reaching the Elbe.
3. Roman historians at times use the plural *quidam*, 'some', where there is good reason to suspect that only one authority is being alluded to.
4. For the much debated passage concerning the *capaces imperii* see Syme 694 and the discussion in Goodyear's Commentary ad loc.
5. See below, p. 201.
6. The favourite reading of Domitian were the *commentarii* and *acta* of Tiberius; it is unlikely that he would have gone for the latter ('transactions') to the cumbersome *acta senatus*.
7. Cf.6.7.5 where Tacitus speaks of his determination to record details that have been omitted by most historians.
8. The inference is valid, whether *publica acta* is a generic term including both the *acta senatus* and *acta diurna* or a third type of documentary material.
9. If the text is sound, this probably means 'senatorial writers'.
10. It is difficult to believe that it was not. But a single passage should not be used to construct an edifice of general principle. Professor Goodyear writes to me: 'The truth, I believe, is this: in some sections (concerning senatorial business) T. builds mainly on the *acta*, in other sections (including some which involve the senate) he builds on early historians, but may from time to time also consult the *acta*.' Though we have not enough evidence to prove that belief, it seems to me likely to come near the truth.
11. Judiciously sifted, it provides important information for the modern historian. A. J. Woodman (at n. 69 in his chapter on Velleius in *Empire and Aftermath: Silver Latin* II (ed. T. A. Dorey, Routledge and Kegan Paul, 1975)) argues that Tacitus, perhaps alone of Roman historians, knew Velleius, and drew on him for his portrait of Sejanus; if there is any such dependence, it is very slight.
12. Syme suggests AD 4–16.
13. Perhaps mention should also be made of the Elder Seneca, who wrote a history from the time of the civil wars almost to the date of his death (he outlived Tiberius by a few years). The history was not published during his lifetime, and has left no trace except for an account of Tiberius' death, quoted in Suetonius, *Tib*.73.2 (on the assumption that that incident comes from the history, and not some other work).
14. Cf. Questa (op. cit.) c. 4 (Le principali fonti di *Ann.* I-VI), pp. 125 ff.

15. Further parallels in the same section of narrative concern the 'necrology' of Augustus; the question of the time and responsibility for the murder of Agrippa Postumus; the relationship between Tiberius and the senate from the time of Augustus' death till the point at which Tiberius' position was formally confirmed; Tiberius' attitude towards Germanicus.

16. Cf. Goodyear's Commentary ad loc.

17. *Ann.* 1.7.6 makes it clear that that version was known to Tacitus.

18. In his article on Cassius Dio in Pauly-Wissowa (1899); *RE* III, 1716 ff.

19. Syme argues (272–3 and 691) that the theory tries to explain too much and is vulnerable on at least two counts—its assumption that a dominating portrait of the dead emperor could be imposed by a single literary figure, and its overestimate of the amount of ground that is common to Tacitus and Suetonius or Dio or all three. The former assumption is not *per se* impossible; for the latter point see the next paragraph.

20. But the causal connection that Dio gives to his note about the appearance of the phoenix in the year before Tiberius' death cannot come from Tacitus, and is unlikely to have been Dio's own invention.

21. If the single source theory is pursued, three names come into the reckoning: (i) Aufidius Bassus, whose history ended some time between AD 47 and the early 50s; (ii) Pliny the Elder, whose history (as its title, *a fine Aufidi Bassi*, indicates) began where Aufidius left off; (iii) Cluvius Rufus, consul not later than AD 41. Cluvius served Nero, Galba, Otho and Vitellius in turn without tarnishing his reputation for integrity. *Histories* 3.65.2 states that he was one of the two witnesses to the compact made between Vitellius and Vespasian's brother, Flavius Sabinus. That might seem to point to him as Tacitus' authority for the incident. A closer reading of the passage suggests otherwise. Tacitus speaks of the looks of the two signatories as seen from a distance: Cluvius, presumably, could have given information gained at close quarters. For all three writers see c. I p. 23.

22. See pp. 147 ff.

23. That Tacitus is here drawing on the three named sources *and no others* is the obvious interpretation of 13.20.2. Another interpretation can possibly be forced out of the Latin (so Iolanda Tresch, *Die Nerobücher . . . des Tacitus*, 1965); Tacitus undertakes to name the authorities responsible for variants, but not (where it exists) for the consensus. On this interpretation, at 13.20 the consensus existed in a number of unnamed authors: Fabius Rusticus, Cluvius Rufus and Pliny are authorities for variants outside the consensus.

24. On Tresch's interpretation (see n. 23) all is well. Fabius Rusticus is named because he gives a version different from the consensus. Cluvius Rufus is named along with 'the remaining authorities' because, although he here agrees with the consensus (and therefore does not need separate mention), he has been named at the beginning of the chapter for a detail that does not belong to the consensus. This interpretation is ingenious, but not convincing.

25. I find implausible the suggestion that the names that stand at 13.20 and 14.2 would have been removed, if Tacitus had been able to give his work a final revision—an argument, perhaps, that he died before he had time to carry out such a revision.

26. See p. 206 above.
27. There are also considerable differences, the most notable being that Dio does not even mention the name of Piso.
28. See pp. 180-1.
29. *exitus illustrium uirorum*; Pliny, *Ep.* 8.12.4.
30. At times (it is clear) he would draw on his literary source even to the extent of verbal detail.
31. But see pp. 208-9 above on 14.2.
32. See p. 184.
33. *Ann.* 4.10-11; see p. 131 above.

**X · STYLE**  *pages 214-235*

1. The quotation is from F. P. Wilson, *Elizabethan and Jacobean* (1946), who goes on to say (p. 26) 'It is the style of "so, so, break off this last lamenting kiss", of "Cover her face; mine eyes dazzle; she died young" '. For the 'Senecan amble' see G. Williamson's book of that name (1951) and M. Croll, *Style, Rhetoric and Rhythm* (1966).
2. While the influence of Livy must not be ignored, it is much less pervasive and much less penetrating. Livy's 'milky richness' savoured of complacency; Cicero would surely have approved of him—that is some indication of the gulf that separates him from Tacitus.
3. Whereas we regard periodic sentence structure as dependent on syntactical organization, the Greeks and Romans regarded it more as a unity audible to the ear; the unity is emphasised by assonance and rhythm.
4. The term *variatio* is used by scholars to signify this 'variation' (sc. of syntactical structure).
5. See Appendix 2 (pp. 334-5) in Goodyear's Commentary (Vol. I) for a succinct discussion of these terms as applied to the language of Tacitus.
6. As regards syntax, its most conspicuous features are the omission of coordinating conjunctions (particularly those, such as 'both . . . and', 'not only . . . but also', that stress parallelism), the omission of parts of the verb 'to be' (*esse*), the use of the historic infinitive in place of a finite verb, thus eliminating the inflectional ending conveying person and number.
7. This and the preceding example are Tacitus' own comments; both refer to wives of the imperial household.
8. Or are clearly anticipated by words such as *ita* or *adeo*.
9. The word *an*, which Tacitus here uses for 'or', lends a slight note of interrogation to the alternative, 'or (can it be?)'.
10. A similar piece of heightened writing occurs in another colourful episode, the description of the Druids among the British, as they sought to withstand the Roman invasion of Anglesey (*Ann.* 14.30). It should perhaps be emphasised that Tacitus does not insert a few highly coloured episodes in the middle of a colourless background. In addition to places (such as that illustrated here) where archaisms and poeticisms cluster thickly, there are, as Professor Goodyear puts it to me, 'lesser clusters and a certain sprinkling of tints all over the place'.
11. *Ann.* 1.8.5; see Goodyear ad loc.

12. Though this aspect of Tacitus' work cannot be properly understood without a good deal of Latin quotation, its function and extent can be understood by those with small Latin. It is for such readers that my chapter on 'Tacitus and his predecessors' (in *Tacitus*, ed. T. A. Dorey) was written.

13. In view of the paragraph of Gibbon quoted below, Tacitus' next sentence is also relevant:

> Nor did the provinces seek to reject that state of affairs; for they looked on the rule of the senate and Roman people with suspicion on account of the rivalries of the politically powerful and the greed of the magistrates, there being no help from laws that were overthrown by force, political influence, and finally bribery (. . . *inualido legum auxilio, quae ui, ambitu, postremo pecunia turbabantur*).

14. Idiomatic English would promote several of the subordinate clauses to main clauses and split the whole passage into four or five separate sentences.

15. For a perceptive analysis and comparison see Peter Gay, *Style in History*, 21 ff.

16. See c. IV p. 100 and n. 30.

17. See p. 176 f.

18. Some at least of the words and idioms may come from Tiberius himself; see Norma P. Miller, 'Tiberius Speaks' in *AJPh* 89 (1968), 1–19.

19. But a more surprising point emerges. Tacitus rejects Claudius as an oratorical model, but in an antiquarian excursus on the origin of the name *mons Caelius* ('the Caelian Mount'; *Ann*.4.65) he is prepared to take a phrase directly from the emperor's speech (*Caelium appellitatum a Caele Vibenna*; cf. the Lyons tablet i 22, *montem Caelium . . . a duce suo Caelio ita appellitatus* (sic)).

20. E.g. *Ann*. 2.14–15. Contrast the *Agricola*, Tacitus' earliest work, in which the speeches of both generals, Calgacus and Agricola, are given in *oratio recta*.

21. The rumour conveyed in *oratio obliqua* is a weapon that is particularly congenial to Tacitus, for it enables him to evade responsibility for the truth of what is said.

## XI · POSTSCRIPT *pages 236–243*

1. Over 1250 items are listed in Hanslik's *Lustrum* survey of the period 1939–72.

2. The *Opera Minora* are virtually complete; of the *Histories* we have the first four and a quarter books out of a total of twelve or fourteen, and a little over half of the sixteen or eighteen books of the *Annals*.

3. In thirty-one books, covering the period from AD 96 (the terminal point of Tacitus' *Histories*) to 378.

4. See Reynolds and Wilson 228–9; there is a translation (slightly abridged) in M. L. W. Laistner, *Thought and Letters in Western Europe, AD 500–900*.

5. For a brief sketch see Reynolds and Wilson 86–90.

6. And when it came to subject matter, it was to Suetonius that Einhard turned as a model for his imperial biography of Charlemagne.

7. It originally contained all three minor works; see below.

8. It was discovered just after 1500 in the Benedictine monastery of Corvey, north of Fulda. The argument for its origin from Fulda is palaeographical rather than geographical; at one time it was joined to a ninth century manuscript of Pliny (M), which R. A. B. Mynors, in his edition of Pliny's *Letters* (Oxford, 1963), declares to be of Fulda provenance.

9. About 1135, the librarian of Monte Cassino also shows knowledge of the *Agricola*; cf. H. Bloch in *CPh* 36 (1941) 185-7. That too may (or may not) indicate a link with Fulda.

10. Since a fuller account is available in English in Ogilvie-Richmond (pp. 80 ff.), I confine myself to the barest essentials.

11. *aliqua opera Corneli Taciti nobis ignota*: the words are those of the papal secretary, Poggio Bracciolini, perhaps the most successful of all searchers for classical manuscripts at the beginning of the fifteenth century. For Poggio see Reynolds and Wilson 120-3 and 236-7.

12. He describes the *Germania* as having twelve *folia*, the *Agricola* fourteen, and the *Dialogus* fourteen, followed by a lacuna of 'six leaves', then a further two and a half leaves. If the 'six leaves' were, in fact, six columns, two to a page, that would make one and a half leaves; the total $(14 + 1\frac{1}{2} + 2\frac{1}{2})$ would then be eighteen, the same figure as that given by Niccoli in 1431.

13. The less likely alternative is to assume that Decembrio added Tacitus' name by his own conjecture.

14. In addition to the *quaternio* (quire) of caroline minuscule (ff. 56-63) an erased *unio* (constituting ff. 69 and 76), some of it decipherable by the use of infra-red photography, is also part of the Hersfeld *codex*. The rediscovery of part of the Hersfeld *codex* has helped considerably in the interpretation of the evidence of the fifteenth century manuscript of the *opera minora*. In particular, the existence in the ninth century *codex* of marginal variants of very differing quality throws considerable light on the marginal variants that figure in a number of fifteenth-century manuscripts.

15. From time to time it has been argued that one or more of the fifteenth-century manuscripts contain readings independent of M 2. The attempt by E. Koestermann to demonstrate such an independence for the fifteenth-century *codex Leidensis* BPL 16B (cf. *Philologus* 104 (1960) 92-115) is now generally regarded as misguided. Koestermann's subsequent Teubner editions of Tacitus are, consequently, of little value. The more recent attempt of R. Hanslik and others to show a similar independence for a group of manuscripts (the so-called 'Genuaner') seems to me to be equally ill-founded.

16. It is uncertain whether Boccaccio himself was responsible for the 'removal' of the manuscript from Monte Cassino, but it is clear that he had a hand in the chain of events that brought it to Florence.

17. See, most conveniently, Plate XIV in Reynolds and Wilson.

18. Since T, dated to 1474, is a direct copy of Guarnieri's composite manuscript (fifteenth-century autograph, apart from ninth-century ff. 56-63), whose fifteenth-century section is itself drawn from a fifteenth-century copy of *Hersfeldensis*, it is clear that, apart from ff. 56-63, the *Agricola* section of the Hersfeld *codex* had been lost between 1458 and 1474—probably nearer the earlier date.

19. See pp. 3-4 of Goodyear's Commentary (Vol. I).
20. *Ibid.* p. 10, especially. n. 3.
21. For Rhenanus and Justus Lipsius, the latter *facile princeps* of Tacitean scholars, see Goodyear's Commentary 6-10; J. Ruysschaert, *Juste Lipse et les Annales de Tacite* (1949); Reynolds and Wilson 162-3. It must not be held against Rhenanus and Lipsius that they did not consult the two Mediceans; only towards the end of the seventeenth century, with the work of Mabillon, did the importance of a systematic study of manuscripts come to be realised.
22. See Goodyear's Commentary 11-19 for a brief sketch.
23. See A. Momigliano, 'The First Political Commentary on Tacitus', *JRS* 37 (1947), 91-101 (note especially the bibliography in n. 3); *idem*, *JRS* 39 (1949) 190-2; J. von Stackelberg, *Tacitus in der Romania* (1960; see also Momigliano's review in *JRS* 52 (1962), 282-5); P. Burke, 'Tacitism' in *Tacitus* (ed. T. A. Dorey, 1969).
24. See P. Burke in *History and Theory* 5 (1966), 135-52.
25. In *Discourses* 3.6.1 he quotes approvingly 'a golden sentence of Cornelius Tacitus, where he says that "men should honour the past and obey the present; and while they should desire good princes, they should bear with those they have . . .;".' This directly reproduces the statement of Eprius Marcellus in Tacitus, *Histories* 4.8.2. At *Discourses* 3.19 he stands an aphorism of *Annals* 3.55.5 on its head—that seems to be the only evidence that he knew the recently published *Annals* I-VI.
26. For this and the following quotation see notes 4 and 5 in Momigliano's article in *JRS* 37 (reference in n. 23).
27. Burke (see n. 23) distinguishes four: Tacitus as a stylist, as a historian, as a moralist, and (above all) as a master of politics.
28. Already shown in the prefatory letter of his first edition of Tacitus (1574). He commends Tacitus as a writer 'most excellent and advantageous for the present age' (*saluberrimo et optimo scriptore ad hoc aeuum*) and concludes: *aeuum calamitosum. sed ad quod tolerandum, multum, me iudice, historia ista faciet: solatio, consilio, exemplo* ('An age of disasters, but one for whose endurance our author's history will (in my opinion) contribute much; by solace, advice, example').
29. The beginnings go back to the end of the eighteenth century: 'The reviewer in the *Göttingische gelehrte Anzeiger* of 1788, though full of admiration for Gibbon, emphasised the superiority of German source-criticism' (Momigliano in 'Gibbon's Contribution to Historical Method' in *Historia* 2 (1954), 450-63). Nevertheless, it was in Berlin at the beginning of the next century that the new approach began to make an international impact.
30. So Ranke turned from Thucydides, the subject of his doctoral thesis, to the period 1494-1514.
31. See references to Nissen and Mommsen in c. VIII, notes 9 and 8.
32. In *Philologus* 25 (1867), 92-134; 26 (1867), 92-166; 27 (1868), 113-49.
33. Cf. Tacitus, *Histories* 1.2.1: 'Four emperors killed by the sword, three civil wars. . . .'
34. For both Claudius and Nero he accepted too readily the framework of a hostile tradition, largely senatorial. In the case of Claudius, though there is

no sustained attempt to question the essential accuracy of the tradition that depicts the emperor as the dupe of his women and freedmen, there are times, both in domestic and foreign affairs, when Tacitus shows insight into Claudius' ability to think, and act, for himself. As for Nero, though Tacitus accepts the stereotyped emperor that the tradition depicted, it is on the senate's reaction to the emperor that he focuses his attention, and in that sphere he writes with both sympathy and understanding—that sympathy is extended beyond the senatorial ranks to those who showed *uirtus* in their opposition to Nero's excesses.

Only in his account of the reign of Tiberius is there a continuous attempt to get to grips with the emperor's personality, and even there Tacitus is prepared, almost at the end, to suggest an explanation—that Tiberius had been 'undermined and altered by the force of absolute power' (see p. 143)—which, if he had applied it throughout Tiberius' reign, might have produced a different and more satisfactory explanation of the emperor's character.

35. See notes 4 and 5 in my chapter in *Tacitus* (ed. T. A. Dorey).
36. In view of Bury's later statement it is worth while noting what Gibbon and Macaulay said of Tacitus. In *Decline and Fall* (c. IX in.) Gibbon speaks of 'the masterly pencil of Tacitus, the first of historians who applied the science of philosophy to the study of facts'—of the early part of Gibbon's own work his one-time fiancée, Suzanne Curchod, wrote, 'I see Tacitus was the model and perhaps the source of your work'. Macaulay in his 1828 *Essay on History* wrote: 'Of the Latin historians, Tacitus was certainly the greatest. His style, indeed, is not only faulty in itself (a rich comment, coming from Macaulay!), but is, in some respects, peculiarly unfit for historical composition.' But he then goes on to say, 'In the delineation of character, Tacitus is unrivalled among historians, and has few superiors among dramatists and novelists . . . Claudius, Nero, Otho, both the Agrippinas, are masterpieces. But Tiberius is a still higher miracle of art.'
37. This is perhaps one of the reasons why the character of Tiberius interested him so much more than did those of Claudius and Nero.

# BIBLIOGRAPHY

The immense volume of literature on Tacitus is made manageable by the existence of a number of bibliographical aids. The most important general introduction to Tacitus is the long article by Borzsák (see p.271 below); English readers can best begin with the shorter survey (Greece and Rome Surveys 4) by F. R. D. Goodyear. The most recent bibliographical surveys are by H. W. Benario in *Classical World* 80 (1986), 73-147 and F. Römer in *Anzeiger für Altertumswissenschaft* (*AAHG*) 37 (1984), 153-208. For more recent work see *L'Année philologique*, published about two years in arrears of the titles listed. Current publications are given in the Bibliographische Beilage of *Gnomon*. The whole of a volume, due in 1989, in the series *Aufstieg und Niedergang der römischen Welt* (De Gruyter, Berlin) will be devoted to Tacitus and will include separate bibliographical surveys of each of his five works.

Among the works listed below the two volumes of Sir Ronald Syme's *Tacitus* (Oxford, 1958) are the most outstanding single contribution to the study of Tacitus since the war; it is referred to throughout this book simply as 'Syme'. Where further information is required, it will generally be useful to begin with the entries in the *Oxford Classical Dictionary* (second edition, 1970), abbreviated here as OCD.

## Text
The extant works of Tacitus are contained in three volumes of the Oxford Classical Texts. The *Opera Minora* ('Lesser Works') by R. M. Ogilvie (*Agricola*) and M. Winterbottom (*Germania* and *Dialogus*), published in 1975, provide the best text and *apparatus criticus* available. C. D. Fisher's editions of *Histories* and *Annals* (first published in 1911 and 1906 respectively) are sensible, if a little over-conservative, but the absence of paragraph numbers makes them awkward to use for quick reference. Between 1978 and 1983 Teubner (Stuttgart) has published new editions of all Tacitus' works (*Agricola* by J. Delz, *Germania* by A. Önnerfors, *Dialogus, Histories* and *Annals* by H. Heubner). From Teubner (Leipzig) comes a critical text of *Annals* 11-16 by K. Wellesley (1986).

## Text and Commentary
For the *Agricola* the edition by R. M. Ogilvie and the late Sir Ian Richmond (Oxford, 1967) is the best in any language. J. G. C. Anderson's *Germania* (Oxford, 1938) is excellent, though its archaeological material needs up-dating

and supplementing, e.g. from the massive German commentary of Much-Jankuhn-Lange (Heidelberg, 1967). There is no good edition of the *Dialogus*; the modest edition of A. Michel (Paris, 1962) may be consulted, but otherwise the most useful place to turn to is the brief introduction to the *Dialogus* by M. Winterbottom in the Loeb edition (see below); there is much useful information in the out-of-print edition of W. Peterson (Oxford, 1893).

For the *Histories* the best commentary (without text) is that of H. Heubner (Heidelberg, 1963-82). K. Wellesley's edition of Book 3 (Sydney, 1972) is invaluable. G. E. F. Chilver's *A Historical Commentary on Tacitus' Histories I and II* (without text: Oxford, 1979) has been followed by his commentary of Books 4 and 5, completed and edited by G. B. Townend.

E. Koestermann's commentary (without text) of the *Annals* in four volumes (Heidelberg, 1963-68), is an essential starting-point, though it does not entirely replace the two volumes of H. Furneaux's edition (Introduction, Text and Notes: vol. I (= *Annals* I-VI), 1896; vol. II (*Annals* XI-XVI), revised by H. F. Pelham and C. D. Fisher, 1907). Volume II of F. R. D. Goodyear's major edition of the *Annals* was published in 1981 (to the end of *Annals* 2). The editions of *Annals* I (Methuen, 1959; reprinted by Bradda Books) and *Annals* XV (St. Martin's Press, 1973) by Norma P. Miller are admirably suited to the needs of students. E. C. Woodcock's edition of *Annals* XIV (Methuen, 1939) is strong on syntactical matters, but otherwise disappointing.

**Text and Translation**
The whole of Tacitus is contained in five volumes of the Loeb Classical Library. The revised edition of *Agricola, Germania* and *Dialogus* (1970) has new Introductions and notes by R. M. Ogilvie and M. Winterbottom; *Histories* and *Annals* remain in their original versions by C. H. Moore and J. Jackson, and are now in need of revision. A French translation alongside a Latin text (with *apparatus criticus*) is available in the Budé edition (Collection des Universités de France). The volumes translated by H. Goelzer can be disregarded, but P. Wuilleumier's edition of the *Annals* (1974-78: four volumes) can be recommended.

**English Translations**
Apart from the translations in the Loeb series (see previous paragraph) modern English translations are available in the Penguin Classics for *Agricola* and *Germania* by H. Mattingly (1948), *Histories* by Kenneth Wellesley (1964: reprints from 1972 have an extensive Bibliography), and *Annals* by Michael Grant (1956, frequently reprinted). The *Agricola, Germania* and *Dialogus* are translated by H. W. Benario (Bobbs-Merrill, 1967), and there is a translation of the *Annals* by D. R. Dudley in Mentor Books (New York, 1966). *Ancient Literary Criticism* by D. A. Russell and M. Winterbottom (Oxford, 1972) has a complete translation of the *Dialogus* (pp. 432-59) by Winterbottom.

**Lexica**
There is a complete *Lexicon Taciteum* by Gerber-Greef-John (Leipzig, 1877-

90), and a *Concordantia Tacitea* by D.R. Blackman and G.G. Betts (Hildesheim – Zürich – New York, 1986). For Proper Names see P. Fabia, *Onomasticon Taciteum* (Paris-Lyons, 1900); for further information *Prosopographia Imperii Romani* (1st edition, 1897-98; 2nd edition, in progress (it has now reached the letter L)) should be consulted.

## General and Chapters I and II

Badian, E. 'The early historians', in *Latin Historians* (ed. Dorey, T.A., London, 1966), 1-38

Benario, H.W. *An Introduction to Tacitus* (Athens, USA 1975)

Béranger, J. *Recherches sur l'aspect idéologique du principat* (Basel, 1953)

Boissier, G. *Tacitus and other Roman studies* (London, 1906)

Borzsák, S. 'P. Cornelius Tacitus', *RE Suppl.* 11. 373-512 (also published separately, Stuttgart, 1968)

Christ, K. 'Tacitus und der Principat', *Historia* 27 (1978), 449-87

Dorey, T.A. (editor), *Tacitus. Studies in Latin literature and its influence* (London, 1969)

Dudley, D.R. *The world of Tacitus* (London, 1968)

Flach, D. *Tacitus in der Tradition der antiken Geschichtsschreibung* (Hypomnemata 39: Göttingen, 1973)

Frier, B.W. *Libri annales pontificum Maximorum* (American Academy in Rome, 1979)

Goodyear, F.R.D. 'Tacitus', in *The Cambridge History of Classical Literature* II (Cambridge, 1982), 642-55

Goodyear, F.R.D. *Tacitus, Greece and Rome Surveys* 4 (Oxford, 1970)

Grant, M. *The ancient historians* (London, 1970)

Häussler, R. *Tacitus und das historische Bewusstsein* (Heidelberg, 1965)

Hanslik, R. 'Die Ämterlaufbahn des Tacitus im Lichte der Ämterlaufbahn seiner Zeitgenossen', *Anzeiger d. Österr. Ak. d. Wiss.* 1965, 47-60

Jens, W. '*Libertas* bei Tacitus', *Hermes* 84 (1956), 331-52

Klingner, F. 'Tacitus und die Geschichtsschreiber des I. Jh.s', *MH* 15 (1958), 194-206

Klingner, F. 'Tacitus', *Die Antike* 8 (1932), 151-69

Laistner, M.L.W. *The greater Roman historians* (Berkeley and Los Angeles, 1947)

Leeman, A.D. 'Structure and meaning in the prologues of Tacitus', *YClS* 23 (1973), 169-208

Lintott, A.W. 'Roman historians', in *The Oxford History of the Classical World* (Oxford, 1986), 636-52

Löfstedt, E. 'Tacitus as an historian', in *Roman Literary Portraits* (Oxford, 1958), 142-56

Luce, T.J. 'Tacitus' conception of historical change', in *Past Perspectives: studies in Greek and Roman historical writing* (ed. I.S. Moxon etc.: Cambridge, 1986), 143-57

McDonald, A.H. 'The Roman Historians', in *Fifty years and twelve of classical scholarship* (Oxford, 1968)

McDonald, A.H. 'Theme and style in Roman historiography', *JRS* 65 (1975), 1-10

Mendell, C.W. *Tacitus, the man and his work* (New Haven, 1957)

Michel, A. *Tacite et le destin de l'empire* (Paris, 1966)

Millar, F. *The emperor in the Roman world (31 BC–AD 337)* (London, 1977)

Momigliano, A. 'Tradition and the classical historian', *H & T* 11 (1972), 279-93

Otis, B. 'The uniqueness of Latin literature', *Arion* 6 (1967), 185-206

Paratore, E. *Tacito* (2nd edition, Rome, 1962)

Percival, J. 'Tacitus and the principate', *G&R* 27 (1980), 119-33

Pöschl, V. (ed.) *Tacitus* (Wege der Forschung 97: Darmstadt, 1969)

Questa, C. 'Sallustio, Tacito e l'imperialismo romano', *Atti e memorie dell' Arcadia* 6 (1975-76), 1-43

Rawson, E. 'Prodigy lists and the use of the Annales Maximi', *CQ* 21 (1971), 158-69

Shatzman, I. 'Tacitean rumours', *Latomus* 33 (1974), 549-78

Suerbaum, E. 'Interpretationen zum Staatsbegriff des Tacitus', *Gymnasium Beiheft* 4 (1964), 105-32

Syme, R. *Sallust* (Berkeley and Los Angeles, 1964)

Syme, R. *Tacitus* (Oxford, 1958)

Syme, R. *Ten studies in Tacitus* (Oxford, 1970)

Syme, R. 'Juvenal, Pliny, Tacitus', *AJPh* 100 (1979), 250-78

Syme, R. *The Augustan aristocracy* (Oxford, 1986)

Talbert, R.J.A. *The Senate of Imperial Rome* (Princeton, 1984)

Theiler, W. 'Tacitus und die antike Schicksalslehre', in *Phyllobolia Van der Mühll* (1946), 35-90

Till, R. 'Tacitus als Ethnograph und Geschichtsschreiber', *Dialog* 10 (1977), 96-119

Usher, S. *The Historians of Greece and Rome* (London, 1969)

Walsh, P.G. *Livy* (Cambridge, 1961)

Wilkes, J. 'Julio-Claudian historians', *CW* 65 (1972), 177-92, 196-203

Wille, G. *Der Aufbau der Werke des Tacitus* (Amsterdam, 1983)

Wirszubski, C. *Libertas as a political idea at Rome* (Cambridge, 1950)

Woodman, A.J. *Rhetoric in classical historiography* (Portland, Oregon, 1988)

Wuilleumier, P. and Fabia, P. *Tacite, l'homme et l'oeuvre* (Paris, 1949)

## Chapters III: The Lesser Works

Bardon, H. 'Tacite et le *Dialogue des Orateurs*', *Latomus* 12 (1953), 166-87

Barwick, K. 'Der *Dialogus de oratoribus* des Tacitus, *S-B Sachs. Akad., phil.-hist. Kl.* 1954

Bringmann, K. Aufbau und Absicht des taciteischen *Dialogus de oratoribus*', *MH* 27 (1970), 164-78

Bruère, R.T. 'Tacitus and Pliny's *Panegyricus*', *CPh* 49 (1954), 161-79

Büchner, K. 'Tacitus: *Germania*', in *Studien zur röm. Literatur*, vol. 8 (1970), 230-52

Büchner, K. 'Tacitus: *Dialogus*', in *Studien zur röm. Literatur*, vol. 8 (1970), 253-98

Burn, A.R. 'Tacitus on Britain', in *Tacitus*, ed T.A. Dorey (1969), 35-61

Costa, C.D.N. 'The *Dialogus*', in *Tacitus*, ed. T.A. Dorey (1969), 19-33

Fritz, K. v. 'Tacitus, Agricola and the Problem of the Principate', *CPh* 52 (1957), 73-97

Güngerich, R. 'Der Dialogus des Tacitus und Quintilians *Institutio Oratoria*', *CPh* 46 (1951), 159-64

Güngerich, R. 'Tacitus' *Dialogus* und der *Panegyricus* des Plinius', in *Festschr. B. Snell* (1956), 145-62

Gugel, H. *Untersuchungen zu Stil und Aufbau des Rednerdialogs des Tacitus* (Innsbruck, 1969)

Häussler, R. 'Nur eine kleine Lücke im *Dialogus*', *Hermes* 91 (1963), 382-3

Häussler, R. 'Zum Anfang und Aufbau des *Dialogus de oratoribus*', *Philologus* 93 (1969), 24-67

Jankuhn, H. 'Archäologische Bemerkungen zur Glaubwürdigkeit des T. in der *Germania*', *Akad. Wiss. Göttingen, Nachrichten* 1966, 411-86

Michel, A. *Le 'Dialogus des Orateurs' de Tacite et la philosophie de Cicéron* (Paris, 1962)

Nesselhauf, H. 'Tacitus and Domitian', *Hermes* 80 (1952) 222-45

Norden, E. *Die germanische Urgeschichte in Tacitus' Germania* (Berlin, ed. 3, 1923)

Reed, N. 'Tacitus's and Dio's Sources on the Boudiccan Revolt', *Arepo* 3 (1970), 5-9

Reitzenstein, R. *Aufsätze zu Tacitus* (Darmstadt, 1967)

Richmond, I.A. 'Gnaeus Iulius Agricola', *JRS* 34 (1944), 34-45

Steinmetz, P. 'Die literarische Form des Agricola des Tacitus', in *Der altsprachliche Unterricht Beih. 1 zu R.* 14 (1971), 129-41

## Chapter IV: The Histories

Briessmann, A. 'Tacitus und das flavische Geschichtsbild', *Hermes-Einzel-schriften* 10: 1955
Brunt, P.A. 'Tacitus on the Batavian revolt', *Latomus* 19 (1960), 494-517
Courbaud, E. *Les procédés d'art de Tacite dans les Histoires* (Paris, 1918)
Fuhrmann, M. 'Das Vierkaiserjahr bei Tacitus', *Philologus* 104 (1960), 250-78
Hanslik, R. 'Die Auseinandersetzung zwischen Otho und Vitellius bis zur Schlacht bei Bedriacum nach Tacitus', *WSt* 74 (1961), 113-25
Klingner, F. 'Die Geschichte Kaiser Othos bei Tacitus', *Berichte u. Verhandlungen* Sächs. Akad. d. Wiss., phil.-hist. Kl. 92.1 (1940), 3-27
Koestermann, E. 'Der Ruckblick Tacitus Historien 1.4-11', *Historia* 5 (1956), 213-37
Koestermann, E. 'Die erste Schlacht bei Bedriacum 69 n. Chr.', *RCCM* 3 (1961), 16-29
Passerini, A. 'Le due battaglie presso Betriacum', in *Studi ... offerti ... à Emanuele Ciaceri* (1940), 178-248
Schunck, P. 'Studien zur Darstellung des Endes von Galba, Otho und Vitellius ...', *Symb. Osl.* 39 (1964), 38-82
Shotter, D.C.A. 'The starting-dates of Tacitus' historical works', *CQ* 17 (1967), 158-63
Wellesley, K. 'Three historical puzzles in *Histories* III', *CQ* 50 (1956), 207-14
Wellesley, K. 'Moonshine in Tacitus', *RhM* 100 (1957), 244-52
Wellesley, K. 'Suggestio falsi in Tacitus', *RhM* 103 (1960), 272-88
Wellesley, K. *The Long Year: AD 69* (London, 1975)
    N.B. There is a full bibliography in editions subsequent to 1972 of K.
    Wellesley's translation of the *Histories* (penguin Books).

## Chapters V-VII: The Annals

Alexander, W.H. 'The Tacitean *non liquet* on Seneca', in *Univ. of California Publ. in Class. Philol.* 14 (1952 (1952) 269-386
Beaujeu, J. 'L'incendie de Rome en 64 et les Chrétiens', *Latomus* 19 (1960), 65-80 and 291-311
Benario, H.W. 'Tacitus and the Principate', *CJ* 60 (1964), 97-106
Brunt, P.A. 'Charges of provincial maladministration under the early principate', *Historia* 10 (1961), 189-227
Brunt, P.A. 'Procuratorial jurisdiction', *Latomus* 25 (1966), 461-89
Büchner, K. 'Tacitus über die Christen', *Aegyptus* 33 (1953), 181-92
Chilton, C.W. 'The Roman law of treason under the early principate', *JRS* 45 (1955), 73-81
Flach, D. 'Die Rede des Claudius De Iure honorum Gallis dando', *Hermes* 101 (1973). 313-20
Fuchs, H. 'Der Bericht über die Christen in den Annalen des Tacitus', *Vigil. Christ.* 4 (1950), 65-93
Fuchs, H. 'Nochmals "Tacitus über die Christen"', *MH* 20 (1963), 221-28
Gill, C. 'The question of character-development: Plutarch and Tacitus', *CQ* 33 (1983), 469-87
Gilmartin, K. 'Corbulo's campaigns in the East'. An analysis of Tacitus' account', *Historia* 22 (1973), 583-626
Ginsburg, J. *Tradition and Theme in the Annals of Tacitus* (New York, 1981)
Giua, M.A. 'Tiberio simulatore nella tradizione storica pretaciana', *Athenaeum* 53 (1975), 352-63

273

Griffin, M. T. 'The Lyons tablet and Tacitean hindsight', *CQ* 32 (1982), 404-18

Griffin, M. T. *Nero: the end of a dynasty* (London, 1984)

Hanslik, R. 'Der Erzählungskomplex vom Brand Roms und der Christenverfolgung bei Tacitus', *WSt* 76 (1963), 92-108

Hennig, D. *L. Aelius Seianus* (Munich, 1975)

Heinz, D. *Das Bild Kaiser Neros bei Seneca, Tacitus, Sueton und Cassius Dio* (Diss. Bern, Bie. Schuler: 1948)

Henry, D. and Walker, B. 'Tacitus and Seneca', *Greece and Rome* 10 (1963), 98-110

Holson, P. 'Nero and the fire of Rome. Fact and fiction', *Pegasus* 19 (1976), 37-44

Kajanto, I. 'Tacitus on the slaves. An interpretation of the *Annals* 14.42-45', *Arctos* N. S. 6 (1969), 43-60

Keitel, E. 'The role of Parthia and Armenia in Tacitus *Annals* 11 and 12', *AJPh* 99 (1978), 462-73

Keitel, E. 'Tacitus on the deaths of Tiberius and Claudius', *Hermes* 109 (1981), 206-14

Keitel, E. 'Principate and civil war in the Annals of Tacitus', *AJPh* 105 (1984), 314-26

Klingner, F. 'Tacitus über Augustus und Tiberius. Interpretation zum Eingang der *Annalen*', *SBAW* (1953), 7

Knoche, U. 'Zur Beurteilung des Kaisers Tiberius durch Tacitus', *Gymnasium* 70 (1963), 211-26

Koestermann, E. 'Die Majestätsprozesse unter Tiberius', *Historia* 4 (1955), 72-106

Koestermann, E. 'Die Feldzüge des Germanicus 14-16 n. Chr.', *Historia* 6 (1957), 429-79

Koestermann, E. 'Die Eingang der Annalen des Tacitus', *Historia* 10 (1961), 330-55

Koestermann, E. 'Ein folgenschwerer Irrtum des Tacitus (*Ann.* 15.44.2 ff.)?', *Historia* 16 (1967), 456-69

Last, D.M. and Ogilvie, R.M. 'Claudius and Livy', *Latomus* 17 (1958), 476-87

Levi, M.A. *Nerone e i suoi tempi* (Milan, 1949)

Levick, B. *Tiberius the politician* (London, 1976)

Levick, B.M. 'A cry from the heart from Tiberius Caesar?', *Historia* 27 (1978), 95-101

Levick, B.M. 'Antiquarian or revolutionary? Claudius Caesar's conception of his principate', *AJPh* 99 (1978), 79-105

Levick, B.M. 'Poena Legis Maiestatis', *Historia* 28 (1979), 358-79

Marsh, F.B. *The reign of Tiberius* (Oxford, 1931)

Mehl, A. *Tacitus über Kaiser Claudius* (Munich, 1974)

Mehl, A. 'Bemerkungen zu Dios und Tacitus' Arbeitsweise und zur Quellenlage im "Totengericht" über Augustus', *Gymnasium* 88 (1981), 54-64

Mierow, Ch. Ch. 'Tiberius himself', *PhQ* 22 (1943), 289-307

Miller, N.P. 'Tiberius speaks. An examination of the utterances ascribed to him in the *Annals* of Tacitus', *AJPH* 89 (1968), 1-19

Momigliano, A. *Claudius: the emperor and his Achievement* (2nd edition, Oxford, 1961)

Passerini, A. 'Per la storia dell'imperatore Tiberio', in *Studi giuridici in memoria di Pietro Ciapessoni* (Pavia, 1948), 195-233

Pippidi, D.M. *Autour de Tibère* (Bucharest, 1944; repr. 1965)

Rogers, R.S. *Studies in the reign of Tiberius* (Baltimore, 1943)

Rogers, R.S. 'Tiberius' reversal of an Augustan policy', *TAPhA* 71 (1940), 532-36

Rogers, R.S. 'A Tacitean pattern in narrating treason-trials', *TAPhA* 83 (1952), 279-311

Rogers, R.S. The case of Cremutius Cordus', *TAPhA* 96 (1965), 351-59

Rogers, R.S. 'Five over-crowded months? AD 62', in *Studies in Honor of B.L. Ullman* (Rome, 1964), 219-22

Ronconi, A. 'Tacito, Plinio e i Christiani', in *Studi in on. di U. E. Paoli* (1955), 615-28

Ross, D.O. 'The Tacitean Germanicus', *YClS* 23 (1973), 209-27

Schillinger-Häfele, U. 'Claudius und Tacitus über die Aufnahme von Galliern in den Senat', *Historia* 14 (1965), 443-54

Schmidt, E. A. 'Die Angst der Mächtigen in den Annalen des Tacitus', *WS* 16 (1982), 274-87

Scramuzza, V.M. *The emperor Claudius* (Cambridge, Mass 1940)

Seager, R.J. *Tiberius* (London, 1972)

Seif, K. P. *Die Claudiusbücher in den Annalen des Tacitus* (Mainz, 1973)

Shotter, D.C.A. 'Tiberius and Asinius Gallus', *Historia* 20 (1971), 443-57

Shotter, D.C.A. 'Ticitus, Tiberius and Germanicus', *Historia* 17 (1968), 194-214

Suerbaum, W. 'Der Historiker und die Freiheit des Wortes. Die Rede des Cremutius Cordus bei Tacitus *Ann.* 4.34-5', in *Politik und literarische Kunst im Werk des Tacitus* (ed. Radke, Stuttgart, 1971), 61-75

Syme, R. 'How Tacitus wrote *Annals* I-III', in *Roman Papers* III (Oxford, 1984), 1014-42

Timpe, D. *Der Triumph des Germanicus. Untersuchungen zu den Feldzügen der Jahre 14-16 n. Chr. in Germanien* (Bonn, 1968)

Townend, G.B. 'Claudius and the digressions in Tacitus', *RhM* 105 (1962), 358-68

Tränkle, H. 'Augustus bei Tacitus, Cassius Dio und dem älteren Plinius', *WSt* 82 (1969), 108-30

Vessey, D.W.T.C. 'Thoughts on Tacitus' portrayal of Claudius', *AJPh* 92 (1971), 385-409

Urban, R. 'Tacitus und die *Res Gestae divi Augusti*', *Gymnasium* 86 (1979), 59-74

Walker, B. *The Annals of Tacitus. A study in the writing of history* (3rd ed., Manchester, 1968)

Warmington, B.H. *Nero, Reality and Legend* (London, 1969)

Webster, G. *Boudica; the British Revolt against Rome AD 60* (London, 1978)

Wellesley, K. 'The *dies imperii* of Tiberius', *JRS* 57 (1967), 23-30

## Chapter VIII: The Sources (Histories)

See also Bibliography to c. IV (esp. Briessmann)

Büchner, K. 'Die Reise des Titus', in *Studien zur römischen Literatur* 4 (1964), 83-98

Fabia, P. *Les Sources de Tacite* (Paris, 1893)

Flach, D. 'Die Ueberlieferungslage zur Geschichte des Vierkaiserjahres', *Ancient Society* 4 (1973), 157-76

Groag, E. 'Zur Kritik von Tacitus' Quellen in den Historien', *Jahrbücher für cl. Phil.*, Suppl.-Band 23 (1897) 761 ff

Hosper-Jansen, A.M.A. *Tacitus over de Joden* (*Hist. 5.2-13*) (Utrecht, 1949)

Martin, J. 'Zur Quellenfrage in den Annalen und Historien', *Würzburger Studien zur Altertumswissenschaft* 9 (1936), 21 ff

Mommsen, T. 'Cornelius Tacitus und Cluvius Rufus', *Hermes* 4 (1870), 295 ff

Townend, G.B. 'Cluvius Rufus in the *Histories* of Tacitus', *AJPh* 85 (1964), 337-77

Treu, M. 'M. Antonius Primus in der taciteischen Darstellung', *Würzb. Jahrb.* 3 (1948), 241-62

## Chapter IX: The Sources (Annals)

Anna, G. d' 'Osservazioni sulle fonti della morte di Agrippina minore', *Athenaeum* 41 (1963), 111-17

Flach, D. 'Tacitus und seine Quellen in den Annalenbüchern I-VI', *Athenaeum* 51 (1973), 92-108

Flach, D. 'Die taciteische Quellenbehandlung in den Annalenbüchern XI-XVI', *MH* 30 (1973), 88-103

Mensching, E. 'Zu den namentlichen Zitaten in Tacitus' Historien und Annalen', *Hermes* 95 (1967), 457-69
Momigliano, A. 'Osservazioni sulle fonti per la storia di Caligola, Claudio, Nerone', *Rendiconti della R. Accademia dei Lincei*[6] 8 (1932), 293 ff
Questa, C. *Studi sulle fonti degli Annales di Tacito* (Roma, 1963[2])
Syme, R. 'Tacitus: some sources of his information', *JRS* 72 (1982), 68-82
Townend, G.B. 'Some rhetorical battle-pictures in Dio', *Hermes* 92 (1964), 467-81
Tresch, J. *Die Nerobücher in den Annalen des Tacitus* (Heidelberg, 1965)

## Chapter X: Style

Adams, J.N. 'The language of the later books of Tacitus' *Annals*', *CQ* 22 (1972), 350-73
Adams, J.N. 'The vocabulary of the speeches in Tacitus' historical works', *BICS* 20 (1973), 124-44
Develin, R. 'Tacitus and techniques of insidious suggestion', *Antichthon* 17 (1983), 64-95
Eriksson, N. *Studien zu den Annalen des Tacitus* (Lund, 1934)
Goodyear, F.R.D. 'Development of language and style in the *Annals* of Tacitus', *JRS* 58 (1968), 22-31
Kuntz, F. *Die Sprache des Tacitus und die Tradition der Lateinischen Historikersprache* (Diss. Heidelberg, 1962)
Löfstedt, E. 'On the style of Tacitus', *JRS* 38 (1948), 1-8
Löfstedt, E. *Syntactica* I[2] (Lund, 1942); II (Lund, 1933)
Martin, R.H. 'Tacitus and his predecessors', in *Tacitus*, ed. T.A. Dorey (1969), 117-47
Martin, R.H. 'Structure and Interpretation in the *Annals* of Tacitus', (forthcoming in *Aufstieg und Niedergang der römischen Welt* (De Gruyter, Berlin))
Miller, N.P. 'Style and content in Tacitus', in *Tacitus*, ed T.A. Dorey (1969), 99-116
Quinn, K. 'Tacitus' narrative technique', in *Latin Explorations: critical studies in Roman literature* (London, 1963), 110-29
Ryberg, I.S. 'Tacitus' art of innuendo', *TAPA* 73 (1942), 383-404
Sörbom, G. *Variatio sermonis Tacitei . . .* (Uppsala, 1935)
Sullivan, D. 'Innuendo and the "weighted alternative" in Tacitus', *CJ* 71 (1976), 312-26
Whitehead, D. 'Tacitus and the loaded alternative', *Latomus* 38 (1979), 474-95
Wölfflin, E. 'Jahresberichte über Tacitus 1-3, *Philologus* 25-7 (1867-68)
Woodman, T. (= A.J.) 'Self-imitation and the substance of history: Tacitus, *Annals* 1.61-5 and *Histories* 2.70, 5.14-15', in *Creative imitation and Latin literature* (ed. D. West and T. Woodman: Cambridge, 1979), 143-55

## Chapter XI: Postscript

Benjamin, E.B. 'Sir John Hayward and Tacitus', *The Review of English Studies* 8 (1957), 257 ff
Benjamin, E.B. 'Bacon and Tacitus', *CPh* 60 (1965), 102-10
Bloch, H.A. 'A manuscript of Tacitus' *Agricola* in Monte Cassino about AD 1135', *CPh* 36 (1941), 185-87
Brink, C.O. 'Justus Lipsius and the text of Tacitus', *JRS* 41 (1951), 32-51
Burke, P. 'Tacitism', in *Tacitus* (ed. T.A. Dorey, 1969), 149-71
Burke, P. 'Popularity of ancient historians', *History and Theory* 5 (1966), 135-52
Butler, P. 'Tacitisme et machiavélisme dans l'oeuvre de Racine', in *Classicisme et baroque dans l'oeuvre de Racine* (Paris, 1959)
Etter, E.L. *Tacitus in der Geistesgeschichte des 16. und 17. Jh.s* (Diss. Basel, 1966)

Goodyear, F.R.D. 'Readings of the Leiden Manuscript of Tacitus', *CQ* 15 (1965), 299-322

Hanslik, R. 'Versuch einer Wertung der Tacitushandschriften', in *Antidosis* (*Festschrift W. Kraus*) (Vienna, 1972), 139-59

Koestermann, E. 'Codex Leidensis BPL 16B, ein vom Mediceus II unabhängiger Textzeuge des Tacitus', *Philologus* 104 (1960), 92-115

Martin, R.H. 'The Leyden Manuscript of Tacitus', *CQ* 14 (1964), 109-19

Mendell, C.W. and Ives, S.A. 'Rycke's manuscript of Tacitus', *AJPh* 72 (1951), 337-45

Oliver, R.P. 'The first Medicean MS. of Tacitus and the titulature of ancient books', *TAPhA* 82 (1951), 232-61

Oliver, R.P. 'The Second Medicean MS. and the Text of Tacitus' *ICS* I (1976), 190-225

Rubinstein, N. 'An unknown letter by Jacopo di Poggio Bracciolini on discoveries of classical texts', *Italia medioevale e umanistica* 1 (1958), 383-95

Ruysschaert, J. *Juste Lipse et les Annales de Tacite* (Louvain, 1949)

Schaps, D. 'The found and lost manuscripts of Tacitus' *Agricola*', *CPh* 74 (1979), 28-42

Stackelberg, J. von *Tacitus in der Romania. Studien zur literarischen Rezeption des Tacitus in Italien und Frankreich* (Tübingen, 1960)

Syme, R. 'Roman historians and Renaissance politics. Society and history in the Renaissance' (*The Folger Shakespeare Library*; Washington, 1960), 3-12

Till, R. *Handschriftliche Untersuchungen zu Agricola und Germania* (Berlin, 1943)

Wankenne, A. 'Napoléon et Tacite', *LEC* 35 (1967), 260-63

# INDEX

Emperors and their families, authors, and a few well-known figures (e.g. Sulla, Pompey, Sejanus) are listed under their conventional English names; in other cases cross-references are given, where uncertainty might arise. Dates, unless otherwise stated, are AD. Where the whole of a chapter is given to a single work (e.g. *Histories*) or person (e.g. Tiberius), no separate instances of that work or person are listed from that chapter in the Index.

*acta diurna* (daily gazette)  122, 201, 212

*acta publica*  201

*acta senatus*  200, 201, 206, 207, 209, 210, 212

Acte  165

Acton  195

*ad Castores see* Castors

*adrogans*  225

*adulatio* (flattery)  126, 128, 164, 178

advocates' fees  145

Aelius Lamia  139

Aelius *see* Sejanus

Aemilius Lepidus, M. (the Triumvir)  111, 112

Aemilius Lepidus, M. (cos. 6)  108, 113, 126–7, 129, 136–7, 139, 226, 231

Aemilius Scaurus, M. (cos. 115 BC)  17

Afranius Burrus  160, 163, 164, 166, 171, 172, 177, 178, 188, 208

Africa  130

*Agricola*  32, 37, 39–49, 50, 53, 55, 56, 59, 65, 67, 94, 176, 199, 237, 238

Agricola *see* Iulius

Agrippa Postumus  109, 110, 114, 162, 203

Agrippina the Elder (wife of Germanicus)  131, 132, 135, 140, 141, 199

Agrippina the Younger (mother of Nero)  140, 145, 146, 151–3, 155, 158–61, 162–6, 170–2, 177, 199, 200, 208, 212, 228

Alexander the Great  107

alphabet, Claudius on  146

*amici Caesaris*  33

Ammianus Marcellinus  236

Anglesey  174

Anicetus  170, 171

*annales maximi*  17

*Annals*  94, 103; extant books  104; title  104, 237, 238, 242

Annius Gallus (cos. by 69)  79, 80, 96, 191

Annius Verus, M. (cos. 97, 121, 126)  34

Anteius Rufus, P.  166

Antias *see* Valerius

anti-Ciceronianism  214, 230

Antistius Sosianus  176

Antonia (mother of Germanicus)  122, 212

Antoninus Pius (emperor 137–61)  34

Antonius, M. (the Triumvir, Mark Antony)  111, 112

Antonius Primus, M.   85–92, 98, 99, 100, 102, 197
Antonius Saturninus (cos. 83?)   28, 32, 56
Aper, M.   59–65
Apicata   131
'appendix' type sentence   221–3
Appuleia Varilla   121
Aquilius Regulus   33, 100, 196
Arabia Petraea, annexed   31
*arbiter elegantiae*   185
Armenia *see* Eastern Question
Arminius   116
Arrius Antoninus (cos. 69, 97)   34
Arruntius, L. (cos. 6)   119, 143, 200
Arruntius Stella (cos. 101 or 102)   36
Arulenus Rusticus, Q. Iunius   33, 36, 210
Asellio, Sempronius   17–8, 24
Asinius Gallus, C. (cos. 8 BC)   113, 119, 203
Asinius Saloninus   128
Ateius Capito, C. (cos. 5)   119, 126, 128
Ateius Labeo   128
Attius Suburanus (cos. 101, 104)   34
*auctoritas*   175
Aufidius Bassus   23, 202
Augustus (emperor 27 BC–AD 14)   105, 108–12, 114, 115, 124–5, 132, 145, 148, 153, 160, 162, 166, 203, 204, 242
Aurelius Fulvus, T.   34
Aurelius, Marcus (emperor 161–80)   34

Bacon   240
Baebius Massa   30, 33
balance *see concinnitas*
Barea Soranus (cos. 52)   179, 185, 186
Baugulf of Fulda   236
Bedriacum   80–2, 87, 88, 102, 192, 194
Benedict   237
Beroaldus   238, 239

Berytus   85, 86
Boccaccio   238
'borrowings' (literary) *see* resonances
Boudicca (Boadicea)   157, 163, 173–5, 215, 219
Bracciolini, Poggio   237
brevity   215–20
Brinno   96
Britain   36, 39–46, 148, 153, 155, 156–8, 163, 173–5, 210
Britannicus   145, 152, 159–61, 163, 165
Brixellum   81, 82
Brundisium, treaty of   112
Brutus, M. Iunius   128, 135
Burke, P.   239, 240
Burrus *see* Afranius
Bury   241, 242
Byzantium   159

Caecina Alienus (cos. 69)   33, 75–80, 86, 92, 191, 193, 195
Caecina Severus (cos. 1 BC)   126, 223
Caelian Mount   229
Caesar (Julius Caesar)   18, 20, 55, 111, 124, 127, 148, 150, 194, 201, 221
Caesennius Paetus, L. (cos. 61)   180, 181
Calgacus   43–4
Caligula (Gaius, emperor 37–41)   55, 117, 131, 133, 143, 162
Calpurnius Piso Frugi, L.   16–7
Calpurnius Piso, C.   178–9
Calpurnius Piso, Cn. (cos. 7 BC)   116, 119, 122–4, 200
Calpurnius Piso, L. (cos. 15 BC)   138, 139
Caninius Rebilus, C. (cos. 37)   167
Canuleius, C.   232
Capri   132, 140, 142
Caratacus   156–7
Carthage   106
Cartimandua   89, 157
Cassiodorus   236
Cassius (the tyrannicide)   128, 135

Cassius Dio   83, 88, 92, 112, 118, 127, 138, 141, 143, 155, 160, 169, 171, 172, 175, 178, 181, 182, 188, 191, 196, 203–10, 212
Cassius Longinus, C. (cos. 30)   169, 175, 185
Castors   80, 192
Catiline (Sergius Catilina)   20, 106–7, 168, 226
*Cato*   60–62
Cato *see* Porcius Cato
Catus (procurator)   175
Caudine Forks   97, 98
Charlemagne   236, 237
Christ   6, 183
Christians   6, 179, 182–3
Cicero, M. Tullius (cos. 63 BC)   14, 15, 17, 19–20, 21, 48, 59, 61, 62, 64, 65, 100, 189, 202, 214
Ciceronian tone in Tacitus   231
Cinna, L. Cornelius   115
City Prefect *see praefectus urbi*
civil administration under Tiberius   130
Civilis, *see Iulius*
*ciuilis, ciuiliter* · 229
Classicianus *see* Iulius
Claudius (emperor 41–54)   109, 162, 163, 164, 166, 207, 212, 231–2
Claudius Quadrigarius, Q.   18–9
*clementia*   154, 157, 164–5
Clutorius Priscus   126–7, 231
Cluvius Rufus (cos. before 41)   23, 190, 208–10, 212
*codex, codices see* manuscripts
Coelius Antipater, L.   17, 24
Colchester   174
Cologne   98, 155, 170
*colonia*   148
colourful vocabulary   223
*comitatus*   51
*commedia dell'arte*   13
'common source'   190, 192
*comparatio deterrima*   112
*concinnitas*   214
*consilium principis*   147, 149, 151, 154, 167

*constantia*   175
*copia uerborum*   214
Corbulo *see* Domitius
Cornelius Palma, A. (cos. 99, 109)   31
Cornelius Africanus, P. Scipio   15
Cornelius Sisenna, L.   18
Cornelius Sulla (cos. 52)   177
Cornelius Tacitus (procurator of Gallia Belgica)   26, 57
Cossutianus Capito   145, 169, 186
Crassus *see* Licinius
Cremona   79, 86–8, 90, 93, 191, 192
Cremutius Cordus   23, 129, 133, 135, 137
Curiatius Maternus   33, 59–66
Curtius Montanus   100, 197

daily gazette *see acta diurna*
Decembrio, Pier Candido   237
*Decumates agri*   55
*delatores*   94, 135–6, 168, 196
Demetrius   186
*Dialogus*   26, 44, 58–66, 237, 238
Didius Gallus (cos. 36)   157
Dillius Vocula, C.   23, 97, 98, 198
Dio *see* Cassius
*dissimulatio*   229
*dissimulator*   107
*dominatio*   115
Domitia Lepida   159
Domitian (emperor 81–96)   26, 28, 31, 32, 33, 34, 35, 36, 37, 39, 40, 45–8, 55–6, 59, 67, 91, 92, 93, 100, 135, 143, 145, 199, 231
Domitius Afer, Cn. (cos. 39)   172
Domitius Corbulo, Cn. (cos. 39 (?))   155, 164, 167, 169, 173, 179–81, 207, 210, 225
Domitius Tullus, Cn. (cos. 79 (?), 98 (?))   34
Drusus (brother of Tiberius)   55, 148–9
Drusus (son of Tiberius)   105, 115, 122, 125, 129–31, 140, 141, 142, 200, 212, 229

Drusus (son of Germanicus) 131, 132-3, 140

Duris 15

Drusus (false) 206

Eastern Question 145, 153-4, 163, 164, 167-9, 173, 179-81, 205, 210

*editio princeps* 238

elections, consular 120

elevation 234

Elizabethan 214

Ennius, Q. 22

Epicharis 184

epigram 129, 219-20

Eprius Marcellus, T. (cos. 62, 74) 33, 60, 62, 94, 100, 186, 196, 233

Fabius Iustus, L. (cos. 102) 58, 60

Fabius Pictor, Q. 13

Fabius Rusticus 23-4, 36, 208, 209, 212

Fabius Valens (cos. 69) 75, 86, 89, 191

Fabricius Veiento, A. (cos. II 80; cos. III 83 (?)) 33

Faenius Rufus 166, 183

*Fasti Amiternini* 120

fastidiousness 172-3, 215

Fire of Rome 179, 181-3

Firmius Catus 136

*flamen Dialis* 130

Flavius Sabinus (brother of Vespasian) 90, 91, 102

*fortuna* 106

freedmen 52, 130, 144, 145, 151, 166, 167, 233

freedom 53, 57, 119, 120, 128, 187

freewill and determinism (excursus) 138

Frontinus *see* Iulius

Fulcinius Trio 205

Fulda 236, 237

Gaius (grandson of Augustus) 109

Gaius (emperor) *see* Caligula

Galba (emperor 69-70) 68, 70-8, 84, 92, 102, 172, 190, 195, 202

*Gallia Comata* 148

*Gallia Narbonensis, see* Narbonensis

Gallic nobles (Claudius' speech) 147, 149-50, 152, 160, 207

Gellius, Aulus 17, 19

German affairs 55, 115-7, 120, 153, 155, 167-9, 210

*Germania* 39, 44, 49-58, 237, 238

Germanicus 55, 105, 107, 110, 111, 115, 116-8, 119, 120, 122-4, 127, 129, 135, 140, 142, 151, 201, 204, 205, 212, 223, 229, 230

Gibbon 227-8, 242

*gloria* 48, 147, 194, 223

Gotarzes 153-4

Gracchi 124

Gracchus, Ti. Sempronius 18

Guicciardini 239

Greece, Nero's tour of 187, 188

Hadrian (emperor 118-37) 31, 34, 35

Hannibal 230

*haruspices* 146

Helvidius Priscus (father) 33, 36, 60, 93, 100, 186, 196

Helvidius Priscus (son) 33

Herennius Senecio 33, 36

Hersfeld 237

*Historia Augusta* 236

*Histories* 60, 104, 130, 168, 199, 202, 209, 237, 241, 242

history (digression on) 137

Hordeonius Flaccus 97, 98, 197

innuendo 109, 222

invented speeches *see* speeches

Isocrates 14, 19

Iulius Agricola, Cn. (cos. 77 (?)) 27, 28, 36, 39-49, 174, 216

Iulius Caesar *see* Caesar

Iulius Civilis 89, 93, 95-8, 101, 197

Iulius Classicianus, C. 175

Iulius Florus 125

Iulius Frontinus, Sex. (cos. 73 (?), 98, 100)   32, 37, 56
Iulius Sacrovir   125
Iulius Secundus   60
Iulius Ursus L.   34
Iulius Ursus Servianus, L.   34
Iulius Vindex   28
Iunia (widow of Cassius)   128
Iunia Silana   165-6
Iunius Blaesus (cos. 10)   133
Iunius Silanus, M. (cos. 46)   162
*Iuppiter Liberator*   184, 186
Iuvenalis, D. Iunius *see* Juvenal

Jerusalem   101
Jewish revolt   187, 188
Jonson, Ben   240
Josephus   90, 92, 159, 195
Juvenal   33, 37, 38, 152
juxtaposition, pejorative   229

Lappius Maximus, A. (cos. 86, 95)   32
*laudatio funebris*   14
Law   108, 124-5
Lepidus *see* Aemilius
*libertas see* freedom
*libertas senatoria*   187
Libo Drusus, M. Scribonius   119, 120-1, 200
Licinius Crassus, L. (cos. 95 BC)   17
Licinius Macer, C.   18
Licinius Mucianus, C. (cos. 65, 70, 72)   70, 78, 84-7, 89, 92, 93, 95, 99, 100, 195-7, 217, 231
Licinius Sura, L. (cos. 97 (?), 102, 107)   34-5
Lipsius, Justus   238, 239, 240
Livia   105, 109-12, 114, 123, 132, 141, 142, 145, 203, 212
Livia (Livilla), wife of Drusus   131, 132, 134, 141, 142
Livy   19, 22-3, 44, 97, 98, 109, 149, 190, 192, 202, 221, 230, 232, 241, 242
London   174
Lucceius, L.   20

Lucilius Bassus   86, 89, 92, 195
*ludi saeculares see* Secular Games
Luxury (digression on)   128
Lyons tablet   147-9, 150, 232

Macaulay   242
Macer   206
Machiavelli   239
Maecenas   125
*maiestas* (treason charge)   118, 120-1, 126-7, 134-6, 176
Mamercus Scaurus   205, 206
Manuscripts: *Hersfeldensis*   237, 238
   first Medicean (M1)   237, 238
   second Medicean (M2)   237, 238
Marius   81, 194
Marius Celsus (cos. 69)   76, 80, 81, 191, 192
Marius Priscus (cos. 84)   29, 30
Martial   36
Martius Macer   79
Maternus *see* Curiatius
Mauretania   153
Meherdates   153-4
Memmius Regulus, P. (cos. 31)   17
Messalla *see* Vipstanus
Messalina   144, 150-2, 159, 161
Mithridates (Bosporan)   154
Mithridates (Iberian)   153
*moderatio*   139, 225
Mommsen, T.   78, 190, 241, 242
Monte Cassino   237
*mores*   22, 41, 51, 147
*mos maiorum*   13, 185
Mons Graupius   43, 216
Montaigne   240
Mucianus *see* Licinius
Mucius Scaevola, P.   17
mutiny, in Germany   115, 117; in Pannonia   115, 117

Narbonensis   26, 35, 148
Narcissus   151, 159
Nero (son of Germanicus)   131, 132
Nero (emperor 54-68)   35, 67, 91, 99, 103, 109, 145, 152, 158-60, 207-10, 212, 228, 232, 233

'new men' *see noui homines*
Nerva (emperor 96-8) 28, 29, 33, 34, 37, 39, 40, 49, 50, 67
Niccoli, Niccolò 237
Niebuhr, R. 240
Nissen, H. 190
Novaesium (Neuss) 97, 98
*noui homines* 15, 28, 139
obituaries 105, 107, 119, 125, 126, 128, 138-9, • 140, 167, 175-6, 218
*Octavia* 178
Octavia 152, 159, 163, 165, 170, 178
Octavian (from 27 BC Augustus (q.v.)) 112
Octavius Sagitta 168, 169
*Opera Minora* 237, 238
*Origines* 16
Orosius 236
Ostorius Scapula, P. (cos. before 47) 156-7
Otho (emperor 69) 68, 70-84, 95, 102, 169, 172, 190-2, 194, 195, 202, 209, 230

Paetus Thrasea *see* Thrasea
Pallas 151, 165
Panormita 237
Parthia *see* Eastern Question
*pater patriae* 118, 122
periodic sentences, in Tacitus 226-9
*permodestus* 220, 225
Petillius Cerialis Q. (cos. 70, 74) 28, 96, 98-100, 174, 198
Petronius (*arbiter elegantiae*) 185-6, 225
Petronius Turpilianus, P. (cos. 61) 173
*Phaedo* 186
Philippi 128
phoenix 138, 205, 206
Phylarchus 15
Pichena 238
*pietas* (filial duty) 111, 112, 171
Piso Licinianus 71, 73

Piso *see* Calpurnius
Pisonian Conspiracy 179, 183-4, 209, 210
Placentia 79, 193
Plancina 123
Plato 19, 186
Plautius, Aulus (cos. 29) 156
Plautius Lateranus 164
Pliny, the Elder 23, 30, 189, 190, 197, 199, 202, 208-10
Pliny, the Younger (C. Plinius Caecilius Secundus, cos. 100) 23, 26, 27, 29, 30, 31, 33, 34, 35, 37, 39, 201, 210, 236
Plutarch 37, 71-6, 78, 80-5, 101, 102, 169, 190-6, 202, 209
Poenius Postumus 174
Poetovio 86
Polybius 15, 19, 190, 236
Polyclitus 173, 175
*pomerium* 158
Pompey (Pompeius Magnus, Cn.) 18, 82, 124, 194
Pompeius, Sextus 112
Pomponius Labeo 205
Pomponius Secundus, P. (cos. 44) 155
Pontius Pilate 183
Poppaea 168-70, 177, 178, 185, 209, 225, 233
Poppaeus Sabinus, C. (cos. 9) 119, 139, 205, 206
Porcius Cato, M. (cos. 195 BC) 15-6, 21, 25, 41
*praefectus urbi* 34, 35, 138, 139, 167, 169, 175
Prasutagus 174
prodigies 158, 218
Publicius Certus 30
Publius Celer 99
*pudor* 23, 194
Puteolanus 238

quaestorship (history of) 146-7
Quinctilius Varus, P. (cos. 13 BC) 116, 224
*quindecimviri* 27, 146

*quinquennium Neronis*  163, 188
Quintilian  13, 21, 22, 26, 36-7, 61, 214

Racine  240
Ranke  104, 241
Red Sea  31
*Res Gestae*  111
resonances, Sallustian (*see also* Sallust) 225-6
Rhenanus, Beatus  238
Royal Society, The  240
Rubellius Plautus  166, 177, 185
Rudolphus of Fulda  237
*rubrum mare*  (Red Sea)  31
rumour  46
Rutilius Gallicus, C. (cos. 70 or 71, 85 (?))  34
Rutilius Rufus, P. (cos. 105 BC)  17

Sacrovir *see* Iulius
Sallust (C. Sallustius Crispus)  18, 20-2, 25, 40, 41, 44, 74, 82, 85, 90, 101, 106, 111, 124, 127, 137, 140, 154, 159, 168, 176, 202, 214, 216-7, 224, 225-6, 231
Sallustian language (tone, etc.) *see* Sallust
Sallustius Crispus, C. (minister of Tiberius)  114, 125
Sallustius Lucullus  32
Salvius Otho Titianus (cos. 52)  77, 80, 81, 191, 192
Scaurus *see* Aemilius
Schwartz, E.  204
Scipio *see* Cornelius
Secular Games  27, 145
Sejanus (L Aelius Seianus, cos. 31)  105-6, 107, 123, 125, 129-37, 139-41, 143, 168, 188, 200, 202, 207, 212, 226
Sempronia  168
Sempronius Asellio  17-8, 24
Seneca, L. Annaeus  22, 24, 102, 160, 163-8, 171, 172, 177, 178, 184, 186, 208, 212, 214, 232, 233, 240

Senecan amble  214
Servilius Nonianus, M. (cos. 35)  23, 172, 202
*seruitium see* slavery
Servius Tullius  109
*SHA see Historia Augusta*
Sidonius Apollinaris  236
Silius, C.  135, 136
Silius, C. (Messalina's lover)  146, 150, 151
Silius Italicus, Ti. (cos. 68)  36
*simulator*  107
*sine ira et studio*  25
Sisenna *see* Cornelius
slavery  52, 54, 110, 120, 187
Socrates  186
Spain  35
*species* (appearance)  112, 117, 225
*speciosus*  120
speeches, invented: *oratio recta*  230-3, *oratio obliqua*  233-4
Spurinna *see* Vestricius
Statius, P. Papinius  34, 36
Stoic opposition  33
Stoicism  83, 184, 186, 187
*subdolus*  105, 112, 120
Subrius Flavus  183
Suetonius Paullinus, C. (cos. 42 (?)  79, 80, 157, 173-5, 191, 193, 210, 216, 225
Suetonius Tranquillus, C.  37, 71, 73, 74, 76, 83, 86, 90, 91, 92, 101, 102, 109, 112, 132, 133, 134, 142, 144, 146, 149, 159, 160, 165, 169, 172, 181, 182, 187, 188, 190, 191, 196, 203-5, 208-9
Suillius Rufus, P.  136, 145, 168
Sulla, L. Cornelius  18, 81, 115, 194
Sulpicius Asper  183
Sulpicius Severus  236
sumptuary legislation (proposed)  127
survey of the empire under Tiberius  130
Swift  240
Syme, R.  206, 209, 242

*tabulae pontificum* 14
Tacitism 239, 240
Tacitus, career 26–32
Tacitus (emperor, d. 276) 236
Tanaquil 109
Tarentum, treaty of 112
Tarquinius Priscus 109
Tertullian 236
Tettius Iulianus, L. (cos. 83) 32
Theophrastus 105
Thrace 130
Thrasea Paetus, P. Clodius (cos. 56) 33, 36, 93, 145, 169, 172, 176, 177, 179, 181, 184–7, 210, 222, 223, 231, 233
Thrasyllus 138
Thucydides 21, 213
Tiberius (emperor 14–37) 35, 55, 144, 148, 153, 162, 163, 187, 188, 199–207, 212, 222, 226, 228, 229, 231–3
Tiberius Alexander 84, 85, 195
Tigellinus, Ofonius 76, 177, 182, 185, 188
Tigranes 173, 180, 181
Tiridates 180, 188
Titianus *see* Salvius
Titinius Capito 210
Titius Sabinus 135
Titus (emperor 79–81) 78, 93, 99, 101, 195, 199
Trajan (emperor 98–117) 29, 31, 32, 34–7, 39, 40, 49, 56, 67, 163, 193, 243
treason trials *see maiestas*

*uirtus see virtus*
Ummidius Quadratus, C. (cos. 40) 181

Valerius Antias 19
Valerius Asiaticus, D. (?) (cos. 35, 46) 148, 207
Valerius Catullus Messalinus, L. (cos. 73, 85) 33
Valerius Flaccus 36

Vannius 155
*variatio* (syntactical asymmetry) 220
Varus *see* Quinctilius
Velleius Paterculus 202
Venutius 89
Veranius, Q. (cos. 49) 174
Verginius Rufus, L. (cos. 63, 69, 97) 23, 28–9, 32
Verulamium (St Albans) 174
Vespasian (emperor 69–79) 26, 33, 34, 45, 62, 69, 70, 77, 78, 82, 84, 85, 87, 89, 92, 93, 95, 99, 100, 128, 181, 195, 196, 199, 231
Vestricius Spurinna, T. (cos. 73 (?), 98, 100) 32, 79, 193–4
Vesuvius, eruption 30
Vetera 96
Vettulenus Civica Cerialis, C. (cos. 76 (?)) 32
Vibius Crispus, Q. (cos. III by 83) 33, 62, 196
Vibius Maximus, C. 36
Vienne 148
Vinius, T. (cos. 69) 68, 73
Vipstanus Messalla 60–5, 87, 99, 100, 189
*viri militares* 32
*virtus* 20, 22, 23, 25, 40, 41, 42, 48, 53, 57, 76, 105, 147
Visellius Varro 135
Vitellius (emperor 69) 68, 70, 71, 74–8, 82, 84–6, 90–2, 93, 95, 102, 190, 194–6
Vitellius, L. (cos. 34, 43, 47) 152
Vitorius Marcellus 36
Vocula *see* Dillius
Vologeses 154, 179–81
Volusius Saturninus, L. (cos. 12 BC) 125
Volusius Saturninus, L. (cos. 3) 167

Wölfflin, E. 241

Xenophon (physician) 159

Zenobia 154

# INDEX OF PASSAGES
# TRANSLATED OR DISCUSSED*

## I · TACITUS

### AGRICOLA

| | |
|---|---|
| 1.1–4 | 40–1 |
| 3.1 | 37 |
| 3.3 | 40, 67 |
| 20.2–3 | 42 |
| 21.2 | 44 |
| 24.3 | 45 |
| 28 | 43 |
| 30.3 and 5 | 219 |
| 30.5 | 44 |
| 33.2–34.3 | 44–5 |
| 37.2–3 | 216 |
| 40.2 | 46 |
| 42.3 | 219 |
| 42.3–4 | 32, 47–8, 65 |
| 43.1–2 | 46–7 |
| 45.3 | 48 |
| 45.5 | 47 |
| 46.4 | 49 |

### GERMANIA

| | |
|---|---|
| 18.1–3 | 51 |
| 19.1 | 51 |
| 27.1 | 52–3 |
| 37 | 49, 54–5 |
| 43.4 | 54 |
| 45.6 | 54 |

### DIALOGUS

| | |
|---|---|
| 1.1 | 58 |
| 9.6 | 59 |
| 12.1 | 59 |
| 35 | 63 |
| 40.2 | 63 |

### HISTORIES

| | |
|---|---|
| 1.1.1 | 64, 68 |
| 1.1.3 | 68 |
| 1.1.4 | 69, 220 |
| 1.2.1 | 45, 69 |
| 1.2.3 | 220 |
| 1.3.5 | 220 |
| 1.4.1 | 24, 69, 74 |
| 1.10.1–2 | 217 |
| 1.11.3 | 68 |
| 1.25.1 | 71 |
| 1.28 | 71 |
| 1.32.1 | 71–2 |
| 1.35.2 | 72 |
| 1.36.3 | 72 |
| 1.40.1 | 72 |
| 1.41.2–3 | 73 |
| 1.49.2–4 | 74 |
| 1.51.1 | 74, 78 |
| 1.52.4 | 75 |
| 1.64.1 | 75 |
| 1.84.4 | 77 |
| 2.1.1 | 77–8 |
| 2.7.2 | 78 |
| 2.18–9 | 79 |
| 2.23.4–5 | 79–80 |

---

*I am indebted to my colleague, Mr. I. S. Moxon, for assistance with this Index and with reading of the proofs.

| | |
|---|---|
| 2.32.1 | 80 |
| 2.37.1 | 81–2 |
| 2.50.1 | 83 |
| 2.101.1 | 86, 92, 195 |
| 3.1.1 | 86 |
| 3.25.3 | 88 |
| 3.36.1 | 88 |
| 3.86.2 | 92 |
| 4.6.1 | 94 |
| 4.14 | 97–8 |
| 4.27.3 | 97 |
| 4.38.1 | 93, 99 |
| 4.39.2 | 99 |
| 4.42.2–6 | 100 |
| 4.58 | 98 |
| 4.60.1 | 96–7 |
| 4.73.3 | 99 |
| 4.74.3–4 | 99 |

*ANNALS*

| | |
|---|---|
| 1.2.1 | 108–9, 226–7 |
| 1.6.1 | 162 |
| 1.7.1 | 110 |
| 1.7.3 | 221 |
| 1.7.4 | 220 |
| 1.11.2 | 113 |
| 1.16.1 | 108 |
| 1.65.1–2 | 224 |
| 1.72.1–2 | 118, 229 |
| 1.72.2 | 220 |
| 1.73.4 | 220 |
| 1.75.1 | 119 |
| 1.81 | 120 |
| 2.61 | 31 |
| 2.87 | 122 |
| 3.3.1 | 122, 222 |
| 3.3.2 | 122 |
| 3.6.3 | 142, 220 |
| 3.18.4 | 144 |
| 3.19.2 | 124 |
| 3.30 | 125 |
| 3.65.1 | 126 |

| | |
|---|---|
| 3.69.5 | 230 |
| 3.76.2 | 128–9 |
| 4.1.1 | 106, 108, 129 |
| 4.3.3 | 220 |
| 4.9.1 | 229 |
| 4.31.1–2 | 229 |
| 4.33.2 | 24 |
| 4.33.3 | 137 |
| 4.33.4 | 38 |
| 4.57.1 | 142 |
| 4.66.1 | 229 |
| 6.45.1 | 230 |
| 6.48.2 | 143 |
| 6.51.3 | 105, 139–42 |
| 11.20.1 | 155 |
| 11.24 | 149 |
| 11.27.1 | 150 |
| 11.30.2 | 151 |
| 13.1.1 | 162, 228 |
| 13.20.2 | 208 |
| 13.45.1 | 168 |
| 13.53.1 | 169 |
| 14.1.1 | 170 |
| 14.4.1 | 220 |
| 14.13.1 | 234 |
| 14.19 | 217–8 |
| 14.32.3 | 216 |
| 14.37 | 218–9 |
| 14.49.3 | 222–3 |
| 14.61 | 170 |
| 14.53–6 | 177 |
| 14.64.3 | 178 |
| 15.3.1 | 181 |
| 15.31 | 180 |
| 15.42.1 | 183 |
| 15.44.2 | 182–3 |
| 15.47 | 218 |
| 15.47.1 | 183 |
| 15.48.1 | 183 |
| 15.68.1 | 183 |
| 16.21.1 | 186 |
| 16.35.1 | 186 |

## II · OTHER AUTHORS

### CICERO

| | | |
|---|---|---|
| Ad Fam. | 5.12.3 | 20 |
| Brutus | 45 | 63–4 |
| De legibus | 1.5 | 15, 19 |
| De oratore | 2.62 | 189 |
| De oratore | 2.64 | 22 |

### CASSIUS DIO

| | |
|---|---|
| 63.15.2² | 83 |

### ENNIUS

| |
|---|
| 22 |

### JUVENAL

| | |
|---|---|
| 7.51–2 | 37 |

### LIVY

| | | |
|---|---|---|
| Praefatio | 2 | 22 |
| Praefatio | 9 | 22 |

### PLINY THE YOUNGER

| | | |
|---|---|---|
| Epistulae | 1.13.1 | 37 |
| Epistulae | 2.11.17 | 29 |
| Epistulae | 7.33.1 | Title page and p. 30 |
| Epistulae | 9.10.2 | 59 |
| Epistulae | 9.23.2 | 26 |

### PLUTARCH

| | | |
|---|---|---|
| Galba | 4 | 85 |
| Galba | 27.1–2 | 72–3 |
| Otho | 7.23ff. | 80 |
| Otho | 9 | 81–2 |
| Otho | 18 | 83 |

### SALLUST

| | | |
|---|---|---|
| Cat. | 10.1 | 106 |
| Cat. | 25 | 168 |
| Jug. | 85.17 | 22 |
| Jug. | 101.11 | 217 |

### SHA

| | |
|---|---|
| 10.3 | 236 |

### SENECA

| | |
|---|---|
| Epist. | 114.17 | 22 |

### SUETONIUS

| | | |
|---|---|---|
| Galba | 20 | 73 |
| Otho | 12.2 | 83 |
| Nero | 49.1 | 187 |